Shop

Boys House
30 by 50

Bark house

Shop

Shop

Waggon House

Shop

Smith Shop

Visiting House
36 by 40

Office

Curring Shop

HARRY N. ABRAMS, INC., PUBLISHERS

JOHN T. KIRK

THE
SHAKER
WORLD
ART, LIFE, BELIEF

THIS BOOK IS DEDICATED TO TREVOR FAIRBROTHER

PROJECT DIRECTOR: MARGARET L. KAPLAN
EDITOR: ELAINE M. STAINTON
DESIGNER: JUDITH MICHAEL
PHOTO EDITOR: LAUREN BOUCHER

Page 1:
Church Family Elder Daniel Crosman
overlooking Mount Lebanon, about 1870
(figure 183)

Pages 2–3:
The Second Meetinghouse, New Lebanon,
New York, after March 1874 (figure 51)

Library of Congress Cataloging-in-Publication Data
Kirk, John T.
The shaker world: art, life, belief / John T. Kirk.
p. cm.
Includes bibliographical references and index.
ISBN 0–8109–4472–3 (clothbound)
1. Shakers.   2. Shaker art.   I. Title.
BX9771.K55 1997
289' .8—dc21   96–52014

Printed and bound in Japan

Harry N. Abrams, Inc.
100 Fifth Avenue
New York, N.Y. 10011
www.abramsbooks.com

CONTENTS

ACKNOWLEDGMENTS

A significant pleasure for me during the years I have spent researching and writing this book has been getting to know and working with Jerry Grant, who was the Assistant Director and Curator of the Shaker Museum and Library in Old Chatham, New York, during most of the development of the book. Before the existence of computers, he typed thousands of entries from his readings of Shaker materials onto index cards; since the introduction of microfilm and computers his retrievable grasp on all aspects of Shaker life has grown prodigiously. Jerry's appearance in the text and notes only suggests his generosity and involvement. Without him this book would not have been possible.

My study of Shaker material began when I was asked to lecture at the Shaker Museum and Library on what the Shakers had originated in the field of the decorative arts. I was asked to do this because in an early book I criticized the practice of promoting the Shakers as a people who had worked outside the general history of design. To prepare for the talk I spent some days with the museum's collections, and the informative voice of Jerry Grant. This experience helped me develop a clearer understanding of the dependence and the independence of Shaker practices. After the talk, the museum provided a small grant so that I could explore the possibility of developing an insightful exhibition or book that would further knowledge of Shaker materials and the museum's collections. Previously, a Guggenheim Fellowship had allowed me to study the relationship of early American furniture and recent American art. That research informed my work on the Shakers, particularly my study of the similarities between the "Classic Shaker" look and the art made in America since 1950. That comparison appears as the last section of the book.

Anyone reading the book will realize the many authors, collectors, dealers, and curators who have added their insights to this study, for I have tried to make that obvious. Most of the objects would not be available if collectors had not held them in trust and made them accessible. Robert and Katherine Booth, Ed Clerk, Vi and Wendell Hess, J. J. Gerald McCue, Stephen Miller, Ruth and Erhart Muller, Gustave Nelson, Winola Stokes, Helen Upton, and Ann Whipple have been generous with their knowledge and their collections. Tim Rieman provided information and allowed me to use some of his photographs. June Sprigg shared her knowledge and enthusiasm for Shaker things, particularly those now at Hancock, Massachusetts. Others in the museum and other scholarly worlds who helped include: Donna Baron, John Bivins, Todd Burdick, Susan Buck, Jean Burks, Ed Churchill, Larrie Curry, Robert Emlen, Renee Fox, Phyllis Galician, Stacy Glass, Mary Ellen Hern, Holly Izard, Richard Kathmann, Shelley Langdale, Susan Montgomery, Jane Nylander, John Ott, Sam Pennington, Marjorie Procter-Smith, Mary Lyn Ray, Vicki Sand, Peter Schjeldahl, Sandra Scripture, Roberta Smith, Tom Sokolowski, Maggie Stier, Scott Swank, Andy Vadnais, Gib Vincent, Glendyne Wergland, Karen Winter, and Larry Yerdon.

At the Sabbathday Lake, Maine, Shaker community Leonard Brooks, and especially, Brother Arnold Hadd were generous with their time and knowledge. Many others have contributed in numerous ways: Dick Albright, Suzanne Courcier, Stephen Fletcher, Robert Gober, Spencer Gordon, Karen Keane, Liz Lunning, David Schorsch, Robert Wilkins, and Robert Wilson.

My colleagues at Boston University have withstood a barrage of questions and have assisted in many ways: Arleen Arzigian, Richard Candee, Naomi Miller, Keith Morgan, Elizabeth ten Grotenhuis, Susan von Daum Tholl, and Fred Licht. Many people have helped by reading or editing parts or all of the manuscript: Susan Buck, Peter Halley, John Hamilton, Hugh Howard, Greg Leftwich, William Moore, Mark Peterson, Stephen Stein, and William Vance. Jane Garrett suggested basic changes to the manuscript. Gerry Ward edited the manuscript as it neared completion. Jerry Grant organized and clarified the quotations and notes, and Virginia McEwen edited them. Cecilia Hanley again and again turned nearly unreadable script into beautiful, organized pages. I wish to thank Kathi Drummy for her creative work on the computer preparing the final version for the editor. It has been a pleasure to work with Michael Fredericks, who produced almost all of the beautiful new photographs.

I am indebted to Margaret Kaplan who, with the assistance of Julia Moore, convinced Harry N. Abrams to publish the book, and has made the project a creative and happy experience. Working with people at Abrams has been a joy. I especially wish to thank the photo editor, Lauren Boucher, the text editor, Elaine Stainton, and Judith Michael, who designed the book.

The Shaker World is dedicated to Trevor Fairbrother; for more than two decades he has made life interesting.

John T. Kirk
Seattle, Washington, 1997

This study provides an understanding of Shaker life and its relationship to the objects the Shakers have made and used during their more than two hundred years as a religious phenomenon. Most of us who care about Shaker design encountered Shaker art and life in the published works of Edward Deming Andrews. Although these were important in establishing the Shakers as an area of study, their bias has made it impossible to focus clearly on the artistic originality of the Shakers. They fostered the idea that Shaker art was created in isolation from anything produced near the communities in which the Shakers lived. As a result, those dedicated to studying Shaker objects have held them to be primarily the product of a peculiar sect living in celibate communities with a special understanding of God's will. A link between Shaker and non-Shaker artifacts was not advanced by scholars of the rest of the decorative arts, for they have accepted the doctrine of Shaker specialists and respected their turf. The observable truth, it seems to me, is that much of what the Shakers produced was very like vernacular work made around Shaker communities, and that Shaker work and related local worldly material fit into a general history of design. And further, I believe that Shaker designs cannot be understood without an awareness of the Shakers' changing beliefs, patterns of living, and attitudes toward design. The overriding purpose of this book is to provide a study I should have read when I first looked at Shaker artifacts and mistakenly dismissed the material as not very original and not very interesting.

Olive Hayden Austin, of the Hancock, Massachusetts Church Family. (see p. 243)

Shaker things made from about 1810 to 1860 are usually designated Classic Shaker. While they are often visually and culturally thrilling, these objects are more fully understood and richly perceived if they are seen as taking part in the Anglo-American cultural, theological, and aesthetic developments from the late eighteenth century to the Civil War. The Shakers have never sought or developed a fixed theology, social structure, or aesthetic stance. For them God is active and constantly giving new insights and understandings in everything they believe and do. Their designs result from taking the prevailing aesthetic of the region around their communities and adjusting it to suit their theological injunctions.

During their first years as a communal sect, from the late 1780s to about 1810, the Shakers in large part used objects the Believers brought to the newly developed communities, and those they made then are not unlike what was produced by non-Shakers living around them. By 1810 most American rural communities had adopted a vernacular expression of the neoclassical style that stressed taut, square, rectilinear, oval, and circular units. The Shakers pushed this aesthetic to a uniform simplicity to produce what is now held to be Classic Shaker; everything they made for domestic use until about the time of the Civil War—from furniture to the spirit-inspired gift drawings—employed bright neoclassical colors: blue, red, yellow, and green.

This form of classicism continued longer in Shaker hands than in "the world," because changes in community life brought new restrictions. During the late 1820s and early 1830s many worldly things, such as non-Shaker books, almanacs, newspapers, and new fancies—from silk hatbands to silver pens and earrings for both men and women—had been introduced into Shaker communities, and Shaker leaders imposed strict rules to eliminate them. Also, because the frenzied religious activities of the late 1830s and 1840s made the Shakers vulnerable to outside criticism, the leaders for a time demanded even stricter privacy than was required before or after these years. The resulting reduced contact with outside developments encouraged the continuation of established ideas, and while the rest of the world moved on to Greek, Gothic, and then rococo revivals, the Shakers continued their commitment to the outmoded neoclassical style. When the Shakers again embraced the world about 1860, they absorbed the vernacular expressions of the rapidly changing current styles. But even when they showed their awareness of new artistic expressions, an underlying Shaker belief in order and regimentation usually informed their designs.

In the late nineteenth and the early twentieth centuries, what the Shakers made for personal use or for sale reflected the modest objects of the high Victorian and colonial revival styles. Under the influence of the "colonial" ideal, the Shakers both painted things white and stripped their furniture of its original colors to expose the wood.

Present-day Shakers reject the idea of a classic Shaker look. Rather, they continue to see their religion and their art as evolving. As Brother Arnold Hadd at Sabbathday Lake said to me, "There is no classic Shaker period; we are still making things."

In any project that sweeps through a range of artifacts and time periods, the question must arise whether we are dealing with art objects. As the title and various parts of the text suggest, I have taken the broadest view of what constitutes art, and include in that designation anything made to be viewed aesthetically.

My primary goal was to assemble objects into enlightening groups, and examine them within theological and historical contexts, in order to make evident what Shaker designers achieved. This precluded a strict historical narrative. I have tried, nonetheless to have the text move sequentially through Shaker history, unless there are logical groupings of objects, or an idea or circumstance from another part of the sequence enlightens a larger issue. The first two chapters set the historical and theological stage for understanding the objects. The following chapters give equal importance to Shaker art, life, and belief, for each informs us about the other two. Ultimately this study is an attempt to see the makers and users of the material as a people possessed of a special belief and way of life who, nonetheless, had to deal with being humans in this world.

Fancy Goods for Sale, Canterbury,
New Hampshire, 1920s (detail, figure 223)

THE SHAKER WORLD

Chapter I

ANN LEE: CHARISMATIC FORCE, AND
THE ECSTATIC ORIGINS OF SHAKER BELIEF

ANN LEE AND ENGLAND

To understand the unfolding of Shaker design over the past two hundred years, it is essential to understand Ann Lee. Her role as a central force in Shaker thought and practice began when she took control of a tiny English Christian group about 1770. What she did, said, and allowed, and how these acts have been understood and interpreted, lie at the center of Shaker theological, social, economic, political, and artistic practices. She was a charismatic leader. Although she did not preach to large groups, her beliefs and forceful presence created a frenzied but focused path to salvation. Except for a few years after Ann Lee's death at Watervliet, New York, in 1784, Shaker activities have openly circled around her. For a time after her death, winning converts and structuring the complex and enthusiastic groups of Believers in small towns across New England and upper New York State took precedence over a public focus on her. After the groups had formed into communities, the Shakers acknowledged Ann Lee as the center of Shaker thought and her life as the promised Second Coming of Christ. Thus God was both male and female, and the Millennium—the thousand years of peace with Christ before the end of the world—had begun. During her life the beliefs necessary for membership among the saved were confession of sins to her, or a leader she designated, and celibacy, if you could sustain it. After her death, common property and strict celibacy were added to confession as the core tenets of the Church.

There are very few contemporary records about Ann Lee and her first followers, and most of what we know comes from oral reports written down after her death. Most of these are from her followers. Other views come from letters, journals, newspapers, accounts written by visitors, and writings by those who left the Shakers and wrote of their life as former members, sometimes, but not always, with bitterness. To construct a picture of the early years it is necessary to weave a tapestry from Shaker and outsider perspectives, with an understanding that both are colored by the devotion and the agendas of the writers. Oral traditions, even those written down only a decade or two after the events, cannot be fully trusted, but early testimonies from differing sides of an issue generally agree on much that occurred. Thomas Brown, who wrote a not-too-bitter exposé of the Shakers in 1812, found those who had left the faith "gave the same account of many things that I had received from those in the faith."[1]

As Clarke Garrett has pointed out, "the eighteenth century witnessed possibly the greatest extent and diversity of episodes of spirit possession since the early Church. Prophecy, visions, and ecstatic trances visited the Jews and Moslems of southeastern Europe, and among the French Jansenists the ecstatics known as the Convulsionaries introduced a remarkable and bizarre repertory of behaviors which, despite persecution, persisted through most of the century."[2] Outbreaks of frenzied spirituality, individually or in a group, could be short-lived or might continue for hours, with visions, hearing and seeing angels, convulsions, whirling for long periods, leaping, dancing, clapping of hands, shaking, groaning, sighing, shouting, beating of breasts, laughing until almost strangled, speaking in unknown tongues, falling to the ground, or singing wordless songs. Since its earliest years Christians had experienced many instances of God's intervention, as when Saint Paul on the road to Damascus saw a great light from heaven, and falling to the ground, heard a voice saying, "I am Jesus." According to the Book of Acts, those with him, although able to hear, were unable to see.[3]

Although there were many theological differences among the spirit-led groups that could cause friction and disagreement, most had in common a dependence on the guidance of the Holy Spirit, which could speak directly and transform individual thought and actions. A new personal beginning was possible, because God now dwelled actively in the believer, and placed him or her among the saved, or on the path to salvation. The converted were one with God and, like children, in need of and open to instruction. The differences between these groups tended to be in degrees of experiences, when or how they might occur. One debated point was how the promised Millennium was to be understood. Most agreed that those who wished to be among the elect

CHRONOLOGY OF SHAKER EVENTS DURING ANN LEE'S LIFE

1736	Ann Lee born in Manchester, England
1742	Ann Lee baptized
1747	Jane and James Wardley start group described as Shakers
About 1758	Ann Lee joins the group of about thirty Shakers
1762	Ann Lee marries
About 1766	Ann Lee becomes a more active follower
About 1770	Ann Lee reveals her understanding that copulation is the cause of sin, becomes the leader, and takes title Mother
1774	Ann Lee, seven followers, and Ann Lee's husband arrive in New York
1775–76	Property leased in Watervliet, Albany County, New York
1780	Joseph Meacham joins, Dark Day occurs, and interest in the sect increases
1781–83	Ann Lee and small group begin a more than two-year missionary sojourn with Harvard, Massachusetts, as their base, where they acquire the Square House; (in 1781, Lord Cornwallis surrenders to George Washington at Yorktown; in 1783, the Treaty of Paris ends the Revolutionary War)
1783	Ann Lee and close followers return to Watervliet
1784	Ann Lee dies

must repent soon, because the Millennium was fast approaching. This premonition had been part of many of the great Christian upheavals from the time of the first Church. If God was now so active in bringing souls to Him, if a sermon could convert tens or hundreds, and the new believers could convert ever larger numbers, the world would soon be ready for judgment. The Shakers believed Christ had returned and the thousand years had already begun.

The early writings by the Shakers trace as a major influence on their beginnings the works of the French Prophets, called Camisards, who moved out of France to various countries in 1685, when Louis XIV revoked the Edict of Nantes, which had secured religious tolerance for the Protestant minority. For the French Prophets, which included women, all social bonds, including family relationships, were to be put aside so the Spirit could lead without impediments: "[It was] by Inspiration that we forsook our Parents and Relations, and whatever was dearest to us in the World, to follow Jesus Christ, and to make War against the Devil and his Followers . . . ; this was the Source of that Union, Charity, and Brotherly Love, which reign'd among us."[4]

By Shaker tradition, Ann Lee was born on or about February 29, 1736. Church records confirm that she was baptized in Manchester Cathedral on June 1, 1742; her name at that time was spelled Anne Lees. She was the oldest of eight children. Her origins are obscure; for example, we do not know her mother's given name. Her father John Lees was a blacksmith who also did tailoring. As a young woman Ann Lee worked in a cotton mill, preparing cotton for the looms, and cutting velvet. Perhaps later she was a cutter of hatters' fur, and for a time, she was a cook in an infirmary. Probably in 1758, when she was twenty-two, she joined a small group of about thirty people who met in members' homes to worship under the guidance of God's Spirit. The group was headed by Jane and James Wardley, and led by Jane, who was given the title of Mother. The Wardleys may previously have been associated with the Society of Friends, known as Friends, or Quakers. Quaker records do not mention the Wardleys as members, but Shaker tradition asserts a relationship. They may have had at least as strong ties with early Methodists, or any of the many local religious groups formed around charismatic leaders.

For much of the century the area in the north of England around the towns of Bolton and Manchester had been a hotbed of religious activities. Methodist societies were established in both towns in 1747, the year in which the Wardleys may have separated from the Quakers. Jerry Grant has raised the question whether the first Shaker historians sought to play up a link to the Quakers who, by the time the Shaker faith began, had become socially and religiously acceptable, rather than the rambunctious Methodists they greatly resembled. By using early Shaker records, Grant has made a case that the presence of the Methodists in the area around Manchester, rather than the Quakers, most influenced the early Shakers' behavioral styles, and that the Shakers, while suppressing links to more radical influences, emphasized their roots in the Society of Friends because it had become a respectable faith.[5]

The Quakers experienced unstructured, ecstatic, spirit-led relationships with God when they developed as a sect during the third quarter of the seventeenth century. George Fox, who began the sect in 1647, and other early Quakers were as aggressive in stating their beliefs as the century-later early Shakers. As these Quakers preached the presence of the indwelling Spirit of Christ that could possess each believer, they at times moved into the shadow of blasphemy. The courts asked whether they were saying that one or more of their members was the second Christ, or only that they were overtaken by His living Spirit. Many followers did in fact believe that Fox was the second Messiah, and Margaret Fell, who married Fox in 1668, treated him from their first meeting as the returning Christ. For their seemingly outrageous activities, many Quakers were beaten and they were often imprisoned. The early leader James Nayler was lashed 310 times, had his tongue bored through, was branded with a B, and when he recovered, was whipped again.[6]

For the Quakers the directness of God's presence in individuals made priests or ministers in a traditional sense unnecessary, and outward sacraments redundant. Women were as important as men, for they too could be God's servants. Although some men and women were acknowledged as gifted communicators of God's word and given the title of minister, anyone could be used as a vehicle. By the time the Wardleys organized their group near Manchester, the Quakers had structured themselves into an ordered religion with rather quiet worship services. Members met and waited in silence for the Spirit to speak in an orderly manner, greatly reducing, while not eliminating, emotional spontaneity. According to the first published Shaker theological statement, printed in 1790, the Second Coming of Christ occurred in 1747, the year Jane and James Wardley separated from the Quakers and formed their own society in Bolton, near Manchester.[7] By the time Ann Lee joined, their group was already known as the "Shaking Quakers," and at times just

"Shakers," because of the ecstatic, emotion-filled activities the members underwent as the Spirit filled them during worship or daily activities. During ensuing decades the sect's title evolved, but usually it included "Shakers," at least as an explanatory word.[8] Like many contemporary Christian groups that existed outside formal structures, the first Believers enjoyed being detached from liturgical worship. If the Spirit of God could speak directly to each soul, and the Bible and non-institutional leaders could interpret, persuade, and instruct, a set of beliefs and formal places of worship were not necessary. Ordered behavior and fixed places of worship became necessary only when permanence was preferred to freedom.

Ann Lee's Rise to Leadership; Celibacy

For about nine years after joining the Wardleys in about 1758, Ann Lee struggled through great anguish and despair. In January 1762 she married, probably in Manchester Cathedral, and possibly with reluctance, Abraham Standerin, a local blacksmith. Both were unable to write, and signed the banns of marriage with crosses. (It is possible that one or both was able to read since the two skills were taught separately in the eighteenth century, but that seems unlikely.)[9] The births of four babies were difficult for Ann Lee, and each child died in infancy. After the death of her fourth child in 1766 she became more actively involved with the Shakers. From about the time of her marriage she had felt an increasing sense of shame and judgment, and gradually she came to believe that only by mortifying her flesh could she find the state of grace she so desperately sought. Shaker tradition records a long struggle of "deep mortification and suffering, her flesh wasted away, and she became like a skeleton . . . . In this manner she was more or less exercised in soul and body for about nine years, during which period the way of God, and the nature of his work, were gradually [revealed] . . . ."[10] It became clear to her that the sexual joining of Adam and Eve had separated men and women from God, and that "cohabitation of the sexes" was the source of evil. Like other religious persons before her, Jane Wardley shared Ann Lee's belief about the rightness of celibacy, but she did not think it was a necessary state for all Believers. As Wardley told Ann Lee, "James and I lodge together; but we do not touch each other any more than two babes. You may return home and do likewise."[11] Ann Lee's husband, probably also a member of the sect, complained to the group about her developing understanding that sexual intercourse was the cause of sin, and around 1770 she announced her conviction of this to the group. From that time she rose in authority to become the leader, taking the title Mother Ann. While the Wardleys had encouraged sexual restraint and confession of sins, Mother Ann required the members to confess to her, or a leader she appointed, and to become celibate, if they could manage it. Jesus had said, "The children of this world marry, and are given in marriage: But they which shall be accounted worthy to obtain that world, and the resurrection from the dead, neither marry, nor are given in marriage: Neither can they die any more: for they are equal unto the angels; and are the children of God, being the children of the resurrection."[12] The Protestant Reformation, working against the Roman Catholic Church, had rejected celibacy as a major force in the religious life, but in the eighteenth century, both in Germany and England, celibacy had again become an acceptable way to live near God. John Wesley, the founder of Methodism, did marry but wrote: "Blessed are 'they who have made themselves eunuchs for the kingdom of heaven's sake,' who abstain from things lawful in themselves in order to be more devoted to God."[13] Ann Lee chose celibacy, but like Saint Paul she found that for others "it is better to marry than to burn, and those who marry do well; but those who marry not do better."[14] She also continued to advocate, like Saint Paul, male authority over women. Paul wrote to the Corinthians that he had chosen celibacy, for it was the highest order, but if lust remained a controlling factor, marriage was necessary. When only one partner wanted to be celibate, the couple should stay married, with the husband having authority over the wife.[15]

In 1812 Thomas Brown, who for an extended period had associated with the Shakers, recorded what he had been told were Ann Lee's words on male supremacy: "If the wife believes, and not the husband, according to the order of the church she must still abide with the husband, and take up her cross according to the faith . . . . If the husband will voluntarily give her up, the church will then receive her to live among believers. But if the husband believes, and not the wife, he is counselled to forsake her, and to have no union with her; and if he pleases he can take his children from her."[16] Brown reported what was probably not an unusual occurrence: after a James Smith had joined the Shakers, his wife Polly and their children were tricked into staying a time with the sect. When Polly Smith left because she did not believe, she was not permitted to take her children, because her husband had committed himself and them to Shaker care.[17] When counseling the American Believer Lucy Markham, Ann Lee encouraged her to work on her husband: "You must be obedient to your husband; he has a simple faith, and you must strengthen his faith, and be obedient to him, as the Church is to Christ: for the husband is the head of the wife, even as Christ is the head of the Church."[18] Although these remembered words suggested some reluctance to face head-on the social and legal structure of marriage, the Shakers in America were repeatedly accused of dividing families. They knew Jesus had foretold such divisions, if God was to be followed, and they were adamant that they alone had the path to salvation. Many outsiders were suspicious of a religion with a woman at its center, but Lee turned this to a theological advantage by acknowledging that men were the decision makers and called Christ first and herself second: "and the woman, being second, must be subject to her husband, who is first; but when the man is gone, the right of government belongs to the woman: So is the family of Christ."[19]

In 1769 *The Virginia Gazette* of Williamsburg published an account of an unstructured Shaker worship service while it was still led by the Wardleys:

> *Our correspondent at Manchester writes a very strange account of a religious sect who have lately made a great noise in that town. They took their rise from a prophet and prophetess who had their religious ceremonies and tenets delivered in a vision, some years ago. They hold theirs to be the only true religion, and all others to be false. They meet constantly three times a day, at the house of some one of their society, and converse . . . until the moving of the spirit comes upon them, which is first perceived by their beginning leisurely to scratch upon their thighs or other parts of their bodies; from that the motion becomes gradually quicker, and proceeds to trembling, shaking, and screeching in the most dreadful manner; at the same time their features are not distinguishable, by reason of the quick motion of their heads, which strange agitation at last ends in singing and dancing . . . . These fits come upon them at certain intervals, and during the impulse of the spirit they disturb the whole neighborhood for some considerable distance, and continue sometimes whole nights in the most shocking distortions and commotions, until their strength is quite exhausted, from which uncommon mode of religious worship they have obtained the denomination of* Shakers.[20]

Like many spirit-led sects the Shakers actively denounced other religious groups, and freely interrupted their worship services. They felt free to break laws, because they believed the legal system had been a temporary necessity until Christ came again. Now, true Believers were under God's law, which was above those formed by men. For such conscious offenses they were fined, physically abused, and at times jailed, but they accepted such difficulties as a natural result of pushing against the established, imperfect order.

ANN LEE AND HER CHURCH IN NEW YORK

Perhaps because their number was not increasing rapidly, and because of a vision that came to an important member named James Whittaker, Ann Lee took her group to America. In his vision Whittaker had seen America as a large tree representing the Church of Christ, where every leaf shone with such brightness that the tree looked like a burning torch. The Shakers' passage to the New World was paid for by John Hocknell, a former Methodist, and one of the few wealthy members. On May 19, 1774, Ann Lee, with seven followers—her brother William Lees, her niece Nancy Lees, Mary Partington, John Hocknell, his son Richard Hocknell, James Whittaker, and James Shepherd—and her husband Abraham Standerin, who may never have been a "substantial Believer,"[21] sailed from Liverpool for New York. According to Shaker tradition, after three months of an unusually difficult voyage their ship the *Mariah,* under a Captain Smith, arrived in New York City on August 6, 1774. This is corroborated by Gaine's Marine List, Custom-House, New York, which indicates the *Maria,* with Captain J. Smith, arrived from Liverpool on August 5. [22] Probably the Shakers cleared customs aboard the ship and came on land August 6, the day the Shakers call "Landing Day."

Without Ann Lee's charismatic leadership the Shakers who remained in England lost their energy as a group. A few of the remaining members came to join the Believers in America; the rest faded from view. The small group in America was fragile. Ann Lee's husband would soon leave her; after her death two members would secede and two others would depart to marry each other, but the group held the seeds of a Society that would develop nineteen substantial communities. To the Shakers in America, Anne Lees Standerin became Ann Lee, or simply Mother Ann. By Shaker tradition Ann Lee's name was shortened upon arrival in New York, but recent scholarship indicates her name was not shortened until after her death.[23] In Shaker writings the "s" was also dropped from the surnames of her brother William (or half-brother, according to Thomas Brown),[24] and niece Nancy. Civil and military records, covering the Shakers' legal infractions and their pacifistic stance, however, continued to cite the leader of the Shakers by her married name.

In New York Ann Lee and her husband found employment as a domestic servant and a blacksmith. By Shaker tradition John Hocknell went north with William Lee and James Whittaker in 1775 to lease from the Manor Rensselaerwych, in Albany County, two hundred acres of swamp and wilderness for Ann Lee and most of her followers. Hocknell also leased an adjacent farm for John Partington, the other wealthy member, who was to follow shortly, and possibly one for himself.[25] The land they leased is about eight miles north of Albany. Called Niskeyuna by the Indians, it was later given the Dutch name Watervliet when townships were laid out in Albany County.[26] The small band was settling in a dangerous area, for during the next seven years the British encouraged Native-American raids on the settlers in this region along the Hudson River to help combat the Revolution. For income William Lee and James Whittaker took jobs in their old trades of blacksmith and weaver.[27]

According to Shaker tradition Ann Lee visited the Believers near Albany several times, but she mostly remained in New York City, where she suffered greatly, both from poverty and unhappiness of soul. She lost her job when she nursed her husband through a serious illness, after which he left her. He decided he wished sexual relations with a woman, and if his wife chose celibacy he would join another. In December of 1775 John Hocknell returned from England, where he had gone to collect his family and John Partington, whose wife Mary had come with Ann Lee. They landed in Philadelphia and traveled overland to Watervliet, where probably by the spring of 1775, they were all settled in a new log house on cleared and planted land.[28]

Although the first Shakers did not send out missionaries, they began what would become a regular practice of allowing visitors to watch their worship services. These were to a great degree spontaneous, however, they were also a form of religious theater designed to impress and thus help in converting the spectators. In 1778 a military surgeon recorded in his journal a visit to the "Shaking Quakers, or dancing quakers" at Watervliet. The worship service was led by "a female by the name of Ann Lee" who "has had the address to seduce several individuals of our country to her party . . . . They spend whole nights in their revels . . . . Both sexes, nearly divested of clothing, fall to dancing in extravagant postures, and frequently whirl themselves round on one leg with inconceivable rapidity, till they fall apparently lifeless on the floor. A spectator asserts that the fantastic contortions of body in which their pretended religious exercises consist, bear the semblance of supernatural impulse."[29] The Boston *Gazette and Country Journal* of November 2, 1778, included a description of the Shakers: "There is a sect whose conscience leads them to gross immoralities, and abominable prophaness. Every Sabbath they have their meeting, when their mode of worship consists in dancing stark naked; one of them presiding whom they call their God."[30]

A great influx of settlers moved into western Massachusetts and the area across the Hudson in upper New York State after the end of the French and Indian Wars in 1763. Religious revivals broke out among the new settlers in 1779. In both Hancock, Massachusetts, and New Lebanon, New York, religious ferment was so intense that the Millennium was expected soon. One of the leaders at New Lebanon was the Baptist elder Joseph Meacham, who had come from Enfield, Connecticut, where his family had long been part of energetic religious activities. In 1780, having heard positive things about the Shakers, Meacham and three others traveled the forty-five miles to Watervliet to see what was happening. By Shaker tradition Meacham spent a day questioning James Whittaker about Shaker beliefs, and convinced that at last here was the long sought Spirit of Christ in His Second Coming, the four confessed their sins and returned home to tell others what they had found.[31] The conversion of Meacham was crucial in Shaker development, for he was a trained preacher and used to large revivalist groups. In time he would help develop the structure that gave the sect permanence.

Seekers came to Watervliet in increasing numbers and many confessed their sins and joined the sect. What they found at the center of the Church, as recorded in 1812, was not the emaciated figure described in England, but "a woman rather short and corpulent. Her countenance was fair and pleasant, but often assumed a commanding, severe look; she sang sweetly, with a pleasant voice, but would frequently use the most harsh, satirical language, with a masculine, sovereign address." In 1823 she was more glowingly remembered: "Mother Ann Lee, in her personal appearance, was a woman rather below the common stature of woman; thick set, but straight and otherwise well proportioned and regular in form and features. Her complexion was light and fair, and her eyes were blue, but keen and penetrating . . . . Her manners were plain, simple and easy; yet she possessed a certain dignity of appearance that inspired confidence and commanded respect. By many of the world, who saw her without prejudice, she was called beautiful; and to her faithful children, she appeared to possess a degree of dignified beauty and heavenly love, which they had never before discovered among mortals."[32]

In America there was a distinction between Ann Lee and her English companions, and her new converts. Only a few Americans, such as Joseph Meacham and Lucy Wright, were allowed into the inner circle. With her English Shakers around her, Ann Lee was a loving and concerned mother, a tough spiritual guide, and a judge who was certain she was right. Ann Lee did not preach to large groups. Perhaps she was following the conventional role of women, or she may not have enjoyed or found herself convincing as a preacher. Her force was as a charismatic leader, the central spirit-led soul, who set an example and exuded an energy that convinced many who encountered her. During worship she sang, usually wordless songs, and her voice was described as sweet. When others joined and sang their own songs she set the tone and rhythm. She was a graceful and an inspired dancer and helped make dancing central to Shaker worship. She readily spoke to individuals and small groups about what they should believe and do, and she was fierce in admonishing backsliders. She believed she had found perfection and was *the* way to God: "I am the first Elder in the Church—I have seen God, and spoke with him, face to face, as we speak one to another."[33] She was unusual among religious leaders in saying, that as with Jesus, a seeker need not struggle to know God since, "I have done it for you."[34] Her own struggle to perfection, like Christ's crucifixion and resurrection, was a means for others to find the way; through her "we had found a way out of sin."[35] She was not sure those who joined became perfect like herself; she was not even certain of her closest associates, but certainly they were on the road.

There had been many prominent women in the history of the Christian Church. Some, like Anne Hutchinson in the seventeenth century, had actively protested against the prevailing religious and social customs. Many of these were called witches, or tools of the Devil, for in pushing against prevailing women's roles they seemed unnatural. Because of her aggressive behavior, Ann Lee was frequently called a witch, a messenger of Satan, as she set people against each other and overturned established beliefs and practices.

Probably Ann Lee did not believe that she herself personified the Second Coming of Christ, but saw the converted body of Believers as the Second Coming, and herself as the prophet through whom Christ spoke: "It is not I that speak, it is Christ who dwells in me." Possibly in England about 1770, Ann Lee had said "I am Ann the Word."[36] Later, her male followers would remember Ann Lee as having said Christ was her "husband," or "Lord and head"; the women would recall Ann Lee having called Christ her "lover."[37] She was known as "Mother," "Mother of the new creation," and with biblical reference, "the Elect Lady," and the "woman clothed with the sun."

On May 19, 1780, the area from Rhode Island to Albany, New York, and up into New Hampshire, experienced what would be known as "Dark Day." At eleven o'clock in the morning the sky turned a strange yellow and in an hour it was so dark that candlelight was necessary. By afternoon the sky was a "higher and more *brassy*" color, and there were occasional flashes that resembled the Northern Lights. The night that followed was pitch black. The recorded smell of smoke suggests to modern scholars that an excessive burning of land to clear newly settled areas was the cause of the dark, but for many at the time it seemed like an omen.[38] Like other sects that had learned to turn events to their advantage, the Shakers used the portentous occasion to create converts. Issachar Bates, who became a prominent Shaker, later wrote:

And that day was as dark as night—no work could be done in any house, without a candle! and the night following was as dark accordingly, altho there was a well grown Moon . . . . The people were out wringing their hands, and howling, "the day of judgment is come!" . . . for darkness covered the whole face of the land of New England!

And what next!—Right on the back of this—On came the Shakers! and that made it darker yet . . . for they testified, that an end was come on them; and proved it, by their life of separation from the course of this world; and by the wicked persecutions they endured, from this adulterous generation.

. . . On the part of the Shakers, it was singing, dancing, shouting, shaking, speaking with tongues, turning, preaching, prophesying, & warning the world to confess their sins & turn to God; for his wrath was coming upon them . . . . On the other part it was cursing, blaspheming, mocking, railing lying threatening, stoning, beating with clubs & sticks, & firing pistols.[39]

The Shakers see this event as the beginning of the sect's public testimony, and from that time the numbers visiting them at Watervliet greatly increased. Some who joined became so spirit-filled that they ran through the woods "hooting and tooting like owls," or believing themselves angels, and thus invisible, removed their clothes and ran about causing havoc.[40]

Ann Lee and Shakers since her call spirit-instigated actions "gifts," a broad term that embraces many things, from a general understanding to an "immediate revelation." Gifts may manifest themselves in diverse ways, including singing, dancing, shaking, shouting, leaping, speaking in an unknown tongue, and prophesying.[41]

During the summer of 1780 some of the leaders were imprisoned because their pacifism suggested they might be British spies, and from late July to early December Ann Lee was imprisoned with them in Albany. It is a Shaker tradition that Ann Lee and Mary Partington were transferred to the Poughkeepsie jail, from where they preached to crowds through the bars, and that many were converted.[42]

VISIBLE EMPOWERMENT

The Shakers recognized the force of visually empowering those who had begun the path to belief. The women put their hair under a cap and bonnet and hid their breasts by pinning a neckerchief across them (figure 59). Men had their hair cut short in front (figure 62). Like circumcision, although less permanent, such visible alterations gave potential Believers a sense of stepping from one life into another. For the leaders it showed another approaching victory, and cut hair made a quiet return to the world less easy. In 1780 Valentine Rathbun, founder of the Baptist Church in Pittsfield, Massachusetts, allowed his hair to be cut as part of his inquiry into Shaker beliefs. After cutting it: "they come round him and touch him with their fingers here and there, and give him a sly cross, and in a very loving way put their hands on his head, and then begin to preach their doctrine to him."[43] He did join, feeling he had been promised a leadership position, but being found unqualified for elevation he apostated after only three months. In 1781 Rathbun published a stinging denouncement of the Shakers in a pamphlet: *An Account of the Matter, Form and Manner of a New and Strange Religion, Taught and Propagated by a Number of Europeans, Living in a Place called Nisqueunia, in the State of New-York.*

The Shaker haircut for men did not always occur with solemnity. In 1783 a deaf-mute, Jude Carter, whose wife had joined the sect and refused to again sleep with him, "made a grievous complaint, [at Harvard, Massachusetts] by signs, that the Shakers had robbed him of his silver buckles, cut off his hair, and got away his wife."[44] The Shaker cut of men's hair remained an active signifier of inclusion in the faith well into the twentieth century, and Brothers could recognize each other at a train station, or anywhere, by the short bangs across the forehead and long hair behind.

GATHERING SOULS: WORSHIP SERVICES, SUFFERING AND PERSUADING

In his attack on the Shakers in 1781, Valentine Rathbun caustically described the worship service at Watervliet before the Church started its travels:

[E]veryone acts for himself, and almost every one different from the other; one will stand with his arms extended, acting over odd postures, which they call signs; another will be dancing, and sometimes hopping on one leg about the floor; another will fall to turning around, so swift, that if it be a woman, her clothes will be so filled with the wind, as though they were kept out by a hoop; another will be prostrate on the floor; another will be talking with somebody; and some sitting by, smoking their pipe, groaning most dismally; some trembling extremely; others acting as though all their nerves were convulsed; others swinging their arms, with all vigor, as though turning a wheel, etc. Then all break off, and have a spell of smoking, and some times great fits of laughter . . . . They have several such exercises in a day, especially on the Sabbath.[45]

During the spring of 1781 Ann Lee, her brother William Lee, James Whittaker, and Mary Partington took their powerful message to areas of New England, often to places where they already had followers to welcome them. The trip would last for almost two and a half years.

Hundreds would join the sect, and many of the sites that developed concentrations of Believers later became established Shaker communities. In Enfield, Connecticut, for example, Joseph Meacham was waiting with his father, a former Baptist minister, and his brother David. The latter two had been convinced while visiting the Shakers at the Albany jail. As the group moved about, their forceful presentation of radical ideas caused many listeners to riot, and members were fined for causing disturbances or beaten for what seemed outrageous acts. It is a tradition that James Shepherd was beaten and whipped for a distance of seven miles. Ann Lee was dragged out of a house, thrown into a sleigh, and experienced "acts of inhumanity and indecency which even savages would be ashamed of . . . . Their pretense was to find out whether she was a woman or not."[46] Once at the instigation of a mob she was inspected by a jury of two women "who reported that she was a woman."[47] At Hancock, Massachusetts, Ann Lee and her followers were arrested for blasphemy. When Ann Lee's body was exhumed at Watervliet in 1835 for reburial on Shaker land, it was found that she had sustained a fractured skull, probably the result of the violence directed toward her.[48]

As the Church moved through northern Connecticut, Massachusetts, and parts of Rhode Island, the leaders worked on large gatherings, but they were particularly successful when concentrating on individuals such as Elizabeth Woodman at Harvard, Massachusetts, who recounted how, "One time Mother Ann spoke to me and said come out from that old man of sin and be like an angel and serve God. Elder William [Lee] says It is your lust that makes you afraid. Elder Whittaker says take up your cross and follow Christ in the regeneration[.] Elder Calvin [Harlow] said confess your sins turn out your works of darkness and come to the light and find everlasting happiness."[49]

The group spent extended periods at Harvard. According to Shaker tradition, they drew such large crowds that they often fed up to two hundred of the curious. This image, which recalls Jesus feeding the multitudes, was recorded a decade or two after it quite possibly took place. Its biblical echo suggests a later adjustment of the facts to increase the similarities between Jesus and Ann Lee. (In an early nineteenth-century Shaker book, Ann Lee, the blacksmith's daughter, was linked with Jesus, the carpenter's son.)[50] But support for the accuracy of later recorded events comes from many sources, suggesting that although they might be shaded by time and later needs, the core events in the stories are true. For example, in support of the account of the crowds at Harvard, it is recorded that so many people watched the worship service that the Believers had to go into the woods to cut logs to prop up the dance floor.[51]

Choosing Harvard as their center, the Shakers purchased for nearly $1,700 a building known as the "Square House." It had belonged to Shadrack Ireland, a preacher who in 1753 was transformed when he experienced a belief in his perfection and immortality. Subsequently he gathered around him a small group of perfectionists who believed themselves immortal. They built on the edge of Harvard a square house in which Ireland and some of his followers lived. When Ireland died in 1778 his followers placed his body in the basement, covered it with lime, and awaited a transformation; after a year he was quietly buried in a cornfield.[52] The house not only fitted the description of a building Ann Lee had seen in a vision while in England, but it was also a link to those of Ireland's followers who were ready to transfer their allegiance to a new perfectionist leader.

The Shakers welcomed people of all backgrounds, degrees of education, and ability, but they realized the value of converting those who could help them proselytize. Thomas Brown, who joined as an out-member—not living in a community—and preached for the Shakers, struggled for some years to fully submit himself to Shaker authority. He confessed his sins several times but was unable to satisfy the Elders. They felt he had not achieved unquestioning submission to them as the only path to God and source of learning. During one of his many visits to Watervliet and New Lebanon, a Believer told Brown why the Elders labored so with him: "It is easier to gain a thousand ignorant, unlearned persons, than one who is learned and well read; but when such an one is gained, he is worth a thousand of the former . . . ."[53]

William Plumer, who had been a preacher and a student of the law, visited the Shakers at Harvard, Massachusetts, during the summer of 1782. Later, in 1785, he became a member of the New Hampshire legislature, then governor, and eventually a member of the United States Senate. His descriptive letters provide one of the first mentions of the sermons that encouraged outsiders to join the Shakers while reinforcing their ideas in recent converts. Plumer also noted that the Shakers' openness to inquiries depended on who was asking the questions, and he included a fine description of the whirling dances:

They are very kind and attentive to strangers, so long as they have any prospect of converting them to their faith; but as soon as a man contradicts or asks questions hard to answer, they become sullen,— pronounce him "damned" and avoid his company . . . .

They say that Christ promised to give his church in all ages the power of working miracles; and that in fact they have healed the sick, cured cripples, and restored speech to the dumb . . . . They generally assemble every evening, and frequently continue their exercises till after midnight. I went with them one evening to their meeting, and though they had cautioned me against being surprised at their worship, yet their conduct was so wild and extravagant that it was some time before I could believe my own senses. About thirty of them assembled in a large room in a private house—the women in one and the men in the other—for dancing. Some were past sixty years old. Some had their eyes steadily fixed upwards, continually reaching out and drawing in their arms, and lifting up first one foot and then the other, about four inches from the floor. Near the centre of the room stood two young women, one of them very handsome, who whirled round and round for the space of fifteen minutes, nearly as fast as the rim of a spinning wheel in quick motion . . . .

Sometimes one would pronounce with loud voice, "Ho, ho," or "Love, love"— and then the whole assembly vehemently clapped hands for a minute or two . . . . At other times the whole assembly would shout as with one voice, with one accord. This exercise continued about an hour; then they all retired to the sides of the room for a few minutes. Then the young lady who was the principal whirler walked into the middle of the room and began to dance. All the men and women soon joined her—dancing, singing, whirling, shouting, clapping their hands, shaking and trembling, as at first. This continued near an hour.

After a second intermission two of the Elders, one after the other, addressed the audience; one of them delivering a very ingenious discourse in defense of their tenets and worship, with an exhortation to persevere in the ways of the Lord. He was a man of strong, clear, distinguishing mind, and an easy, yet impressive speaker. More than half of his discourse was in the strong, persuasive language of the Scriptures. . .

Then the assembly renewed their former exercises for more than an hour. This done, several of the young people, both men and women, began to shake and tremble in a most terrible manner. The first I perceived was their heads moving slowly from one shoulder to the other—the longer they moved, the quicker and more violently they shook. The motion proceeded from the head to the hands, arms, and whole body, with such power as if limb would rend from limb. The house trembled as if there were an earthquake.[54]

Ann Lee and other leaders of the Church actively sought the conversion of the living and found it appropriate to allow the dead to benefit from the salvation that the Second Coming of Christ initiated. Elder Rufus Bishop, who gathered testimonies about the first leaders in 1812, recorded: "Mother Ann and the Elders with her uniformly taught the doctrine of a free offer of the gospel to all souls, whether in this world or in the world of the spirits. That none could be deprived of the offer of salvation because they had left the world before Christ had made His appearance; or because they had lived in some remote part of the earth, where the sound of the gospel had never reached their ears. Their labors in the world were not confined to this world, but extended to the world of the spirits, and their travail and sufferings for the salvation of departed souls were often distressing beyond description."[55] In part to convince the unbelieving, Ann Lee and other Shaker leaders did on occasion miraculously heal the sick and the maimed.[56] In a similar way leaders such as George Fox, and the Mormons during the first half of the 1830s, relied on echoing the miraculous acts of Jesus to inspire those who needed convincing.[57]

In the fall of 1782 the Church decided to extend its missionary work by sending out pairs of American converts. In New Hampshire, they discovered ready souls at both Enfield and Canterbury, and in that area found the beginning stages of communal living. Nearby at Loudon, the Freewill Baptists had ordained a deacon who in 1780 assessed the members' wealth, asking them to contribute proportionally to the group and to build homes for those who could not afford them. Sharing was not new to the Shakers; John Hocknell while still in England had supported poorer members. Communal living had been established at Watervliet by 1782 when the Church "held the property which they had there, as a Joint Interest . . . . they gave what they had gained by their industry . . . for the good and benefit of the whole society . . . . That there should be a free table kept there, and other necessaries for the entertainment of those that went to see them—that the poor might have an equal privilege of the gospel with the rich . . . ."[58] The impetus to share was encouraged by James Whittaker, for in that same year he decreed to the group at Ashfield,

Massachusetts: "The time is come for you to give up yourselves and your all to God—your substance, your temporal property—to possess as though you possessed not."[59] In Loudon and Canterbury the Shakers developed communities on large "collective" farms privately owned by individuals, one with thirty, the other with forty Believers, where the members worked without wages and shared what they produced.[60] In the spring of 1783 American Shaker missionaries went into what would become the state of Maine.

While the English leaders could cause outrage and violence as they did their work, the American missionaries seem not to have generated equal hatred and derision. Possibly the combination of their Englishness, during a war against Britain, the message of confession and celibacy, which suggested the dreaded Roman Catholic Church, along with the presence of a central woman, pushed some audiences to actively hate the English missionaries.

DRINK AND NAKED DANCING

In September of 1783 Ann Lee and her close followers returned to Watervliet, where many came to see them. Rumors of Ann Lee's use of alcohol had persisted for years, and now she and other Elders, particularly her brother William, were regularly perceived as drunk. Possibly alcohol had become a means of stimulating visions and gifts, much as marijuana and LSD were occasionally used in the 1960s to facilitate a greater sensitivity to inner and outer stimuli. In the 1780s drinking was very much a part of rural culture, and organized pulpit preaching against it did not develop until early in the nineteenth century.

Throughout his involvement with the Shakers, from 1796 to 1803, Thomas Brown pressed the leaders about the persistent rumors that in addition to drinking, the earlier Shakers had danced naked at Watervliet. The leaders, including Mary Hocknell, who had been with Ann Lee in England and America, denied it. Brown took his inquiry to the apostate Daniel Rathbun, who had known Ann Lee and traveled with James Whittaker to gather Believers. Rathbun told Brown he had asked Whittaker whether to speak the truth about the nakedness and he was told it could be denied because "they were not naked in one sense, being clothed with spiritual garments, 'clothed with salvation.'"[61] Finally an older Shaker did confirm to Brown that there had been naked dancing at Watervliet. That the leaders, who insisted they be accepted as the only source of truth and path to sinlessness, could lie bothered Brown more than the nakedness, and he consequently ended his close involvement with the Shakers.[62] Since excessive drink and naked dancing were noted only at Watervliet the combination was probably a short-lived practice. Stein suggests excessive drinking may have been a problem in various communities into the early 1800s.[63]

In July of 1784 William Lee died. He had been a devoted follower of Ann Lee and one of the most fervent participants in ecstatic worship. At times he was contentious, especially when he thought his sister preferred James Whittaker and might make him the "Lead" after her death.[64] During his later years William Lee drank excessively, and perhaps after his death the amount of drinking and naked dancing decreased. Ann Lee died two months later, on September 8, 1784, just a year after ending her exhausting travels. For more than twenty years she had been torn by often violent spirit-led gifts. For almost two and one half years she had traveled, not staying more than a few months in any one place, and she was often physically abused. However, her death was unexpected. Some of her followers had thought that she might possibly live forever, or at least until the end of the world.

Ann Lee had led her Church to a land where it could take advantage of the revivalist spirit that longed for a distinct path to salvation. She was not the first religious leader to utilize the emotional excitement of spirit-led, ecstatic worship, nor the first to say Christ spoke through him or her, but she did place herself closer to God than other leaders had, by saying, "I have done it for you," and suggesting that she, like Jesus, was filled with Christ's Spirit, and therefore part of the Godhead and a direct means to salvation. By maintaining the superiority of men over women, she made herself heir to Jesus. She established measurable factors by which the Believer knew he or she was saved. Chastity had long been an option for those who wanted to increase their virtue, but Ann Lee made it the central "cross" and added initial and continuing confessions. Thus, those who joined *knew* they were among the chosen, and the leaders who heard confession knew who was saved.

Chapter II

"BROUGHT INTO GOSPEL ORDER"

The exciting, strenuous early years of the Shaker religion produced no objects now recognized as Shaker-made, and we know only a few Shaker-used pieces saved as icons and signifiers of the energized lives of the first Shaker saints in America. During the structuring years that followed, as Believers were "brought into Gospel Order," roads, fields, buildings, furniture, textiles, clothing, and all other design features were organized into conscious grids and linear patterns. The objects the Shakers made were required to be both theologically correct and capable of production in great numbers as a rush of new members settled into new buildings. What they made spoke of uniformity, easy replication, order, and control. Happily for the Shakers, the neoclassical styling of the turn of the century lent itself to their needs, for it gloried in simple shapes, and, in its rural guise, it favored plain surfaces; its very nature encouraged easy duplication of form.

ORDER AND CONTROL

The Shakers began in joyful acceptance of spirit-led ecstatic experiences that brought constantly unfolding understanding. During her lifetime Ann Lee's forceful presence and stinging judgment kept unrestrained worship under her ultimate control. Although she was not always sure all the gifts to the members were from God, she defined who was a Believer. She spoke against laws, for they blocked spontaneity; as the authority and jury, she moved people in and out of salvation. After her death the new leaders turned to rules and patterns formulated to give the sect a controlled vitality. The establishment of unifying beliefs and community structures secured the survival of the sect even as it contradicted the fundamentally experiential nature of the faith. As most religions and societies have discovered, unstructured spontaneity leads to a fracturing that may end in chaos, anarchy, or disappearance. For permanence, spontaneity must be incorporated into patterns and guidelines that prevent members' whirling away on individual trajectories. While preventing clashes, rules also allow those in authority to judge who is inside and who is outside of the group. After the Revolution, secular Americans lived within laws established by the majority; for the Shakers, however, authority lay at the top of the structure. An example of how the leaders established control and created unity is seen in the ways they made visible their preference for the right side over the left. The Millennial Laws of 1821 (see Appendix, Chapter XIII: 3 and 4) ruled that when sitting quietly at the beginning of worship, a Believer must fold his or her hands with the right thumb over the left; the right knee went down first when kneeling. These Laws were not published, or generally known, when the apostate William Haskett, in *Shakerism Unmasked* (1828), recalled them with some accuracy, and included two more right-over-left injunctions not in the Laws: boots went on the right foot first, and the right foot went on the first stair when ascending.[1]

But even as the Shakers tightened control over temporal matters, they believed that God would continue to reveal new understandings. The inevitable tension between physical control and spiritual openness created much of the excitement, and many of the problems, that the Shakers experienced during the next half century. In 1857 the prominent American historian Benson John Lossing helped the Shakers counteract many negative writings about them with a positive article in *Harper's New Monthly Magazine*. He accompanied his text with eighteen woodcuts based on drawings and watercolors he had made (see figures 50, 52, 53, 134 and 135). Lossing noted how the Shakers lived ordered lives but would not codify their theology: "They have no creed, because they believe that the operations of the Divine light are unlimited."[2] Although by this time Shaker theology was codified and systematized in several of their publications, Lossing may have been reflecting the belief that there must always be an openness to gifts that promote new insights and understandings.

JAMES WHITTAKER, LEADER: 1784–1787

After Ann Lee's death authority passed briefly to James Whittaker, who began the structural patterns that later became complex and forceful under Joseph Meacham and Lucy Wright. Whittaker was the natural candidate to lead after Ann Lee, in part because the slightly earlier death of her brother William removed him as a contender. Whittaker was the Shakers' best preacher and he had been trusted by Ann Lee, who delegated to him the task of explaining Shaker beliefs to individuals and to large and small gatherings. His only drawback was his fanaticism, particularly about women. He saw no value in marriage under any circumstances, and if women tried to touch him, "he would spring from them." He believed, however, "when we get into heaven you may hug and kiss me as much as you have a mind too."[3] In 1785 Whittaker wrote to his parents in England, describing himself a "minister of the gospel in the day of Christ's second appearance. All earthly profits and pleasures; all earthy generation, and propagation which are the delights of all men in their natural birth . . . have I forsaken for Christ's sake . . . that sordid propensity to, or ardent desire of copulation with women . . . . All we . . . being separated from all effeminate [i.e., homosexual] desires, and sensual pleasures, are in possession of the only hope of eternal life: my God has delivered me, redeemed my soul, filled it with heavenly glory, and the power of an endless life." To justify his unmarried state to his unbelieving parents, he affirmed he multiplied by religious conversions: "I have begotten many thousands of children."[4] For Whittaker heaven and earth were very different places. On earth stringent living was part of perfection; in heaven men and women would be involved romantically, and other delights, such as gold, would be natural.[5]

Feeling that it was the right time for a massive missionary effort to the world, he ordered a large ship to carry missionaries to other lands, but after various false starts, the project was abandoned, and Whittaker concentrated on encouraging communal sharing among Believers. Through letters and extensive travel he sought to make the Church a collective organization rather than a group of individuals.

The most visible and perhaps most lasting effect of Whittaker's three years of leadership was the creation of the first Shaker building erected almost exclusively for worship. The log house at Watervliet, and the Square House in Harvard, had served both as meeting and dwelling houses. In the new and later meetinghouses, only members of the Ministry had rooms. For the site of the new meetinghouse, he chose New Lebanon rather than Watervliet because the land was better there and New Lebanon was more convenient to the developing communities.

The meetinghouse, built on the George Darrow farm, was raised on October 15, 1785, and first used on Sunday, January 29, 1786. It was a plain, gambrel-roof building (at right in figure 50), constructed to be without interior walls or columns that would impede worshipful dancing. It was first erected where the larger "arched roof" meetinghouse, begun in 1822 and dedicated in 1824, now stands at left in the illustration. (As shown there both buildings face east. When on its original site, the first meetinghouse faced south.)

The worship service had already been divided, with the women at one end and the men at the other, or in separate rooms if they were small. Eighteen days after Ann Lee's death on September 8, 1784, the Marquis de Lafayette visited the Shakers at Watervliet and an accompanying French diplomat described a somewhat quieter service than is found in earlier descriptions: there were about one hundred forty Believers in a large wooden hall, with men at one end and women at the other. The service began with three sermons: They spoke of celibacy, declared that Believers were "inaccessible to sin," and stated that at her death Ann Lee had gone directly to heaven. During the dancing many "pirouetted on a single leg, with surprising rapidity."[6] At Enfield, Connecticut, in 1785, several preachers spoke, declaring that Christ's Second Coming "was manifested in the flesh" by the Shakers. After each sermon, solemn wordless songs were sung, along with groaning, sighing, and shaking. There was violent dancing, again with the men at one end of the room and women at the other. The participants were streaming sweat.[7] In the new meetinghouse, Whittaker firmly fixed the separation of the sexes by decreeing: "And these are the Orders that ye are to observe and keep. Ye shall come in & go out of this House with Reverence and Godly fear. That all men shall come in and go out at the west doors and gates [at the left when standing outside and facing the front of the original building]. And all women at the east doors & gates. That men and women shall not intermix in this House or yard nor set together. That there shall not be any whispering or talking or laughing or unnecessary going out and in in time of publick worship."[8]

Not every Believer was happy with what was happening to the sect. There were defections during Ann Lee's last year at Watervliet because of the gifts of drink and nakedness. After her death others departed, some because they had thought she would not die; others missed her forceful presence. Some left during Whittaker's leadership because of his fanaticism. Four of the original handful of English Shakers departed: Richard Hocknell and Nancy Lee married each other, and in 1788 John Partington and James Shepherd withdrew. Later Shepherd became destitute, rejoined the sect, and lived as an insignificant member.[9]

Whittaker died on July 21, 1787. During his nearly three years of leadership he began to organize the frenzied worship and social activities that defined the Believers under Ann Lee, built the meetinghouse, and encouraged the development of shared lives and property in "community neighborhoods." Soon these Shaker communities would dot the landscape.

MEACHAM AND WRIGHT, LEADERS: 1787–1796

There were four possible successors to Whittaker, all American: Joseph Meacham, his brother David, Calvin Harlow, and Lucy Wright. The sole woman seems not to have been considered, but when in a short time she rose in authority it would be remembered how close she was to Ann Lee. Before his death Whittaker designated all three men as the "joint ministry." Joseph Meacham took over at New Lebanon while his brother and Harlow traveled to instruct other communities.[10] At New Lebanon Meacham showed such skills of leadership that the other two acknowledged him as head, and it was recalled that Ann Lee had said "Joseph is my first Bishop; he will have the keys of the Kingdom; he is my Apostle in the Ministry, my first Bishop; what he does, I do."[11] She had prophesied that he would one day lead: "It will not be my lot, nor the lot of any that came with me from England, to gather and build up the Church; but it will be the lot of Joseph Meacham, and others, to gather the Church."[12] With the meetinghouse in New Lebanon as the center, Meacham encouraged Believers to move to land around it, and many came "into unity," although it meant living in huts, cabins, barns, and the few houses that existed. On Christmas Day, 1787, they ate their first communal meal. The majority of the first to live there arrived in 1788.

Meacham elevated Lucy Wright to "lead in the female line," creating a rigid separation of the sexes in a dual structure. With equal authority they became "beloved Parents in Church relation, and first in relation to the whole visible body of the Believers." Then Meacham added Henry Clough and Thankful Hamlin as assistants, thus establishing the tradition of two men and two women in the Central Ministry.[13]

Meacham gave no reason for his promotion of Wright, but rather announced it as a "gift," which made it an uncontestable act of God. It was logical to have both male and female spiritual leaders since, through Jesus and Ann Lee, Christ's Spirit had been manifested in male and female messiahs, who personified God's male and female aspects. To support Meacham's action, anecdotes were recalled that linked Lucy Wright to Ann Lee. (Wright had been married to Elizur Goodrich before they joined as early converts. She, like Ann Lee, resumed her maiden name.)[14] It was remembered that Wright had been left in charge of the women at Watervliet while Ann Lee traveled, and that she had favored Wright as a possible successor. Wright had tended Ann Lee during her last illness, and once when Wright asked Lee to return to bed she was told: "I will; I will be obedient to you Lucy; for I am married to you, and I will go with you."[15] Meacham saw himself as above Lucy Wright, but he acknowledged that a woman could be first among equals, writing to her near his death that after him she would become "the *Elder or first born.*"[16]

WOMEN AND MEN

Meacham's placing a woman again at the center of the Church allowed women a degree of freedom, creativity, and responsibility unusual at the time. But while the women were parallel to the men, they were not equal. Men dominated Ministerial correspondence and theological writing, and most Shaker patents were issued to men. Male Office Deacons were called Trustees, and they controlled the community's money and property, while the women of the same rank were known as Office Sisters. Until late in the nineteenth century the Office Sisters were prohibited from holding property in trust, which shows an acceptance of the laws of coverture that in most states made it difficult, until after the 1840s, for women to own property.[17] When the Believers walked within the meetinghouse in "Church Order," their procession moved in double file, with the Elders followed by the Brothers, and then the Sisters. Each sex was organized with position and age leading.[18]

The basic job descriptions for the sexes remained as in the world: men did the heavy work, "the thick work," on the farms, and had their own line of businesses, such as chairmaking. They also did tailoring and at an early date, weaving. Later weaving became women's work. Shaker women cooked, cleaned, did most of the weaving and sewing, and took part in developing religious, domestic, and community order. They also created their own lines of business, such as bonnet making, and controlled the income they produced. They also did some finishing work on men's tasks, such as painting some of the window sashes and finishing furniture. As a visitor recorded in 1797, "above all" they did "ceaseless laundry. Cleanliness is one of the tenets of this society."[19]

It is not surprising that there was no radical realignment of jobs, for breaks with convention are usually in accord with their time and place; the stances taken by the feminists of the late nineteenth and twentieth centuries could not be imagined in the late eighteenth century. The degree to which the role of women evolved was not unlike the degree to which the buildings, furniture, textiles, and other designs changed. In most cases, what the Shakers made is closely related to, but discernibly different from, what the world produced.

The Quakers had made women equal to men, but the Shakers created a structure that gave women a controlling interest in half of the vertical line of ascent to a top position equal to that held by a man. The ability of women to control half of a complex social structure did allow them to develop organization and leadership skills usually confined to men. When, at the end of the nineteenth century, women in the sect greatly outnumbered men, and feminist understanding began, they took over many of the tasks once performed by men. In the twentieth century women have been the primary actors in most Shaker communities and have performed formerly male tasks. For example, the last Shaker chairmaker was Lillian Barlow, who took over that responsibility in 1934 and made chairs until her death in 1942 (see figure 196).

FAMILY, COMMUNITY, AND "CHURCH ORDER"

By 1790 Meacham and Wright, known as First Father and First Mother, were firmly in control. They had the meetinghouse, the start of communal living, and an ever-tightening, structured authority. Gradually the other communities followed the New Lebanon model, and when a community was loathe to give up the freedom of the self-directed spirit-led life and worship, Meacham strode in to take charge. Upon his arrival at Hancock in 1790 he told those who gathered that "there was not one soul upon earth could find relation to God without him," and he chose twenty men and twenty women to be the first, or leading, order.[20] Between February 19, 1791, and August 17, 1792, the Harvard Community was inspected by thirty-four visitors from New Lebanon, including Joseph Meacham and his assistant Henry Clough.[21] When Canterbury, New Hampshire, apparently resisted organizing in the manner he dictated, Meacham moved most of their members, many of whom had been together for ten years, to other communities and replaced them with Believers from New Lebanon and Enfield, New Hampshire.[22] Ann Lee, who had believed the end of the world was rapidly approaching, would not have allowed such restriction, but her charismatic control was gone and the world had not ended.

"Gospel Order" (also called Church Order) consisted of several factors that broke each Believer's former patterns of family, friends, and economic independence, while placing approval of every act in the hands of the leaders. First, while joyfully receiving a new life in God, members were removed from the worldly social patterns of the extended family and non-Believing friends. Second, the family unit was dissolved. Children were housed away from their parents, and husbands and wives separated—at least as far as living across the hall from each other. Third, a spatial division spread the members across the landscape into self-sufficient "Families" of approximately thirty to one hundred Believers—about half male and half female—which were placed up to a quarter of a mile apart. The number in a Family often depended on the size of the dwelling house.

The Family was the primary unit to which each Believer belonged, and with which he or she agreed to a formal covenant. The Family formed the base of the organizational pyramid that rose to the Central Ministry located at New Lebanon. Each part of the organization had as its authority two Elders and two Eldresses. In addition, each Family had two Deacons who were in charge of the land the Family farmed and the men's enterprises. Two Deaconesses oversaw the Family's kitchen, housekeeping, and the women's line of businesses. The other members of the

Family could relax and feel provided for, as Thomas Brown observed in 1812: "A deacon in each family, transacts the temporal business: others have no worldly concern, as food, raiment, and all things necessary, are by him provided . . . ."[23] Trustees dealt with worldly matters both legal and monetary. Families were usually named according to their geographical relationship to the meetinghouse or for a geographical feature: for example, the South, West, or Hill Family. Each Family worked independently of the others and developed its own special product, such as chairs or brooms. Members of one Family did not speak to those in another without the consent of a leader; they met at the meetinghouse, but social exchange was by permission only. Goods were sold or exchanged between Families, for each Family was a discrete economic unit, as was each community.

The sense that these newly-structured units were Families was encouraged by joining those with kinship ties. Priscilla J. Brewer has found that Family members were often related biologically: "Over half the original 1790 Hancock Church Family came from just five extended families . . . ." And "In 1832, the New Lebanon First Order totaled eighty-one residents, thirty-six of whom (44.4 percent) shared a surname with a fellow Family member." That everyone slept and ate in close proximity reinforced the Family as a unit. "When New Lebanon's First Order moved into its new[ly enlarged] 'Great House' in September 1832, sixteen 'retiring [bed] rooms' were shared by the eighty-one Believers in the family, or about five people to a room."[24]

Realizing that some degree of pattern communication between the sexes would help diffuse tensions caused by their separation, Meacham in 1793 introduced "union meetings" where several times a week four or five pairs of Brothers and Sisters met to discuss topics of general concern. Those paired were of similar age and interests, but the pairs ranged in age to keep a group balance. Often the Sister of each pair took care of the Brother's clothing, while the Brother did chores for her, such as fixing or hauling.[25]

As Whittaker had decreed the separation of the sexes, even to entering at different ends of the meetinghouse, Meacham carried the same rule into the animal and plant world. He prohibited the mingling of animal species in pastures and barns, and the grafting of one fruit tree onto another species. To keep Believers' affection focused on God and their new Family, animals were not to be made into pets because "it would corrupt the animals by raising them out of their order."[26] It also removed the possibility of seeing them engage in sexual activity.

The Families within a community were divided into three types. The Senior Order, which contained the Church Family, was for the more spiritually advanced. The Junior Order was made up of younger people, who often worked on the land. Those in the Novitiate Order had not committed themselves and retained control of their property. They were there to try the life while the leaders judged their spiritual qualities and depth of commitment. The novitiates lived some distance from the others, for the leaders realized that seekers, like those who joined, had different degrees of religious and intellectual understanding and some might interfere with the smooth running of the community. In 1817 Rufus Bishop, in the Ministry at New Lebanon, wrote describing these three types of Believers to David Darrow, in the Ministry of Ohio:

We find, that among those who embrace the testimony, there are different degrees of faith and sense, especially in their first setting out—and [they] may justly be ranked in three classes. One class receives faith, but instead of turning their backs to the world, they keep their faces toward the world, striving to keep their friendship and fashions as far as possible. This is a poor, or bad mark for a believer, and ten chances to one if he does not stumble and fall backward.

Another class is drawn into the faith more by the principle of love, they love the messengers of peace through whom they were begotten into the faith, they admire the manner of their address, and even the color and form of their garments are the most desirable; so that they see no alteration or improvement for the better. This is beautiful and praise-worthy, especially in young believers.

A third class (or rather those of a riper travel) are looking for a continual increase, not only in spiritual things, but in temporal also—they are looking for a new heaven, and a new earth—(not instantaneously created) but progressively according to the will of God manifested in the lead. And although our former Parents could see by the gift of God, the future order and glory of Christ's kingdom on earth yet neither they nor we could come into the full possession and enjoyment until it was gained by travel.[27]

Eventually there were nineteen substantial communities, and some smaller ones, reaching from Maine to Indiana and Kentucky (see figure 1). Each was centered around a Church or Center Family. The communities were divided into Bishoprics, manageable groups of adjacent

THE SHAKER COMMUNITIES

1 Watervliet, New York 1787–1938
2 New Lebanon, New York 1787–1947
3 Hancock, Massachusetts 1790–1960
4 Harvard, Massachusetts 1791–1918
5 Enfield, Connecticut 1790–1917
6 Tyringham, Massachusetts 1792–1875
7 Alfred, Maine 1793–1932
8 Canterbury, New Hampshire 1792–1992
9 Enfield, New Hampshire 1793–1923
10 Sabbathday Lake, Maine 1794–
11 Shirley, Massachusetts 1793–1908
12 Gorham, Maine 1808–1819
13 West Union (Busro), Indiana 1810–1827
14 South Union, Kentucky 1807–1922
15 Union Village, Ohio 1806–1912
16 Watervliet, Ohio 1806–1910
17 Pleasant Hill, Kentucky 1806–1910
18 Savoy, Massachusetts 1817–1825
19 Whitewater, Ohio 1824–1907
20 Sodus Bay, New York 1826–1836
21 Groveland, New York 1836–1895
22 North Union, Ohio 1822–1889
23 Narcoossee, Florida 1896–1911
24 White Oak, Georgia 1898–1902

1. THE SHAKER COMMUNITIES

communities linked to facilitate their administration. The Bishopric Ministry consisted of two Elders and two Eldresses, who moved regularly between the communities for which they were responsible, staying in their private residences in the meetinghouses of each community. Usually the Bishopric Ministry appointed Church Family Elders and Eldresses of the communities they controlled, and authority and appointments fanned out from them to the dependent Families' leaders. For all this, authority lay in the Central Ministry in New Lebanon, which appointed the Bishopric Ministries. (The Central Ministry also served as head of the New Lebanon Bishopric.) Although each group of four Ministers, from the Central Ministry down to the Family level, was known as the Ministry and called so as a group—as in "The Ministry is coming tomorrow"—there was, in a very Shaker hierarchical manner, further structuring within the group of four. The senior male and female Ministers were addressed as Elder and Eldress, as in Elder Joseph and Eldress Lucy, and the junior pair as Brother and Sister, as in Brother Henry and Sister Ruth. During the first years the Central Ministry lived with the Church Family. In 1792 they withdrew to live apart in the meetinghouse and work in their own shops, where they did jobs — such as tailoring and making oval boxes — they could leave for long periods when they were living at their other communities. To make themselves more special, they ceased hearing confessions, leaving that kind of involvement to Family Elders and Eldresses.[28]

The structure of the Society is easily diagramed, although for a variety of reasons—including the lack of a qualified person—positions might go unfilled for some time. Likewise, a Believer could hold more than one position, or the job might be left open. The organization of the Hancock Bishopric in the 1820s is given in figure 2. Its leaders reported to the Central Ministry at New Lebanon while they had under their care three communities: Tyringham and Hancock, Massachusetts, and Enfield, Connecticut. The scheme further shows the organization of the Hancock Community: Senior Order, Junior Order, and Novitiate Order. Each had two Families.

GOVERNMENT AND ORGANIZATION
OF THE HANCOCK COMMUNITY AND CHURCH FAMILY

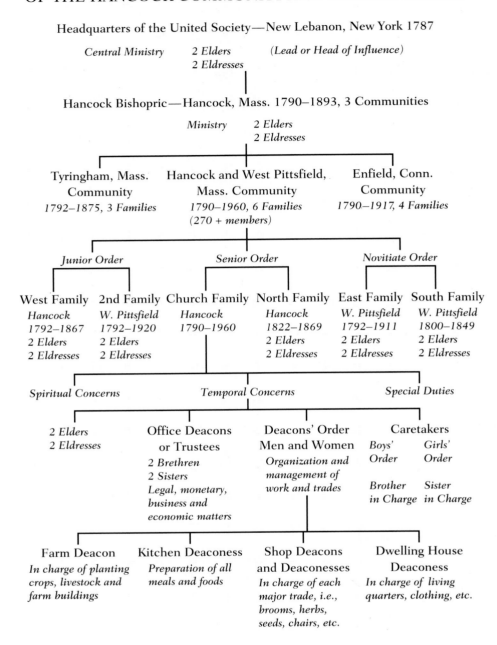

Headquarters of the United Society—New Lebanon, New York 1787

Central Ministry 2 *Elders* *(Lead or Head of Influence)*
2 *Eldresses*

Hancock Bishopric—Hancock, Mass. 1790–1893, 3 Communities

Ministry 2 *Elders*
2 *Eldresses*

Tyringham, Mass. Community	Hancock and West Pittsfield, Mass. Community	Enfield, Conn. Community
1792–1875, 3 Families	1790–1960, 6 Families (270 + members)	1790–1917, 4 Families

Junior Order | *Senior Order* | *Novitiate Order*

West Family	2nd Family	Church Family	North Family	East Family	South Family
Hancock	*W. Pittsfield*	*Hancock*	*Hancock*	*W. Pittsfield*	*W. Pittsfield*
1792–1867	*1792–1920*	*1790–1960*	*1822–1869*	*1792–1911*	*1800–1849*
2 Elders	*2 Elders*		*2 Elders*	*2 Elders*	*2 Elders*
2 Eldresses	*2 Eldresses*		*2 Eldresses*	*2 Eldresses*	*2 Eldresses*

Spiritual Concerns | *Temporal Concerns* | *Special Duties*

2 Elders 2 Eldresses	Office Deacons or Trustees	Deacons' Order Men and Women	Caretakers
	2 Brethren 2 Sisters Legal, monetary, business and economic matters	*Organization and management of work and trades*	*Boys' Order* / *Girls' Order* *Brother in Charge* / *Sister in Charge*

Farm Deacon	Kitchen Deaconess	Shop Deacons and Deaconesses	Dwelling House Deaconess
In charge of planting crops, livestock and farm buildings	*Preparation of all meals and foods*	*In charge of each major trade, i.e., brooms, herbs, seeds, chairs, etc.*	*In charge of living quarters, clothing, etc.*

2. ORGANIZATION OF THE HANCOCK
COMMUNITY AND ITS CHURCH FAMILY

The Church Family was first in the Senior Order and it is further described.

Hervey Elkins, who was a member of the Enfield, New Hampshire, Community (founded three years after Enfield, Connecticut) from his childhood to about 1850, when he left, delineated the line of authority as he wrote a sympathetic account of the Society. As in the military, each rank reported to the rank above; ideas or problems were carried by inferior to superior up the chain of command and no deviation from the proper order was tolerated. On signing the Family covenant—a Shaker is covenanted to an individual Family—all property is given to the Church and "Members also stipulate themselves by this signature to yield implicit obedience to the Ministry, Elders, Deacons and Trustees, each in their respective departments of authority and duty . . . . The Shaker government, in many points, resembles that of the military. All shall look for counsel and guidance to those immediately before them, and shall receive nothing from, nor make application for anything, to those but their immediate advisors."[29] The rules governing behavior within the Society were written down as "Milenial Laws, or Gospel statutes and ordinances, adapted to the day of Christ's second Appearing; Given & established in the Church, for the protection thereof: By the Ministry & Elders. New Lebanon, August 7th: 1821." The second rule is: "All trials [sufferings, temptations] must be opened according to the appointed order of God; and Believers are strictly forbidden to open their trials to those who are not set in order to hear them."[30]

The fourth feature of Meacham and Wright's "Gospel Order" was the commitment of all property: land, buildings, money, and household goods. Like dissolving the personal family unit, this eliminated personal sentiment and individual control, and made members dependent on the new Family unit and its position within the scheme. It also accrued greater power to the leaders. When the Shakers first gathered they had little but land and the ability to work, and from the days of Ann Lee a commitment to labor was central to Shaker life. Before she elevated Calvin Harlow to a position of authority Ann Lee required him to learn a manual trade so that he could contribute to the welfare of the group. Later he rose to be first Elder in the Hancock Ministry.[31] With work seen as part of the sacred life, laziness was not tolerated, and the Shakers soon became comfortable in new buildings. By the early nineteenth century they were envied for their secure lives in neat, clean villages by neighbors who might live in much more haphazard settings.

The fifth part of "Gospel Order" was the commitment to a covenant. The idea of a religious covenant had been part of the Puritan Church; those who "owned" the covenant agreed to be under the watch and discipline of the church. At first the Shaker covenant was an oral agreement to a statement by Meacham. In it, all agreed to hold everything in common, not to bring the Church into debt, and to abide by the leaders in all temporal matters. Believers did not have to abide in spiritual matters for there they were responsible to the actions of God's Spirit. In 1795 the covenant was put into a written form and signed by twenty men and twenty-two women. As the number of Families grew, each Family signed its own copy. It became standard for a youth to decide at twenty-one whether to sign or go into the world.[32] This signing gave those gathered into Gospel Order the legal status of a "Religious right." The phrasing, "All the members that should be received into the Church, should possess one Joint Interest, as a Religious right," meant that covenanted members who later wished to leave could not sue for part of the community's property, or for wages for the work they had done while in the community: "Therefore it is our Faith never to bring Debt or blame against the Church, or each other, for any Interest or Services used should bestow to the Joint Interest of the Church, but Covenanted to freely give and Contribute our time and Tallents, as Brethren and Sisters . . . ."[33] Some seceders did sue for wages, but none were able to win: "Through his [Meacham's] instrumentation the Believers were gathered 'into a body religious, not a body politic, or a body corporate . . . . Their real and personal estate could not be treated as a joint tenancy, nor a tenancy in common, therefore it was made a consecration—a consecrated whole.' "[34] Although there has never been a successful claim against the Church, the Society has usually worked out amicable arrangements with those who left. If they felt responsible, as for a Believer who had come as a child, they would do much more than for someone who left soon after joining. It was customary to return "in kind" movables brought to the community. For someone who had been a member for some time, a gift of clothing and one hundred dollars was not unusual. Returning the exact things was rarely possible, for most worldly things would have been sold to the poor, used up, or discarded. Land, except for perhaps an outlying piece, was not returned to the former owners who left, for it had become part of the "whole."

Between 1795 and 1799 about twenty members left New Lebanon. Some did not wish to give up their property by signing the covenant. For a few, the advancement of a woman to a controlling role, a "petticoat government," was not acceptable.[35] For many the new ordering of life and religious services was too unlike what Ann Lee had allowed, and the rules continued to tighten. When members asked Lucy Wright why things permitted under Ann Lee were now forbidden she answered:

Young people must not expect to please themselves with every fancy, or think to have every notion they would naturally want, or to have their own ways; but they must remember that they are called to be exemplary in all things.

Brethren and Sisters, you hear a great deal about the cross; perhaps a great deal more than you want to hear, many times; but every one ought to consider that all they have gained toward the kingdom of heaven is by the daily cross; and all who do not carry the daily cross in all their thoughts, words and actions cannot travel far in the way of God.

Some think they have harder times than others; but such ought to consider whether there is not something in them which needs greater crosses to subdue. And don't you flounce or frown till you see whether you do not need all you have and more.

[Some say] Mother [Ann] and the Elders [allowed greater freedom and] why can't we do so now? If they allowed such things who can blame us? But I want you to remember that such things are not allowed; we do not allow disorder.[36]

By 1800 ritual pattern had fixed the worship experience into a formal ballet. "[T]hey sat silent a few minutes, then arose and stood in their order, and sung a tune without words; after which, four or five sung a more lively tune, to which the others *danced*. After dancing about half an hour, they all kneeled in silence a few minutes; as soon as they arose, their leader spoke of an intermission." During the break in the service they went across the road to the dwelling house.[37]

What had begun under the Wardleys and Ann Lee as the commitment of confession under the lead of the Spirit of Christ, had become a religious and social establishment. During the early years the Shakers, as did other small ecstatic protesting Christian groups, exhibited cult-like features as they whirled around the figure of Ann Lee. She was the mesmerizing leader who oversaw mind-bending rituals, and used outside threats to create a defensive cohesion. Now, a quieting Society settled down as a distinct sect fixed by rules, ownership of land, and the moderating influence of the many new members who had not known the frenzied years.

SHAKER THEOLOGY

Meacham wrote the first reasoned and written statement of Shaker theology: *A Concise Statement Of Principles Of The Only True Church, According To The Gospel Of The Present Appearance Of Christ. As held to and practiced upon by the true followers of the Living Savior at Newlebanon, &c.* Published in 1790 by the Shakers, six years after her death, it did not mention Ann Lee. It did affirm that the Second Coming had occurred but defined it as the Spirit of Christ living in his people, those he had chosen to be his body, the "Living Savior" at New Lebanon. Meacham cited four stages of God's grace through Christ that brought the world to the first years of the Millennium. The first was a promise of Christ:

given or made known to the patriarchs by promise . . . [and made evident in] Ezekiel's vision of the holy waters . . . . The second dispensation was the law that was given of God to Israel, by the hand of Moses; which was a further manifestation of that salvation which was promised through Christ by the gospel . . . . But when they disobeyed the command of God, and committed sin, and became like other people, the hand of the Lord was turned against them . . . . The third dispensation was the gospel of Christ's first appearance, in the flesh: and that salvation which took place in consequence of his life, death, resurrection, and ascension at the right hand of the father . . . so that he has become the author of eternal salvation to all that obey him . . . . [B]ut there was another day prophesied of, called the second appearance of Christ . . . . Even so shall it be in the day when the son of man is revealed . . . and make a final end of sin; and establish his kingdom upon earth: but as the revelation of Christ must be in his people, whom he had chosen to be his body, to give testimony of him and to preach his gospel to a lost world . . . . The fourth dispensation or day is the second appearance of Christ, or final, or last display of God's grace to a lost world, in which the mystery of God will be finished and a decisive work, to the final salvation, or domination of all the children of men. (Which according to the prophecies rightly calculated, and truly understood, began in the year of our Saviour Jesus Christ, 1747.)

The date of the Second Coming is the year the Wardleys separated, by Shaker tradition, from the Quakers. Salvation and deliverance from sin and death lie in believing and obeying the gospel of Christ, by confession, forsaking of sin, "and denying ourselves and bearing the cross of Christ, against the world, flesh, and devil." Christ's Gospel is further explained as "denying all ungodliness and worldly lusts."[38]

It is uncertain why Ann Lee, or even a central female leader, was not mentioned in this first Shaker publication. In Whittaker's letter to his parents of 1785, which was published with Meacham's *A Concise Statement,* he too stressed Christ's second appearance while failing to mention Ann Lee or that a woman was central to the faith. However, in private Meacham did discuss the appropriateness of Christ appearing in female form.[39] How the *public* argument was structured may have been a conscious effort to ease people past a female manifestation of Christ once Ann Lee was gone. When in 1794 a visitor at New Lebanon asked whether Ann Lee was the founder of the Shakers, it was denied.[40] It seems that the more difficult beliefs were kept secret during public statements but openly professed among the inner circle. Thomas Brown, in his 1812 *An Account of the People Called Shakers,* recalled that when he first asked about Shaker beliefs in 1798, he was told the Second Coming of Christ is spiritual in his people. But, other, older members gave him the "very strong meat" that affirmed Ann Lee as the Second Coming as prophesied in the Bible. "They believe that the fulfillment of most of the prophesies, centres in the first and this second coming of Christ."[41] In 1796 Joseph Meacham wrote in a letter to Lucy Wright, "Christ Jesus our Lord & Mother are the two Chief anointed ones that stand before God in Relation to the salvation of all souls & as god hath Fulfilled his Promise in them both the Foundation is Laid in the headship of man For the Restitution of all things."[42] By 1809 Ann Lee was openly professed as the second appearance of Christ, and after 1816 Shaker publications regularly recorded that in Ann Lee "Christ did visibly make his second appearance."[43]

Meacham, like Ann Lee and Whittaker, was obsessed with sexuality, and the need to overcome the greatest cross, "the flesh." He believed sexual arousal and ejaculation could be eliminated through penance and physical mortification. Writings by the Shakers and apostates record efforts late in the 1780s by some Shaker Brothers to "destroy the whole order of nature," through physical exhaustion. But though physically weak some still experienced spermatorrhea, in which semen emerges without an orgasm. The inability to halt the emission of what was believed to be "unclean and hateful," caused the Brothers to give up this aspect of perfection.[44]

By 1794 there were eleven organized communities scattered over four states: New York, Connecticut, Massachusetts, and New Hampshire, and the area that would become the state of Maine in 1820, and it was possible again to think of evangelizing. For Meacham, life in the Millennium was one of mortifying the body, eschewing nature in favor of new and perfected behavior, and it was logical that he would try to perfect missionaries spiritually as he had perfected communities temporally. Having seen how hard it could be for older people to accomplish perfection, he focused on the young, whom he found more malleable and able to suppress natural instincts. He developed a core of youthful Believers who were to subjugate their will to a life of discipline and march forth to convert the world. Their training was spiritual rather than academic, for formal education was limited to a few months. Boys were taught in the winter when they were not needed in the fields, and girls in the summer. Only the Bible and two other types of books were allowed: spelling and mathematics. Because Meacham's strictures were so severe and his demands so concentrated, the youths rebelled, and during 1796, the year of Meacham's death, twenty of them left New Lebanon. In 1798 the idea of a perfected order of youths striding out to convert the world was abandoned.[45]

LUCY WRIGHT, LEADER: 1796–1821

In writing of Lucy Wright in 1796, Meacham acknowledged her as his successor as the central force: "Thou, tho' of the weaker sex . . . will be the *Elder or first born* after my departure." In the spring of 1796 he resigned in Lucy Wright's favor and died that August.[46] With the death of Meacham, power was again in the hands of a woman. Some had hoped that Henry Clough, second to Meacham in the male half of the Lead Ministry, would become the more powerful figure, but he had never been a forceful leader, and until her death in 1821, Lucy Wright was the controlling person, and she became the individual most responsible for creating the Shakers of the first half of the nineteenth century. Wright combined the religious vision of Ann Lee with the practicality of Meacham. She knew the excitement and religious importance of ecstatic worship and had for a decade seen the value of structuring the society. Lucy Wright was not as fond of restrictions as Meacham, and she restored many of the earlier religious practices. Individual gifts were to be expected and honored: convulsions, speaking in tongues, and "dancing in the back [earlier] manner."[47] The dances and wordless songs remained patterned, but they were performed with more joy and spontaneity. To the dance Wright added hand motions imitating the "'motioning' of Angels." She also encouraged angelic "bowing."[48] Meacham had written a theological statement that excluded Ann Lee; under Wright, Lee again became central, perhaps more than ever before. It strengthened Wright's hand to have a woman join Jesus as the way to God, and Ann Lee was regularly recognized as a second manifestation of Christ, a female messiah.

The first leaders, from Ann Lee through Lucy Wright, have remained the most revered members of the faith. What they said and did was recalled and written down to be saved as valuable to the faithful, and the gleanings are still regularly read by Believers. To gather written accounts, Elder Rufus Bishop sent out letters in 1812, asking anyone who had known Ann Lee to write testimonies about her life, and to record her words so they might be preserved and used to encourage and instruct. These were not to be made public but were to serve the faithful as written records of a saint who could not record her thoughts. In 1816, under the guidance of Seth Youngs Wells, the gleanings were organized and published in a small edition of about twenty copies as *Testimonies of the Life, Character, Revelations, and Doctrines of Our Ever Blessed Mother Ann Lee, and the Elders with Her*. The books were to be kept from outsiders, who might use the wonders described—from visions to miraculous healings—against the Church. From then on, sayings by important living saints were carefully recorded. For example, Lucy Wright's last recorded words, said about fifteen days before her death, speak of the heavenly golden chain in which each link of the spiritual life is important: "To my sense Believers are held together in union by a *golden Chain*. This chain is composed of the gifts and orders of God and every order is a link in the chain; and if you break any of these orders, you break this chain and are exposed to be led astray, But while you are careful to keep the gifts and orders of God, you are surrounded with this golden chain, and are secure from evil."[49] (The role of gold and gold chains is discussed in Chapter VII.)

Many of the objects used by the early leaders have been iconized and handed down as symbols of achieved sainthood. An example is the saddle used by Lucy Wright and given by her to a promising leader, Hannah Goodrich. Goodrich was born in the town of Hancock in 1763. Her father, a deacon in the Baptist Church, visited the Shakers in Albany in 1779 and, reporting them "as being in possession of the beautiful apostolic gifts," he joined. In 1780 Hannah and her brother Daniel went to Watervliet, and Ann Lee and the Elders so impressed her that she too believed. In 1792 twenty-nine-year-old Hannah Goodrich was a member of the Hancock Community when the Central Ministry at New Lebanon appointed her to the Bishopric Ministry over Canterbury and Enfield, New Hampshire, and she received the title of Mother. "The saddle which Mother Hannah Goodrich used on her first journey from Hancock to Canterbury is still preserved at the last named place. It formerly belonged to Mother Lucy Wright, who presented it to Mother Hannah."[50]

Sabbathday Lake, Maine, honors the saddlebags that, according to tradition, Lucy Wright presented to Sarah Kendall, formerly of the Harvard Community, when she was sent to assume a leadership role over the newly gathered Believers at Alfred, Maine, in 1793.[51] Gifts of significant objects were exchanged as signs of love and as signifiers of authority. Lucy Wright died on February 7, 1821. Fifteen days later Ruth Landon at New Lebanon wrote to Molly Goodrich, Eldress at South Union, Kentucky, about Eldress Ruth's elevation to Wright's former position of female Lead in the Central Ministry. As both a remembrance and a sign of her new authority, she sent with the letter a cap that had belonged to Mother Lucy.[52]

One of Wright's most important acts was to send missionaries into the revivalist ferment developing in Kentucky and the neighboring states since 1799. Like the English Shakers, she recognized the value of thrusting preachers into groups seeking nearly the configurations of beliefs that the Shakers offered: the immediacy of God, powerful personal experiences—in Kentucky people were dancing, rolling about, jerking, and barking during services—the approach of the Millennium, and the ability of the Believer to know he or she was saved. In 1805 three Shaker missionaries left on foot for Kentucky with a horse to carry the baggage, and there were many ready to hear them. An early convert and future leader, Richard McNemar, later wrote: "For upwards of fifteen years my soul has been on the wheel, forming into union with professed followers of the lamb, but never did I find my mate, until I found the spirit from New Lebanon."[53] At Ann Lee's death there had been one thousand Believers; when Wright died there were four times that number.

Lucy Wright dispatched David Darrow to lead the many who had converted in the West. There, during the next twenty years, Father David, as he came to be known, oversaw the development of four communities in Ohio, two in Kentucky, and one in Indiana.[54] Darrow's importance in Shaker life remained obscure until Stephen J. Stein's recent history showed Darrow to be as creative and important in the West as Wright was in the East. Although Darrow continued to acknowledge Wright's authority and seek her guidance, Stein has demonstrated that Darrow was equal to both Meacham and Wright in influencing the development of the Society. Within a year of his death in 1825 the Central Ministry, conscious that the western Shakers might seek independence, abolished the elevating titles of Mother and Father for the heads of communities and members of the Ministry. This helped keep ultimate authority in the East.[55]

Among the first converts in the South were African-American slaves. Ann Lee had wished everyone to convert, even those who had died. Once when speaking of seeing heavenly spirits she said: "I have seen the poor negros, who are so much despised, redeemed from their loss, with crowns on their heads [in heaven]."[56] On occasion owners and their slaves joined and became equal in the Society, and it was noted that former masters often served former slaves. If an owner left the Society and wished to take back a slave, the Shakers sought to free the slave to remain a member by paying wages to him or her for work done. The money was then used to purchase his or her freedom: "Today we purchased Jonas Crutcher a colored man who had been a believer about nineteen years. We kept him hired here while his owner retained him a slave. We have bought him to prevent his being sold South. He was accepted on equal terms."[57] They had used the wages to pay the owner's price. Throughout the nineteenth century there were African Americans in most Shaker communities (two appear at the right of figure 59). In the middle of the century the African American Rebecca Jackson was Eldress of a Family of mostly African Americans in Philadelphia (she is discussed in Chapter VIII). In the North the number of African-American Believers would total about thirty to forty.[58] However, they were seen by some Shakers as different, and this feeling persisted throughout the nineteenth century. In 1843 Richard Bushnell, Elder of the North Family, New Lebanon, wrote to Archibald Meacham at Watervliet: "We want no more to do with coloured people than duty requires[,] neither should we wish to neglect [our duty] towards them if made known to us—but heretofore we have experienced no good results from taking them in among us."[59] For at least some of the members the clothing African-Americans wore was thought to be properly different: In 1872 "Sister Aurelia came to our shop with another new fashioned cap with a wide forepart and crown set in. We thot it very nice for a sick person and a corpse and we did not know but she was inspired to get up something plain and easy for the colored sisters."[60]

By engaging the seekers at the Kentucky revivals the Shakers gained more than converts, for the Kentuckians' emphasis on exotic gifts reinvigorated that aspect of Shaker worship. From them, the Shakers learned the value of worded songs as developers and conveyers of theology. By 1800 the Shakers had a few publications that defined their beliefs, but an emphasis on sung communication was better suited to their experiential and developing religion. Although new songs were rehearsed before they were sung in unison at worship services, the ideas they expressed could be refined and changed over time. The first Shaker hymnal of Shaker texts, *Millennial Praises,* was published in 1813, and there Seth Youngs Wells wrote about hymns "for words are but the signs of our ideas, and of course, must vary as the ideas increase with the increasing work of God."[61]

By 1810 the ideas that undergirded Shaker beliefs and activities into the 1860s were firmly in place. The rigid control of Whittaker and Meacham had given way to more spontaneity under Wright. Although gifts were received within a fairly tight framework of controlling rules and practices, there was greater freedom. The eleven communities in the East were well organized and economically sound, and membership was growing. After the death of Lucy Wright in 1821, the Central Ministry became a true collective. Never again would one individual supervise such dramatic changes as had occurred during the thirty-five years dominated by Meacham and Wright. What the leaders inherited was a governmental structure that worked surprisingly well. Nearly all the substantial communities the Shakers developed were in place, and they were recognized as clean, well run, and economically successful. The buildings and the objects in them had, since at least 1810, the distinctive look recognized as the Shaker manner of handling design.

Chapter III
SHAKER DESIGN: SOURCES, CENTRAL CONTROL, REGIONAL DIFFERENCES

O ur review of the ecstatic Shaker years and the subsequent ordering of the Society makes possible an understanding of the design aesthetic that the Shakers developed during the first years of the nineteenth century. The order established by Meacham and Wright during the 1790s affected thought, worship practices, the placement and actions of people, and how Shaker-made things looked as the physical landscape was made to accord with the behavioral one, even though this was contrary to the openness to spirit direction that was the basis of belief. Everything from the layout of the settlements to the design of a chest of drawers was intended to reflect and record a perfected social structure. Communities were asked to build and plant appropriately. When Meacham visited the Harvard Community in 1791, to prepare it for gathering into Gospel Order, he told the members their fields and gardens should be planted in straight rows because "this will be preaching to the world for they admire the beautiful outward order of the people of God."[1] In 1795, when Shirley, Massachusetts, was a community of two hundred Shakers living on three thousand acres, an outside observer recorded: "The walls are excellent & high & upon an horizontal line, & as straight as they can be laid."[2] This ordering is seen in a later view of Canterbury, New Hampshire (figure 3). When workers at New Lebanon built an office building with a square roof, Meacham declared the form not in "church order" and it was replaced overnight with a gambrel roof, like that on their first meetinghouse.[3] In 1793 the Shakers at Harvard could be described as: "Neat in their apparel and furniture. Their houses which they have erected in this town, are large and commodious and approaching something like elegance."[4]

Fully part of the nineteenth-century American push to better how one lives, the Shakers strove to improve their physical circumstances. The structure of their communities provided the time and there was encouragement for individuals to develop new devices that would make life and

3. PHOTOGRAPH: THE NORTH FAMILY, CANTERBURY, NEW HAMPSHIRE
Inscribed on back: "North Family" and "Taken down in the 1920s"
About 1890; before 1894
H. about 6³/₈" W. 9⁵/₁₆"
Canterbury Shaker Village, Canterbury, New Hampshire

labor easier. They were very aware of what was happening in the world, and kept informed about the latest inventions and adopted those they found useful.[5] The Shakers were successful farmers and artisans, and they sold the surplus from their fields and barnyards to the world. From the beginning, they also produced objects for sale, among them leather goods, ax- and hammerheads, nails, scythe handles, baskets, churns, boxes, sieves, measures, spinning wheels, reels, hand cards (used in preparing wool for spinning), chairs, smoking pipes, whiplashes, textiles, copperware, and brooms.

When the Shakers first came into Gospel Order they lived in whatever was available and used what objects the Believers brought with them. There are many lists of what accompanied them, for the Shakers became good recordkeepers. In part this was because of the complex legal issues that the sharing of property created. These would take years to sort out, and careful accounting was part of the required legal record. In 1793, for example, Samuel and Elizabeth Johnson brought to New Lebanon ("Do" means ditto, or the same as above):

4. CHAIR
Worldly chair which, by tradition, was used at Harvard by Ann Lee
Probably Harvard area, Massachusetts
1750–90; Shaker additions about 1830
Seat pine; legs, stretchers, and left arm support maple; rest of upper part ash or hickory. Bottom half of handholds pieced on. Original parts have a heavy coat of red paint, Shaker parts a thin coat of red.
H. 30⅛" W. 24" D. of rockers 25⅞"
Fruitlands Museums, Harvard, Massachusetts

Two Cows	£10- 0-0	one bead Quilt	£0-10-0
Four Swine	2- 8-0	A Tosting Iron	0- 4 -0
one Barrel one half Pork	5- 0-0	An old Horse	3- 4 -0
one case of Draws	1-10-0	Money which had been lent	
Two old Chery Tables	0-12-0	to the town of West Stockbridge	
Two Fether Beads bolsters		was collected and brought back	
and Pillows	5-10-0	here and delivered to Amos	
Two under Do and two Pillows	0- 9-0	Hammond	2-12-0
Six pares of Sheets	4- 0-0	also a lot of Land which I sold	
five Pairs of Pillow Cases	1- 5-0	to Daniel Goodrich for	73- 6-8
Nine Towels	0- 9-0	and collected the Money and	
one Flowered Coverlet	1-10-0	delivered it to Amos by the	
one toe Do one Duck Blanket	1- 6-0	Liberty and Priviledge I had	
one old brass kittle	1- 0-0	Elizabeth Johnson the Second	
one Iron Pot one Tea Kittle	0-13-0	hath had	
two Small Do and one Skillet	0-12-0	A Bead and Beading [mattress	
one Pair of Hand Irons [andirons]	0-16-0	and covers, not a bedstead]	5- 0 -0
Shovel and Tongs	0- 8-0	A New Chest	0-12-0
An ax	0- 8-0	Lebanon January 25th 1803	
A warming Pan	0- 8-0	I have made a Statement for Distribution of	
a frying Do and two pails	0- 5-0	my Estate according to a Rule of the Church	
one Pair of Iron Flats	0- 4-0	viz. (a Daughter one Part, a Son two Parts,	
Puter Plate 23½ a ⅙	1-15-3	their Mother four Parts, and the Father Eight)	
three Pounds of Feathers	0- 9-0	One Part is 53 Dollars 29½ Cents[6]	

Furniture was rarely a major item on these lists. Food, cooking utensils, and textiles for warmth were more necessary in the old and the new situation. The above listing is without a bedstead. Furniture did arrive: in 1791 Joshua and Louise Burch brought four chairs, one table, one stand; in 1793 Susana Draper, five chairs, and "sundreys old furniture"; in 1793 Josiah Tallcot a clock, "Sundry Articles Household Furniture." In 1792 a Brother who withdrew from New Lebanon took away with him "1 High Case of Draws, 1 Teatable, 1 Chist with a Draw in it."[7] In 1796 over one hundred tools were returned to two craftsmen, a wheelwright and a joiner; they included chisels, saws, hammers, a glue pot, and planes with shaped blades for making moldings.[8]

Only a few worldly objects used by the early Shakers are known. Those associated with Ann Lee hold a special place in Shaker history. Small pieces of the textiles she used are carefully preserved, and at least two chairs are associated with her. According to tradition, the worldly sack-back Windsor chair in figure 4 was her chair when she spent long periods during her missionary years at Harvard, Massachusetts. It was made during the second half of the eighteenth century and painted with a heavy coat of red. Later, the legs were shortened and rockers added and perhaps the medial stretcher was changed; all these parts have only a thin coat of red. Although not Shaker-made, it has a Shaker-added feature. In Shaker-made chairs the rockers are normally placed in slots cut into the center of each leg. The rockers in those made in the Harvard Community after about 1830 were secured by one rivet and burr through each leg. In this chair, with rockers added to the sides of the legs, each leg employs two rivets and burrs.

5. CHAIR
Probably Shaker-made; history of ownership at
Watervliet; similar finials used at Watervliet and
New Lebanon, New York, and in the world
Top slat incised: "Mother Ann Lee. 1776"
1790–1810
Maple and hickory; paint removed; legs extended
at base
H. 40½" W. 19½" D. of seat 14½"
Paint removed and legs extended by the donors.
Philadelphia Museum of Art, Philadelphia,
Pennsylvania: gift of Mr. and Mrs. Julius Zieget

The chair in figure 5 has a history of ownership at Watervliet, but it may not be Shaker-made. It employs reel-shaped turnings in the back posts as found in worldly chairs made about 1780–1810. The finials are like those used in both the world and on early Watervliet and New Lebanon chairs. At some point the chair was shortened. Unfortunately, collectors extended the legs, and removed the original red paint. (The top slat retains a late nineteenth or early twentieth-century incised inscription: "Mother Ann Lee. 1776." This may be the chair mentioned in *The Shaker* of May 1876, where it was noted that since the Church Family of Mount Lebanon was to show new Shaker chairs at the Philadelphia Centennial, "We have thought it a good idea, that they should take with them Mother Ann Lee's chair, now in possession—what there is left of it— of Shakers at Watervliet, N.Y. It has been so constantly used, that the legs are worn up to the lower rounds, all round."[9]

USING SKILLED WORKERS

Many new objects were needed and people with useful skills were put to work in the trades they knew. Beginning with Edward Deming Andrews, most scholars have written that if Believers were too happy in their work, and thus not a sufficiently humble vehicle of God, they were transferred to another job.[10] On the contrary, the Shakers were too practical a people to indulge such a practice, and manual skills from the time of the blacksmith's daughter Ann Lee were valued. (Part of the confusion arises from the fact that some work was seasonal, and Brothers could work at a variety of jobs throughout a year.) For example, a tailoring shop at New Lebanon was managed by one of the first converts, David Slosson, a tailor by trade before he joined.[11] In 1787 Reuben Hosford, an experienced hatter, made hats at New Lebanon and for five years he sold them to Shaker communities and to the world. In 1792 he was sent to Hancock to organize a center of Shaker hat-making.[12] David Rowley, one of the best known early furniture makers at New Lebanon, had worked between 1800 and 1806 for Daniel Gay, a cabinetmaker in his native town of Sharon, Connecticut. Then he practiced as an independent journeyman in Lebanon Hollow, New York. In 1809 he became a Shaker, and until his death in 1855 he produced furniture at New Lebanon.[13] Shaker Brothers working in a single craft remained so consistent that about 1850 Isaac Newton Youngs could draw up a long list of Brothers who had remained for years in the trades of tanning, blacksmithing, tailoring, hatting, shoemaking, joinery and carpentry, saddle making, box making, coopering, clothier's work, kitchen work, weaving, and card making (used in preparing wool). Youngs noted that his extensive list was far from exhaustive.[14]

CHIPPENDALE, NEOCLASSICAL, AND SHAKER STYLING

The objects the Shakers brought from the world were in a mixture of styles. Pieces listed as old in an inventory, as in "Two old Chery tables" mentioned in the 1793 inventory just given, could have been seventeenth-century, William and Mary, Queen Anne, or Chippendale (which in rural areas lingered in fashion until the end of the century) in style. The latter design attitude was part of the international rococo taste developed in the middle of the eighteenth century, which called for an active line breaking out into space with great vigor. As it filtered into rural vernacular hands it encouraged forceful, active designs such as that found in the cupboard seen as figure 6. There a bold form is crowned by a large cornice, and the doors (with H-hinges) have great surface plasticity: the panels are boldly raised, projecting their thick centers forward. Early Shaker-made things reflected such local styling and, as in the world, used local woods. And, until about 1860, all domestic Shaker furniture was finished with a colored surface. Like the worldly cupboard in figure 6, the Shaker-made cupboard with a New Lebanon history in figure 7 has raised panels and H-hinges. Opening the doors of the Shaker piece gives easy access to only the middle area of the shelves; this, along with the depth of the raised panels and H-hinges, suggests an early date. (Soon, as in figure 47, an open door would make much more of the shelf space immediately available.) The cornice is thin and this may indicate a Shaker theological move to simpler forms, or it may be part of the late eighteenth century's lean, neoclassical simplicity.

The Shakers altered many of the worldly pieces they used. The chest of drawers seen as figure 8 was made acceptable by removing brass pulls from the two false drawer fronts on the chest section and the two real drawers below. Wooden pulls were added to the real drawers. Later, following a custom developed by the Shakers at Harvard, a drawer was inserted between the bracket

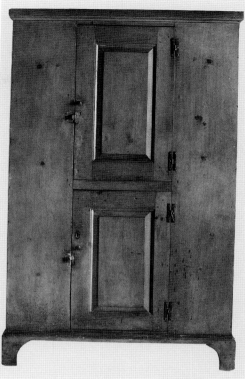

feet. The worldly mahogany table in figure 9, made 1750–90, with lathe-turned legs and feet, originally had four rails connecting the legs, and no drawer. Shaker hands cut away one of the long side rails, added a useful deep drawer, and a thin rail below it. When the drawer is removed the mortices in the square parts of the legs that once held the long side rail are visible; they still hold the cut-off tenons. A chalk inscription on the bottom surface of the top gives what might be an illegible name, and the date 1835. If, before its reworking, the table followed the worldly custom of the time, the four original rails had modest shaping at the ends of their lower edges. (It must once have appeared very like the worldly table in figure 10, although that piece was made with a drawer.) The Shakers cut away the lower shaping of the remaining rear and side rails. Then they made those rails the depth of the square part of the legs. To do this they left the upper three inches of each original rail untouched, but below that line they chiseled away the faces of the rails and placed on the reduced wood new, thin, plain mahogany boards. (While 3⅜ inches in height, the new pieces are only three-eighths of an inch in depth. To keep these thin boards firmly in place, the ends were beveled and slid into beveled grooves in the legs.) The front of the new drawer is butternut; the knob is cherry; the new interior wood is pine. The plainer and more useful Shaker conversion had two wooden pegs placed in each end rail. (There are tiny metal balls along the lower edges of the rails, which may have held a bag or a skirt; their date is unknown.) When Edward D. and Faith Andrews published this wonderful Shaker conversion in their second article, in *Antiques* (April 1929), they accepted it as "an uncommon, possibly a unique [Shaker] example."[15] It is a unique and wonderful Shaker conversion.

9. TABLE
Worldly table, probably from Massachusetts or
Rhode Island, altered by the Shakers, probably
at New Lebanon, New York
Original piece 1750–90; Shaker additions 1835;
inscribed in chalk on bottom surface of top:
"[probably a name] 1835"
Original piece mahogany; Shaker additions:
drawer front butternut, knob cherry, additions to
rails mahogany; secondary wood: pine
H. 26¼" W. 32¼" D. 22 ⁵⁄₈"
Private collection

10. TABLE
Newport, Rhode Island
1750–90
Mahogany and chestnut
H. 26¾" W. 30½" D. 23"
Descended in the Otis-Doggett families
of Southeastern Massachusetts
Courtesy of Israel Sack, Inc., New York, New York

NEOCLASSICISM

A new emphasis on classicism developed in Europe in the third quarter of the eighteenth century as part of the Enlightenment's urge to join reason and idealism to classical purity. Since every individual was of equal value, and reason and the intellect were to govern, art should be uncompromising in recapturing the ideals of Greece and Rome.

The first phase of the new classicism produced intellectually idealized forms, with an overlay of antique motifs, to project calm, rational behavior by reasonable people. In the new style, ovals, circles, spheres, squares, rectangles, and references to antique objects such as shields, echoed rational thoughts and historical symbols. As an instance of the intellectualized new forms, in 1777 Goethe designed for his garden at Weimar, Germany, an Altar of Good Fortune (figure 11). The sphere represented ever-moving, restless desires poised on a cubic block of virtue. Design had been reduced, and timeless containment set on a rational, equal-sided, space-defining base. Significantly, the sculpture was placed in a natural landscape as real and thriving, as full of growth, wonder, and emotions, as the intellectually active virtues controlled within the sculpture.

To research the classical style, some English designers, such as Robert Adam, went to Italy, and some also to Greece, to absorb the forms and motifs of ancient architecture and other artifacts. When Adam returned to England in 1758 he became one of the most sought-after architects and interior designers. Until his death in 1792 he transformed existing structures and created new buildings for British aristocrats. His lofty design attitude filtered down to the merchant level by the 1780s, and two furniture designers produced pattern books to help makers and buyers create fashionable, if more modest, classical furniture. George Hepplewhite's widow published his *The Cabinet-Maker and Upholsterer's Guide* in 1788, and Thomas Sheraton produced his *The Cabinet-Maker and Upholsterer's Drawing-Book* between 1791 and 1793. Sheraton's book was issued in revised versions into the next century. These publications carried the new look beyond Britain, and became the first pictorial sources used widely in America. Previous designers, such as Thomas Chippendale, had produced London design books, but none had the impact of these works. The new publications suggested just the right degree of complexity to suit the merchant class of England, and the upper economic level of America that paralleled it in income and taste. In these designs, carved, inlaid, or painted motifs decorate simple geometric shapes. Further, in 1790 America was ready for a look that projected its new republican idealism by harking back to Greece and Rome.

The Hepplewhite design for a Pembroke table (figure 12) shows this intellectual phase of Enlightenment furniture. The basic form makes no reference to an historical table. What suggests the classical world are the tightness of form, the use of ovals and urns for the inlaid or (if desired) painted decoration, and the light against dark colors employed. Both urban and rural shops that produced such pieces could make less elaborate versions for those who wished to patronize them but preferred, for matters of taste or economics, less enriched forms. Plainer but still stylish tables, like that in figure 13, were used in lesser rooms in elaborately furnished houses, or as a prominent piece in more modest homes. This small mahogany drop-leaf table was made and labeled by Robert Lawton of Newport, Rhode Island, in 1798.

Even more modest examples were made in both town and country shops. They employed local woods, such as cherry, maple, or birch in New England, and in the middle and lower states, walnut. If the wood was colorful—cherry or walnut, for example—the finish was usually clear. Tables with light-colored woods as their visible parts, such as maple, birch, or pine, were normally painted a rich color. On occasion even colored woods, such as cherry, had their color intensified by a red-colored stain or varnish. The inexpensive, rural, vernacular table in figure 14 was made, labeled, and dated 1813 by William Lloyd, cabinetmaker of Springfield, Massachusetts. It employs cherry on the outside and maple and pine inside as secondary woods. The small metal pull on the drawer is original. Such vernacular versions of early neoclassical styling, with plain tapered legs and simple tops, proved so useful, attractive, and easy to produce that the form remained an option even when new fashions stumbled over each other to catch the eye. They continued to be made from New England to the western states at least as late as 1900. The Shakers found such forms practical, easy to produce in quantity, and sympathetic to their theological injunctions.

11. ALTAR OF GOOD FORTUNE
Design by Johann Wolfgang von Goethe for his garden at Weimar, Germany
1777

SHAKER NEOCLASSICISM

The Shakers wished to live a life of mortification as part of an achieved perfection to prepare themselves for an opulent life in heaven with Jesus and Ann Lee. Visions of some of the heavenly objects they would enjoy are shown in the watercolors included as figures 163 through 166. On earth, the Shakers usually sought to expunge unnecessary details from thoughts, daily living, and designs. In practical terms, a streamlined design made it easy to multiply similar pieces for the many new converts, while providing a sense of equity.

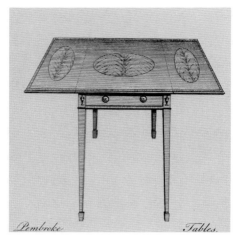

12. PRINTED TABLE DESIGN
Design by George Hepplewhite, London, England
September 1, 1787
From The Cabinet-Maker and Upholster's
Guide . . . ., *third edition, produced by Alice*
Hepplewhite, 1794

Above, right:
13. TABLE
Labeled and dated by Robert Lawton, Newport,
Rhode Island, 1798
Mahogany and pine
H. 27" W. 30¾" D. 18"
Preservation Society of Newport County: gift
of Mr. and Mrs. Ralph E. Carpenter

Opposite:
14. TABLE
Labeled and dated by William Lloyd, Springfield,
Massachusetts, 1813
Cherry, maple, and pine
Closed: H. 29" W. 35" D. 19"
Old Sturbridge Village, Sturbridge, Massachusetts

15. TABLE
Purchased from Hancock, Massachusetts,
1810–40
Cherry, pine, and yellow poplar
Closed: H. 28¹/₁₆" W. 41⁷/₈" D. 16¾"
Collection of the Shaker Museum and Library,
Old Chatham, New York

Thus, Shaker design, as it emerged around 1800 to 1810, mixed two parallel and complementary themes: the elimination of unnecessary features and the expression of the neoclassical aesthetic. The congruence of these two impulses produced what is now called the "Shaker look," or "Classic Shaker."

The cherry drop-leaf table in figure 15 was made by the Shakers at Hancock fairly early in the nineteenth century. It uses a cherry pull with a threaded shaft on the drawer. The bottom of the drawer is pine, and its sides and back are yellow poplar. (Small wooden pulls are a feature associated with, but not limited to, Shaker furniture; see the worldly painted pine piece with maple pulls in figure 21.)

LATE CLASSICAL STYLING

By 1790 in Europe and 1800 in America, designers moved from intellectual classicism to the more archaeologically correct Greco-Roman style where antique motifs decorated antique forms. Many chairs followed the Greek *klismos* form, their saber-shaped legs recalling chairs on Greek vases. (These appear on Shaker gift drawings, where they represent the kind of objects that the Shakers would use in heaven; see figure 165.) Lyres, eagles, cornucopias, and other classical references, which during the earlier intellectual phase of neoclassicism had been relatively flat, became richly three-dimensional and robust: legs might echo the limbs of lions or goats, or end in dolphins' heads. Swags and leafage were carved in deep relief; the styling is more reflective of Roman than Greek designs.

Paralleling this passionate exuberance was one of equal richness, but its elaboration was added by placing gold-colored decoration on flat rectilinear surfaces. As in the earlier intellectual classicism these were smooth, tight, and basically simple designs, but they differed in stressing a layering of squared and rectangular shapes arranged so that the squares and rectangles stepped forward from the main mass. The early nineteenth-century commode with two doors in figure 16 is in the French style championed by such Paris designers as Percier and Fontaine, who rose to prominence around 1800, during the height of Napoleon's power. The piece in figure 16 was made in New York City, about 1810, by the French-trained cabinetmaker Charles-Honoré Lannuier. In France such pieces made for the court often sat directly on the floor, without paw feet, and exhibited more gold-colored ormolu decoration. The New York piece directly copies a French design created for a more modest setting, published as plate 48 in *Collection des Meubles et Objets de Goût,* by Pierre de le Mésangère, in 1803. The New York version layers the following areas: slightly vertical rectangular panels enclosed by raised rails, drawer, panels flanking the drawer, pilasters, and lower rail. The blocks below the pilasters project even further. On many court-level French pieces these blocks would be seen as front feet, since they and the lower rail rested directly on the floor. The main constructional difference between the New York piece and the published design is that the doors in the design are totally flat, without enclosing rails.

In England one of the most famous uses of this tight, layered style is the east facade of the stable block of the 1814 Chelsea Hospital in London, designed by John Soane. In America this styling affected the whole range of contemporary artistic expressions, from the furniture of the New York cabinetmaker Duncan Phyfe, to the buildings of the Boston architect Charles Bulfinch. After the fall of Napoleon in 1814–15, the restored French monarchy, in seeking to have less pretension than the emperor, continued the flat rectilinear look with beautiful veneers, but decreased the amount of complex ormolu mounts. Other continental countries, employing easily smoothed hardwoods such as mahogany, pear, and cherry, produced the restrained upper-middle-class style we call Biedermeier. With layered rectangles, gentle curves, and classical references in smooth shapes, this style provided hospitable furnishings suitable for the bourgeoisie, who set them against plain walls, bare floors, and white curtains.

THE "SHAKER LOOK"

Similar to Lannuier's and others' layered furniture designs, and to Charles Bulfinch's architectural designs—which included granite walls made of layered slabs—the facade of the New Lebanon cupboard over drawers in figure 17 moves in and out in rectangles: the door panels are set below the surfaces around them and the drawer faces project toward the viewer. This is one of the earliest dated Shaker pieces, and one of the first to use flat panels in its doors. A penciled inscription on the upper surface of the bottom board reads: "January 29th 1817/ JB & GL."

16. COMMODE
New York, New York
Stamped: "H. Lannuier New York"
1810–15
Mahogany; parcel-gilt; marble
H. 39¼" W. 47¾" D. 24"
Courtesy of Christie's, New York, New York

17. CASE WITH CUPBOARD OVER DRAWERS
New Lebanon, New York
Inscribed on top of bottom board: "January 29th 1817/ JB & GL"
Pine painted red
H. 83" W. 43" D. 17½"
The Society for the Preservation of New England Antiquities, Boston; Cogswell's Grant, Essex, Massachusetts; gift of Bertram K. and Nina Fletcher Little.

18. CHEST OVER TWO DRAWERS
Eastern Massachusetts, probably Boston area
1790–1810
Mahogany and pine
H. 32½" W. 40½" D. 17¼"
Historic Deerfield, Inc., Deerfield, Massachusetts

19. CHEST OVER TWO DRAWERS
Labeled and dated June 23, 1836, by S.W.
Spooner, owner of a furniture and feather store in
Brattleboro, Vermont
Pine painted red; for later changes see text
H. 39" W. 42" D. 18½". The top edge of the
chest has recently been planed, the hinges are
reset and have new screws, and areas have later
paint over the original paint. Possibly it was
originally finished with a dark line edging the
front of the chest area, to provide a paneled look;
a dark band shows through the later paint.
Old Sturbridge Village, Sturbridge, Massachusetts

20. CHEST OVER TWO DRAWERS
New Lebanon, New York
1820–40
Pine painted red; mahogany knobs attached with
blunt-end screws from inside drawers; bone or
ivory keyhole surrounds
H. 37¼" W. 43¼" D. 19½"
Collection of Robert and Katharine Booth

Figures 18 through 20 trace the changes that occurred as designs moved from an American high-style approach, through local vernacular designs, to Shaker work. The eastern Massachusetts chest over two drawers (figure 18) was made about 1800 of mahogany and pine. Although full chests of drawers were fashionable from the 1680s, many customers of all social and economic patterns continued to want the convenience of a storage chest over one or more drawers. This chest over drawers is fairly stylish: it exhibits a refined attention to details executed in an expensive, imported wood, and the drawers are edged with applied cock-beading.

The red-painted pine chest over two drawers shown in figure 19 is a worldly vernacular expression labeled by S.W. Spooner, owner of a "furniture and feather store" in Brattleboro, Vermont. The piece is dated June 23, 1836, and like thousands of others made during the eighteenth and early nineteenth centuries, has three useful storage areas and a bright, durable finish. This example reflects lean classical styling by being severely contained without much interruption to its surface, and in using simple arched bracket feet. The flat wooden drawer knobs have the shape of fashionable brass pulls of this date (as in figure 38).

The chest over two drawers in figure 20 was made by the Shakers in New Lebanon between 1820 and 1840. It is of pine, finished with a thin coat of red paint. (The use of paint and colored and clear varnish is discussed in Chapter VII.) This piece continues the basic features found on pieces made in the world. Straight-angled bracket feet were used at this date on many New England pieces,[16] and they appear on a number of Hudson River Valley pieces owned by the New York State Museum in Albany. What is not standard outside of Shaker communities is that the

21. CHEST OVER DRAWER
New England
1750–1810
Pine painted red; maple knobs; nails used sparingly, most boards secured in place with wooden pins
H. 27¹/₂" W. 51" D. 19"
Private collection

Opposite, above left:
22. STAND
New England
1760–1810
Cherry
H. 27" Diam. of top 15¹/₂"
Historic Deerfield, Inc., Deerfield, Massachusetts

Opposite, above right:
23. TWO STANDS
Probably New Lebanon, New York
1820–50
Cherry
H. 26⁵/₁₆" Diam. of top 17¹/₂"; H. 26" Diam. of top 19"
Collection of the Shaker Museum and Library, Old Chatham, New York

projecting lips around the drawers are finished to a smooth quarter-round, rather than as a molding with a sharp fillet (although the smooth form appears on the non-Shaker piece in figure 21). Particular to Shaker designs is the proportioning of the drawer heights. Unlike most worldly designs the bottom drawer is much deeper than the top drawer (the bottom drawer is 10¹/₈ inches high, the top one about half that at 5¹¹/₁₆ inches). Usually worldly drawer heights decrease by about 1 inch to 1¹/₂ inches as they move upward. (A similar differential in drawer heights was used in the higher styled piece in figure 18. This is an exception in the world, but standard in Shaker hands. The Shakers' freedom to break normal canons of drawer heights is discussed further in Chapter VI.) The lower edge of the end-cleats of the top of the Shaker piece project down slightly over the outsides of the chest. Perhaps this was to minimize the passage of dust or to provide a deeper piece to help control warpage. The front and rear edges of the lid do not have a similar treatment.

A like mixture of design retention and change is found in a comparison of worldly and Shaker cherry stands. The dish-top cherry stand in figure 22, although beautifully balanced in form and detail, is so generic in idea and execution that it must, until further documentation is found, be called New England and broadly dated from 1760 to 1810. The form of the pillar, with

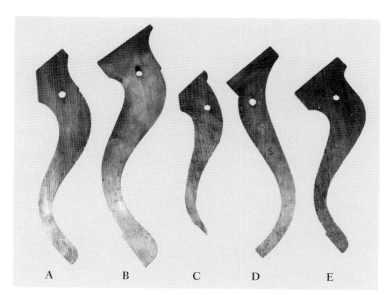

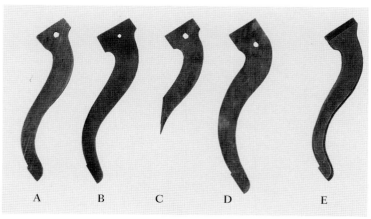

24 A–E. CANDLESTAND AND TEA-TABLE
LEG TEMPLATES
*Used by Nathaniel Dominy V in East Hampton,
New York*
*1790–1830; (moving A at left to E at right, D is
for a form of a leg used after 1800)*
Pine
A: L. 13³/₄" W. 9" D. ³/₁₆" *(initialed "JD" both
sides)*
B: L. 15¹/₂" W. 9³/₈" D. ³/₁₆"
C: L. 10 ⁹/₁₆" W. 7⁷/₈" D. ³/₁₆" *(broken and
initialed "JD" both sides)*
D: L. 13¹/₂" W. 9¹/₂" D. ³/₁₆" *(stamped "14" and
"4³/₄" on one side)*
E: L. 12¹/₂" W. 7⁷/₈" D. ³/₁₆" *(inscribed one side
"5¹/₄ Wide/13¹/₂ Long")*
Winterthur Museum, Winterthur, Delaware

25 A–E. FOUR STAND LEG TEMPLATES
AND ONE STAND LEG
Pleasant Hill, Kentucky
1810–1850
A and B: Yellow poplar; C–E: Walnut
A: L. 13¹/₂" W. 3¹/₄" D. ⁵/₁₆"
B: L. 13³/₄" W. 3⁹/₁₆" D. ¹/₄"
C: L. 9⁷/₈" W. 3¹/₈" D. ¹/₄ "
D: L. 14³/₈" W. 3⁵/₈" D. ¹/₄ "
E: L. 13¹/₂" W. 3⁵/₁₆" D. ¹³/₁₆"
*Shaker Village of Pleasant Hill, Harrodsburg,
Kentucky*

an urn at the base and a ring at the top, was universally used. (The Square House purchased for Ann Lee in Harvard, Massachusetts, has a newel post that employs a similar shape.) The pair of Shaker stands in figure 23 was purchased from Hancock, but are typical of dozens made between 1820 and 1850 at New Lebanon. (That community closed in 1947 and the Central Ministry moved, with much of the community's portable goods, to Hancock.) The Shaker stand differs from those of a worldly design in using a simplified column, and a round plate under the top with a threaded hole into which the post screws on wooden threads. The round plate is secured with metal screws to the top. Worldly stands usually have a rectangular cross-cleat with a plain hole holding the top of the post. The post is held fast in the cleat by a wedge driven from above before the cleat is screwed to the top. Although the practice was rare outside Shaker communities, non-Shaker stands using round cleats and threaded posts were made in various parts of New England in the middle of the eighteenth century. Many of them had wooden pins securing the legs in place.[17]

The shape of the legs found on the Shaker stands was employed throughout the colonies and then the young republic. The leg templates, or patterns, shown as figure 24, come from the Dominy family shop of East Hampton, New York, where they provided outlines for stand and larger tea-table legs from about 1790 to 1830.[18] The Shaker templates in figure 25 were found in the attic of the carpentry shop at Pleasant Hill, Kentucky, built in 1815: two are walnut and two use yellow poplar. The walnut leg for a stand shown with them, at the right, was found in a different building in that community.[19]

The conventional twentieth-century opinion of Shaker furniture is that it eliminates all unnecessary features. This is not true. Many of the objects the Shakers made and used could easily have been more reductive in design. The Shakers used certain decorative features by choice, and in other instances worldly shop practices, habits of production and finish, moved quite naturally into Shaker work without being judged by the leaders for appropriateness: large cornices crown many case pieces made well into the nineteenth century; many drawers have complexly molded lips that overlap the case (figure 83); other drawers are finished with real or simulated cock-beading that serves no purpose but to give a finished look to the drawer edges (figure 38; in the world cock-beading can provide a protective edge around veneer); the vertical front corners of many larger cases have three-quarter-round moldings (figure 7); many bracket feet have complex forms; and decorative, non-functional finials decorate the tops of back posts of chairs. The list could be very long, and perhaps suitably end with furniture and architectural woodwork finished with painted decorative graining (figures 153 and 154).

CENTRALIZED AUTHORITY: PAINT, FURNITURE, AND DRESS

New Lebanon became the center of the Shaker world until it closed in 1947, and from there the Central Ministry sought to dictate designs as a means of undergirding unified thought and behavior. (The community's name changed officially to Mount Lebanon in 1861, when it received its own post office.) Often new designs were submitted for approval; some were allowed and others rejected. On occasion designs were disallowed without ever being officially presented. For example, on June 30, 1820, Isaac N. Youngs recorded in a personal journal at New Lebanon, "Having made two milking stools, I thot; (as it was a common custom) I would stain them with paint, I did so, put them to dry, in a place where Abiathar saw them, he soon after . . . spoke to me of them saying, dont you paint any more—after a while I saw they were taken away[,] found they were given to the Deaconess; and I soon found the ministry [was] stirred up about the matter, and having found the stools in general painted, ordered, the paint to be scoured off every stool." (The following month the Ministry issued an edict listing items not to be painted, and first were milking stools.) Youngs was upset as much at the high-handedness of the act as the decision against paint: "It worked my feelings some . . . stools taken away without my knowledge, & I could not help think that it was actuated more by zeal than by candor & fair dealing, & whether it was . . . wisdom to scour all the paint off seeing the labour that it was to do it . . . ."[20] Paint was at times used to disguise theologically unacceptable details. On the Fourth of July, four days after recording the removal of paint, Youngs wrote: "Finished a striking clock. No. 8. I began it in May 1819 & worked at it by little at a time & I reckoned it took me about 40 days to make the clock & case." On the twenty-sixth of that month he noted: "The feelings of the elders & especially El[de]r Sister are so exercised about the mahogany clock door, that I have at last painted it over—they tho't Mother w[ould] feel better satisfied if there was something done about it."[21]

Since the watchful eyes of supreme authority governed what was in use at New Lebanon, it was logical for things to be taken from there as models to be copied at other communities. Hannah Goodrich, as mentioned in Chapter II, had received Lucy Wright's saddle when she was initiated into the order of the Ministry that oversaw Canterbury and Enfield, New Hampshire, in 1792. She continued in that position until 1820, during those years when Lucy Wright was the most powerful member of the Central Ministry, and she often took from New Lebanon specimens to be copied in her communities. This practice was remembered in 1882 with admiration:

At the early date of which we are writing, it was considered quite an attainment to be able to present an article of manufacture that would reflect an honor upon the makers. The Believers at New Lebanon stood first in this as well as in many other things, and Mother Hannah took pleasure in the cultivation of so worthy an object.

While on her visits to New Lebanon, she would obtain some article to take home as a model of religious care as exercised by the Brethren and Sisters of the Parent Society.

In the journal of the Church of Canterbury, it says,—"We often received specimens of the various kinds of manufacture as samples, made in the most substantial and perfect manner, such as leather, seives, clothing, boots and shoes, pails, small oval boxes, hoes, nails and other articles.

"The Trustees were not permitted to sell any article whatever, at any price, unless it was free from blemish. We were to be an example of righteousness in all our temporal management and workmanship."[22]

Designs developed in other communities were submitted, through the proper stages of authority, to the New Lebanon Ministry for approval. During the 1850s Elder Grove Blanchard of the Harvard/Shirley Bishopric Ministry corresponded with the Ministry of the Hancock Bishopric for their thoughts about changes in chair designs. At first that Ministry expressed the hope that they could see and discuss the chair prototypes during a visit at Harvard. Some days later, they asked if examples of the new chair designs could be brought to them at Enfield, Connecticut, one of the communities they governed. Then, knowing permission really lay with the Central Ministry at New Lebanon, they suggested samples be sent there. In January 1854 the "new style of chair which it was proposed to introduce among Believers" was inspected at New Lebanon and "the rocking chair is condemned except for the sick and the small chair admitted with some modification." [23]

Throughout their history the Shakers have at times accommodated what they produced for sale to worldly tastes. Some Shaker-made furniture employed hidden dovetails (a form of construction in which the parts of the joints are invisible when assembled). As this did not accord with the requirement for an open display of features, the construction is rarely found in pieces made for Shaker use, but it was used in at least one piece made for the world: "I work in the Shop & blind dovetail a writting Desk for my Niece in Charlestown," wrote Alfred Collier of the Harvard Community on November 27, 1857.[24] By 1836 the Believers at Enfield, New Hampshire, were making table covers for the world that resembled oilcloth but, being more pliable, could be folded as readily as linen cloth. "It is made of common sheeting, painted with gum elastic and other ingredients, in a very tasteful manner, with borders of garlands, wreaths and vines, presenting an unique and very handsome appearance."[25] But it was always risky to please the world, even when it provided needed income, particularly if the leaders wanted an occasion to force greater restraint. In an 1812 letter to the Ministry at Union Village, Ohio, the Central Ministry condemned making fancy things for sale to the world:

We should also be glad to hear how it is with the Ministry & people at Pleasant Hill. We understand that Comstock says they make very superfluous baskets—of diverse colors! which they sell to the world, to a great amount altho' they are worthless things. We consider such things to be a dishonor to the gospel. Ebenezer Crowel [?] brought a knife here which he said was made there, its price (if rightly recollected) was 2¼ Dollars!! Can such things be justified among the people of God? Mother [Lucy Wright] says they feel to her like an abomination in the sight of God.

The testimony of the gospel allows of no superfluities among the people of God. And it is an established rule in the Church, our selves. Mother desired you would bear testimony against all such Babylonish merchandize as long as you have power to speak, & purge it out.[26]

Ideas for designs were communicated in letters. In 1846 Thomas Damon at Hancock answered an inquiry about a desk design from George Wilcox at Enfield, Connecticut. What is

26. DRAWING OF A CHEST OF DRAWERS WITH A DESK DRAWER
Made by John Kelleher at Mount Lebanon, New York
About 1937
Watercolor, graphite, and colored pencil on paperboard
H. 11" W. 9"
The desk drawer is taller than the drawers above and below. This shows the mid-century New Lebanon piece was not first made as a chest of drawers and then converted into a desk by altering the center drawer.
National Gallery of Art, Washington, D.C., Index of American Design

described is a chest of drawers in which the front of one drawer drops forward, when it is pulled out, to serve as a writing surface (as in figure 26). Although the hiding of construction and use-features is far rarer in Shaker hands than in the world, a piece that could be returned after use to a balanced design answered the Shakers' sense of perfect beauty. But the Shakers were always nervous when they were bending the rules. Thomas Damon's passage describing the piece notes how to deal with overt cleverness in design: when there is a law prohibiting self-expression it *must* be obeyed, but without a law, free expression is satisfying:

> *Not having anything of importance to write about, I will proceed to comply with your request respecting the desk although I fear you will hardly obtain 5 cts. worth of information. Length 23 in. Width 21½ in. as wide as the bench would admit. Depth, back side 4½ in. front side 2¾ in. including lid & bottom. The desk is made precisely as any common desk, and slides in & out exactly like one of the drawers. When it is shoved in, it slides sufficiently far to admit of a* false drawer face *(about ½ in. in thickness) which is hung with brass butts so as to turn down to admit the desk's sliding out & in . . . freely: this and all the rest that I have said relative to it, would no doubt have occurred to your mind, but as you requested the particulars I have been thus explicit. You will please suit yourself as to size and formation, "For where there is no law there is no transgression."*[27]

Disguising a desk to appear as a full chest of drawers combined practicality with uniformity of appearance. The 1834–37 Church Family's Stone Dwelling House at Enfield, New Hampshire, has built-in chests of drawers with pairs of closet doors above and below a stack of drawers. For many of the units, one of the pair of top doors does not open—it is nailed in place. Thus visual balance is allowed to override simple functionalism. A Harvard-made case of drawers with pairs of stacked drawers below a two-door cupboard has a useful long drawer, in the next-to-bottom tier, which was made to *look* like the two drawers set side-by-side. Thus in that piece there is a conventional balance of shapes on the outside, while a large storage area is maintained on the inside.[28] Such false fronts were fairly common in the world. For example, the worldly chest over two drawers in figure 8 appeared more readily as four drawers before the Shakers removed the brass pulls that enriched all four horizontal divisions.

Sometimes sketches of designs were sent by mail. Isaac Newton Youngs included in an 1830s letter to Benjamin Seth Youngs at South Union, Kentucky, descriptions with inserted drawings of the end of a long student's desk and a teacher's desk—both shut and open—used at New Lebanon (figures 27 and 28).[29]

A uniformity in clothing was perhaps more important than uniformity in furniture, for it, like of scholars provided for. These draughts are calculated for 48 scholars at desks, besides room for two classes of small children of 6 each, making in all 60. #

No. 2 on several accounts is the better of the three forms, as the desks in that form can all be made alike, with less labor than to make a part different for the monitors, for those at which the monitor sits on the end, need to have the desk lid, at his end, slanted towards his seat &c. The four desks are 8 feet long, 20 inches wide, about 2 feet 1 inch high on the front. 8 inches deep on the front; 6½ on the back, without the lid & top: top flat, 7 inches — lid slants 2½. Back board projects a little above. thus

The platform at the teachers end of the room is intended on these draughts to run the whole width of the house, the first & ... in two parts of equal width, forming two steps 5 inches high each; the teacher's desk stands on the lower form, & the chair in which to sit at the desk on the upper form. In front, & at each end of the desk there is a partition, or a railing & balustrade, which come up to the upper platform, & enclose the desk, at such height as suits — say 2 feet 8 inches. At each corner, on the upper platform, are two type boards, the manner of which you will doubtless remember more or less. The benches at these boards we will suppose stationary, in such a manner that they may be easily taken up if necessary, without leaving any obstacle on the floor. —

As to the teacher's desk, such a form as ours is perhaps as good as any. It is so calculated as to stand up, or sit down to write. It is 4 feet long & 20 inches wide & nearly 4 feet high on the back. It has two leaves to fold or shut up, both so formed that when open they are right to set in a chair, on a platform 8 inches high, & when shut, to stand at, on the floor, having a slant of about 3½ inches in 15. Thus. Below the bottom of the desk upper part of the desk there are drawers for paper ... The leaf contains an apartment to put in papers &c. On the inside, there are partitions, shelves &c, for various articles.

Left:
27. LETTER WITH DRAWINGS OF STUDENT AND TEACHER'S DESKS
From Isaac Newton Youngs, New Lebanon, New York, to Benjamin Seth Youngs at South Union, Kentucky
1830s
Ink on paper
H. 9¾" W. 7¹¹/₁₆"
The Western Reserve Historical Society, Cleveland, Ohio

28. STUDENT'S DESK
New Lebanon, New York
1830s
According to tradition, it was removed from the attic of the 1839 schoolhouse of the New Lebanon Church Family, by Edward Deming Andrews.
Oak, pine, and cherry with a dark red-brown surface outside; red wash inside
H. 28½" L. 95" D. 19½"
Hancock Shaker Village, Pittsfield, Massachusetts

hair and bonnet styles, easily signified inclusion and exclusion. In July 1817 Rufus Bishop of the Ministry of New Lebanon wrote to David Darrow in the Ministry of Ohio about new changes permitted in dress:

> *Mother [Lucy Wright] has felt a gift to have some improvement made in the wearing apparel of brethren and sisters (without following the fashions of the world)—it has been gained by a spontaneous union of the body, and has ever since given a more general satisfaction than any change of the kind since the first of our faith; and we are fully persuaded that our change was altogether for the better.*
>
> *Our Hats are altered but little; the crowns are raised about ¹/₂ inch, and the brims (especially of every day hats) are about half an inch less. Our great Coats and Surtouts are not so large at the bottom. In our Strait bodied Coats we leave out about ¹/₂ yard of useless cloth in the hind part of the skirt (this I confess was at the first mortifying to my old traditional sense, for the more cloth I could han[d]somely get into the folds and skirt of a coat, the better it suited me.) We have also excluded a number of useless buttons and buttonholes—Our Jackets are not so long nor strait, nor our Trowsers quite so large. Our Color for Coats &c. was shifted merely out of necessity—Indigo was scarce, and besides this, our cloth would crack and fade, but this was not all; we poor taylor[s] had so far worn out our eyes that we felt unable to work so much blue.*
>
> *Now you will see that we feel as fully settled not to follow the fashion of the world, as our good brethren at Ohio; and that we are equally determined to follow our present lead whom God has placed in Zion for our protection, nor is our confidence without foundation, for God has greatly blessed her with wisdom, and her children in obedience. But I must turn my tone, or you will by and by think I am full of preach.*[30]

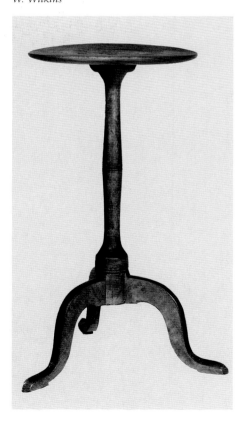

29. STAND
Sabbathday Lake, Maine
1820–50
Birch top and post, maple legs; painted red
H. 26¹/₂" Diam. of top 13⁷/₁₆"
Collection of Suzanne Courcier and Robert
W. Wilkins

REGIONAL ACCOMMODATION AND COMPROMISE

Objects made in the New Lebanon–Hancock areas were similar to each other (and akin to those produced in non-Shaker communities around them), and their design attitude and constructional features migrated to other Shaker communities as objects and ideas were carried abroad. Believers were sent out to teach skills, and makers moved to live and work for extended periods—often years—in other communities. But the impact of regional traditions quite automatically conditioned the design sense of distant Shaker communities, and many objects produced away from the central authority look more like local vernacular expressions than those associated with the center of the Shaker world. The Harvard Shakers seem to have been more conscious of worldly ideas than those in other communities. They were willing to use worldly pieces after only minor alterations (see figure 8), and what they built appears to have a greater degree of worldly sophistication. For example, Alfred Collier made, possibly in 1861, a tall square-taper-leg desk, painted it green (an unusual color for Shaker furniture), and added a neoclassical brass escutcheon and pull. It was very fashion-conscious even though by the world's standards it was stylistically decades out of date.

The designs produced in the Maine communities during the first half of the nineteenth century, while fitting into the general New England character found in upper New York, Connecticut, and Massachusetts styling, have the more active lines and strong coloring of local Maine vernacular pieces. Robert Emlen found Joshua H. Bussell's plans of Alfred, Maine (see a detail in figure 126), so colorful and exotic that "an analogy might be made to the painted furniture produced during this period by the Shakers' rural neighbors in southern Maine."[31] Why the part of Maine where the Shakers settled was more visually active is uncertain, but recent scholarship suggests its more exotic aesthetic may result from that area's more esoteric religious expressions.[32]

The red-painted dish-top Sabbathday Lake stand (figure 29) has characteristics not found on stands from other communities: the very slender post has a central swelling marked by a ring turning. (The post is 1¹¹/₁₆ inches at the central ring; it thins out to 1⁷/₃₂ inches above and 1⁵/₁₆ inches below.) The decorative swelling appears also on Maine Shaker tables with four legs, and many worldly Maine chairs and tables have similar swelling areas. (Perhaps this form reflects the curving shapes on contemporary bamboo-turned objects.) The feet and lower half of the legs of the stand (figure 29) have ridged centers. As on many Shaker ones, and a few non-Shaker stands, the top of the post threads into a round cleat that is screwed to the top.[33]

In general, the furniture produced in Ohio and Kentucky was more like local products than New England work. The chest of drawers in figure 30 was made at Union Village, Ohio, and signed and dated "November 9th 1827" by Daniel Sering. It is close in design and woods to non-Shaker furniture made in Ohio and Kentucky. The Shaker piece uses walnut or butternut, and yellow poplar as the secondary wood. A similar use of walnut (with yellow pine inside), molded drawer edges, turned wooden knobs, and skirt shaping appears on the miniature non-Shaker chest of drawers from the central piedmont area of North Carolina, shown as figure 31. (Its drawer knobs are replaced, but follow a local pattern.) Likewise, the Shakers made corner cupboards in Ohio and Kentucky where they were a common worldly form, but not in the eastern communities.

Although little is as yet known about Ohio and Indiana vernacular worldly chairs, John Bivins has found in the files of the Museum of Early Southern Decorative Arts, Winston-Salem, North Carolina, a number of photographs of worldly slat-back chairs with local features that appear on western Shaker chairs, but not on those made by eastern Shakers. The distinctive form of the finials and the barrel-like turnings under the arms (with a central ring decoration) on the Pleasant Hill, Kentucky, chair (figure 32), appear on the worldly example from Piedmont, Georgia (figure 33). (The Georgia example was converted into a wheelchair, as was the Shaker example in figure 124.) While that places the non-Shaker piece some distance from Shaker communities, the barrel shape with a central ring appears on a published worldly Kentucky rocking slat-back,[34] and on Shaker chairs made in Ohio. The Union Village, Ohio, rocking chair (figure 34) has slats with straight top edges with downward curves at the ends. That slat shape is found on worldly chairs from Tennessee (figure 35) and South Carolina. Many non-rocking Ohio Shaker chairs have the bases of their legs turned to strongly incurving feet, a feature found on Tennessee (figure 35) and South Carolina slat-back chairs. None of these features appear on Shaker chairs made in the East. (Undoubtedly more research on furniture made nearer western Shaker communities will produce striking comparisons.)

Special construction features appeared in some communities, mostly introduced by craftsmen who received their training elsewhere before they joined. For example, at Hancock and Enfield, Connecticut, many of the drawer sides are tapered: narrower at the top, to provide a lean look above, and a wider surface at the base on which to run the drawer (figure 36). This feature is

Above left:
30. CHEST OF DRAWERS
Union Village, Ohio
1827
Signed and dated on one drawer: "Daniel Sering Maker/November 9th 1827," and on the back of another drawer: "Daniel Sering/November 9th 1827"
Walnut or butternut, and poplar
H. 51¾" W. 43⅝" D. 22"
The Warren County Historical Society, Lebanon, Ohio

Above right:
31. MINIATURE CHEST OF DRAWERS
Central Piedmont area, North Carolina
About 1820
Walnut and yellow pine; pulls replaced
H. 17½" W. 14¾" D. 10¾"
Museum of Early Southern Decorative Arts, Winston-Salem, North Carolina

known on a worldly chest-on-chest made about 1800 by Reuben Beman, Jr., recorded in 1785 as a cabinetmaker in Kent, Connecticut.[35] Many of the New Lebanon case pieces use beveled edges on the stiles (the verticals) and rails (the horizontals) around the panels, and this construction is also found on the Enfield, Connecticut, piece seen as figure 85. To achieve these bevels quickly, the front, and usually the back, edges of the stiles were beveled their entire length. The ends of the rails were cut at an angle so they could cover the bevels where they meet the verticals (see figure 37). It is not a complicated joint to make, since it needs only the beveling and then the rails cut with angled ends. This constructional feature appears in some early English architectural paneling, in late seventeenth- and early eighteenth-century English furniture, particularly that made in the Yorkshire area, and in many chests made along the Connecticut Valley from 1680 to 1730.[36] Differences from one community to another were often more obvious. For example, the Shakers usually protected the edges of keyholes from wear by lining them, as in the world, with brass, either inset into the wood or applied to the surface (figure 38), or an inset of bone or ivory (figure 20). Some of the latter employed at Enfield, Connecticut, are heart-shaped. A list of such variations would be long.

Inconsistency between communities was not always a matter of distance making communication difficult. As Beverly Gordon has pointed out regarding Shaker clothing: "Materials that were available in one part of the country were not necessarily available in another, and regional tastes and styles also varied. Individuals were usually able, furthermore, to adapt small details to their personal taste."[37]

Architecture varied from one community to another in part because of the availability of differing building materials. Apparently in 1811, the New Lebanon Ministry conveyed council to the South Union, Kentucky, Ministry on the construction and design of buildings to "keep union," that is, to fit in with approved designs. Nearly seven years later Benjamin S. Youngs at South Union returned some council of his own:

It would seem that what is wisdom & prudence with one people in a certain situation, is not always wisdom & prudence with another people in another situation. Countries and climates, people & laws, manners & customs, local situations & circumstances, advantages and disadvantages peculiar to each—all are different—and each requiring a different method of arrangement from the other in the line of outward economy . . . . This is much the case with us in regard to building materials—we are much put to it for a little building timber, as it is extremely scarce here . . . but good building stone of different kinds & the best kind of materials for brick, we have convenient & in plenty.[38]

Communities also differed in when they made physical changes. In 1834, for example, the Shakers at Canterbury replaced the simple benches in their dining room with Windsor chairs.[39] At Union Village, Ohio, the *Daily Record of the Church Family*, recorded on July 13, 1847, "low chairs obtain'd to set on at the dining table instead of benches which had formerly been us'd—an advance in comfort and convenience."[40] A journal from South Union, Kentucky, records on January 1, 1849: "Brethren on this Blessed New Years Day begin to make chairs for the dining room and so get clear of the benches."[41] At Pleasant Hill, Kentucky, it was in 1864 that "We introduce chairs instead of benches in our dining rooms." They were purchased rather than community-made.[42]

In a review of a complexly integrated group of communities, particularly one focused primarily on the eastern part of the Society, it is tempting to provide specific beginnings and endings for events and aesthetic developments. But the objects came from the minds and hands of individuals, many with strong personalities, who came from a variety of backgrounds, and lived in varied settings. In each community the Shakers employed local materials and many local customs, thus, although Believers wished to live in unity, this did not always occur.

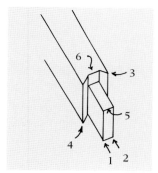

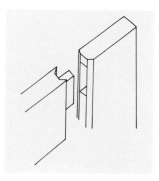

Steps:
Saw cuts 1-4
Chisel cuts 5-6

36. DETAIL OF DRAWER JOINT SHOWING TAPERING OF DRAWER SIDES
Typical of joinery made at Enfield, Connecticut, and Hancock, Massachusetts
1820–50
Pine
Collection of the Shaker Museum and Library, Old Chatham, New York

37. DRAWINGS OF BEVELED MORTISE AND TENON JOINTS
Typical of joinery made at New Lebanon, New York
Drawings by the author

Chapter IV

THE SHAKERS AND BEAUTY

From their beginning the Shakers dismissed fancy things. Discussing gold beads, jewels, silver buckles, and other ornaments of the kind, Ann Lee said: "You may let the moles and bats have them; that is, the children of this world; for they set their hearts upon such things; but the people of God do not want them."[1] The Shakers sold the gold and other valuables that came to their communities, and gave the valueless ornate to the poor. Throughout the history of Shaker life there have been times of greater freedom followed by a tightening of restrictions. For example, in 1802 the Ministry at New Lebanon realized it had gone too far in adopting worldly conveniences and inventions. To protect themselves against too rapid and unnecessary changes they decided not to take in new ideas or items for use unless they were gifts, revealed as God-directed additions. To ensure that new items would be a bit out of date when adopted, they instigated for objects the same procedure used for allowing new ideas: sending the request slowly up the chain of command. A member desiring an item requested it in writing to the Family Deacon, the Deacon took it to a Family Elder, the Family Elder gave it to the Ministry Elder and the Ministry Elders had six months to decide its appropriateness. Thus things were not of the newest fashion when the Shakers got to use them.[2]

Sometimes the early Shakers destroyed what offended them. An apostate recorded in 1812: "Their superfluous furniture, such as ornamented looking glasses, &c. in a number of instances, were dashed upon the floor and stamped to pieces; ear and finger-rings were bitten with all the symptoms of rage, and then sold for old metal. All this was done to testify their abhorrence of that pride which introduced these things among mankind—and likewise as a type of the destruction of Babylon."[3] In 1818 Brother Isaac Newton Youngs wrote about getting rid of the superfluous: ". . . it is natural for us to gather a great deal of rubbish, conveniences etc., and it often has been the gift in times past to have a burying . . . to purge out some things that we had gathered."[4]

In the 1840s the Shakers took brass knobs off some furniture and substituted turned wooden pulls, but that was during the strictest purge they would undergo as they sought to eliminate backsliders and the weak of heart. We do not know if the offending knobs were on Shaker-made things, or on worldly objects brought to the communities. By 1840 they were probably Shaker-made, as on the red-painted Shaker case of drawers in figure 38. The piece was made in Union Village, Ohio, about 1830, and its distance from the wrath of the Central Ministry may be the reason it still has the brass pulls. (In its use of round brass pulls and ungraduated drawer heights, it follows high style neoclassical conventions.) But even at New Lebanon some decorative knobs were tolerated. On June 23, 1869 a visitor "Called at the sisters work shop which is kept as neat as a palace, and furnished with ample accommodations. Saw some small white knobs, and some brass ones on the little drawers of boxes, tables &c. A clock told the time of day in almost every hall and room."[5] (At this date, however, there was again greater use of worldly ideas, as we will see in Chapter IX.) Shakers could alter what they purchased to have it accord more closely with their aesthetic, as seen in figure 9, and a number of looking glasses purchased or brought by converts from the world had their projecting ears cut off to leave only a simple rectangular frame.[6] In a related fashion they simplified many of the worldly clocks they purchased.[7] But fashion and comfort were not totally ignored; for example, in 1825 the New Lebanon Brothers "Nicholas [Bennett] and Garret [Lawrence] go [into the world] in pursuit of an easy chair." Three days later they "return from Vermont bring home an easy chair."[8] (Easy chairs had upholstered seats, arms, backs, and wings either side of the backs. In the eighteenth and early nineteenth centuries they were, in the world, used in bedrooms. When depicted in contemporary paintings, they are usually occupied by an elderly person.)

38. CHEST OF DRAWERS
Union Village, Ohio
About 1830
Maple and pine painted red; brass knobs
H. 38" W. 38¼" D. 18"
Canterbury Shaker Village, Canterbury, New Hampshire

THE MILLENNIAL LAWS

Because of the recorded words of Ann Lee against ornamentation, the later purging out of many enrichments, and an incorrect stressing of the Shakers' aggressively restrictive Millenial Laws of 1845, many scholars of Shaker life and art have been far too ready to believe that all artistic detailing and awareness of beauty were expunged from Shaker communities.

Beginning early in the nineteenth century the Shakers developed an oral tradition of rules to guide Believers' behavior. During the last years of Lucy Wright's life, Freegift Wells of Watervliet developed more extensive rules, but Wright required that they remain an oral tradition. Six months after her death they were written down, and perhaps each community received one handwritten copy. Known as the "Milenial Laws, or Gospel statutes and ordinances, adapted to the day of Christ's second Appearing . . . New Lebanon, August 7th: 1821" (see Appendix), they provided firm but not overly detailed instructions. They were revised and greatly expanded and extended in 1845, during the latter years of the religious upheavals of the Era of Manifestations, when rigid controls were thought by some to be appropriate. But they were seen even at the time as extreme by many individuals and some communities, and those skeptics continued to prefer the 1821 laws that set guidelines without attempting to intrude on every act.

Modern understanding of Shaker activities before 1845 was made more difficult because Edward Deming Andrews (who has been the greatest influence on how the Shakers are viewed in the twentieth century), mistakenly thought all copies of the 1821 Laws were lost.[9] He therefore published in *The People Called Shakers* (1953) the apostate William Haskett's memory of them, which appeared in *Shakerism Unmasked* (1828). Haskett's list added some Laws that were not on the Shaker list and left out others. Also, he gave them a falsely restrictive cast by stating each in the negative: "It is Contrary to Order" heads each section of his version. Since Andrews did not have the 1821 Laws, he published in full the extreme Laws of 1845. Probably few Believers followed them in every detail, but since their publication by Andrews, Shaker scholarship has repeatedly focused its evaluations around them, which skewed the understanding of the early years.

In a conversation with Brother Arnold Hadd of Sabbathday Lake, he told me that the 1845 Laws were the work of Philemon Stewart, whom he considered "not a stable person," and said they had little effect on the communities in Maine. "For example," he said, "they require that all beds be painted green, but none were made here. The only one we own [at Sabbathday Lake] came from Mount Lebanon."[10] Reviewing the mid-century laws is helpful when seeking to understand what the Shakers were really doing in 1845, for they provide evidence of what the Shaker leadership wanted eliminated. Attention is paid to nearly every action: "No one should carelessly pass over small things, as a pin, a kernel of grain, etc. thinking it too small to pick up, for if we do, our Heavenly Father will consider us too small for him to bestow his blessing upon."[11]

Even with rules upon rules about getting rid of things, or not allowing them to enter the communities, a practicality remains evident in the 1845 Laws: "Blankets or Comfortables [soft quilts] for outside spreads, should be blue and white, but not checked or striped; other kinds now in use may be worn out."[12] Some of the Laws seek to ensure compassion for older members: "No one may mock, ridicule or treat with disrespect, the aged, infirm, and decrepit. Ye shall not turn away the poor who ask alms of you, knowing that your Heavenly Father will provide for you."[13]

While not receiving strict obedience, the 1845 Laws did affect behavior. For example, they state: "No one should write or print his name on any article of manufacture, that others may hereafter know the work of his hands," and fewer pieces of furniture and other objects made after 1850 are signed with their maker's name. For example, in 1843 Isaac Newton Youngs included his name on the title page of a book he wrote on the rules of music. In a second edition printed in 1846, he moved his name to the end of the introduction.[14] These Laws state: "The Ministry may in no wise blend in common with the rest of the people; they may not work under the same roof, live in the same house, nor eat at the same table. But their dwelling place shall be in the meeting house, even in the most holy Sanctuary."[15] At Pleasant Hill, Kentucky, the Ministry had been taking turns eating with the various Families. After the 1845 Laws they built onto the north end of the Centre Family Dwelling a small dining room for the Ministry's use.

BEAUTY

Early Shaker phrases such as "Hands to work and hearts to God" have been taken out of context to prove that Shakers not only forsook beauty but disparaged it. Book titles like *Religion in Wood*, *The Gift to be Simple,* and *Work and Worship Among the Shakers* underscore the purposefulness of Shaker acts, while suggesting there were no worldly influences or personal and group aesthetic choices that conditioned design, production, and use of what they created. One of the best known Shaker songs, "Simple Gifts," begins " 'Tis the gift to be simple, 'tis the gift to be free," but the song is not about simplicity. The "gift" is the act, or intrusion, of God. The human response God required is "to come down where we ought to be . . . . To bow and bend," and "To turn," that is, to joyfully subjugate individual will to obedience.

Purging and restriction do not, however, eliminate beauty. It is always present. It is an instinct. People have a drive to be surrounded by what they find appropriate. As anthropologists have found, native tribes in secluded places combine objects from the outside world with indigenous things to create new visual expressions that are appropriate to the maker's eye. Many prisoners adjust their cells to visually comfortable spaces. The Shakers were, and are, not against beauty, but against ostentation; they have consciously, and unconsciously, made thousands of aesthetic choices.

Outsiders are not equipped to say what was and is beautiful to a Shaker, for only a Shaker can determine this, and each generation and each community, each Family and each person, would give different answers. But non-Believers can read their words, study their choices and decisions, and perceive the achievements within the broad artistic and cultural development. What they did is evidence of a fairly consistent concern for aesthetic, as well as functional issues, from about 1800 to the present.

Cultural historians strive to explain how an instinct for beauty comes about—is it natural or learned? Art historians ask what the historical and artistic influences were, and then many do a formal reading of the works, speaking of balance, mass, and line. But such considerations may not have been part of the maker's vocabulary or conscious thought. What the Shakers made flowed naturally from both experiences and intentions, which are finally inseparable. In 1805 Benjamin Seth Youngs wrote concerning God's order, and used the word "artist" twice: "in building a house, or constructing any machine, each part naturally lies in apparent confusion till the artist brings them together, and puts each one in its proper place; then the beauty of the machinery and the wisdom of the artist are apparent."[16]

Andrews gathered together in *Shaker Furniture* a group of Shaker phrases:

Regularity is beautiful.
There is great beauty in harmony.
Order is the creation of beauty. It is heaven's first law, and the protection of souls.
Love of Beauty has a wider field of action in association with Moral Force.
Beauty rests on utility.
All beauty that has not a foundation in use, soon grows distasteful, and needs continual replacement
    with something new.
That which has in itself the highest use possesses the greatest beauty.[17]

The beauty evoked in all these quotations has to do with order, but it is judged by perception of unity and appropriateness. This appropriateness included "proper" shapes and colors, judgments, and, indeed, natural as well as learned aesthetic instincts.

In the Shakers' *A Summary View of the Millennial Church* (1823), "True gospel simplicity" was explained: "its thoughts, words and works are plain and simple . . . . It is without ostentation, parade or any vain show, and naturally leads to plainness in all things."[18] This does not exclude conscious beauty, or the satisfying of the eye's enjoyment of form, balance, and unity. Marjorie Procter-Smith, an insightful historian of Shaker theology, finds "that beauty is not intrinsic to their existence, which is functional . . . . the beauty of artifacts resides in their usefulness, and is in service to that usefulness."[19] In stressing theological intention she seems to be overlooking the natural flow of aesthetic concerns possessed by anyone who consciously designs objects.

How the Shakers linked aesthetic choices and careful repetitions is seen in the integration of furniture and architectural details found in the new Dwelling House that Believers built at Hancock in 1830. For the dining room they made long cherry tables (figure 88), each with three columns decorated top and bottom with reel and ring turnings (figure 39). The newel posts in the original floors of the south staircase tower of the Dwelling House almost exactly follow the configuration of the table columns (figure 40). (The same form of newel post is found in the late eighteenth-century Gilbert House, located three and a half miles away, in New Lebanon, which is discussed in Chapter VII as a possible source of Masonic images for Shaker gift drawings.) The ceiling of the Dwelling House dining room is supported by two large cherry columns. They are less decorated, and like the classical Doric order, they have at the top only an echinus—or quarter-round-like cap above a fillet—and no projecting base; the columns sat directly on the floor. (The very bottoms of the posts are now enclosed by a new floor laid over the old floor. It is possible to see through gaps in the new floor that a groove was turned into the posts, about an inch from the original floor, when they were on the lathe.) These posts and the cherry balustrades were not stained as the pine woodwork "with a bright orange color" but, like much Shaker-used cherry, received a red stain below a varnish finish.[20] The added color intensified the redness and, thereby, the visual force of the shapes of the careful designs. (This balustrade has been disastrously refinished, and the dining room columns stripped to raw cherry, but where the cherry architectural detailing remains untouched, particularly in the attic, it shows the red stain and the thin clear finish found on the table.)

The dining room of the Centre Family Dwelling at Pleasant Hill, Kentucky, built between 1824 and 1834, also has two columns in the middle of the room to support the ceiling. The columns are placed on tall eight-sided plinths that echo the raised-paneled wainscoting on the walls (see figure 41). The room is further enriched by four half-columns placed as pairs against the east and west walls. Without structural necessity they repeat the form of the two columns in the center of the room, and allow diners to feel themselves within an echoing colonnade. The woodwork of the room is painted a strong gray above a rich red baseboard.

Pillars, particularly in pairs, were an important part of the architectural language the Shakers used to discuss theological and organizational issues. They refer to the many cedar pillars Solomon used in the buildings he made, but most particularly to the two pillars of brass he placed in the porch of the Temple in Jerusalem, through which anyone entering had to pass. The pillar on the right as the visitor came *out* was called Jachin, meaning "he that strengthens and makes stedfast," that on the left Boaz, meaning "in strength." The Shakers associated the one on the right with Jesus, and that on the left with Ann Lee. "Thus, Christ in his first appearing, was a pillar,

39. DETAIL OF DINING TABLE SHOWN AS FIGURE 88
Hancock, Massachusetts
About 1830
Cherry with a red stain and clear finish
Collection of the Shaker Museum and Library, Old Chatham, New York

40. NEWEL POST
Hancock, Massachusetts, Brick Dwelling House, south stairtower
1830
Cherry, refinished
H. of column between square sections 15"
Hancock Shaker Village, Pittsfield, Massachusetts

41. DINING ROOM WITH COLUMNS
Pleasant Hill, Kentucky, Centre Family Dwelling
1824–34
Shaker Village of Pleasant Hill, Harrodsburg,
Kentucky

strong and steadfast; and his second appearing was in the strength of the first." Joseph Meacham and Lucy Wright were called "first Father and Mother of our redemption, who are the invisible first Pillars upon which the spiritual house of God is built."[21] Elders and Eldresses were designated twin pillars of the community. The special terms of inner and outer courts, based on Jewish temple organization, designated the power relations of the Shaker hierarchical groups. The higher or inner court received special treatment. According to the 1845 Millennial Laws, "It is advisable for the center families in each bishopric, to avoid hiring the world to make household furniture, except for the outer court."[22]

A conscious effort to establish beauty through a harmony of straight, angled, rectangular, arched, and curved shapes is found in the staircases and doorways of the main Pleasant Hill Centre Family buildings. The central hall of the Centre Family Dwelling (1824–34) is famous for the harmonic integration of what could have been disparate features: the rise of the staircases, arched and rectangular doorways, and straight lines established by chair-rail moldings and peg rails (figure 42). A similar combination of beauty and practicality occurs in the building's second-floor staircase balustrade (figure 43). Its square-shaft balusters are painted blue-green; their bases, and the handrail above them, are painted a visually strong red color, which echoes the red baseboards edging the hall and the staircase. The desire for an uninterrupted linear repeat of the balusters was so strong that to anchor the wooden railing the creators made the fifth square-shaped baluster from each end out of iron. While disguised to appear like a wooden part, the iron rods hold the uninterrupted flowing movement firmly in place. This disguising of the nature of the material used calls into question the often repeated assertion that Shaker principles invariably demanded a truthful display of materials.

The arch over a door to the meeting room contains Gothic pointed windows. Here a desire for a particularly beautiful feature pushed the Shaker designer beyond the simple limits of the

42. HALL, FIRST FLOOR
Pleasant Hill, Kentucky, Centre Family Dwelling
1824–34
Shaker Village of Pleasant Hill, Harrodsburg,
Kentucky

43. HALL, SECOND FLOOR
Pleasant Hill, Kentucky, Centre Family Dwelling
1824–34
Shaker Village of Pleasant Hill, Harrodsburg,
Kentucky

materials at hand. Since the two larger Gothic shapes were bigger than available window glass, each is fitted with two pieces (one above the other) butted together. The twin spiral staircases in the nearby Trustees' Office (1839–41) are famous for their conscious beauty (figure 44).

Today we are rightly hesitant to discuss quality in design of earlier objects, for we necessarily insert personal and present-day concerns. But a comparison of Ministry and non-Ministry objects shows that there is a higher quality of aesthetic judgment, workmanship, and materials in those made for the leaders. Therefore, their intention to be finer is observable.[23]

Although many scholars of Shaker works set them outside normal design processes, most are ready to relate them to designs by the Bauhaus. The linking of these concentrated efforts to join aesthetic and practical issues is supposed to reinforce the opinion that the Shakers' sole concern was with simplicity over aesthetics. But with both the Shakers and the Bauhaus, simplicity and utility involved a myriad of intellectual and aesthetic choices. It does not take much attention to detail to see aesthetic concerns at work in one of the Shakers' most famous forms, their chairs. The tops of the slats of these pieces are unnecessarily arched to provide visual lift to the design. Likewise, although the back posts do not need finials for chairs to perform their function, nearly every community made them with finials of a distinctive shape. On occasion, the desired look pushed the design well beyond the character of the materials used. For example, the X-ray photograph shown here as figure 45 reveals a metal rod inserted into the top of the back post of an Enfield, Connecticut, chair. Such rods allowed the maker to turn a finial with a very thin neck below its upper mass, pushing the finial design well beyond the natural strength of the wood. The Enfield child's chair in figure 46 expresses its maker's interest in beauty not only in elegant finials with metal rods, but in its use of figured maple.

Opposite:
44. STAIRCASE
Pleasant Hill, Kentucky, Trustees' Office
1839–41
Shaker Village of Pleasant Hill, Harrodsburg, Kentucky

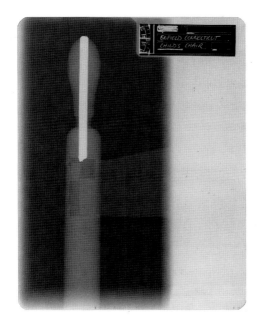

45. X-RAY PICTURE SHOWING METAL ROD IN FINIAL
Enfield, Connecticut
Courtesy of Timothy Rieman

46. CHILD'S CHAIR
Enfield, Connecticut
1830–50
Figured maple; rush seat
H. 33³/₈" W. 15³/₈" D. of seat 10³/₄"
Collection of Bernard Brown

The cupboard in figure 47 is one of the greatest Shaker achievements in reductive design. It stresses tall, lean elegance with a minimum of detail. The extraordinary thin top combines aesthetic and constructional features: its narrow line was produced by rabbeting, or cutting away, the lower third of the top board, which is only three-fourths of an inch thick. Into this recess are nailed the back, sides, and two front boards. This construction produced a sturdy union, while leaving a half-inch top line to crown the cupboard; to add a beautiful line it was rounded. The top door closes within the rabbet. The ends of the thin board between the two doors are neatly set into the vertical boards of the case. The cupboard's decorative features are the thin, rounded top board, the quarter-round shape of the moldings around the flat panels, and salmon-pink paint. The color remains vivid inside, although it is dark outside because a finishing coat of varnish has turned gray-brown.

As detailed in the long 1817 quotation from Rufus Bishop in Chapter III, Shaker clothing received the same ordering as everything else in the Shaker world. It was unified particularly for worship, where similarity pleased Believers while adding to the spectacle watched by the many who came to see them dance. The clothing for men certainly did not eschew conscious beauty. At the beginning of the nineteenth century the leaders approved for men's Sabbathday coats: decorative stitching, sleeve cuffs 6 inches long; on the front, six or eight buttons 1 inch in diameter, and three real and three not-cut-through buttonholes, each 3 inches long. The backs had folds marked with buttons. With the coats removed for dancing, color was added to the drama: the vests, of the same cloth as the coats, had twelve buttons. The sleeves of the full-cut shirts were held close to the arms by very long blue silk ribbons that fastened around the arm above the elbow (see figure 59, where the ribbons are shorter). The neck stock was made of $2\frac{1}{2}$- to 3-inch stiff white or blue silk, and fastened with a buckle at the back of the neck.[24] (Evidence of a dramatic coloring of clothing used during worship in the 1850s is seen in figures 134 through 137.)

Color was everywhere in Shaker life. At this time checked and striped clothing abounded, and heavy iridescent cloth was produced by mixing varying warps and woofs: brown and blue, green and blue, white and red, and red and blue (figure 226), which makes a vivid blue-red-pink-purple effect. Bright blue was associated with worship, but it appeared in clothing and on other articles for daily use. Often, with a kind of vanity, bright colors and patterns were used for linings of more somber garments: for example, bright blue lined some red-brown skirts, and patterned cloth often lined collars made of plain cloth. "White stocks were generally worn on the Sabbath, and were considered a part of the uniform, while the blue were for more common use. In 1810 the white stocks gave way to white cotton, linen, or silk neckerchiefs which are used more or less to the present date [1858]."[25] Fashions changed in part to simplify, and in part because the blue was fading and cracking due to the color process. The Shaker desire for fine clothing that employed the best cloth and tailoring contributed at times to the need to purge ostentation. But a list made in 1840 by a Hancock Eldress indicates that by then Sisters there had at least two sets of fine clothing for winter and two for summer. There are 130 items for each sister mentioned.[26]

The tension between conscious restriction and a desire for beauty created the balance that is at the heart of the Shakers' aesthetics. A fine example is seen in their rugs, which were a great source of color in rooms and halls. Blue and red were favorites, but orange, green, brown, black, gold, rose, and purple were common.[27] To make them appear both simple and rich two or more colors were often twisted together and called one color. In 1841 a Sister had an "inspiration" from the spirit of Lucy Wright that told her "two colours are sufficient for one Carpet." But each stripe may be made of "red and green, another of drab and grey, and yet another of butternut and grey," and different areas of a carpet could have different "pairs" of colors. The "binding yarn may also be of two colours, and also the binding if necessary."[28]

Shaker attention to beautiful color and pattern was prized across all activities and habits: the beauty of Mary Hazard's penmanship made her a busy scribe at New Lebanon; horsehair sieves often employed two colors of horsehair woven to produce a pattern; many Shakers liked the effect of bird's-eye and tiger-maple wood. On occasion, a painted version of patterned woods, employing elaborate graining, appeared early on furniture, later on furniture and interior woodwork, and as a finish on seemingly endless seed boxes made at the end of the nineteenth century.

Although Ann Lee had said "let the moles and bats" have gold beads, jewels, and other similar ornaments, early in the nineteenth century Shaker men and women began to wear "Gold earrings, [which] had crept in by slow degrees, under the pretense that they were good for a headache." Although this practice was soon disallowed,[29] it demonstrates a concern for personal enhancement. For unifying reasons, the Shakers developed a fixed hairstyle for men, and this can be seen

Opposite:
47. CUPBOARD
New Lebanon, New York, Center Family
Medicine Department
1825–50
Pine painted salmon pink; outside with darkened varnish
H. 84¼" W. 36¼" D. 16¼"
Collection of the Shaker Museum and Library, Old Chatham, New York

as a simple push for unity; but a concern to have hair in an appropriate balance of traditional shapes caused the Shakers to invent, at New Lebanon in 1816, "hair caps" for balding brethren.[30] Isaac Newton Youngs is known to have worn one.[31] These impulses for decorative enrichments were the result of human and learned instincts. Times of purging lessened the degree to which they were found, but an awareness of beauty was always present in Shaker communities. A description of the herb business at New Lebanon about the time of the Civil War demonstrates how the Shakers could reconcile rules and a consciousness of beauty:

> Forty years ago it was contrary to the "orders" which governed our lives to cultivate useless flowers, but, fortunately for those of us who loved them, there are many plants which are beautiful as well as useful. We always had extensive poppy beds and early in the morning, before the sun had risen, the white-capped sisters could be seen stooping among the scarlet blossoms to slit those pods from which the petals had just fallen . . . . The rose bushes were planted along the sides of the road which ran through our village and were greatly admired by the passersby, but it was strongly impressed upon us that a rose was useful, not ornamental.[32]

In this wonderful description that reads like a scene Winslow Homer or Childe Hassam might have painted, intentions of perfection are mixed with an admiration of the beautiful. Beauty was part of the Shakers' spiritual understanding, and for them heaven, and earth-bound Believers' experiences of heaven, were fraught with beauty. In the 1843 *A Holy, Sacred and Divine Roll and Book* (figure 145), various Believers recorded spirit manifestations they had experienced or observed. For some, such as Daniel Myrick, the term "beauty" is used in a spiritual sense, as when he speaks of God "clothing her [the Church] in beauty."[33] For others, beauty was used as part of a visual metaphor: after hearing "A heavenly trumpet very loudly sounding," Harriet Goodwin "looked toward the northwest, and there beheld a beautiful rainbow; and on the rainbow, stood four thousand holy and mighty Angels."[34] Earlier in her testimony Goodwin had written about buildings where she saw "a beautiful sign; it reached the whole length of the house, and appeared to be about six feet wide." It was the color of gold and a voice spoke, declaring in part, "The dwellings of my people shall I cause to glow with beauty."[35] In the text on the Mulberry Tree gift drawing by Hannah Cohoon (figure 166), the "bower" and the "short green grass" are called "beautiful." On March 12, 1841, the spirit of Mother Lucy Wright included in her words to the Sisters: "Again, dear sisters, I think the late manner you have got into of pleating your old drugget and worsted gowns in small pleats, and not pressing them down, is very suitable for what it is for. But I do not like to see them worn into meeting Sabbath days—it breaks the uniform and does not look pretty."[36] On January 5, 1842, the spirit of Father William Lee sent the Sisters over eighteen years old "a very beautiful white silk neck handkerchief for each and every one of you. They are bordered with gold and have pale blue fringe. And the picture of all your heavenly Parents' mansions is drawn on them."[37]

It was not beauty but the trap of worldliness from which the Shakers fled. They did write, "let it be plain and simple, and of the good and substantial quality which becomes your calling and profession, unembellished by any superfluities, which add nothing to its goodness and durability."[38] Similar words were used by many eighteenth-century Americans when they ordered goods from Europe and wanted to obtain the nice over the too grand. In the nineteenth century these words could have come from the pen of any number of English or American design reformers. During their push for better human instincts to guide the conditions of workers and what they produced, many writers saw objects as having a moral content; the Shakers' prescription for good design fit neatly within an international drive to embody moral values in everyday things.

In the 1870s, Charles Nordhoff visited religious communities across America and wrote *The Communistic Societies of the United States,* one of the most helpful compendiums for understanding how the Shakers fit into the pattern of American communal sects. When visiting Mount Lebanon, Nordhoff spoke with Elder Frederick Evans, who told him: "No, the beautiful as you call it, is absurd and abnormal. It has no business with us. The divine man has no right to waste money upon what you would call beauty, in his house or his daily life, while there are people living in misery."[39] This late nineteenth-century concern is for the impoverished living outside the communities. Earlier Shaker restrictions had resulted from a concern for their own religious state. Elder Frederick's operative words are "beautiful as you call it," and "what you would call beauty," meaning—during this time of high Victorian styles—complicated, eclectic, additive features. It was not a rejection of beauty as he saw it. At Canterbury Nordhoff observed that "The dining-room was ornamented with evergreens and flowers in pots."[40]

WORLDLY RESPONSES TO SHAKER SETTINGS: DICKENS, HAWTHORNE, AND OTHERS

In 1853 the apostate Hervey Elkins wrote in his *Fifteen Years in the Senior Order of Shakers* of the wonder and beauty of his time with the sect:

> *Viewed from the plain below, in the grey, dim twilight of a soft and serene atmosphere, when all nature was wrapped in the unique and beautiful solemnity of an unusually prorogued autumn, these fires [they had just set to burn trash], emerging in the blue distance, from the vast amphitheatre of hills, were picturesque in the highest degree. How neat! how fascinating! and how much like our conceptions of heaven the whole vale appeared! And then to regard this work of cleansing and beautifying the domains of Mount Zion, as that preparatory to the visitation of the Most High, is something which speaks to the heart and says: "Dost thou appear as beautiful, as clean, and as comely in the sight of God, as dost these elements of an unthinking world?"*[41]

In various parts of his text, Elkins described Shaker songs as "beautiful," and when commenting on dwelling rooms, he mentioned an "elegant but plain stove."[42]

Shaker objects and environments carry coded messages so strong that they have regularly evoked sharply differing interpretations, sometimes from the same author. In part what was said depended on how the writer was thinking about America in general. The writings of the British author Charles Dickens were vastly popular in America and he had long anticipated a successful visit here. He arrived in Boston in January of 1842 and the town made a favorable impression. But he grew more anti-American as he moved to other areas, disliking what he perceived as uncouth and profit-oriented people. Dickens's dislike of America was heightened by the United States' refusal to make reciprocal agreements with Great Britain regarding international copyrights. Dickens's books were popular, but he was not gaining income commensurate with his fame. The laudatory attitude of the press began to turn as Dickens expressed his growing displeasure, and the mood shifted to mutual loathing. After returning to England he wrote *Martin Chuzzlewit* (1843–44), in which he scathingly attacked the American character.

Dickens visited the New Lebanon community in 1842. At this time the Shakers had closed their worship to outsiders because of the revivalist fervor now designated the Era of Manifestations (1837–50), for at this time the services were so filled with emotional frenzy that, it was feared, any viewing by outsiders would provoke public mockery. Kept out of the worship services he had heard about, Dickens added the Shakers to the other Americans he disliked. In his vitriolic *American Notes for General Circulation* (1842), in which exaggeration for humorous effect was interwoven with dislike, he described his night in a hotel in the town of Lebanon, and the visit the next day to the Shakers at New Lebanon, in equally caustic tones: the hotel was "inexpressibly comfortless" with bed chambers resembling "whitewashed cells, which opened from either side of a dreary passage; and were so like rooms in a prison that I half expected to be locked up when I went to bed, and listened involuntarily for the turning of the key on the outside . . . . [I]ndeed, these bedrooms were so very bare of even such common luxuries as chairs, that I should say they were not provided with enough of anything, but that I bethink myself of our having been most bountifully bitten all night." At New Lebanon: "[W]e walked into a grim room, where several grim hats were hanging on grim pegs, and the time was grimly told by a grim clock, which uttered every tick with a kind of struggle, as if it broke grim silence reluctantly, and under protest. Ranged against the wall were six or eight stiff, high-backed chairs, and they partook so strongly of the general grimness, that one would much rather have sat on the floor than incurred the smallest obligation to any of them . . . . They are governed by a woman, and her rule is understood to be absolute, though she has the assistance of a council of elders. She lives, it is said, in strict seclusion, in certain rooms above the chapel, and is never shown to profane eyes. If she at all resembles the lady who presided over the store, it is a great charity to keep her as close as possible . . . ." Dickens based his description of the worship service that he was not allowed to see on a "print of this ceremony which I have in my possession . . . ." It was like the one shown in figure 59.[43]

Most Americans reacted strongly to Dickens's account of themselves, and after the Civil War, when the English author wanted to visit the country again, he waged a campaign for popularity by projecting himself as a more understanding commentator. He admitted that to understand Americans was a more complex undertaking than he had acknowledged during his first attempt at the age of thirty, and during a five-month tour in 1867 and 1868, profited by nearly a quarter of a million dollars from the seventy-five performances he gave.

Nathaniel Hawthorne's thoughts about the Shakers changed as he dealt with his own sexuality. In 1831 Hawthorne visited the Shakers at Canterbury, where he watched them dance. In a letter of August 17, 1831, he described what he saw to his sister Louisa and lightly satirized the Shakers to amuse his family: in a meeting he saw "thirty or forty Shaker ladies, some of them quite pretty, all dressed in very light gowns, with a muslin handkerchief crossed over the bosom and a stiff muslin cap, so they looked pretty much as if they had just stept out of their coffins." About the men, he wrote: "There was nothing very remarkable in the men except their stupidity, and it did look queer to see these great boobies cutting all sorts of ridiculous capers with the gravest countenances imaginable." But by the end of this letter he had changed his emphasis:

This establishment is immensely rich. Their land extends two or three miles along the road, and there are streets of great houses, painted yellow and topt with red; they are now building a brick edifice for their public business, to cost seven or eight thousand dollars. On the whole, they lead a good and comfortable life, and if it were not for their ridiculous ceremonies, a man could not do a wiser thing than to join them. Those whom I conversed with were intelligent, and appeared happy. I spoke to them about becoming a member of the Society, but have come to no decision on that point.[44]

On September 9, 1831, in a letter to his cousin John Dike, Hawthorne wrote about Dike's marriage plans, and his own aversion to the idea of marriage: "I presume your marriage will take place very shortly, if it has not taken place already. If it were my case, I should feel very strangely, the moment the knot was tied. I have some idea of joining the Shakers, as I had an opportunity of inspecting one of their villages, during my journey, and was much pleased with their manner of life. However, there will be time enough for that after I have tried how I can content myself in the married state."[45] A letter from him dated November 4, 1831, mentions ". . . when I join the Shakers, I will send her [a Mrs. Ede's] a great slice of rye-and-indian bread."[46]

In his story "A Shaker Bridal" (1838), Hawthorne addressed the different emotional and career needs society assigned to men and to women. The protagonists in the sketch, Adam Colburn and Martha Pierson, were committed to each other but Adam could not achieve the financial success he felt necessary for marriage. In despair, he led them into Shaker commitments. Adam soon acquired a reputation as an efficient manager of temporal affairs, and as an effective preacher, fulfilling society's idea of a successful male. Martha "was not less distinguished in the duties proper to her sex." While they were still "in the summer of their years," the dying Elder of their community asked the Elders from all the eastern communities, including New Lebanon, to join him in inquiring whether Adam and Martha would accept leadership roles in their own community; no Eldresses are mentioned. Adam, who had a "severe" and "rigid" aspect, accepted and vowed to "strive, with my best strength, for the spiritual and temporal good of our community." Martha, at this seeming achievement, could not at first speak. Then she seconded Adam's commitment as though it were her own, "grew so pale, that she looked fitter to be laid in her coffin," and shuddered. As in a wedding, the Elders asked them to join hands at this moment of elevation after which Adam dropped Martha's hand and "folded his arms with a sense of satisfied ambition." Martha grew ever paler until "like a corpse in its burial clothes, she sank down . . . her heart could endure the weight of its desolate agony no longer."

In exploring society's sanctioned roles for men and women, Hawthorne used what he believed to be the structure of Shaker authority, and the particular qualities of Shaker men and Shaker women. But he misunderstood the pattern of Shaker authority: a dying Elder of a community would have had another Elder and two Eldresses working with him, and they would not have asked leaders from all the eastern communities to help them make a decision; they would have sought guidance from the Central Ministry. Also, Eldresses, who were never that different from men in their responsibilities, would have been fully part of any decision involving a Sister. Ultimately, the sketch says more about Hawthorne's fear of sex than about Shaker customs. It may also record his personal concern that two aspects he wished to embrace—strength and submissiveness—could not be joined, nor could submissiveness triumph separately.

Some who knew Hawthorne doubted he would marry, but he did so in 1842. Shortly after his marriage he visited the Shakers at Harvard, Massachusetts, with Ralph Waldo Emerson, and made no significant mention of the inspection in his journal. In August of 1850 he met Herman Melville, who was reverential to the older Hawthorne. The shy, usually distant and reserved

Hawthorne immediately asked Melville, who was a homosexual, to spend a few days with him and his wife. There followed a series of visits in which Melville was the most persistent. Hawthorne's wife Sophia saw the friendship as a father-son relationship and may not have recognized a homoerotic undercurrent. In August of 1851 Hawthorne visited Hancock with Melville and others, and they were shown about by a Brother:

> This old man was one of the fathers and rulers of the village; and under his guidance, we visited the principal dwelling-house in the village. It was a large brick edifice, with admirable convenient arrangements, and floors and walls of polished wood, and plaster as smooth as marble, and everything so neat that it was a pain and constraint to look at it; especially as it did not imply any real delicacy or moral purity in the occupants of the house. There were spit-boxes (bearing no appearance of ever being used, it is true) at equal distances up and down the long and broad entries. The sleeping apartments of the two sexes had an entry between them, on one side of which hung the hats of the men, on the other the bonnets of the women. In each chamber were two particularly narrow beds, hardly wide enough for one sleeper, but in each of which, the old elder told us, two people slept. There were no bathing or washing conveniences in the chambers; but in the entry there was a sink and wash-bowl, where all their attempts at purification were to be performed. The fact shows that all their miserable pretense of cleanliness and neatness is the thinnest superficiality; and that the Shakers are and must needs be a filthy set. And then their utter and systematic lack of privacy; their close junction of man with man, and supervision of one man over another—it is hateful and disgusting to think of; and the sooner the sect is extinct the better—a consummation which, I am happy to hear, is thought to be not a great many years distant.[47]

This passage does not display the amusing banter the Shakers had caused Hawthorne to write two decades earlier. Edwin Haviland Miller has speculated that Hawthorne's new fearfulness of Shaker societal practices may have resulted from the sexual tension developing between himself and Melville. To support his thesis that Hawthorne was in a quandary about his sexuality, Miller details the autobiographical and homoerotic nature of Hawthorne's writings, noting particularly the timid and sexually tormented character Arthur Dimmesdale in *The Scarlet Letter*, published the year he met Melville.[48] It is not clear Hawthorne ever seriously considered becoming a Shaker, but the sect did provide a foil he could wield as he thought privately about sexual ambiguity and celibacy, and wrote privately and publicly about traditional and nontraditional roles for men and women.

In 1856 Benson John Lossing visited New Lebanon, and the appreciative extended article he wrote for *Harper's New Monthly Magazine* helped correct how outsiders viewed the Shakers. He found: "Order and Neatness there held high court with a majesty I had never before seen." Describing a Family worship service: "This family worship service continued about an hour and a half, when I retired to the room assigned me, filled with new emotions, for I was in the midst of social and religious novelties." He described the larger community service: "Their movements in the dance or march, whether natural or studied, are all graceful and appropriate; and as I gazed upon that congregation of four or five hundred worshipers marching and countermarching in perfect time, I felt certain that, were it seen upon a stage as a theatrical exhibition, the involuntary exclamation of even the hypercritical would be, 'How beautiful!' " "System is everywhere observed, and all operations are carried on with exact economy." "Having property in common, the people have no private ambitions nor personal cares." "In morals and citizenship they are above reproach; and they are loved by those who know them best."[49]

As time has passed, each generation has developed new and sometimes divergent views that reflect new issues of religion, idealism, individualism, social order, women's rights, and quality in life and art. In 1847 John S. Dwight wrote that the Shakers wanted "the spiritual *without* the material, not the spiritual *in* the material."[50] This is true, but the material was not therefore ignored or treated lightly.

The following chapter looks at the objects the Shakers made in light of our best understanding of Shaker intentions of how they should live. Chapter IX deals with how the Shakers' living areas really looked. We will see that by the end of the nineteenth century, the Shakers had developed two kinds of spaces: some areas, such as meeting and dining rooms, were minimally appointed arenas to be shared with the public—these furthered the idea of a simple-living people. In contrast, their private rooms rapidly joined the complex room arrangements associated with the high Victorian and Edwardian eras.

Chapter V

VISUAL AFFIRMATION OF ORDER:
A GIFT DRAWING, A CASE OF DRAWERS,
A MEETINGHOUSE, A BARN, AND DANCES

The Shaker commitment to "True Gospel Simplicity" placed them squarely within the Enlightenment's commitment to order and patterned clarity in both life and art. Much of the Western world was mining the past for intellectual, political, and aesthetic inspiration and justification. People everywhere happily revived a classical vocabulary of lines, grids, squares, circles, and ovals to bring harmony to their visible world. For example, designs for new institutional buildings, such as boarding schools, hospitals, madhouses, and prisons, which housed large numbers of inhabitants, joined the new belief in the dignity of people with rationally developed designs that employed the new shapes for everything. This chapter closely examines a diverse group of Shaker artifacts and expressions to show how the sect fit neatly into the contemporary attitude toward forms and patterns. But it should be remembered that while such rationality was the goal of Shaker living patterns, it would remain contrary to the expectations of an experiential faith that valued unfolding spiritual knowledge, often through ecstasy and spirit manifestations.

A GIFT DRAWING

The aligning of units into geometric patterns was second nature to Shaker minds during the first half of the nineteenth century. Even during the emotional time of the Era of Manifestations, many of the drawings that recorded visions are organized and divided into areas any architect would understand.

On March 16, 1843, the spirit of Adam left heaven and visited New Lebanon to provide Believers with a plan of heaven (figure 48). All of its features were numbered, and Adam dictated to the recording instrument an index that explained each part. The *Holy City* plan was given to Believers so that they could reflect it in God's redemptive city on earth, which the Shakers knew was New Lebanon. The Holy City was directly over New Lebanon, and the city on earth was to grow from three miles square to twelve miles square and include Hancock. The distance between the two communities is four miles.

> *The plan of the City of the New Jerusalem, or of the living God, called the* Holy City, *is a perfect patron [i.e., pattern] of the High City of the* Holy Selan *in the Heavens.*
> *The Holy Selan is right over this the Holy City on earth. There is many cities between, along thro the Heaven.*
> *The Temple of the Living God and Eternal Mother Wisdom at the Holy Selan is right over this their temple in the Holy City on earth.*
> *This Holy city is three miles square now, and as the work of God increases, this city will also spread every way from the center till it comes to its final & perfect size, which is now marked out by a wall; the city will then be 12 miles square, and include Hancock within its beautiful walls.*

Laid out with a compass and carefully ruled, the city plan is balanced in the same way that many pieces of Shaker furniture are balanced: parts feel equalized because of the quiet tension of not-quite-alike parts (see figures 83 through 85). The design employs circles—some containing four- and seven-sided units—squares, and rectangles. The center of the visual complex that "First Father Adam" provided was the "sanctuary or Meeting house, [it] is where the center of the temple is marked out" (1 on the plan). "Here stands the temple of the Living God & Eternal Wisdom," to the Shakers, the male and female aspects of God.

The elaborate description of architectural details, including an array of pillars, manifests the

Opposite:
48. "HOLY CITY"
New Lebanon, New York
Inscribed on back in ink: "Sacred Sheet From Mt. Lebanon"
March 16, 1843
Pencil and watercolor on paper
H. 32" W. 24⅝"
Philadelphia Museum of Art, Philadelphia, Pennsylvania: gift of Mr. and Mrs. Julius Zieget

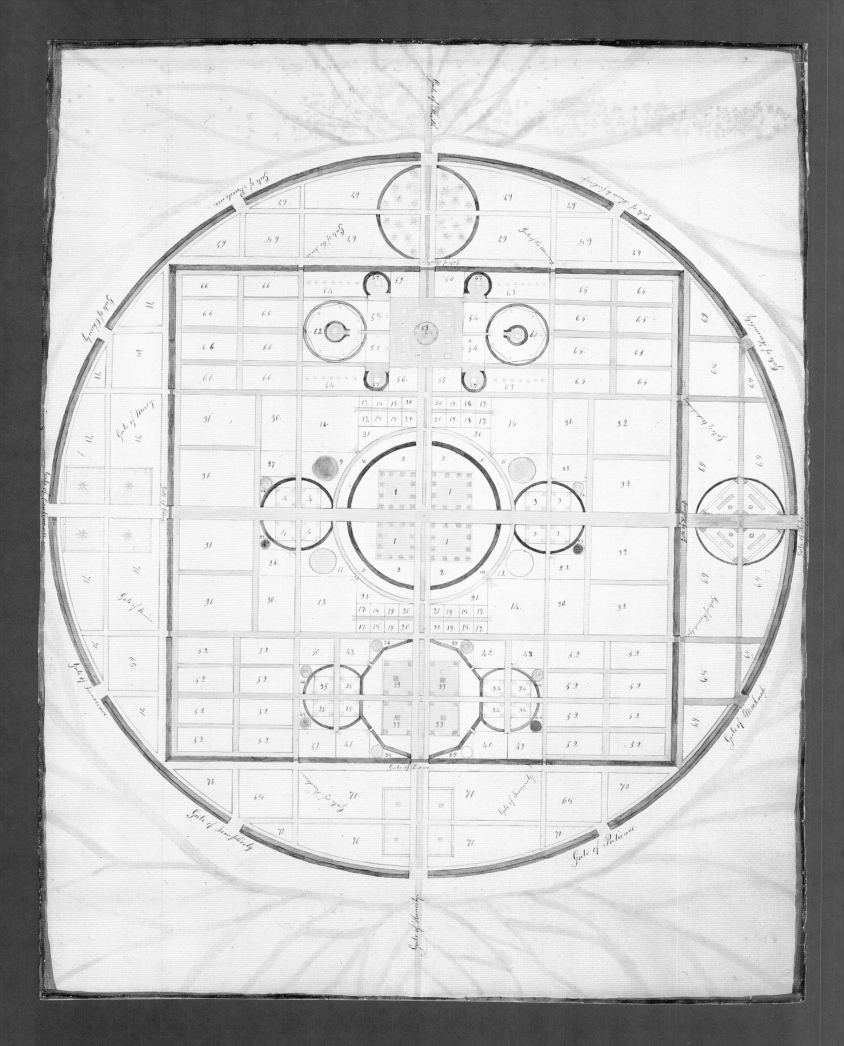

expectations provided in the book of Revelation, particularly in Chapters 21 and 22, which echoed the building and furnishing of Solomon's Temple as described in the Old Testament. The Court of the Saints (3 on the plan) has four pillars that "are significant of the four leading characters or elders that direct & lead the court; two males & two females, There being four in each quarter shows that the whole house is governed by an established Lead of four, which is the eternal law of God for the Lead of Saints . . . ." The outer court (4 on the plan) is the Deacon's "place of residence while visiting the holy city." The eternal Father and the eternal Wisdom, each has a separate fruit garden and flower garden. There is "Mothers flower garden" for Ann Lee and "The Saviors flower garden" for Jesus; each also has a fruit garden. The Saints have similar pairs of gardens.

As in Shaker communities, the "dwelling of the Young believers, who have set out to travel in the work of God, & put away their sins," is at the edge of the pattern (69 on the plan), and those walls are red, which signals judgment, among other things. (The assigned meanings of colors are given in Chapter VII, p.129 ff.) Like the "holy grounds" the Shakers would be directed to clear for special spiritual hilltop services beginning in the spring of 1842, the plan includes a sacred ground, which, like the clearings on earth, is marked with a stone and a fountain, which in heaven is forty feet wide.

The plan is bisected by a river flowing smoothly both east and west (up and down on the drawing). The gold street on either side of it measures thirty feet in width; the main street crossing this is one hundred feet wide. The outer wall, mostly of jasper, as in Revelation, is edged outside with a "dark color [black, which also edges the four sides of the drawing]," which "shows that all is darkness without." (The original name of the South Union, Kentucky, community was Jasper.)[1]

The protective outer wall has twelve gates named: "In consequence of the 12 christian virtues, which are the 12 foundation pillars of the Church & law of Christ . . . ." "Over each gate, upon the arch of the gate, is a watch tower, on the top of each tower, there is standing an angel, holding a trumpet and a spear." These angels call the unsaved while being ready to protect those who have found salvation.[2]

A CASE OF DRAWERS

The tall case of drawers in figure 49 is one of the earliest dated Shaker objects. It was made at New Lebanon, and is dated 1806 in paint on the back. Without a cornice or crowning top line, it projects a tight, stripped, minimal form. Six long drawers, with two vertical lines of turned knobs, rise to an upper, more complex area that has six short drawers with four vertical lines of knobs. Most of the drawers decrease in height as they ascend. (Beginning at the bottom they are: $8^{3}/_{16}$, $8^{5}/_{16}$, $8^{3}/_{8}$, $8^{1}/_{4}$, $8^{1}/_{4}$, $8^{3}/_{16}$, $7^{1}/_{4}$, $7^{7}/_{16}$, and $6^{5}/_{8}$ inches.) The profusion of rectangular shapes in the upper portion acts like a cornice, providing a visual lift to the design. In practical terms, each user probably had an equal number of short and long storage areas. The projecting base follows one of two worldly shop practices adopted by the Shakers: enclosing boards, as in figure 49, rather than the tighter form where the sides project down to form the feet, found in figure 80. (But to help support the weight, the side boards of figure 49 do carry down inside the enclosing boards to rest on the floor.) The slightly projecting base provides visual stability under the great upward thrust of the case. (A similar piece now at Pleasant Hill has broader knobs.)[3] This form, with its almost rude immediacy, explains the Shakers' ability to expunge most but not all superfluities. The base's molded edge, and the decorative shaping of the legs, demonstrate that even when a designer strove to produce as austere a form as possible, some traditional shop practices naturally continued.

BUILDINGS

Lofty ideals could produce unbuildable buildings. In 1784 the Frenchman Etienne-Louis Boullée designed as a monument to the neoclassical hero Isaac Newton a giant tomb in the shape of a sphere. The huge ball was to hold the body of Newton "as by the extent of your wisdom and the sublimity of your genius you determined the shape of the earth; I have conceived the idea of enveloping you in your own discovery."[4] Never built, the monument expressed the longing, like Goethe's contemporary garden sculpture seen in figure 11, to unite logically simple forms even when the function was only the realization of a perfect idea. Similarly, Boullée's 1793 plan for a projected museum features circles, squares, and an interplay of the two like that found in God's plan for the Holy City on earth.[5]

49. CASE OF DRAWERS
New Lebanon, New York
Dated in paint on back: "1806"
Pine colored red; maple knobs
H. 84" W. 48" D. 19"
The sides continue to the floor behind the bracket feet
Hancock Shaker Village, Pittsfield, Massachusetts

In America during the late eighteenth century, as in Europe, both large- and small-scale buildings were conforming to new design concerns. In 1796 the English-trained architect Benjamin Henry Latrobe arrived in America and began work in Virginia. There his most important early building was the 1797–98 State Penitentiary. In it he joined simple interlocking geometric shapes with the amenities of light, air, and sanitation. The cell block for men was a semicircular structure three stories high and one cell deep; the cells had vaulted ceilings and opened onto a balcony on the inside of the semicircle. Each cell had a primitive water closet. The ends of the semicircle were joined by a straight wall, forming a closed D-shaped court. The keeper's house was located at the center of the straight wall, which allowed him a panoptic surveillance of all activities the Central Ministry at New Lebanon might have envied. Beyond the straight wall two rectangular buildings, with their own courts, housed a women's prison and separate infirmaries for men and women.[6] Although the Shakers wanted more practical spaces than the projected tomb for Isaac Newton, and smaller buildings than Latrobe's jail, a related idealism pushed them to produce an extraordinary sense of a contained volume in two of their most important buildings: the 1822–24 meetinghouse at New Lebanon, and the 1826 round barn at Hancock, Massachusetts.

MEETINGHOUSES

New Lebanon was the center from which Shaker patterns of life, spirituality, and art flowed, and it was natural that the first meetinghouse, begun in 1785 and consecrated in 1786, became the central icon of the Society. It had been raised before any community had been brought into Gospel Order, however it spoke of individual and group achievements in the material and spiritual worlds, and was the first large-scale Shaker-made object. It was logical, therefore, that its builder, Moses Johnson, would create nearly identical meetinghouses in ten more communities in the next eight years (1786–94). Like early Shaker-made furniture, this prototypical design reflected mid-eighteenth-century worldly styling. Still, while other sects generally used pitched roofs for meetinghouses, the Shaker building resembles contemporary vernacular houses and barns made under the influence of mid-century Georgian designs: it has a rectangular shape, clapboards, double-hung windows of a balanced arrangement, four-paneled doors, and braced interior beams. The use of the gambrel roof allowed a greater volume of space for the Ministry living over the worship space. That roof was in the English, rather than the Dutch, style, having upper and lower slopes of equal length: the upper one is pitched at 30–40 degrees, while the lower is a steep 60 degrees. (Its end is seen at the right of figure 50.) It had a men's door and women's door on the long side for the general public, and doors at each end for Brothers, Sisters, and the Ministry. Inside, men and women used different ends of the building. Such provisions for separating the sexes were common in nonconformist meetinghouses and synagogues. Some early Quaker meetinghouses have a partition that slides down to close off one side from the other, and a Baptist meetinghouse in Bristol, Rhode Island, had a rail down the center to secure the division of the sexes.[7]

A visitor described the Shirley meetinghouse in 1795:

We first viewed the meeting House, which drew our attention, because beautifully painted white on the sides & even over the roof. The doors were green. Within, the wood work is painted of a deep blue, & the seats are of a chocolate colour. The Seats are moveable benches, placed round the room, while the area is clear like a Dancing Room. There are two Stoves inserted into the two chimnies at the end of the Building . . . . The two doors on the north side fronting the road, open into the House, & we ascend by these steps of hewn stone placed upon a broad flat stone, & which were brought 9 miles. At each end & near the corners are doors with the same steps, which open immediately upon the Chamber Stairs, & lead to the apartments of the elders. These we were not permitted to visit. In the Meeting Room were pendant brasses to receive lights if they should be at any time necessary. These brasses were flat plates not formed like our Chandeliers but to set candle sticks upon, which are brought into the Hall. They shove up, so as easily to be put entirely out of the way . . . . The Meeting House is in the Center of a Square, which is railed in by a handsome fence of rails . . . . The whole surface of the square is laid in turf, brought from an adjacent field. And that it might not be injured by rain from the building, spouts & gutters lead off the waters into a stone drain, which conveys them into the Street under the surface of the ground.[8]

Many of the early Shaker structures were hastily built of inadequate materials on weak foundations. For example, in 1804 the main timber supports under the walls of the 1792 Canterbury meetinghouse were replaced by hewn granite.[9] If larger houses or barns were needed as communities increased in membership, they might be pulled elsewhere for different uses and larger ones erected on their previous sites. By 1805 nearly all the early buildings at New Lebanon had been replaced with better aligned, more spacious, and more adequately constructed ones.

THE SECOND MEETINGHOUSE AT NEW LEBANON

In 1822 the first meetinghouse was pulled to the north and turned to face east. On the old site was built a large meetinghouse in the neoclassical style (figure 50). When the new one was finished, on June 20, 1824, "The whole society in New Lebanon attended meeting in the New

50. SECOND AND FIRST
MEETINGHOUSES
New Lebanon, New York
By Benson John Lossing
Inscribed: "Shaker Meeting House, Lebanon,
Aug 18, 1859" and "House 80 x 65/
Porch 35 x 27"
Ink and watercolor on paper
H. 4½" W. 8½"
The Huntington Library, San Marino, California

51. PHOTOGRAPH OF THE SECOND
MEETINGHOUSE
New Lebanon, New York
By James Irving of Troy, New York
After March 1874: it shows irons "to hang a crane
on for suspending painting stages" installed by
Daniel Boler, April 1, 1874
H. 11" W. 13⅞"
Collection of the Shaker Museum and Library,
Old Chatham, New York

Meeting house; also two loads from Hancock and Elders from Canterbury the Ministry from Alfred & Deacons from Watervliet, also many of the world. A rainy wet day."[10] Another account of the first meeting records about a thousand from the world. "The next Sabbath there were at least three hundred Shakers, and two thousand spectators."[11] The old meetinghouse (to the right in figure 50) served as a school, and then a seed house; it is now the headmaster's house of the Darrow School. During the years it acquired a flat roof, and then a pitched roof.

Like contemporary Shaker furniture that lacks a heavy cornice-molding, the mass of the new building is tight. There are no complex, jutting overhangs playing against recessions to move the eye in and out; all is tense, rigid, and contained; even the jutting canopies over the doors seem like quickly drawn curves (figure 51). Inside there are broad side walls pierced with huge windows below a vaulted ceiling (figures 52, 53, 59, and 62). European and American religious buildings during the eighteenth and nineteenth centuries featured similarly open spaces, but usually with fixed benches. Earlier in Europe such areas were often without benches or chairs so people could stroll about or stand in groups during services. In the eighteenth century, and increasingly in the nineteenth century, many European and American public rooms and dance or entertainment halls provided open, empty rooms that could be employed in a number of ways.

**52. INTERIOR OF SECOND
MEETINGHOUSE**
New Lebanon, New York
By Benson John Lossing
August 1856
Pencil on paper
*Inscribed: "Interior view of the Meeting house
from the women's [i.e. Sisters'] side [i.e. end]."
Color notes include: walls a robins egg blue;
wainscoting of white pine varnished; doors a deep
ultramarine blue inside and out; outside of
meetinghouse white.*
H. 8½" W. 12¼"
The Huntington Library, San Marino, California

**53. INTERIOR OF THE SECOND
MEETINGHOUSE**
New Lebanon, New York
By Benson John Lossing
*Inscribed: "Interior of the meeting house/Aug.
18.1856"*
Ink and watercolor on paper
H. 6" W. 8½"
*Winterthur Museum, Winterthur, Delaware:
The Edward Deming Andrews Memorial Shaker
Collection*

The 1797–98 design by Benjamin Latrobe, in figure 54, was a proposal for a grand ballroom in a theater in Richmond, Virginia. The closely contained volume, with its rigid arrangement of arches and niches, has large windows on one side and at the end. Its right wall would have abutted other rooms. The walls are painted yellow, a color the Shakers used on much of their furniture and architectural woodwork. Simpler halls, without apses at the end, were scattered throughout many worldly towns and villages the Shakers knew. For example, the second floor of the mostly eighteenth-century Frary House at Deerfield, Massachusetts, has a vaulted ballroom that was used for dances, concerts, plays, and meetings by special groups. There, in 1797, the Board of Trustees of the Deerfield Academy held its first meeting. Being an eighteenth-century space, it has a more playful arrangement of surfaces than the subsequent neoclassical taste would dictate. Closer to the Shakers' new religious arena was the Masonic hall seen as figure 55. It was part of the home

54. PROPOSED BALLROOM FOR A
THEATER IN RICHMOND, VIRGINIA
By Benjamin Henry Latrobe
1797–98
Ink and watercolor on paper
H. 16" W. 21⁷/₈"
Library of Congress, Washington, D.C.,
Prints and Photographs Division

55. PHOTOGRAPH OF MASONIC HALL
IN THE GILBERT HOUSE
Lebanon, New York, taken 1984
Courtesy of Phyllis Galician

built by Elisha Gilbert in 1783 in New Lebanon Center, only three and a half miles from the center of Shaker activity. Its walls are covered with more than fifty Masonic symbols. (The closeness of these to symbols used in Shaker gift drawings is discussed in Chapter VIII.)

During worship services the new meetinghouse might be packed with people. Benson John Lossing records four to five hundred Believers in 1856, and the crowd of non-Believers could sometimes number over a thousand. The outsiders came not just to see ecstatic gifts, for other, far larger, sects provided greater displays of exotic behavior. The Shakers, however, provided spectacular theater as ritualistically dressed men and women moved in danced patterns.

The public sat separated by sexes on a series of rising, fixed benches on the east side of the building, through which they entered (at the left of figure 52). In figure 59 a woman sits in worldly dress at the left, and a top hat and walking stick designate a man beyond the image to the right. They are seated on loose benches placed in front of the fixed ones, probably because of an overflow of worldly people, and are shown facing three of the five west windows. When making the plate the engraver failed to reverse the image so that it would be correct when printed: the Sisters and their bonnets and capes (hung on pegs), and the worldly woman, should be on the right, at the northern end of the room. The Brothers and their hats and jackets should be on the left, at the southern end. Shakers too infirm to dance used the single fixed bench on the facing west wall. (It is on the right in figure 52, which also shows, upside down at the top, the five windows above the single fixed bench. In the upside-down part, the "men" and "women" written in the left and right windows, were Lossing's notes of who used each end of the room.)

In 1856 Lossing visited New Lebanon in preparation for his article in *Harper's,* producing drawings and watercolors from which engravings were made. Except for the various versions of the print shown in figure 59, these were the first interior views of Shaker rooms. Figure 52 shows Lossing's drawing of a Brother in a frock coat sitting on a bench in the meetinghouse. (His detailing of Shaker clothing is seen in figure 134.) His watercolor of this view (figure 53) correctly shows the walls, above the wainscoting, and the ceiling as blue. The pegs for hats, bonnets, and other clothing make rows on the walls. The Shakers began worship on movable benches and then cleared them away to provide an open space for dancing and unimpeded reception of ecstatic gifts. Outside, the two doors below hemispheric canopies facing the street served for the world: men entered the left door, women the right. This kept all the men at the south end of the building and women at the north end. The "porch" or wing has three doors, set close together. The Ministry entered through the center door, the Brothers the right door, and the Sisters the left. The Ministry lived in the upper floors of the porch.

The massive building impressed both Shakers and non-Believers. In 1825 Horatio Gates Spofford wrote in *A Gazetteer of the State of New-York, etc.:* "Their new Meeting House erected in 1823, is a model of architectural beauty and simple grandeur, well worth the notice of church architects. The main edifice is 80 by 65 feet, all in one room, without beams or pillars, having a conical roof, covered with tin; and the porch, 34 by 27, roofed and covered in the same way. They are of wood, but the foundations, and flights of steps, outside, are of marble."[12] During his 1856 visit to New Lebanon, to prepare his *Harper's* article, Lossing was lodged across from "the house for public worship, a spacious framed building, painted white, with an arched roof." When Charles Nordhoff visited there in 1874 he called it a "great boiler-roofed church."[13]

The meetinghouse was used twice on Sundays. In the morning, at 10:00 or 10:30, all the Families, except the Church Family, were present at a meeting open to the public. On June 30, 1851, four small louvered windows were added between the large room and the Ministry's living area so they could watch the meetings unobserved. (One is shown in figure 246.) The Church Family used the meetinghouse in the afternoon and selected other Families to join them; the public was excluded from the afternoon services. After about 1850, when membership was declining, the Church Family did attend in the morning to increase the number of Shakers present; the First and Second Orders of the Church Family alternated Sunday appearances at the public morning meeting.

THE ROUND BARN

In 1826 the Church Family at Hancock consciously or unconsciously employed neoclassical principles when they built their round barn. As with Latrobe's 1797–98 jail in Richmond, rational principles and a desire for geometric spaces produced a logical functionalism. The circular plan of the barn harks back to ancient forms. The Greeks, for example, made round buildings, with stone or tile conical roofs. The Romans, using concrete, developed larger round buildings with domed roofs. The new form appeared in the bathhouses at the Roman port at Baiai, and evolved into the far grander domed Pantheon in Rome in the second century A.D. The Pantheon, first built as an imperial monument and shrine, was consecrated as a Christian church in 609 A.D. Its dome has a round opening at the apex, which, except for the doors, serves as the only source of light. This building, as much as any ancient circular construction, influenced neoclassical architecture.

In addition to the prevailing neoclassicism there was a local precedent of multisided "round" structures for the storage of grain. From the early 1700s there were in upstate New York buildings called "hay barracks" that followed an ancient Netherlandish form that provided a means of raising the floor so hay and rye (and in New York corn) could be lifted above water meadows. They were made of poles, usually forty or fifty feet in height, that supported a pointed roof, over an adjustable floor that could be raised or lowered by means of pulleys. These storage structures were square, rectangular, hexagonal, or octagonal in form. (There were no water meadows on the Van Bergen farm in Leeds, New York, but an overmantel from its house shows at the left two octagonal barracks with adjustable floors. One has the floor raised half-way up the poles.) When

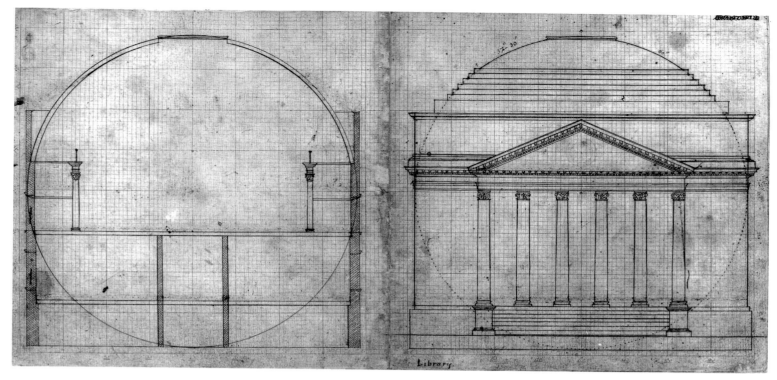

56. DESIGN FOR THE LIBRARY
AT THE UNIVERSITY OF VIRGINIA
By Thomas Jefferson
About 1820
Ink on graph paper
H. 8¾" W. 17¼"
University of Virginia, Thomas Jefferson Papers,
Special Collections Department, Library,
Charlottesville, Virginia

57. VIEW OF HANCOCK,
MASSACHUSETTS
Published in John Warner Barber's, Historical
Collections . . . of Every Town in Massachusetts,
1839
Wood engraving
Hancock Shaker Village, Pittsfield, Massachusetts

58. PHOTOGRAPH OF THE ROUND BARN
Hancock, Massachusetts, probably 1880s
Photograph: H. 8½" W. 5¼"
Collection of the Shaker Museum and Library,
Old Chatham, New York

the floor was raised the area under it could be used as a temporary shelter if boards were nailed below it to the supporting poles.[14] In 1793 George Washington designed and built on his Dogue Run Farm in Fairfax County, Virginia, a sixteen-sided barn. It is the earliest known nearly circular barn in America.[15]

In 1806 Thomas Jefferson, who used neoclassical principles in his design for Monticello (1769–1809), began a small brick octagonal retreat called Poplar Forest, in Bedford County, Virginia, where he could get away from the constant demands of his daily life. Early in the nineteenth century John Clarke created a round brick building about thirty-six feet in diameter on his plantation in Powhatan County, Virginia. Its twelve-foot-high wall supports a conical roof that angles up to a central brick chimney. The presence below it of a central fireplace with three hearths suggests the building was used as slave quarters. Since Clarke pursued progressive and innovative technologies and designs, it is not surprising that he built this tight, neoclassical structure on his plantation.[16]

When the artist John Vanderlyn returned from France in 1817 he created a circular building in New York City in which he showed, for a fee, the panoramic view he had painted of the palace and gardens of Versailles. For this he built on the northeast corner of City Hall Park, facing Chambers Street, a brick and stone version of the Roman Pantheon fifty-three feet in diameter. Its forty-five-foot-high wall supported a dome and the front had a classical portico. Inside visitors climbed to a raised central platform where they were surrounded by a scene covering more that 3,000 square feet of canvas. The building was demolished in 1870.[17] As part of his design for the University of Virginia at Charlottesville, Thomas Jefferson created the Rotunda (1823–27), a half-size, near replica of the Pantheon's main drum and colonnaded portico. When beginning this design on graph paper, Jefferson dotted in a large circle that rose from the ground, and described the shape of the roof. The center point, made by the compass, is in line with the tops of the volutes of the capitals of the large columns (see figure 56).[18]

It seems unlikely the Church Family at Hancock, and the round barn's probable builder Daniel Goodrich, had heard of Goethe or Latrobe, or knew of Vanderlyn's building. But the barn is contemporary with Jefferson's Rotunda, and new principles of thought and design had filtered into rural areas.

The barn built at Hancock is acknowledged to be the first truly round barn built in America. It is nearly ninety feet across, and was built with the help of hired masons. It held about ninety cattle in radiating stalls around a central mow into which hay was pitched from a wagon floor above. An 1857 drawing shows the perimeter with stalls, rather than the present stanchions.[19] At first the barn had a conical roof, as shown at the right in a wood engraving of 1839 (figure 57), with a covered opening at the center. The original design gave the building greater classical unity than is seen today, making it very like a rural idea of the Pantheon. In 1827 it was described thus: "The roof comes to a point at the centre, and sheds off the rain all round something similar to an umbrella."[20] In 1864, a fire made it necessary to rebuild, and a flat roof topped by a cupola was installed. In the mid-1870s a monitor, or twelve-sided superstructure, was added to provide greater ventilation and headroom for the Brothers working with the hay (figure 58). In 1880 a manure pit was dug down around the inside of the wall. This was one of the Shakers' least practical design changes, for although it made the collecting of manure easier, it weakened the walls, with the result that they began to crack. In 1968 all the stonework was pulled down and rebuilt. When the barn was first erected, the Society accepted the design as a gift from God, but it was, like so much the Shakers made, manifestly modern. It is possible that the creation of the building was a conscious effort on the part of the Shakers at Hancock to rival the grand up-to-date meetinghouse just finished at New Lebanon. From the time the barn was built many have come to see it. Round and polygonal barns grew in popularity after 1850, and by 1880 Hancock's barn was well known through its publication in leading farm journals.

DANCES

This section is not intended to be a history of Shaker dance patterns. That topic has been addressed admirably by Edward Deming Andrews in *The Gift to be Simple* (1940), and more completely by Daniel W. Patterson in *The Shaker Spiritual* (1979). The purpose here is to see the shapes and roles of basic visual patterns used in worship services. Square, circular, and other easily followed group dances predate the neoclassical era in which the Shaker patterns developed, but the new style's simple arrangements meshed with and intensified traditional precedents. Individual Families had evening worship services in their own buildings, but on the Sabbath the

59. "SHAKERS, THEIR MODE OF WORSHIP"
Hand colored lithograph published by D.W. Kellogg and Co., Hartford, Connecticut 1832–40
Ink and watercolor on paper
H. 10⁷⁄₁₆" W. 11³⁄₈"
Collection of the Shaker Museum and Library, Old Chatham, New York

community used the meetinghouse, the central communal symbol of union, and the place the public most frequented.

Squares

Unity, sermons, and sexual segregation had made firm inroads into ecstatic-based worship by about 1788 when Joseph Meacham learned, in a vision from angels dancing before the throne of God, the Square Order Shuffle. In it, groups of Believers moved in unison, using square, containing patterns. Part of Meacham's intention was to produce a difficult dance that would aid, through its concentrated effort, in mortifying the flesh of the performers. About 1790 he would introduce the even more mortifying Turning Shuffle. For the Square Order Shuffle, Believers arranged themselves in rows, women at one end facing men at the other, as in figure 59 (as mentioned earlier, the scene has been reversed by the printing process). Alternatively, in the Turning Shuffle, both groups faced those singing wordless songs. The dancers moved with a slow shuffling step backwards and forwards. The pace was a step every four seconds with a turn every eight steps, and visitors commented on the clatter made by the "thick shoes." Isaac Newton Youngs at New Lebanon described the dance: it "consisted in taking three whole steps forward, turning, & taking three back, setting the foot straight forward at each end, & then going forward again three steps, and taking a double step, or 'tip tap,' as it is called, then receding three steps, with a 'tip tap'; this takes the turn part of the tune once; then it is repeated, in the same manner, then shuffle the set part once over."[21] The activity might last each Sabbath for hours in the morning, and again in the afternoon. During breaks in the dancing, a preacher admonished them: "Avoid carnal lusts. Labor to shake off sin; sin is hateful; I hate sin. Power of God."[22]

The change to uniformity did not occur at the same time in each village. The earlier style of more spontaneous dancing persisted at Enfield, Connecticut, until 1791. On special occasions, and during heightened spiritual activity, as during four weeks of strong religious fervor at Enfield in 1807, the individual expression reemerged. The Shakers called this form of dance "promiscuous" dancing, or dancing in the "Back [old] Manner."[23]

In a form called "the hollow square" (first seen in a vision at Harvard in 1825) the basic movement was shuffling steps, and the men and women were arranged thus:

> [T]he two ranks facing each other, on the north and south, advance up towards each other, turn round, and take three steps to the place of beginning, then advance up again and recede backward with the double step, the same as in square order shuffle; this takes half of the time once over, while the other two ranks on the east and west shuffle. In the other half (of the tune) the east and west ranks advance and recede while the others shuffle . . . . There may be two squares in motion at the same time.

> Music was furnished by three men who kept time by "pawing" with their hands "like dancing dogs" and chanting a wordless tune "in voices which might almost have been heard to the end of the valley."[24]

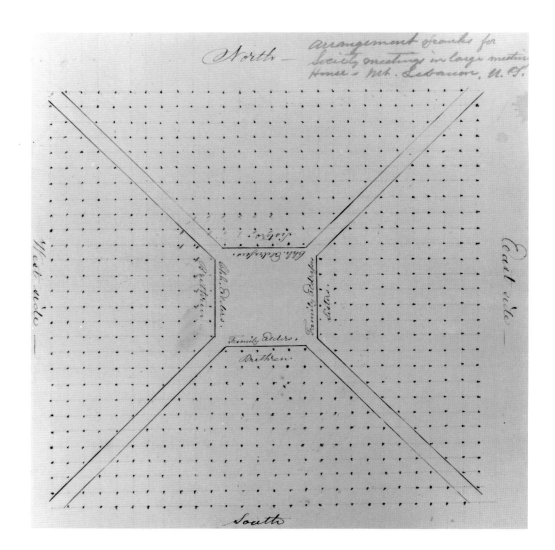

60. AN ARRANGEMENT FOR STANDING
DURING WORSHIP
New Lebanon, New York
Probably between 1824–40
Ink on paper
H. 8³⁄₈" W. 8¹⁄₈"
*Western Reserve Historical Society, Cleveland,
Ohio*

A design for standing within the second New Lebanon meetinghouse (figure 60) places the leaders in the center at the head of ranks of Believers. At the north, Church Eldresses lead Sisters. To the east, Family Eldresses stand in front of more Sisters, while Family Elders at the south begin lines of Brothers. Church Elders complete the design on the west, and stand before the remaining Brothers. The drawing was probably made between 1824 and 1840. (A later note on its upper right corner places the design at New Lebanon.)[25]

There was a group of dances that combined squares, rectangles, and marching, which Elder Henry Blinn called Changeable Marches, either because Believers changed directions often, or because the pattern changed according to the number participating. Among the many diagrams Patterson has provided, five show the placement of the singers, and the movement of Brothers and Sisters dancing in geometric patterns (figure 61).[26]

Circles

After Meacham's death in 1796 squared patterns continued, but Lucy Wright relaxed the intensity of the dance and added circles, narrow and wide lines, and hand gestures and bowing that suggested angelic motions and gathering. In 1813 a new dance required the Believers to go around in a circle single file, and "Along about this time some songs began to be motioned with our hands; various motions for different songs; and to motion with our hands for the various kinds of song sung for laboring, etc."[27]

Two variants of the ring dance were introduced in 1828. In the "continuous ring, the men and women each formed four ranks facing in alternating directions, then they march forward in the song, turning from one rank into the other at the end." In the second, the "endless chain" or "union dance," designed to make the dancers conscious of everlasting fellowship, the Brothers and Sisters placed themselves "in two large circles, facing opposite ways and leaving a small opening or space on one side. The singers were stationed in the center of the circle. When the ranks moved forward they turned at the opening out of one circle into the other, bringing 'every one to meet and see every one in the circles.' "[28] Images of circular dancing were produced in various publications. *Frank Leslie's Illustrated Newspaper* for November 1873 showed the Shakers danc-

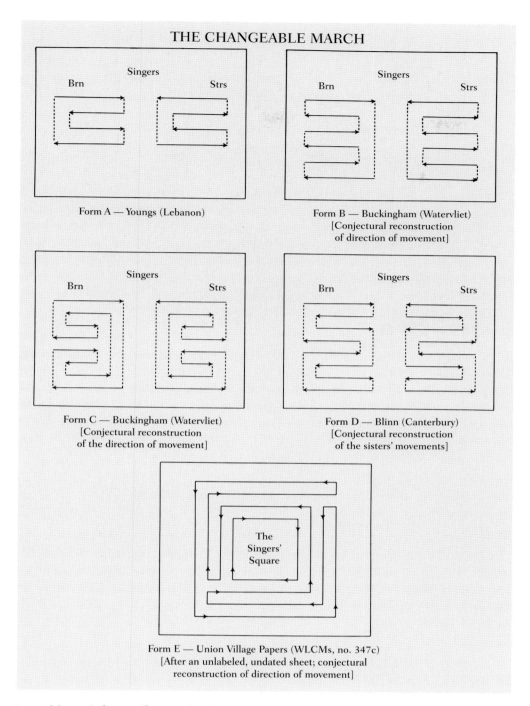

THE CHANGEABLE MARCH

Form A — Youngs (Lebanon)

Form B — Buckingham (Watervliet)
[Conjectural reconstruction
of direction of movement]

Form C — Buckingham (Watervliet)
[Conjectural reconstruction
of the direction of movement]

Form D — Blinn (Canterbury)
[Conjectural reconstruction
of the sisters' movements]

Form E — Union Village Papers (WLCMs, no. 347c)
[After an unlabeled, undated sheet; conjectural
reconstruction of direction of movement]

61. FIVE PLANS OF SQUARE DANCES
OR MARCHES

ing at Mount Lebanon (figure 62). The viewer of the illustration is facing south. The image is wrong in the following ways: the left, or east, was the world's side, and outsiders sat on a staging of five rising benches. The Shakers should be on a single bench running the length of the west wall. It was divided in the middle: the men used the south half, the women the north half. The print is also wrong in the placement of the doors in the end wall. What are shown as two large doors—at the left and right—were really windows, and the smaller doors should be closer together. What appear as rods hanging above the dancers should be seen as stovepipes running the length of the building. (The Lossing drawing, figure 52, is a nearly correct record of the room.)

In 1832 a visitor to New Lebanon was impressed by the neatness of the building, the smooth floor, the pale sallowness of the Sisters in contrast with the healthy, ruddy appearance of the Brothers, and the presence of several African Americans, both male and female, among the worshipers:

The worship commenced by the men arranging themselves in line at one end of the room, and the women on the other, and after a few words were addressed to them by the Elder they all kneeled down in opposite lines, facing each other, and after a period of profound silence, they commenced singing hymns from a book, the words of which were unintelligible to the auditors. After this they rose and marched backwards and forwards facing each other, to a tune which they all sung; then they faced the

62. "NEW YORK STATE. THE SHAKERS OF
NEW LEBANON—RELIGIOUS
EXERCISES IN THE MEETING- HOUSE"
Mount Lebanon, New York
Sketched by Joseph Becker; published in Frank
Leslie's Illustrated Newspaper
(November 1, 1873, p. 124).
Wood engraving
Ink on paper
H. 9¼" W. 14"
Collection of the Shaker Museum and Library,
Old Chatham, New York

wall, with their backs to the audience, and marched in the same manner, backwards and forwards towards the wall.

When this exercise ended they formed two circles, a smaller and larger one, and marched to the tunes sung by the inner circle, which composed the principal singers; their hands also keeping time, either by the alternate motion of swinging backwards and forwards, or by clapping them together as they became animated by the tunes which were sung. This exercise continued about half an hour, when they retired to their seats.[29]

A Pattern Danced by Spirits

Many of the dance configurations were the result of instructions from angels. With the arrival of the extraordinary revivalist Era of Manifestations that began in 1837, the Society experienced repeated visitation by spirits who provided gifts of visions, speaking in tongues, texts and drawings, songs, and dances. In 1853 a dance pattern performed by spirits, where they spun or marched in circles from one point to another, was seen and drawn at Enfield, New Hampshire. The drawing recording the event is inscribed "This song was sung and labored [danced] by the good spirits as is here described Christmas eve 1853 & was seen and learned by Elder Br[other] Timothy R[andlett]" (figure 63).

Marching

Linear marches were introduced in 1817, and consisted of a simple pacing about the room, probably in single file. A little later the march was taken outside at Harvard and it filed through the community: "At 2 o'clock P.M. The [visiting] Lebanon Ministry, our Ministry, the Elders, brethren, and sisters went into the street and marched, and when we got against the Square House, they came out, and the South Family and we marched to the Second Family five abreast. We marched to the west side of the house and stopped. They came out and formed on. Then we marched back and into the meeting house, sat down and rested a spell."[30] Marching was later configured into geometric patterns.

In 1840, as part of the purification process of the Era of Manifestations, a new dance, "walking the narrow path," was introduced. Its strenuous heel-to-toe walking on the cracks of the meetinghouse floor helped eliminate the weak of spirit from continuing in the Society. The role of this walking is discussed in Chapter VIII, for it inspired the gift drawing shown as figure 180.

VISUAL AIDS TO ORDERED DANCES

To facilitate order and pattern, the dances, like the songs, were practiced away from public view, and diagrammatic patterns were placed in at least two floors to guide the performers. The Marquise de La Tour Pin de Gouvernet kept a journal in which she recorded a visit to Watervliet in 1795. While watching the worship service she observed an older Sister establish herself in an armchair, an absence of children, and shiny copper nails in the floor used to guide the movements:

Finally, a bell rang. Our guide told us that this announced the hour of prayer and asked if we would like to be present. We consented very willingly, and he led us towards the largest of the houses, which no exterior sign distinguished from the others. At the door I was separated from my husband and Monsieur de Chambeau, and we were placed at opposite extremities of the immense hall, on either side of a chimney in which was burning a magnificent fire. It was then the beginning of spring and the cold was still felt in these large woods. This hall was about 150 or 200 feet long by 50 feet wide. It was entered by two lateral doors. The building was very light and the walls, without being ornamented in any way, were perfectly smooth and painted a light blue. At each end of the hall there was a small platform upon which was placed a wooden arm-chair.

I was seated at the corner of the chimney, and my guide had enjoined silence, which was all the easier for me as I was alone. While keeping absolutely silent, I had the opportunity to admire the floor which was constructed of pine wood, without any knots, and of a rare perfection and whiteness. Upon this fine floor were drawn in different directions lines represented by copper nails, brilliantly polished, the heads of which were level with the floor. I endeavored to divine what could be the use of these lines, which did not seem to have any connection with each other, when at the last stroke of the bell the two side doors opened, and I saw enter on my side fifty or sixty young girls or women, preceded by one who was older who seated herself upon one of the arm-chairs. No child accompanied them.

The men were arranged in the same manner at the opposite side, where were my husband and Monsieur de Chambeau. I then observed that the women stood upon these lines of nails, taking care not to cross them with their toes. They remained immobile until the moment when the woman seated in the arm-chair gave a sort of groan or cry which was neither speech nor song. All then changed their places, and I imagined that this kind of stifled cry which I had heard must represent some command. After several evolutions, they stopped, and the old woman murmured quite a long string of words in a language which was absolutely unintelligible, but in which were mingled, it seemed to me, some English words. After this, they went out in the same order in which they had entered. Having thus visited all parts of the establishment, we took leave of our kind guide and entered our wagon to return home, very little edified regarding the hospitality of the Shakers.[31]

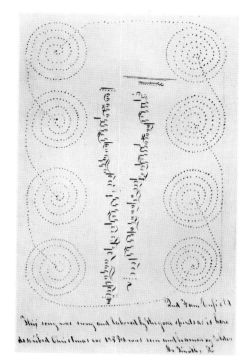

63. DRAWING OF A VISIONARY DANCE
OR MARCH
Enfield, New Hampshire
Recorded by Timothy Randlett
Seen: December 24, 1853
Ink on paper, dimensions unrecorded
Photograph courtesy of theWinterthur Museum,
Winterthur, Delaware: The Edward Deming
Andrews Memorial Shaker Collection

Probably the meetinghouse floor at Watervliet, destroyed early in the nineteenth century, provided more guidance than this visitor observed, for at least one such floor still provides important information about dance-guides imbedded in its wood. (Most of the meetinghouse floors have been replaced over the years; that of the 1822–24 meetinghouse at New Lebanon is not visible, because it is covered by a carpet that runs under bookcases. The floor at Sabbathday Lake, which is possibly original, has no nails.) The floor in the Canterbury meetinghouse has ten rows of wooden pegs and copper nails. The building is a rectangle, with the narrow ends at the north and south, and when built in 1792 it had fireplaces at each end and two inside staircases. There are two original doors in the west wall; the east wall was originally interrupted only by windows. In 1815 the fireplaces were replaced by stoves and the stairs removed. At the same time a doorway was cut into the east wall to give the Ministry access to a new staircase tower in which one of the original staircases was reused. The lines of pegs and copper nails fan out from where that later door is located. The 1795 description just cited suggests the floor guides predate the 1815 doorway. Thus, they may have fanned out from where singers stood in the center of the originally doorless east wall. From that point eight lines radiate out, four in the general direction of one of the doors in the west wall, and four toward the other. Each set of four radiating lines is crossed by a line of pegs running due east and west. Distinctions between the lines was achieved by employing different size and different color wooden pegs, and round-headed copper nails: The lines use 3/4-inch dark pegs, 5/8-inch light pegs, 3/16-inch dark pegs, and there are four lines of 3/16-inch copper nail heads. In both sets of fanned lines, two of the lines follow the same trajectory: a line of 3/4-inch black pegs and a line of copper heads. Each color and size must have denoted a different movement in the dancing.[32]

With the arrival of the Era of Manifestations in 1837, frenzy and excitement returned to the worship services. The new emotionalism was described by Horace Greeley in 1838: "At length, what was a measured dance becomes a wild, discordant frenzy; all apparent design or regulation is lost; and grave manhood and gentler girlhood are whirling round and round, two or three in company, then each for him or her self, in all the attitudes of a decapitated hen, or expiring top."[33]

It is a happy circumstance that the developing needs of the Shakers to establish order, simplicity, and unity was confluent with the western World's embracing of neoclassical principles. The Shakers' expression of the style produced a series of forms and patterns that continues to resonate with those who seek a quiet immediacy of form, surface, and color.

Chapter VI
THE "CLASSIC" OBJECTS

Throughout the years I sought the logic of Shaker designs, Brother Arnold Hadd's admonition, "There is no classic Shaker period, we are still making things," has corrected many easy assumptions. To understand what is "Shaker," I found it necessary to first discover its roots in the Anglo-American history of design. Then it was critical to see what was usually held to be "Shaker" as an extended moment in a living, changing process that has continued for more than two hundred years. But even after one understands those two important conditioning factors, the active power of those famous years, from about 1810 to about 1860, still remains. It is true that many Shaker-made objects are not distinguishable from non-Shaker ones. But the pieces that are discernibly Shaker are imbued with the unique qualities of the sect's design attitude. They exhibit an ethos so powerful that they stand out as new: original in intention and appearance. Shakers and non-Shakers were conscious during those years of what constituted that "look."

The Shakers did hire outsiders to make furniture, sometimes as gifts to other families. For example, in 1859 the North Family of New Lebanon hired a local non-Believer named Shumway to make a case of drawers with a cupboard as a gift to the Church Family as a token of thanks after one of its members, George Wickersham, had helped the North Family design a stone barn. Earlier, in 1827, Thomas Bowman, Sr., who lived in the town of New Lebanon, made, signed, and dated the counter with drawers around a central cupboard shown as figure 64. He and his son, Thomas Bowman, Jr., worked extensively for various Shaker Families.[1] This piece was purchased from Watervliet as Shaker-made. After the Civil War, when many new Shaker-made things reflected late nineteenth-century aesthetics, conservative Shaker designers knew how to employ

64. TAILOR'S COUNTER
Town of Lebanon, New York
Signed and dated by non-Shaker Thomas Bowman, Sr., in 1827
Pine: surface stripped and refinished
H. 32¼" W. 101" D. 28⅝" (with leaf up 38⅝")
Dorothy and Harvey Rextrew began purchasing Watervliet material from Eldress Anna Case in 1928. This piece came from a basement and because of water damage it was stripped and refinished. It was purchased from the Rextrew collection for the Charles and Helen Upton collection in 1959.
Private collection

the telling features of the earlier period. Although they usually added, perhaps unknowingly, some unmistakably late features, they could, at least in part, recapture, or continue, the aesthetic stance of the great design years.

The pieces discussed here exemplify the type of Shaker designs some historians link to those of the Bauhaus, seeing in both groups of objects a conscious exploitation of the nature of the materials and an achievement of a new level of stripped-down functionalism. This is the Shaker work commonly placed alongside Japanese and 1950s Danish modern objects during discussions of the Shakers' use of traditional materials and their evocation of quiet beauty. In the last chapter of this book I will draw parallels between this kind of Shaker design and the work of certain minimalist artists of the 1960s. What the Shakers produced during those years is not, however, just a homogeneous group of pretty pieces. Rather, it contains a variety of expressions, each responding to a different part of the Shaker experience.

I have divided the material into focused sections, and most of these have subsections. The diversity of purposes, intentions, and uses behind these types would allow other arrangements. My divisions are:

1. ORDERED:
The need to organize communities of hundreds, then thousands, of disparate people for the Millennium was answered by a reliance on grids. These matrices located, in a tidy manner, objects on the landscape and inside buildings, and placed people and objects on this landscape in appointed spaces. This order ensured that each thing would be in its proper place and each person receive a proper share. Rooms and such movables as spit boxes, furniture, and textiles, were often numbered or labeled to signify their permanent place.

2. STRETCHED:
The religious undergirding of life allowed new aspects of design to alter traditional forms. By placing themselves outside of traditional visual design attitudes, and being required to handle household objects with great respect, the Shakers could permit objects to be stretched to leaner and longer forms than found in similar things used in the world.

3. FRAGILE:
Many pieces were made to be so fragile they could not have survived without the careful and respectful attention dictated by Shaker rules.

4. RUGGED:
There was a requirement for a Believer to be successful at daily hard work. While seeking unity and ethereal religion in the dwelling and meetinghouses, Shakers were admired as successful farmers and small business people. This aspect of their lives required the rugged artifacts and attitudes that were basic to agrarian and small factory conditions.

5. IMPROVISED:
Like other rural people (or city people who could not, or would not, buy everything ready-made), the Shakers could combine or alter existing objects to solve a felt need.

ORDERED

Any establishment housing large numbers of people must create physical and social patterns, and the Shakers added to this a theological understanding that pushed their needs to lengths not known in the military, penal institutions, hospitals, or other such temporal institutions. For short periods it is possible to put up with inconveniences, but if existence is projected for a millennium, rough edges have to be removed and strictness and sameness imposed. There is great power in repetition. Repeated phrases, dances, songs, and like artifacts make it easy to remember the signifiers of what we are; insiders are unified while outsiders are mystified. Such limitation can be liberating, for controls signal our freedoms as they define our limits. Multiple drawers, like large groups of very similar chairs, costumes, and haircuts, defined the Shakers, and, for them, defined the saved in God's eyes. The Shakers were legally bound together in a united interest, and to eliminate jealousy, as well as to treat all of the saints similarly, the household objects used by everyone on the same level, in the rigid hierarchical structure, looked alike, or nearly alike. Striving for equity—taking your "allotted share"—could be so conscious that petty behavior could take precedence over strict rules against waste, and this remained true into the early years of the twentieth century when a Hancock Brother added sugar, which he did not want, to his coffee. When the Sisters noted that he left sugar in the bottom of the cup and asked him why, he replied that he did not like sweet coffee but wanted to get his fair share.[2]

Laws and Order
By the 1820s, many of the Believers had not known the religious fervor that created the faith, and it was no longer possible to depend on belief and respect, or fear of the leaders, to guide daily behavior. Lucy Wright had been able to rule by personal authority; six months after her death the Central Ministry, at New Lebanon, sanctioned the Millennial Laws (reproduced here as an Appendix).

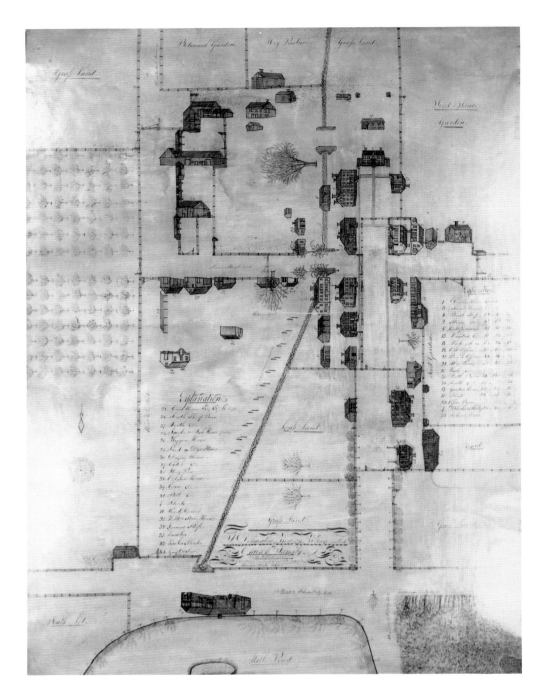

65. "A DELINEATION OR VIEW OF
THE VILLAGE CALLED THE CHURCH
FAMILY"
Watervliet, New York
By David Austin Buckingham
Date: March, 1838
Pencil and ink on paper
H. 30½" W. 22"
New York State Museum, Albany, New York

Opposite:
66. "DIAGRAM OF THE SOUTH PART
OF SHAKER VILLAGE, CANTERBURY"
By Peter Foster
1849
Pencil, ink, and watercolor on paper
H. 16¼" W. 12³⁄₈"
Library of Congress, Washington, D.C.,
Geography and Map Division

The 1821 Millennial Laws dictated that Shaker lives and objects were to be based on right-angle grids without gaps or interruptions: "It is considered good order to lay out and fence all kinds of lots, fields and gardens in a square form where it is practicable, but the proportions, as to length and width may be left to the discretion of those who direct the work" (see figures 65 and 3). "If a brother or sister be missing in meeting or at the table the one who comes next should fill up the place, so that there may be no gap left for the devil to get between."[3] As in the carefully learned patterned dances, there was to be no perceptible deviation. This unity facilitated spiritual development, created guidelines for actions, and, like order in the army, or elsewhere, it made things look neat. Many of the rules addressing relationships with the world were to protect Believers from outside influences, but of equal concern was how the communities appeared—both in order and cleanliness—to those too ready to judge them odd: "Buildings in the Church, which get out of repair, through age and decay, or any other means, must be repaired soon or taken away." "No kind of filthy substance may be left or remain around the dwelling houses nor shops, nor in the door yards; nor in the street in front of the dwelling houses and shops." "When a square of glass gets broke out it must be mended before the sabbath." "Every Saturday night and Monday morning the street opposite the meeting house, and against the dwelling houses must be cleared of hay, straw and dung &c. And the outward yard of the meeting house must be cleaned every Monday morning from all such filthiness."[4] This cleaned up everything before the hordes of worldly folk arrived on Sabbathday morning, or people came to do business during the week.

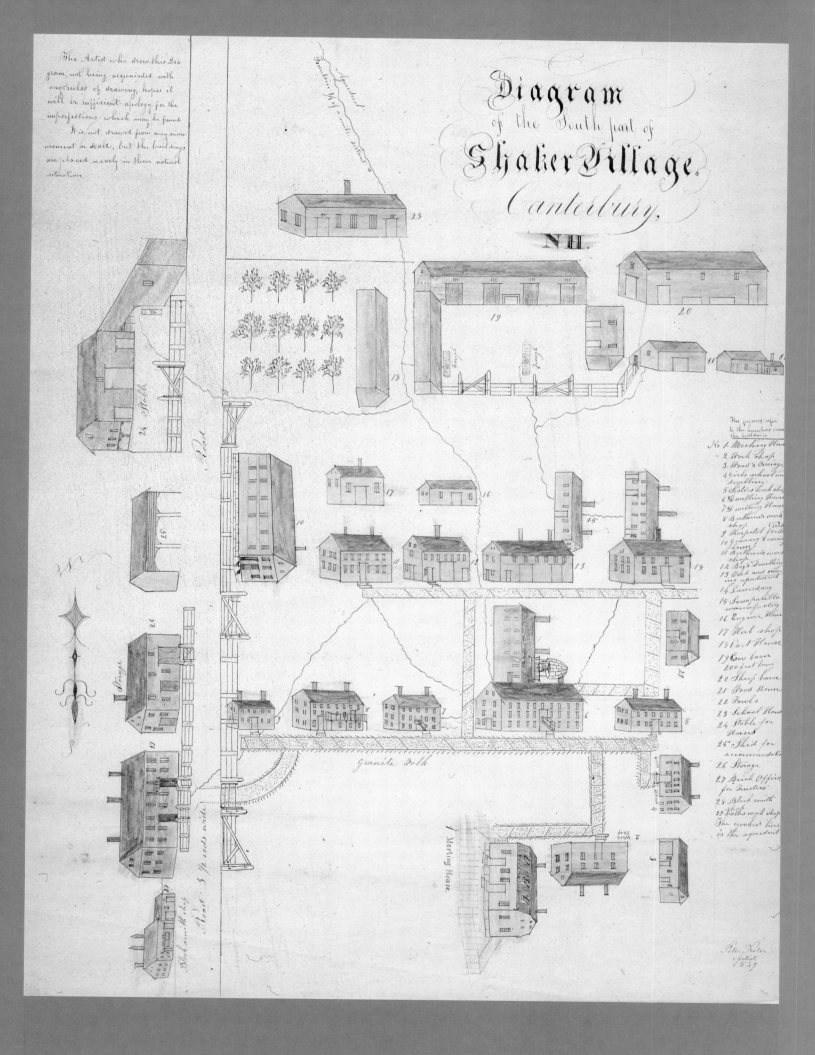

The Artist who drew this Diagram, not being acquainted with any rules of drawing, hopes it will be sufficient apology for the imperfections which may be found

It is not drawn from any measurement or scale, but the buildings are placed nearly in their natural situation.

Diagram
of the South part of
Shaker Village,
Canterbury,
N.H.

The figures refer to the numbers over the buildings.

No 1. Meeting House
" 2. Work Shop
3. Wood & Carriage
4. Girls school and dwelling
5. Sisters Work shop
6. Dwelling House
7. Dwelling House
8. Brethren's work shop, Hospital for the sick
9. Hospital for the sick
10. Granary & weaving
11. Brethren's work shop
12. Boys Dwelling
13. Wheat and spinning apartment
14. Laundry
15. Sarsaparilla manufactory
16. Engine House
17. Herb shop
18. Cart House
19. Cow barn 200 feet long
20. Sheep barn
21. Wood House
22. Fowls
23. School House
24. Stable for Horses
25. Shed for accommodation
26. Storage
27. Brick Office for Trustees
28. Black smith
29. Clothier's work shop
The crooked line is the aqueduct

Peter Foster
Artist
1849

Meeting House.

Granite Bolt

Storage

Road 3½ rods wide

Road

Numbering and Marking

As in other institutional situations, numbering buildings, rooms, and the objects in them was an obvious precaution against confusion. The buildings on many Shaker town plans have numbers and a key provides the building's name or use (see figure 66). Many rooms and daily objects have beautifully stamped, hand-painted, stenciled, or typeset printed numbers or names. In 1853 Hervey Elkins described the numbered unity of the bedrooms along the halls of the Great Stone Dwelling House at Enfield, New Hampshire: "On either side are retiring rooms, all exactly twenty feet square, nine feet high, and of identical furniture and finish, rendering it difficult to determine, but by number, one room from another."[5] The New Lebanon furniture maker Isaac Newton Youngs wrote in 1833 to his brother Elder Benjamin Seth Youngs at South Union, Kentucky: "the rooms are all numbered, but not with any Showy sign or label—then we have large figures printed on paper about an inch in depth for which I made some types on purpos which we paste onto the furniture[:] chairs, brooms—store things &c. &c. that belong to the several apartments which helps much to keep things in their place."[6] (Other institutions, including churches, numbered objects for similar reasons. A painting by Gari Melchers of the late nineteenth century shows the interior of a traditional Dutch Reform Church in Holland with parishioners seated in rows of red slat-back chairs; each chair has a black heart outlined in white on the back of the top slats, and on the hearts are white numbers.)[7]

The box with printed letters and numbers in figure 67, presumed to have been made by Isaac Newton Youngs, contains thirty-six compartments for his paper labels, undoubtedly the "large figures printed on paper" mentioned in the letter to his brother. The inscription inside the lid reads, "December 10, 1833," and has his initials "iny." Each letter is surrounded by loops of Youngs's distinctive flourishes. Made of pine, and dovetailed at the corners, it has a red stain on the outside. Like seed boxes in shape, it is more finely made.[8]

67. BOX OF LETTERS AND NUMBERS
Church Family, New Lebanon
Signed inside lid: "iny," and dated "December 10, 1833"
Probably made by Isaac Newton Youngs; it contains numbers and letters printed by him
Sheets with numbers are 1" high, those with letters about ³⁄₈" high
Pine stained red; printed paper labels
H. 3¹⁄₈" W. 24⁵⁄₈" D. 12¹⁄₈"
Collection of the Shaker Museum and Library, Old Chatham, New York

The Millennial Laws of 1821 do not mention numbering or signing objects. In the more restrictive Laws of 1845, initialing and numbering to facilitate organizing things was allowed, but information was to be kept to the minimum:

1. The initials of a person's name, are sufficient mark to put upon any tool, or garment, for the purpose of distinction. 2. Blue and white thread should generally be used for marking garments. 3. It is considered unnecessary to put more than two figures for a date, on our clothes, or tools, and it is strictly forbidden unnecessarily to embellish any mark. 4. No one should write or print his name on any article of manufacture, that others may hereafter know the work of his hands. 5. It is not allowable for the brethren to stamp, write or mark their own names, upon any thing which they make for the sisters, nor for sisters to do in like manner, upon articles made for the brethren.[9]

Given this stringency it is not surprising that fewer things were signed or dated in the late 1840s and the 1850s. However, these laws were not always closely followed, particularly after 1860 when new, less restrictive laws, were developed. For example, after 1845 Amos Stewart and Orren N. Haskin of New Lebanon, and Eli Kidder of Canterbury, among others, signed furniture they made. Pieces were still inscribed by others as the work of a particular maker, as happened with sewing desks "made by Elder Henry C. Blinn" of Canterbury about 1870 to 1880.[10] (Various signed pieces of furniture from the second half of the century are discussed in Chapter IX.)

As Beverly Gordon has pointed out, Shaker textiles, like other textiles used in eighteenth- and nineteenth-century households, were usually marked with embroidered initials. Shaker textiles had initials that stood either for an individual's name (for example, HB for Henry Blinn), or for a particular Family ("CHH" for Church Family, "E" for East Family, and so forth). The numbers on textiles usually referred to rooms in dwelling houses, and sometimes to the year in which the piece was made. A Shaker towel marked

CHH
18
32

belonged in room 18 of the Church Family and was made in 1832.[11] Often compartments within furniture were numbered, or labeled with their use (see figure 79). Some labels were hand-lettered on paper, but most were letterpress printed. Most chairs numbered for rooms had the number stamped onto the top of a front leg. Some had a painted number or a paper label on the back of a slat. Placed there they would not be worn off by sitters. In his journal entry of Saturday, November 27, 1819, the Watervliet cabinet- and chairmaker Freegift Wells recorded that he: "has been sorting over & marking chairs[—]the chairs in the Deacons room are marked 1 the Dea-coneses room 2 the Brethren's meeting room 3, the Sisters meeting room 4 the Brethrens front chamber 5, the Sisters front chamber 6 the Brethrens north chamber 7 the Sisters north chamber 8 &c."[12] The Enfield, New Hampshire, chair in figure 149 has an exquisite figure 12 stenciled on the rear of its top slat. Three of the set of six chairs in figure 92 retain letterpress labels which read "laundry" on the backs of their middle slats (figure 92A). Numbering continued as a Shaker practice into the latter part of the century. The spit box (for tobacco juice) numbered 25 in figure 68 is probably part of a group of spit boxes made by Daniel Crosman for the Mount Lebanon Church Family Dwelling House built after fires in 1875 devastated their buildings. (When the community received its own post office in 1861, it changed its name from New Lebanon to Mount Lebanon.)

68. SPIT BOX
New Lebanon, New York
Possibly one of fifty made by Daniel Crosman in 1877 for the new 1875 Church Family Dwelling House
Maple and pine; copper tacks; painted yellow, black numbers
H. 3⅝" W. 10½"
Hancock Shaker Village, Pittsfield, Massachusetts

Grids

Repeat patterns were everywhere in Shaker communities. Community buildings were realigned to appear as in figures 65 and 66. Interior living and work spaces for equal purposes were given equal units that were similar in design. The ubiquitous peg rails provided a sense of unity to and between rooms, and when holding like objects intensified the sense of repeated patterns. (See the pattern the peg rails establish in figure 52.)

Textiles are easily designed to grids, for it is a simple matter to use similar lines in the warp and the interlacing weft. An illustration of a Brother's returning room with a grid-patterned wall hanging hooked to pegs appeared in *Frank Leslie's Illustrated Newspaper* for September 1873 (figure 69). Squares had long been part of worldly textiles but as Beverly Gordon points out, what she terms "loom control" designs were ubiquitous in Shaker hands. "The most striking thing about the textiles, and indeed about all Shaker work, is a sense of order. In most cases this is achieved through a structural rather than decorative design, simple lines, symmetry, and regularly repeat-ing patterns . . . . In addition, many textiles are finished with some sort of border around them, and often the borders are as important to the design as the central area; they act as frames which complete the piece and affirm that they are finished statements."[13] The two square neckerchiefs shown here have the typical woven grid: figure 70 is made of natural color linen with a blue grid, and remains as it came from the loom at Sabbathday Lake. Brother Arnold Hadd believes that community stopped using linen for neckerchiefs about 1810, and the heavy weight of the linen in this piece suggests a very early date. The Sabbathday Lake cotton neckerchief in figure 71 has a wide, 1¾ inch hem. Other examples at Sabbathday Lake have among them one with a light brown

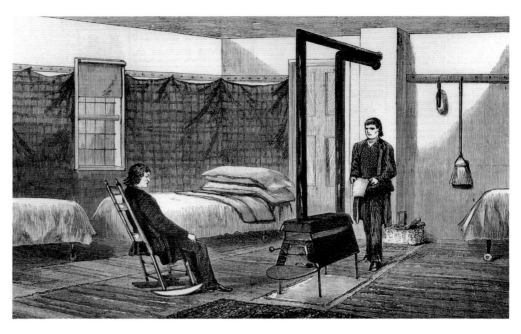

69. "SLEEPING-ROOM OF THE MEN
SHAKERS. THE SHAKERS OF LEBANON,
NEW YORK"
Sketched by Joseph Becker; published in Frank
Leslie's Illustrated Newspaper
(September 6, 1873), p. 417
Wood engraving
Ink on paper
Image: H. 6" W. 9 ⁵/₁₆"
Collection of the Shaker Museum and Library,
Old Chatham, New York

Right:
70. NECKERCHIEF
Sabbathday Lake, Maine
1800–10
Linen, unhemmed; natural linen and blue linen
lines
H. 33¹/₂" W. 32 ⁷/₈"
Collection of the Shaker Museum and Library,
Old Chatham, New York

Far Right:
71. NECKERCHIEF
Sabbathday Lake, Maine
About 1820
Cotton; white with blue grid; 1³/₄" hems
H. 30" W. 29"
The United Society of Shakers, Sabbathday Lake,
Maine

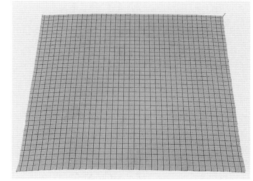
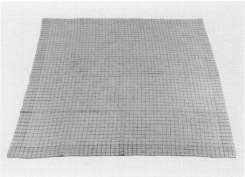

grid, and another with a more subtle pattern: it has a white on white pattern achieved by putting concentrated lines of white thread into an open white weave.

Grids and Gift Drawings

A group of fifteen related gift drawings was probably made between 1841 and 1859 by Polly Collins (1808–84). She was born in Cambridge, Washington County, New York, and arrived at Hancock in 1820 where she was an active instrument, or medium. She recorded pictorial spirit messages and made narrative records of her visions, and occasionally other instruments used her to record their visions.[14] A group of her drawings divides their sheets into rectangular and square units while employing motifs found in the world on such things as embroideries, quilts, and grave-stones. Normally these drawings combine four or more square units with strong lines between them (figures 72 and 73). The resulting patterns relate them to appliqué album quilts where, like pictures in an album, individual, often square, panels are applied to a backing (figure 74). In these quilts, an applied strip running between and around them is usually of a contrasting color. The quilt squares are often decorated with flowers.

In figure 72 the artist has turned broad lines between the near-squares into narrow pathways. This is signaled by the gates placed at each junction. These narrow paths may refer to the diffi-cult narrow path to salvation, as seen in figure 180. Certainly they are pathways to be transversed between gardens of heavenly joy. Collins's 1854 "A gift from Mother Ann to the Elders at the North Family" (figure 73) takes a vertical sheet of paper and edges it with dark heavenly blue at the top and sides. The lower two-thirds is sequestered as a near-square with a bright green top and dark green bottom line. The near-square is divided into three horizontal tiers by a gray and a brown line; the central horizontal band is divided further into three squares by blue vertical lines. The near-square is also bisected by crossed yellow lines that create four large squares. All the small squares and rectangles thus formed on the near-square are filled with embroidery or appliqué-like trees and flowers. In the grid drawing in figure 168 Polly Collins arranged in the top row, left to right, three original saints from England: Mother Ann Lee, Father James Whittaker, and Father William Lee. At the right of that line is Christopher Columbus, who had returned in spirit and joined the Shakers. He is given a lofty position because he discovered America and made the development of the sect possible. (It has been believed that the gift drawings were kept private and never displayed. This may not be true. The early twentieth-century postcard, seen in figure 158, shows one of the drawings just discussed hanging on a Shaker wall. Other gift drawings, their design sources, display, and "discovery" in modern times are discussed in Chapter VIII.)

Walls of Doors, Cupboards, and Drawers

The Shaker passion for order began with Ann Lee, who said, "Provide places for your things, so that you may know where to find them at any time, by day or night; and learn to be neat and clean, prudent and saving, and see that nothing is lost."[15] Another time she said: "Do all your work as though you had a thousand years to live, and as you would if you knew you must die to-morrow."[16] She wanted order but expected God to call the saved during her life. This dual awareness of the need to plan while being open to change has persisted throughout Shaker history.

Doors were important factors in producing a grid effect: large doors on openings between rooms and halls, large closet doors, and smaller cupboard doors. Drawers, like the boxes the Shakers loved, were places to put things and furthered the grid of order. If cupboards and drawers went from floor to ceiling they prevented the despised dust from collecting above and below. In 1832 William Deming of Hancock wrote to Elder Benjamin S. Youngs of South Union about Hancock's new Brick Dwelling House:

We began laying the foundation on the 15th of April 1830 . . . . The work is all well done. There is none to excel it in this country. And the same can be said of the Joiner work—The stuff is very clear; Scarcely a knot can be seen in all the work, except the floors and they are yellow pine and very good. There is 100. large doors including outside and closet doors; 245 cupboard doors—369 drawers [one is dated 1831]—These are placed in the corners of the rooms and by the sides of the chimneys. The drawers are faced with butternut and handsomely stained,—They take up but little room, and are not to be cleaned under . . . . And I think we may say it [the house] is finished from the top to the bottom, handsomely stained inside with a bright orange . . . color. The out doors are green. The outside of the house is painted with four coats of a beautiful red. The plastering is covered with a coat of hard finish & is a beautiful white.

Outside, the bricks had four coats of "beautiful red" paint. (Perhaps the paint was to keep moisture out of the bricks.) The outside doors were green.[17]

In Shaker hands design could go beyond function and become a matter of visually filling an area. The 1834–37 Church Family Stone Dwelling House at Enfield, New Hampshire, had 860 drawers, averaging about nine drawers for every member living there in the middle of the nineteenth century. These were not all personal drawers, rather, most were for long-term storage.[18] An April 8, 1845, letter to New Lebanon from Union Village discussed the shift from freestanding chests, and chests of drawers, to built-ins in the new 1844 Center Family Dwelling House:

It has been the custom in the Church for Brethren and Sisters generally to have a chest for their private convenience, and a bureau in the room, is it best to keep up the practice when we move in the new house or not? There will be a large close room in every dwelling room with two large drawers for each person that lives in the room, and a large cupboard and ample accommodations in the close room for hanging close. Some have felt as tho this was sufficient accommodations, and that the chests and bureaus in the rooms might be dispensed with, as it was quite expensive to keep them up, (some have private Bureaus). But we would be glad to have the Ministrys counsel, and be as much in union as we can in all things.[19]

A wall of Shaker large doors, cupboard doors, and drawers may at first seem an informal layout, but usually they have a simple, logical rhythm of one, two, or three stacks of drawers with a cupboard above each, and the resulting units may be interrupted by large doors. In 1837 a wing was added to Canterbury's Church Family Dwelling, and at the attic level there was a board wall separating the Sisters' and Brothers' sides. (Probably late in the nineteenth century, a door was cut through it.) The storage room in the Sisters' part (figure 75) has two areas that contain a total of one entry door, seven closets, fourteen cupboards (as shown), two very narrow cupboards, six short doors into the crawl spaces, and 100 drawers. In the wall shown, two or three stacks of six drawers, united by a top molding, have a cupboard above each stack. The groupings are inter-

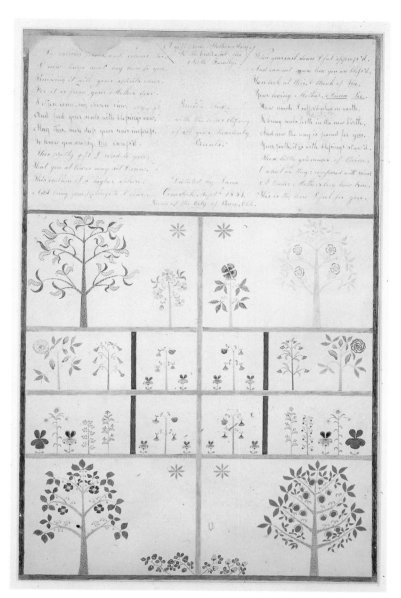

72. "BELOVED SISTER ANNA . . . GIVEN
BY MOTHER LUCY'S PERMISSION . . .
JUN. 1853"
Attributed to Polly Collins
Hancock, Massachusetts
Ink and watercolor on paper
H. 12" W. 8"
Library of Congress, Washington, D.C.,
Manuscript Division

73. "A GIFT FROM MOTHER ANN, TO
THE ELDERS AT THE NORTH FAMILY . . .
DICTATED BY DANA COMSTOCK. SEPT.
1854. GIVEN AT THE CITY OF PEACE.
CHH."
Attributed to Polly Collins
Hancock, Massachusetts
Black ink and yellow, blue, red, green, pink,
and purple watercolor on paper
H. 19" W. 12"
Hancock Shaker Village, Pittsfield, Massachusetts

74. ALBUM QUILT
Probably Baltimore, Maryland
1854
Cotton and silk appliquéd on cotton
L. 122⅝" W. 106½"
Winterthur Museum, Winterthur, Delaware

rupted by closet doors. (The same-height drawer areas in the opposite wall have five drawers of greater depth.) The pine woodwork was painted with a thin coat of chrome yellow. Used primarily for off-season clothing and bedding, these storage units were numbered on white cards, and a record of what was in each space was kept in a notebook with parallel numbers. Visually the slight variations in the units that result from hand construction are intensified by the changing shapes of the numbers. A few drawers have later glued-on cards with a name of an individual Sister. All the larger and smaller doors now have probably twentieth-century brass hooks; some retain hanging tags specifying the contents or the name of a Sister.

While the employment of multiple drawers and doors was not invented by Shakers, and would become standard as storage areas in late nineteenth-century non-Shaker homes, the Shakers' special concern to formulate practical units did alter the normal proportional relationship of parts and thus became a physical manifestation of their theological and philosophical concerns.

The Shakers often placed a floor-to-ceiling case of drawers, perhaps with a cupboard above, in the corners of rooms and, on occasion, isolated a case of drawers by imbedding it in a plastered wall (see figure 208). Built-in cupboards covering an entire wall—or individual units set into a plastered wall with only the front showing—were not unique to the Shakers. Wallace Nutting, in his *Furniture Treasury,* showed a 1740–60 high chest of drawers with pointed feet on cabriole legs let into a wall in the Old Inn, South Woodstock, Connecticut. It is certain the piece was made to be placed in the wall for it has no sides or back.[20] A matching Connecticut chest-on-chest and desk-and-bookcase made without finished sides were sold at a 1990 auction. They too were made to be inserted into walls; when installed only their cherry fronts were visible.[21]

Furniture

Furniture designed with multiple drawers, and perhaps doors, to form a grid, was not a Shaker invention. It had long been used by doctors and others to separate and organize herbs and other small items. Some of these were made to appear in keeping with highly styled furniture and looked much like high chests on cabriole legs, and at least one was made to look like a cabinet on a desk.[22] But most worldly multiple-drawer pieces were simple in form and looked like the red-painted case of drawers in figure 76. It was used by Dr. Josiah Bartlett (1729–95) of Kingston, New Hampshire, signer of the Declaration of Independence and Articles of Confederation, and the state's first governor. He labeled the contents of each drawer. It is unlikely the Shakers would have used such a tall bracket base but in other ways it is like Shaker work.

The small, possibly Vermont, piece in figure 77 was made about 1800–20. It has doors below a fall-front desk and a series of drawers in the top below an open bookcase area. Like much early Shaker work it consists of a series of vertical and horizontal rectangles, and like Shaker designs it has a strong sense of layering the rectangular parts: the fall-front desk, the two lower doors and their board surrounds, and the stepped back drawer and bookcase section. The front is grained to resemble a richly patterned mahogany; the sides are painted a plain red-brown. It has a few moldings: applied half-round moldings around the upper part, and, in a smaller form, horizontally between the drawers; half-round moldings run on the upper and lower edges of the three lower drawers. Black paint edges the drawers to suggest edge-veneers or applied moldings. The configuration of projecting and receding rectangles differs from Shaker work in using an almost casual arrangement of drawers. They have no mathematical or visual progression in their layers of three, five, six, and seven units. The piece was fairly well made, but it lacks the unity of surface and design found in Shaker work: the front is grained, the sides are not; although most of the drawers are nailed together, the lower three are dovetailed. There are broad plane marks on the lid of the desk's fall-front. Such signs of rudimentary work are valued in vernacular worldly furniture where it purveys character, but such individuality is not part of the prized Shaker aesthetic, which employs elegantly controlled smoothness. This places the Shakers squarely within the neoclassical emphasis on polished surfaces.

The Shaker double desk and bookcase shown in figures 78 and 79 has the same profile as the worldly piece in figure 77. It was made in New Lebanon between 1820 and 1840 of pine and is painted with a thin coat of orange-brown. It was probably used by a pair of Elders, Deacons, or Trustees. According to tradition it came from the Second Order of the Church Family. There are bookshelves behind the top doors. The lower two fall forward and create a writing surface. (To make these smooth, the recesses between the panels and the rails around them are filled with thin sheets of wood so that the panels and rails are flush.) Behind the fall-forward doors are two tiers of bookshelves above a tier of pigeonholes: six on the left and three on the right. The left have

paper labels: "Letters," "Quotations," "Religious manuscripts," and so on. Below the pigeonholes, there is a small drawer on each side that pulls out awkwardly; since the drawers strike the rear edge of the fall-doors, they had to have their sides curved so that they could be pulled up to miss the obstruction.

Drawers

What characterizes much rural work is a freedom gained by being distant from the strong influence of European-based proportions, and its attention to traditionally balanced details. Much of what is new and particular in Shaker design was conditioned by even further removal from mainstream urban thought. The leaders were theologically able to say "we will do what we choose to do," and this allowed Shaker designs to be pushed in ways most worldly rural people would think too outside tradition. The scaling of drawers is one of the design features Shakers made their own, for they were determined to have what served their needs rather than what was conventional. They did maintain harmony and rhythm; they would not usually build an inconsistent drawer progression, as in the top of figure 77, but they did ignore the normal rhythmic progression of drawer heights as they mount upward. (If they made a surprising arrangement, it usually produced a new unity, as on the example shown as figure 83.)

Most worldly drawers decrease in a geometric manner, decreasing by 1 to 1½ inches in height with each successive upward tier. But the Shakers made drawers the height that suited what would go in them. Thus, in the chest over two drawers in figure 20, the top drawer is much shallower than the bottom one. In the double desk (figure 78), the bottom two drawers of each stack

75. DWELLING HOUSE ATTIC: DOORS, CUPBOARDS, AND DRAWERS
Church Family, Canterbury, New Hampshire, Sisters' side
1837
Shown in color as figure 258
Canterbury Shaker Village, Canterbury, New Hampshire

76. CASE OF DRAWERS
*Belonged to Dr. Josiah Bartlett of Kingston,
New Hampshire*
1770–90
Pine painted red
H. 55¾" W. 36" D. 9"
Private collection

are of the same height, and much deeper than the two above; the top one is thinner than the second. Another feature of this double desk not expected on worldly vernacular pieces is the difference in the width of the boards between the pairs of doors: the upper two, which swing on side hinges, have a broad strip between them, while the lower two are divided by the front edge of the board that also divides the interior bookcases and pigeonholes. Such a lack of exterior unity would not be seen in a worldly work of this sophistication. It might be said that the clumsiness with which the drawers under the pigeonholes pull out and the differing separation between the pairs of doors denote a make-it-up-as-you-go-along approach. That may, in part, be true, but the play of all the neatly finished verticals and horizontals produces an intriguing pattern; the "eye" behind the design produced a fine Shaker sense of unity. The rounded edge of the thin top (rabbeted like the top of figure 47 to receive the vertical boards and upper doors) is repeated in the projecting rounded edge of the board below the upper pairs of doors. (The ends of that board are scooped away, in a New Lebanon manner, to bring the line of the rounded board back to the surface of the uprights.) This horizontal roundness is repeated on the board that separates the upper from the lower section. The piece exhibits a rich play of rectangles: the vertical flat panels of the top play against the rectangles of their surrounds and the projecting horizontals of the lower, large drawer fronts. The drawers are punctuated at their centers with round knobs. A squatter version of this double desk, now at Pleasant Hill, lacks the vertical grandeur found here. While the one pictured is 48 inches wide and 84¾ inches high, the Pleasant Hill one is 45½ inches wide and 71¼ inches high.[23] The greater reach to the upper section of this taller piece allows a better proportional relationship between slenderer upper panels and the longer drawers; their vertical action pulls the eye up to the elegantly thin top board.

Left:
77. DESK, CUPBOARD, DRAWERS, AND BOOKCASE
New England, possibly Vermont
1800–20
Pine and yellow poplar; front grain-painted with red, brown, and ochre; sides painted red-brown
H. 71½" W. 35¼" D. 13⅛"
Old Sturbridge Village, Sturbridge, Massachusetts

Below:
78. AND 79. DOUBLE BOOKCASE, DESK, AND DRAWERS
New Lebanon, New York; possibly Second Order of Church Family
1820–40
Pine painted orange-brown; brass pulls on small drawers
H. 84¾" W. 48¼" D. 16⅝"
Hancock Shaker Village, Pittsfield, Massachusetts

80. CASE OF DRAWERS
New Lebanon, New York, North Family
Signed: "Galton (?)"
1830–40
Pine painted pinkish-red; cherry knobs; ivory
or bone keyhole surround
H. 70¹/₂" W. 60⁷/₈" D. 19³/₁₆"
Shown also as figure 261
Collection of the Shaker Museum and Library,
Old Chatham, New York

Tight Grids

One of the most original Shaker objects is the case of drawers from the North Family at New Lebanon that appears as figure 80. Sixteen nearly identical rectangles are stacked and held in a tight grid contained by the edges of the case. The straight lower edge ends in crisply angled bracket feet; the eye marches up the knobs to the thin, molded top board. It is audacious in its repeat of like forms that visually break up a large mass into understandable units. It uses only one lock, and the keyhole is protected from wear by a rectangular surround of bone or ivory. In the world this lack of balance would not have been welcomed in such neoclassical tightness, and if there were no second lock, a second escutcheon, with no lock behind, would provide visual balance. But, this piece anticipates the Millennial Laws of 1845, which say "no false locks may be used";[24] only one lock meant only one lock surround. The slightly jarring effect of the one white rectangle high up introduces just a shade of enjoyable discord. In fact, this is not a machine-perfect grid—there are slight variations among the rectangles, for they are handmade, and the distance between them is not exactly the same: the basic height of the drawers is 7¹/₂ inches but a few are ¹/₈ of an inch shallower, and they are not all, at least now, perfectly horizontal. These slight variations, as with handmade silver bowls, means that the forms are not quite perfect, not like units stamped out with a die. This keeps the surface alive and the eye continuously intrigued. As one moves closer, the variations are more obvious, for the surface becomes a series of endlessly shifting shapes. Like the gift drawing in figure 72, the squared parts play against the straight lines that run between and around them. At a slightly recessed level, they allow the eye to travel across, down, and around the projecting drawer fronts. The piece is 70¹/₂ inches high, 60⁷/₈ inches wide, and 19³/₁₆ inches deep. Part of the excitement of this case of drawers is the surprise of finding so large a form on such small feet; had its mass not been broken into a grid of rectangles, it would have appeared too big for them. In fact this piece reaches to the limits of Shaker audacity. A similar piece, except that it lacks the top molding, now needs support under the center, which the weight of the case and drawers has caused to settle.[25] There is a related piece at Hancock that has an additional drawer on each stack of drawers. The extra tier has proven too much for the design, and the eighteen drawers now tilt down toward the center.

Spontaneous Grids

Freedom from worldly design constraints allowed different proportional relationships among drawer heights as they moved up a piece, and it also freed the Shakers to make a different balance between one side and another. In worldly homes, areas such as kitchens and pantries that focused on practicality over harmonious decoration used variously shaped units. In their *The American Woman's Home,* Catharine Beecher and Harriet Beecher Stowe suggested shelving and various rectangular units to fit around the kitchen sink (figure 81). Likewise, businesses and stores, such as the Asa Knight Country Store from Vermont (now at Old Sturbridge Village), used an array of shelving, bins, and drawers of varying size to fit the merchandise. In worldly designs for use in the major rooms of a home, the left and right sides of a piece were the same, until influences from China during the third quarter of the nineteenth century introduced asymmetrical arrangements of squared units. Before that, in worldly domestic rooms not thought of as service areas, such casual configurations would be covered over when not in use. The designs shown in figure 82 are from *An Encyclopaedia of Cottage, Farm, and Villa Architecture and Furniture,* published in London by John Claudius Loudon in 1839. Loudon gathered designs from various sources and published them to encourage good designs in simple work. Both wardrobes have useful, asymmetrical, or not visually balanced spaces, but they were masked by balanced panels when the doors were shut. (The upper wardrobe's deep drawer was for "bonnets, &c.") The Shakers, who stressed exposed practicality, reveled in unbalanced units, both in work and living areas. Fortunately their better designers had the eye to make new, aesthetically pleasing rhythms of the results.

The furniture form shown as figure 83 served a number of purposes, but is usually called a counter. In the 1840s Elisha D'Alembert Blakeman worked at making a "counter & case of drawers under it & cupboard," and "a counter 8 feet long with seven drawers in it & 2 cupboards." In 1873 Giles Avery, working at Watervliet, called a piece to hold a sewing machine a counter. He was "cutting up stuff in the Shop for a sewing machine counter for Eldress Polly." However, one similar to the piece shown in a sewing room (figure 206) was called in 1860 "a table with two rows of drawers."[26] Brother Arnold Hadd reports: "In Maine these objects are always called 'bench' but pronounced 'bunk'." Many historic photographs from the late nineteenth century show such pieces with padded tops to serve as ironing surfaces. The padded one in the sewing room, at Mount Lebanon, has drawers nearly to the floor (figure 206).

81. KITCHEN STORAGE UNITS
Published in Catharine E. Beecher and Harriet Beecher Stowe's, The American Woman's Home: or, Principles of Domestic Science . . . . *(c. 1869; from 1870 ed., New York), p. 34*

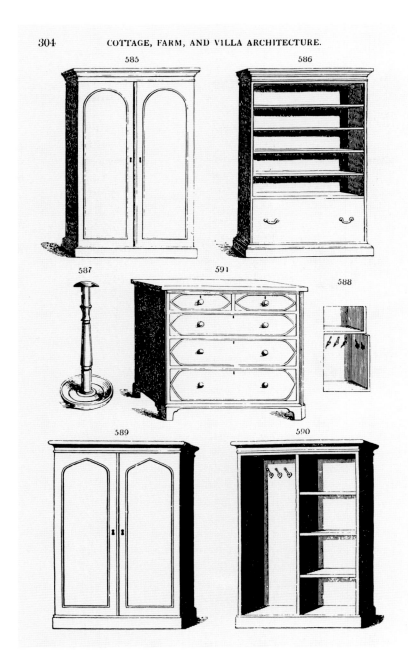

82. STORAGE CASES
Published in John Claudius Loudon's An
Encyclopaedia of Cottage, Farm, and Villa
Architecture and Furniture . . . ., *1839, p. 304*
From Loudon's Furniture Designs, *ed.*
Christopher Gilbert, 1970

The cherry piece shown in figure 83 has a red-stained pine drop-leaf attached to its rear edge. It shows long curving cut-marks that cross each other. These suggest that cloth or paper clothing patterns were cut on it with a sharp knife. It is one of the most brilliant of Shaker designs, for it successfully balances stacks of drawers of varying lengths and heights: on the left four drawers of the same height, on the right two alike bottom drawers below a shallower top drawer. Except at the top and bottom, there is no simply rhythmic or visual relationship where the left and right drawers meet. What unites the parts are the broad spaces between the drawers, the knobs, and the similarity of the edges of the drawers. These edges are not a simple quarter-round as in figure 78; they have a standard worldly finish of filet, or ridge, stepping down to the quarter-round.

The distinctness of this edging and the visual force of the knobs are the most important unifying elements in the piece. As in most furniture designs, the front facade is organized to pull the eye up to the top section. Here the thin line of the top right drawer and the two white keyhole surrounds make the area visually intriguing. The elevation of the complex facade on high, turned legs creates an enveloping space that contains the tension—or push—between the two dissimilar banks of drawers.

The cherry top is made with two boards: the rear one, only $2\frac{5}{16}$ inches wide, is attached to the wider front board by a series of nails driven from the rear edge. Their heads are deeply recessed. The top is cherry but the drop-leaf behind is stained pine. This difference in woods raises the question whether the leaf is part of the original design or a later Shaker addition. Both top and leaf have cleated ends, but those on the top are attached with rabbet joints; those on the leaf are

secured by five wooden pins. (A nearly identical piece is without a drop-leaf.)[27] The drop-leaf is held up by "lopers," or "sliders," thin wood supports held in boxes secured to the sides of the case. When a box is removed, no finish can be seen under it, suggesting they, and thus the drop-leaf, are original.[28] The sliders have wooden knobs with which to push them out. These knobs have wooden extensions that go into the sliders, while the wooden knobs on the drawers are held in place by screws from inside.

The piece is neatly and cleanly executed. Where you can see them, the rails between the drawers, both left and right, stop at the vertical board that separates them. But inside, tenons on the rails pass all the way through the board. Drawer dividers are usually like these on the outside, but inside, they normally rest in front-to-back grooves in the vertical, separating board. Making tenons to pass through the board takes more time than cutting grooves, for it is necessary to bore then chisel a series of neat holes, but the result is stronger.

The sides of the drawers taper in the Hancock and Enfield, Connecticut, manner: they are narrow on the top and wider at the base (see figure 36). The drawers are numbered inside so they can be put into the spaces for which they were made. The numbers mix Arabic and Roman numerals, and some drawers use both. Inside, the drawers show very important evidence of the original finish. The Shakers often intensified the red color of cherry by staining it redder, but much evidence of this practice has been eliminated by fading and over-cleaning. On the pine sides of the drawers, and particularly on the inside of the cherry drawer fronts, there are many red fingerprints that record the maker handling the drawers with red-colored fingers while staining the fronts red. (Rural paintings of the late eighteenth and early nineteenth centuries often depict bright red furniture. Examination of such pieces of furniture reveals that usually red paint covers a light wood such as maple, birch, or pine.) There are vertical grooves in the inside of the side boards of two of the small drawers; they held drawer-dividers (one is missing). The top long drawer had two dividers running front to back added after the piece was finished (small glue blocks to hold them are still there). The present owners replaced the right keyhole liner, which was missing.

The 1830–40 case of drawers shown in figure 84 has a history of being from Harvard,

83. TAILOR'S COUNTER
Enfield, Connecticut, or Hancock, Massachusetts
1825–50
Cherry stained red, pine drop leaf stained red; fruitwood knobs; ivory or bone keyhole surrounds
H. 33" W. 56¼" D. 25⅛"
Collection of Anne and J. N. Whipple, Jr.

84. CASE OF DRAWERS
Probably Harvard, Massachusetts
1830–40
Pine painted dark red; brass knobs
H. 8¹³/₁₆" W. 22¾" D. 8⅞"
Drawers and case constructed with dovetails
Fruitlands Museums, Harvard, Massachusetts

Massachusetts, and is of red-painted pine. None of its drawers are of the same height. The top one on the left is ³/₁₆ of an inch shallower that the one beneath it. On the right the drawers progress upward: 2 inches, 1¾ inches, 1⅝ inches. The dividing strips between the drawers are ⁵/₁₆ of an inch thick, the end boards are ⁷/₁₆ of an inch, and the backboard ⅜ of an inch. The left drawers are 12½ inches long, the right drawers 9 inches. Clearly standardization of parts was not a factor; perhaps available stock created the design. Unlike the similarly slightly haphazard worldly form shown as figure 77, this Shaker piece seems tightly controlled. Its excitement comes from the shift in the scale between the left and right drawers, held visually, as well as physically, by end boards that project up and down beyond the case. The top front corners of these are rounded, which removed corners that might catch a hand placing things on top.

This piece may originally have sat on a surface rather than hanging on a wall, as it is now displayed. Although the bottoms of the side boards are painted, the undersurface of the bottom board is without paint. And, a similar piece from the same source and owned by the same museum has no holes for hanging.

A case with two cupboards and drawers (figure 85) has a history of coming from the East Family of Enfield, Connecticut; it has tapered drawer sides in the Enfield and Hancock manner (see figure 36). The rails of the cupboard doors are made with through-beveled inner edges, as shown in figure 37. The panels are raised, but not to the boldness of form found on the earliest pieces (see figure 7). (A few pieces made as late as 1850 have raised panels; many of these seem to be by makers such as Abner Allen at Enfield, Connecticut, who learned this practice early and continued the habit when it was no longer fashionable.)[29] The top door is two-thirds the height of the lower door; the top and lower large drawer are the same height; the smaller drawers are the same height. These proportional relationships seem to result from intended use. What the design achieves, perhaps without conscious intention, is an extraordinary rhythm and movement: the vertical of the lower door moves up to a tight, complex drawer area. Then the knobs spread the eye out to move up and around the cupboard door above. There appears to be a red coat under the yellow: a thin red paint covers the sides of the drawers, over the dovetailing of the drawer fronts. Probably the interior areas once had later paint: the left edge of the top door has some thick yellow-white paint; its inside surface has been cleaned, and some red color remains under a later clear finish. The present owner took off "the original iron latches" and put on the wooden catches. (They have left rectangular marks on the doors.) Later strips of wood finish the top and bottom of the case. The top three-sevenths of the left side have original yellow color; the lower part once had another piece of furniture built against it. The shadow of its molding has left an unpainted profile on the case near the top left corner of the lower large drawer.[30] This piece is one of the great manifestations of a maker's ability to pull a freewheeling design into a tight sense of order. To what degree the visual delight was planned, or perceived and discussed after being made, we do not know. That it does delight is certain.

STRETCHED

The use of a long line is common in Shaker religious practice, and it echoed the faith that Believers were on a linear progression that would continue until the end of the world. Shaker marches moved bodies of Believers around their meetinghouses and through their communities. The paths between buildings were often consciously narrow. When Charles Nordhoff visited

85. CASE WITH CUPBOARDS AND
DRAWERS
Enfield, Connecticut
1825–50
Pine and butternut colored yellow
H. 87¾" W. 37" D. 19½"
*It once had a shorter part attached at the left; top
and bottom moldings not original; iron latches
removed and turn-buttons added*
Collection of Mr. and Mrs. Gustave G. Nelson

86. PHOTOGRAPH: CHURCH FAMILY,
CANTERBURY, NEW HAMPSHIRE
*By W. G. C. Kimball, Concord, New Hampshire,
1879*
*Half of a stereoscopic view; full card: H. 3⅜"
W. 6⅞"*
*Collection of the Shaker Museum and Library,
Old Chatham, New York*

Pleasant Hill in 1874 he noted: "The walks connecting the buildings are here, as at South Union, Union Village, and elsewhere, laid with flagging-stones—but so narrow that two persons can not walk abreast."[31] A view of the Church Family at Canterbury shows a similar, conscious line of stones (figure 86). After 1840, the Narrow Path ritual encouraged exaggerated elongation. (The ritual is discussed in Chapter VIII.) The length of the halls in Shaker dwelling houses also emphasized stretched spaces as natural occurrences. One hall carpet was 80 feet long.[32] This would not be exceptional in many institutional situations, such as in a hotel, but the Shakers' dwelling houses were homes for God's people on earth. The pine drying rack from the laundry house of the North Family of New Lebanon (figure 87) would not have survived in worldly use, for it is an extraordinary 71⅝ inches in length, and built with minimal strength: each end of the three slats is secured to the wedge-shaped verticals by only one thin nail. In the world this would have been ridiculous, but in Shaker hands it seemed natural. There are tapered holes in the end boards to receive the heads of the screws that secured it to the wall. Marks on the back of the slats show that there were originally two vertical pieces attached 20 inches in from each end.

87. DRYING RACK
*New Lebanon, New York; from the North Family
Laundry House wall*
1830–50
Maple and pine painted dark red
H. 14⅞" L. 71⅝" D. 3½"
*Two vertical strips once attached to back
20 inches in from each end are missing*
*Collection of the Shaker Museum and Library,
Old Chatham, New York*

Tables

Long tables have been used in America since the trestle-base form was introduced from Europe in the late seventeenth century, and institutions housing large numbers of people regularly used them. Like drawer arrangements, the tables from which the Shakers ate took on communal meanings. Ann Lee had said, "Never put on silver spoons nor table-cloths for me; but let your tables be clean enough to eat on without cloths."[33] A short version of the trestle-base table was made for the four members of the Ministry who lived in separated areas, worked in their own buildings, and often ate in a separate room, or if in the general dining room, sat away from the others. The 1832 letter to South Union from William Deming about Hancock's new Brick Dwelling House notes: "The dining room is at the South end with accommodations for 80 persons to sit down at one time. The victuals is conveyed up into the dining room by means of two sliding cupboards. The Ministry has a neat little dining room adjoining the large one."[34] As we have seen, their separation in another room was later insisted upon by the 1845 Millennial Laws.

Trestle tables were particularly appropriate to the use-conscious Shakers for they allowed unimpeded leg room. Most worldly versions of the form use a stretcher between the legs about half-way between the floor and the top, which braces the table fairly well. In adopting the form to their purposes the Shakers made a change that would not have been logical in worldly hands. As with their long meetinghouse benches made without horizontal stretchers, the Shakers expected these tables to be treated with respect, and opened up the lower space, perhaps to make it easier to clean the floor, by placing the stretcher under the top, Thus any strong end-to-end turbulence would have cracked the legs off this table. (At the end of the nineteenth century trestle tables made to hold marble tops at Union Village, Ohio, had much thicker wooden parts, and stretchers near the floor.)[35]

The table in figure 88 is 11 feet 1½ inches long, 34¾ inches wide, and 27½ inches high. The end-cleated top was made of three long boards. It is of cherry, stained red under a clear finish. The three columns have reel and ring turnings at the tops and bottoms of their main shaft. The table was made, probably with three others, for the 1830 Hancock Brick Dwelling House, thus their posts correspond in form and wood to the newel posts in the original lower floors of that building's south stair tower (see figures 39 and 40).

Until about 1900 in most communities, and as late as 1962 at Sabbathday Lake, the Shakers ate in silence, and this suggested a special arrangement that has continued to the present. To facilitate meals without speech, serving dishes and condiments are placed in the center of every group of four people—two on each side. (An 1870s arrangement for Shakers eating at long tables appears as figure 232. In figure 231 the condiments hang in the center of each group of four.) Known as "eating four to a square,"[36] the resulting pattern of units of four, stretched along extended rectangles, fits neatly into the Shakers' predilection for the square, the repeated square, and the extended line. The Shakers first used benches at their dining tables and then, as we saw under regional differences in Chapter III, communities began individually to change to chairs. Many developed a new form of chair that was sufficiently low-backed to fit, like the discarded benches, under the tables. Thus when entering a dining room not in use, the viewer would see a neat space with long thin stretches of tabletops. With the chairs pulled out from tables set for "eating four to a square" the room would communicate a powerful impression of tight repetitions. The short-

88. DINING TABLE
Hancock, Massachusetts, made for dining room of 1830 Brick Dwelling House
About 1830
Cherry with red stain and clear finish
H. 27½" L. 133½" W. 34¾"
A detail of a leg is shown as figure 39
Collection of the Shaker Museum and Library, Old Chatham, New York

89. CHAIR
Watervliet, New York
1850–60
Maple with thin brown color; splint seat
H. 25⅝" W. 18⅝" D. 14"
Collection of the Shaker Museum and Library,
Old Chatham, New York

Opposite, top:
90. TABLE
Possibly Alfred, Maine
1830–60
Pine, birch legs, painted red; maple knobs
H. 32⅜" W. 119¾" D. 21"
When all the way in, the drawer front projects
1⅝" from the rail, and is ⅜" back from the edge
to the top; the projecting sides of the drawer are
painted red. The rear of the back rail is also
painted red. Sometime after it was made,
something was added to the rear of the top; it has
since been removed and more red paint remains
under where it was attached than on the rest of
the top.
Hancock Shaker Village, Pittsfield, Massachusetts

Opposite, bottom:
91. BENCH
Canterbury, New Hampshire
1830–40
Pine seat; birch legs, stretchers, and spokes; maple
top rail; painted red
H. 32¼" L. 72" D. of seat 10¾"
Center leg placed off center: there are 10 spokes
to its left and 12 spokes to its right. Pressure has
pushed left front and center legs through the seat.
Private collection

back, nicely compact dining chair in figure 89 was made at Watervliet between 1850 and 1860. The low back allowed it to be pushed under dining tables to facilitate cleaning, in order to make the room neat and the tables appear long and thin.

An early undated manuscript recorded the rules for patterned meals, including sitting upright and cutting meat into squares: "When you take a piece of bread, take a whole piece (if not too large) and when you cut meat, cut it square & equal, fat & lean, & take an equal proportion of bones—take it on your plate together with the sauce."[37] The behavior of "slugs" (a Shaker term for the lazy and selfish) was inappropriate at well-patterned meals, as part of a satirizing poem by Richard McNemar shows:

To save his credit, you must know,   *Then to make up what he has miss'd,*
That poor old Slug eats very slow;   *He takes a luncheon in his fist.*
And as in justice he does hate,   *Or turns again unto the dish,*
That all the rest on him should wait,   *And fully satisfies his wish;*
Sometimes he has to rise and kneel.   *Or if it will not answer then.*
Before he has made out his meal;   *He'll make it up at half-past ten.*[38]

The splendid worktable with a birch base and pine top in figure 90 is painted red. (A similar table is reported to have been found in the Alfred, Maine, area.)[39] The extraordinary top cantilevers out at the ends, opening up and stretching the design with great audacity. The maple knobs, placed above the center of the drawer, punctuate its rectangular shape. The drawer is designed to be pushed in beyond the edge of the top, but not as far as the skirt rail: it goes in ⅜ inch past the edge of the top but, because of its depth, it stops 1⅝ inches out from the rail. This keeps it usefully near the edge of the work surface, but far enough in to avoid having scraps fall into the drawer. Its horizontal form plays dramatically against the shape of its rail, and the top carries the horizontal line out into space.

Benches and Chairs

The Shakers' freedom to stretch form beyond what would survive in worldly circumstances is clearly shown in their long benches, for they, rather like the early trestle tables, are made without the low lengthwise strengthening stretchers found on worldly examples. The long red-painted bench in figure 91 has an amazingly narrow seat. Only 10¾ inches deep, it was carefully shaped: the rounded top edge of the front of the seat continues on the front corners that curve to the sides. The top surface of the seat is cut to angle down for seating, then up again to provide a thick back edge to hold the spokes. The single center leg at the back is off-center (there are ten back spokes to its left, and twelve to the right), and is vertical in orientation. It appears to be original. The top rail is shaped like those of the low-back Windsor chairs made at Canterbury and Enfield, New Hampshire, about 1840. Such a form would be ill-equipped to provide stability if a group of sitters chose to shift from side to side. That the Shakers developed such precarious forms is evidence of a willingness to create daring designs that would only work within a Shaker approach to life. Later, in less self-conscious Shaker communities, new benches were made with strips connecting the legs, and some of the older ones had supporting strips nailed across their front and back legs.

Lines of similar chairs were used in various places and during many events in Shaker life, which added to the sense of similarity and continuum. Three of the six Canterbury chairs in figure 92 have printed labels reading "Laundry" on the back of their central slats (figure 92A). Although made at Canterbury, they were purchased as a group from Mount Lebanon in 1918.

The exquisite, stretched-tall Enfield, New Hampshire, chair in figure 93 has the three sets of scribe marks on the back posts above the seat used to lay out a normal three-slat chair. When it was decided to make a high-seated chair for use at a high work area, the lower ones were ignored and the seat rails placed higher. The fine shaping of the parts and the elongated placing of units create an elegant, open verticality. The "boots" added to the chair shown as figure 123 give a similar height to the seat, but project another type of Shaker design that speaks of a do-it-yourself mentality.

A few tall-back rocking chairs with five slats were made in Shaker communities as far apart as Union Village, Kentucky, and Canterbury, New Hampshire. The 1840–50 New Lebanon rocking chair in figure 94 has a splint seat. A paper label on the back of the middle slat is printed with a number 3 so that the chair could be returned to room three.

Peg Rails

Peg rails had long been used in worldly homes, businesses, and meetinghouses, but they were ubiquitous in Shaker hands. They were often used in two or more layers, and contributed, like long halls and long rugs, to the impression of stretched vistas in many Shaker interiors. The blue

92. CHAIRS, SET OF SIX
Canterbury, New Hampshire
Three retain a printed paper label reading
"Laundry" on the back of their middle slat
1830–50
Maple stained red, rush seat
Each about: H. 40½" W. 20¼" D. of seat 13½"
Collection of the Shaker Museum and Library,
Old Chatham, New York

92A. LABEL ON THE REAR OF THE
MIDDLE SLAT OF A CHAIR SHOWN
IN FIGURE 92.

peg rail in figure 129 comes from the 1822–24 New Lebanon meetinghouse; it was one of the peg rails seen in Lossing's 1856 drawing of the inside of that building (figure 52). Like the seemingly endless drawers in dwelling houses, these rails were symbols of neatly ordered permanence that stretched without any disruption into a perfectly arranged future. Because the turned parts were regularly called pins, their extensive use in Shaker communities gave rise to the false assumption that the Shakers invented the clothespin.

Brooms

The Shakers began to make brooms during the last years of the eighteenth century, and continued to produce them for sale during much of the nineteenth century. They were sold both locally and as far afield as Hudson, Albany, and Boston. By 1811 the Shakers were selling both the old-style round form and the newer flat broom.[40] In their own communities brooms were constantly in use, particularly during the "cleansing gift" that was part of the Era of Manifestations. In 1887 it was reported that the Shakers covered brooms with cloths to give an extra polish to their floors: "The Shaker broom is always hung up against the wall when not in use. They put a clean white cotton hood on some of their brooms and when thus equipped, used them to dry-polish their smooth

93. CHAIR WITH A HIGH SEAT
Enfield, New Hampshire
1835–45
Birch; cane seat
H. of seat 21¼"
Private collection

94. ARMCHAIR WITH ROCKERS
New Lebanon, New York
1840–50
Maple and birch; splint seat
*H. 51¼" W. 22¼" D. of seat 15" D. of rockers
28⅛"*
*A printed label on the back of the middle slat
reads: "3". Winterthur Museum, Winterthur,
Delaware*

hard wood floors and to remove the last trace of dust from the hard and shining surface."[41] There is a cloth-covered broom for sale in figure 222, but the cloth is just a decorative cover to make the broom look nice. To facilitate the cleaning effort long-handled brooms were made for sweeping ceilings (see figure 95). These were also sold to the world (in 1810 two long-handled brooms sold for $1.12½),[42] in Shaker hands the exaggeration seems natural, for it is easy to imagine a Shaker saying: "If there is dust up there we will get rid of it; we have long brooms."

Ladder, Stadia Rod, Barn

Long "apple picking" ladders that allow access to upper branches of fruit trees are standard in the world. For the Shakers it seemed natural to exaggerate the form in lightness and length. The brown-painted ladder in figure 96 from New Lebanon exhibits an elegant, frail strength; it is both light and strong, although the rungs are only ⁹/₁₆ of an inch thick. At its base it is 13¼ inches wide, it tapers to 8¾ inches at the top, and it is 10 feet 6½ inches in length. One reason it is so light in weight is that the sides are made of pine. A crack that developed in one side was secured with hand-slotted screws, the form of which suggests an early date. The rungs are probably hickory. As in many practical Shaker objects, the ladder's shape gives strong evidence of a consciousness of design. In a characteristic Shaker manner it joins in one object a visceral enjoyment of the practical, a visual interest, and a delightful tactile experience.

Like the ladder, the length of the stadia or surveying rod (see the detail of one end in figure 97) results from its use. Although the form is found widely in the world, the character of this Shaker example is special. It comes from the Church Family, New Lebanon, and is over 12 feet in length. Its 6 inch disk is painted white and black, and can be moved up and down half the length of the instrument. The cross created by the black and white pattern was sighted-on when surveying. Like the drying rack in figure 87, the sharpness of the edges of the strip of wood combines with the practical beauty of the circle to make it seem particular to a Shaker setting. A similar division of a circle, but with red and blue quadrants, appears in a well-known gift drawing.[43]

The Shakers produced many work-buildings of extraordinary length. As always, they would find a way to construct what seems practical, and therefore obvious, to themselves, even when it might surprise non-Believers. The 207-foot-long barn in figure 98 was the cow and grain barn for the Center Family of Union Village, Ohio. It was built about 1891 to 1895.

Textiles with Lines

Textiles can be strong purveyors of patterns, and two of the most easily executed by the loom were favored by the Shakers: the grid, which we have already discussed, and one of lines. Lines appeared on Shaker carpets, clothing, bags, sewing kits, seat tapes, and wall hangings, for example. Tapestries and simpler cloths had been used for centuries to cover cold walls, and for the same reason the Shakers often hung wall cloths from pegs around their beds. The best known version of a Shaker wall cloth, which appears in an 1873 print, uses a grid design (see figure 69). Sabbathday Lake owns a much earlier wall hanging shown as figure 99. Made of heavy linen, it has sewn eyelets at the top and bottom; it was probably looped to pegs above and secured some other way to a baseboard or the floor. Since it is 94 inches high and 55 inches wide, three strips were sewn together to obtain the needed height. Each exhibits a series of three gray-blue lines comprising a central solid one flanked by two narrowly paired lines. These create a horizontal movement against the natural linen ground. In 1887 wall hangings were put into the second meetinghouse at Mount Lebanon behind the visitors' seating area to keep the walls clean.[44] They were probably hung from the pegs.

FRAGILE

Special Handling

A preciousness of behavior, possible because they were isolated from the world, was part of the Shakers' awareness of Millennial perfection. The Roman Catholic mystic Thomas Merton was wrong, in 1966, when he over-idealized the Shaker creative process. His statement that "Thus the craftsman began each new chair as if it were the first chair ever to be made in the world," shows he did not understand the small-factory process that produced most of the chairs, and the

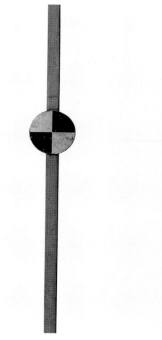

employment of outsiders to do some of the work. Merton was right, however, when he wrote: "The peculiar grace of a Shaker chair is due to the fact that it was made by someone capable of believing that an angel might come and sit on it."[45] Many Shakers did expect, see, and speak to angels, and the Shakers knew as Believers they would join the heavenly throng.

Shakers were expected to treat domestic objects with care to preserve them, and this included their surfaces. (When we look at color we will see that what was touched could be varnished to keep it clean, and what was less handled could not.) The concern for near permanence of form and surface was expressed in the Millennial Laws of 1821: "When brethren or sisters go up or down stairs they should not slip their feet on the carpet, but take them up and set them down plumb, so as not to wear out the carpets unnecessarily . . . . Also, when they turn at the head and foot of the stairs they should not turn their feet while on the floor, lest they wear holes in the floor; but they should turn their feet while clear of the floor . . . . It is not right to lean our chairs back against the wall in our dwelling houses nor any decent building; nor against any beds or furniture. . . . It is also wrong to sit with our feet on the rounds of our chairs."[46] The 1845 Laws go much further: "All should be careful not to mar or destroy the furniture in their shops or rooms."[47] Although such admonitions were in part to discourage idleness, the required consciousness of objects contributed to the Shakers' unconventional attitude toward form and visual balance of parts.

Right:
100. HIGH STOOL
New England
Probably 1825–50
Soft maple originally painted red; stool and its
original splint seat painted gray at a later date
H. 41" W. 19" D. 13½"
Private collection

Far Right:
101. WALKER
Mount Lebanon, New York; the parts are similar
to those in chairs made by the South Family
1875–90
Maple with a clear finish
H. 32½" W. 17 ¾" D. 23⅛"
Collection of the Shaker Museum and Library,
Old Chatham, New York

102. DRYING RACK
New Lebanon, New York, North Family
1830–60
Pine painted yellow; brass hinges
H. 44" W. 27⅜" D. folded 2½"
Collection of the Shaker Museum and Library,
Old Chatham, New York

Invalid Walker, Drying Rack, Lapboard, Bed

For the Shakers, gentleness was a virtue, and its formal expression, even to the extent of an object's appearing fragile, was a desired achievement. Makers must have taken delight in creating useful items that appeared almost ridiculously light. The high stool in figure 100 is a standard worldly item of probably the second quarter of the nineteenth century. Made of soft maple with a splint seat, it has been painted gray over an earlier red coat. In contrast, the Shaker invalid's walker in figure 101 pushes for leanness in a piece made to support a person in frail health. It lacks a firm Shaker history, but it shares many characteristics with chairs made by the South Family of Mount Lebanon in the last quarter of the nineteenth century: the legs are the same diameter and their tops are rounded in the same manner as the front posts of the armless chairs produced there. The length and gentle swelling of the stretchers echo exactly the stretchers placed between the front legs of the rocking chair in figure 195. The lack of scribe marks on the legs to locate the drilling positions for the stretchers, and the use of a clear finish, rather than a colored one, affirm its late date.

Folding drying racks had been standard household and institutional items long before the Shakers formed communities. They were generally simple grids of vertical and horizontal slats. The London cabinet shop of Thomas Chippendale, for whom a whole style of English design is named, produced one very much like the Shaker example in figure 102. It was made for Paxton House, Berwickshire, Scotland, in 1774 in three sections, with bracket feet on the end verticals.[48] The Shaker example pushes thinness of parts almost to silliness: the parts measure only ¹³/₁₆ of an inch square. To intensify the sense of thinness, the inner faces of the verticals above the top horizontal rails are tapered. The rack has a yellow wash and tiny brass hinges. The donor recorded: "This rack was given to me by the Shakers at Mt. Lebanon, N.Y. in January 1947 before the Colony was closed and they moved to Hancock, Mass. Shaker Colony. It was in the Kitchen of the North Family Sister's House."[49]

Many items, such as writing boxes and lapboards, were made of very thin boards. The Shaker Sisters used lapboards to facilitate handwork, and many were made in the 1830s as presentation gifts from Brothers. The 1845 Millennial Laws spoke against such gifts, undoubtedly because they were common occurrences. The lapboard in figure 144 measures 18 inches by 11⅞ inches, and is only ⅜ inch thick. When a board is cut this thin it can easily warp, and care must be taken to be sure it is quarter sawn (i.e., from a board cut as a radius of the log), in which case it will probably stay flat. This lapboard was purchased at Hancock, but its original source is unknown since many objects were moved there in a progression of shifts as communities closed down. It has slightly rounded edges and is painted red below a yellow finish. The surface is so smooth from handling that it feels as if it has a thin coat of butter. One end has two holes that once held a thong or string for hanging. While many of the things the Shakers handled had a lightness of parts, others had features that made parts appear thin. As we have seen in figure 36, the tops of some drawer sides were thinner than their bases, to make them look lean while maintaining a thick base to run on.

The early green bed in figure 103 is of maple with a pine headboard. The rails join each other in tenons, and the round legs pass through the joints as round tenons. Thus, the legs hold the rails together. In worldly beds, and later Shaker beds, it was standard to have heavy rectilinear sections at the top of the legs to hold the rails that tenon into them. Those beds are held together by the ropes that support the mattresses. Typical of much Shaker work, and celibate use, this great Shaker bed has a lean stance with minimal defense against stress. The use of wheels made cleaning easier. In 1863 Freegift Wells changed the rollers on a bed "so as to draw it out endways."[50] The green on two early beds that have been studied scientifically shows two layers of chrome green paint and over that a layer of green paint with varnish added to it.[51] (Green paint is discussed further in Chapter VII.)

103. BED
Probably New Lebanon, or Watervliet, New York, or Hancock, Massachusetts
1800–30
Maple frame, pine headboard; painted green
H. 34" W. 38" L. 74"
Legs held in place by wedges from above, and kept from turning around (so wheels stay in proper alignment) by metal pins passing horizontally through rail tenons and tops of legs; possibly later pairs of screws (from the top down) further secure corner joints.
Art Complex Museum, Duxbury, Massachusetts

Until the second half of the nineteenth century Believers slept two to a bed, and the use of beds, like every Shaker activity, was ordered. In 1812 Thomas Brown noted: "It is contrary to order for a man or woman to sleep alone, but two of the brethren sleep together, and the sisters the same." To get everyone a good night's sleep the 1845 Laws asked everyone in a room to go to bed at the same time, and in their required double beds, they were to "rest in fear of God, without any playing, or boisterous laughing, and lie straight."[52] A visitor accompanying Herman Melville to Hancock in 1851 recorded: "An old Shakeress with a dry Yankee twist in her voice took us to the bedroom &c and explained to us a curious camel's hump raised in the middle of the bed, lengthwise, a kind of imitation Berkshire mountain range where two sisters slept together—that they should not roll on one another."[53] In 1850 Brother Elisha D'Alembert Blakeman, in charge of the boys in New Lebanon, solved a problem of fitting eight boys into less space than four beds would occupy, by making one "long enough for 8 boys side by side."[54] In the mid-1860s, as the population decreased, many double beds were narrowed to a single bed size. A green one at the Winterthur Museum, with a Hancock history, now has no paint on the round ends of the headboard because it was cut down at both ends. The location of the rope holes in the end rails of that bed also show that they have been shortened. The 1873 print illustrated as figure 69 shows narrow beds. (The Shakers had long used narrow beds for hired men and the ill.) In the 1870s or 1880s, when new mattresses were purchased, many beds were lowered. When we discuss the Shakers of the early twentieth century, we will recount a story of a roomful of early beds being cast out of attic windows by the Shakers to get rid of them.

Chairs

Chairs seem always to have been associated with the Shakers, and many records of seeing Ann Lee describe her as sitting in a chair. For example, Timothy Hubbard recalled seeing Ann Lee "sit in her chair, from early in the morning, until afternoon, under great operations and power of God. She sung in unknown tongues, the whole of the time; and seemed to be wholly divested of any

104. PAIR OF CHAIRS
Canterbury, New Hampshire
1850–60
Maple stained dark red; cane seats
Tops of front legs stamped: "4"
Each about: H. 41" W. 18½" D. of seat 13½"
Collection of the Shaker Museum and Library,
Old Chatham, New York

attraction to material things."[55] Figure 4 shows a chair she used at Harvard, Massachusetts.

Early Shaker chairs have the heavy posts found in worldly chairs of the time (see figure 124). It could have been natural for the Believers to continue that sense of weight and stability in a Society expecting their furniture to be in use for a millennium. But instead, their chairs became thinner than most worldly chairs, and in the 1840s four communities added fragile cane seats: Canterbury and Enfield, New Hampshire; New Lebanon; and Harvard. The parts of the Canterbury pair in figure 104 are elegantly slender. The rear legs end in tilters—balls with a flat base that fit into rounded hollows in the base of the legs. They are held in place by leather thongs. Tilters helped fulfill the injunction not to wear out the floors or the carpets "unnecessarily," when leaning back. The leaders knew the Believers were leaning back in their chairs when they ruled against the practice in the 1821 Laws. Not only are the posts, rails, and slats surprisingly thin but the seat lists, or rails, are almost ridiculously insubstantial. They measure only 1 inch from front to back at their centers, and are flattened top and bottom. Moreover, they are pierced with holes to receive the cane. At their centers the slender stretchers are only ¾ of an inch from top to bottom. (The tops of the front legs are stamped with the number 4, signifying that the chairs belonged in room number four.) The high-seated chair in figure 93 appears even more wondrous. It is not surprising that Thomas Merton wrote of Shaker chairs made for angels.

Shaker chairs are now often displayed hanging from peg boards. There are accounts by visitors who observed the practice, and figure 105 shows a late interior with a chair hung upside down. It rests on its easily replaced tape seat, not on a slat or rung, for that would damage the chair's surface.

For the Shakers, rocking chairs were a sign of comfort and often signaled old age. The Millennial Laws of 1845 assured against too much comfort in the bedrooms: "One rocking chair in a [bed] room is sufficient, except where the aged reside."[56] An 1875 riddle by a former Shaker furniture maker reads: "I have a back, legs and arms you see, Though feet were never given me, Yet aged people think me nice; Who'll guess my name by trying twice?"[57] As mentioned earlier, despite restrictions on comfort, in 1825 two New Lebanon Brothers went to Vermont to buy an "easy," well upholstered wing chair, perhaps for the sick and elderly.

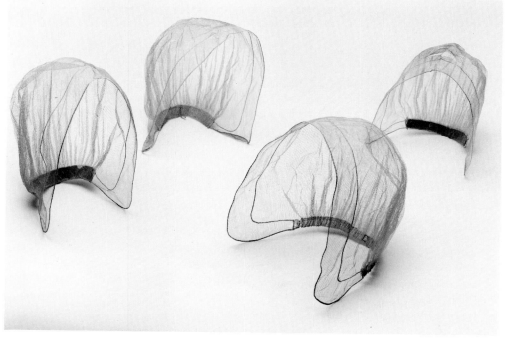

Thin Textiles

Thin textiles are not unique to the Shakers but they fit easily into the general character of Shaker domestic practices, and are therefore appropriately considered in that context. Girls remained bareheaded until they reached about fourteen years of age, when they began to wear caps as a sign of modesty (see figures 105 and 106).[58] An 1829 newspaper article describing Sisters' dress noted: "And on their heads, each one had a white muslin cap."[59] (When the Sisters were outside, a bonnet covered the cap.) The early caps were of homespun cotton or linen, but by 1806 they were of imported muslin.[60] The late caps in figure 106 are of wool. The thin linen nightshirt in figure 107 belonged to Elder Joseph Brackett (1797–1882), of the Maine Ministry, composer of "Simple Gifts," with the famous first line: " 'Tis the gift to be simple" in 1848.[61] It has a minimal

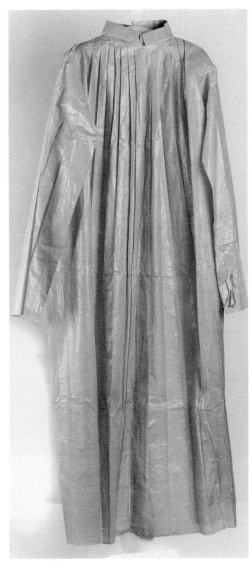

form and attached neck ties. The two blue Xs below the V opening at the throat are laundry marks.

The demanding Millennial Laws of 1845 describe the clothing to be put on the dead: "A corpse should be dressed in a shirt and winding sheet, a handkerchief, and a muffler if necessary,—and for a female add thereto a cap and collar."[62] Figure 108 shows a thin, glazed cambric shroud of about 1850 that came into the Hancock collections from Edward Deming Andrews. Probably it was made by the Shakers, but they might have purchased it, or at least the material to make it; that it is machine-stitched, and the cloth is either hand or machine-made, does not decide the question. The *Workman's Guide* (1838) says shrouds were designed to open in the back; those for women had pleats in the front, while those for men were plain.[63] The flared pleats on figure 108 provide a linear grace.

Iron Pieces

Objects made of iron by the Shakers may have very thin parts. Many Shaker-made door latches appear large when viewed head-on, but from the side the handle may be only ¹⁄₁₆ of an inch thick and the thumbpiece paper thin. Two Shaker door handles appear in profile on the door at the lower center of the gift drawing shown as figure 165.

Shaker stoves are a well known and loved form. For many, the Shakers made wooden molds and sent them to foundries to be cast, and most have cast legs. A few have wrought legs of surprising slenderness. Many of these had their lower ends flattened and turned sideways to form round feet (figure 109). Some had holes in their flat feet through which they could be fastened in place. Wrought legs with flat feet and securing holes were not invented by the Shakers, but were the result of traditional practices. For example, they appear on partly wrought-iron beds made for the Thetford Union Workhouse, Norfolk, England, erected in 1836.[64]

110. ADULT CRADLE
Probably Harvard, Massachusetts
Possibly by Ziba Winchester (b. 1800 left Shakers
1838). A Harvard journal entry of January 13,
1835, may refer to this piece: "Ziba finished the
cradle & brought it into the nurse room to stain."
Pine and maple colored yellow; pair of cherry
batten repairs on outside of foot board; one cherry
repair on outside of headboard
H. 29⅛" W. cradle 28" (rockers 30⅜")
L. without repairs 74"
Fruitlands Museums, Harvard, Massachusetts

RUGGED

To understand the early Shakers it is necessary to find a balance between two parts of their lives, the consciously precious and the everyday rugged. The preceding objects have exemplified a rarefied aesthetic, a joining of an exacting consciousness of form, line, and belief. Most of those pieces were for domestic use, and were used in careful behavioral patterns. But while Believers strove not to mar walls, or to wear out chair rungs, carpets, and floors, and understood the use of slender drying racks and light cane-seated chairs, they were also participating in rudimentary country activities. Although they lived in secure, well-built buildings in ordered towns, and were envied for their prosperity, life in early Shaker villages was in many ways a struggle. The men pursued farming and their various industries, and the women did the laborious and often physically demanding housework, and also had their businesses.

Domestic

Ann Lee and other early leaders were credited with faith healings, and Shakers counted on their own herbal medicines and faith as cures. The 1845 Millennial Laws state: "The order of God forbids that Believers should employ Doctors of the world, except in some extreme cases, or the case of a sick child, whose parents are among the world, and desire such aid; and in such cases, the Ministry or Elders should decide whether it be proper or not." Although the Shakers did consult all kinds of medical authorities from outside their village,[65] the women who cared for the sick and the elderly could find the responsibility demanding. As in the world, the Shakers developed objects to help them. The adult cradle in figure 110 has a history of coming from the Harvard Community and is very like those in a collection of worldly examples gathered at the Shelburne Museum in Shelburne, Vermont. Many of those cradles have holes or pegs in their sides so that the mad could be tied in. Similarly, there were in the world cagelike Windsor chairs into which the sick could be tied.

The Shaker adult cradle in figure 110 is made of pine and maple and is colored with a yellow wash. The bottom board is installed so that body fluids could run off: It is nailed to the rockers, and the foot board is nailed to its top surface, but the bottom board is free of the sides by ⅝ of an inch, and of the head board by 1½ inches. (It has two later cherry cleats to strengthen the foot board, and one broader cleat securing the cracked head board.) It was possibly made by Ziba Winchester, for a journal entry of January 13, 1835 reads: "Ziba finished the cradle & brought it into the nurse room to stain."[66]

The Shakers always stressed cleanliness and, as the 1797 visitor to New Lebanon noted, women worked just as hard as the men, their time being taken up with cooking, weaving, and, as noted earlier, "above all with ceaseless laundry."[67] The Shakers, who were quick to improve their

111. TAILOR'S GOOSE
New Lebanon, New York, probably North Family
1820–50
Iron
H. 5" W. 9⅛" D. 1¾"
Collection of the Shaker Museum and Library,
Old Chatham, New York

environments, soon developed complex power-driven washing machines. At the 1876 International Centennial Exposition in Philadelphia a type of washing machine patented by the Shakers of Canterbury won an award: "N.A. Briggs, Shaker Village, Merrimack Co. N.H. for their strength, size, simplicity and capability for extensive uses."[68] The heavy tailor's goose (so named because of its long handle) in figure 111 probably comes from New Lebanon's North Family, and was used very hot to press heavy cloth. It was particularly helpful in flattening seams. The twist to the handle made this part feel less hot.

Business and Farm

The 1857 print *The Laboratory* (figure 112) was used in Lossing's *Harper's* article, and with others titled *The Hydraulic Press, Vacuum Pan, Crushing Mill,* and *Powdering Mill,* showed the Shakers' inventiveness and commitment to hard work that made them successful business people. A machine for sifting sage leaves after they had been crushed into a powder for use in the sausage business, comes from Hancock (figure 113). It consists of a funnel above a frame that has boards above and a screen below. The broken leaves passed from the funnel through a slit in the boards and onto the screen. The frame was agitated from side to side, which shook the leaves over the screen, and the powder fell through it into the drawer below. Like many light industrial items employed by Shakers and non-Shakers, it combines simple shapes nailed and bolted together to make a practical, visually handsome object. One end has a rod that was hooked to an eccentric wheel; it agitated the top from side to side. At this early date it was probably driven by waterpower.

The Shakers produced herbal medicines in great quantities for themselves, and by 1821 they were selling them increasingly to the world.[69] The production was a natural outgrowth of community doctoring and, like their seed and herb businesses, a natural result of farming for large numbers of Believers. Men ran the heavy machinery and women did most of the tedious work in the herb industry: "cleaning roots, picking and 'picking over' flowers and plants, cutting sage, cleaning bottles, cutting and printing labels, papering powders and herbs, and 'dressing' or putting up extracts and ointments, was done by the sisters. They also made the ointments."[70] The Brothers were more focused on "the thick work." In 1884 a drawing was made for a print that appeared in the 1885 *Shaker Almanac* (figure 114). It shows Sisters preparing herb extracts. In the center of the room they are sitting at a long trestle-base table filling bottles (see bottles and a bottle-drying rack in figure 122). At the right are shipping boxes. The walls are almost covered with pictures, probably advertising posters. At least one is framed, for its top tips forward.

Shaker farm equipment usually shows the same awareness of aesthetic issues as found in their domestic items. The early winnower from Watervliet (figure 115) was used to flip grain so the chaff would blow away. The arches of the nailed-on handles play against the arch of the thin, rising back and the curve of the leather covered bottom. The sculpted walnut New Lebanon grain shovel (figure 116) was carefully strengthened with tin when shrinkage cracks developed. The

113. SAGE SIFTER
Hancock, Massachusetts
1850–1900
Maple and pine; leather; metal screen
H. 43½" L. 64" D. 20¼"
Collection of the Shaker Museum and Library,
Old Chatham, New York

114. *"SHAKERESSES LABELING AND*
WRAPPING THE BOTTLES CONTAINING
THE SHAKER EXTRACT OF ROOTS, OR
SEIGEL'S SYRUP"
Published in Andrew Judson White's, The Joys
and Sorrows of a Poor Old Man, Shaker
Almanac, 1885, *(New York, 1884), p. 13*
Collection of the Shaker Museum and Library,
Old Chatham, New York

115. WINNOWER
Watervliet, New York
1820–40
Oak; leather; handmade iron tacks
H. 10½" W. 33 ⅛" D. 23½"
Collection of the Shaker Museum and Library,
Old Chatham, New York

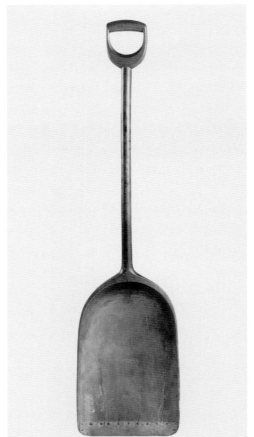

Right:
116. GRAIN SHOVEL
New Lebanon, New York, Church Family
1825–50
Walnut; tin patch; copper rivets
L. 43 1/2" W. 10 1/4" D 2 3/4"
Collection of the Shaker Museum and Library,
Old Chatham, New York

Far right:
117. SNOW SHOVEL
Hancock, Massachusetts
1850–70
Pine; maple handles; metal; colored dark red
L. 55 1/2" W. 15" D. 4"
Collection of the Shaker Museum and Library,
Old Chatham, New York

118. BULL BLINDER
Canterbury, New Hampshire
Mid-nineteenth century
Cowhide; copper rivets; metal buckle
H. 13 1/4" W. 10 1/2" D. 9"
Collection of the Shaker Museum and Library,
Old Chatham, New York

Hancock red-painted snow shovel (figure 117) is similar to commercially made worldly examples, but the Shaker eyes and hands that developed this one kept the lines simple and beautiful. The rectangular form of the metal-edged board plays against the angle of its top board, and that piece holds the shaft, which divides at the top to form an elegant handle.

Other farm artifacts evoke a more earthy, day-to-day practicality. The bull blinder in figure 118 has straps to go over a bull's horns, and cups, each mounted with nineteen brass rivets, to cover the eyes. A lower strap went around the throat. When purchased from Canterbury in 1952 the Eldress said, "It was to prevent the bull from trundling the cow."[71] Other Shaker leather items, such as mailbags, have the same practical, visually intriguing design sense.

Stone was worked by Brothers for such needs as paths, foundations, steps into buildings, stepping stones to facilitate mounting a horse, carriage, or wagon, and dripstones. The latter caught water from downspouts and carried it away from foundations. The marble one in figure 119 possibly came from Hancock. It uses a clean, circular action and a trough that tapers to become narrower as it moves away from the circle. These shapes play against a forceful rectangular mass. A red sandstone example, in the same collection, from the southwest corner of the seedhouse of the Church Family, Enfield, Connecticut, is more worn. According to tradition it was made from the stone hauled down to Enfield from Vermont "for foundation, bridges, etc., by ox-team."[72]

119. DRIPSTONE
Possibly Hancock, Massachusetts
1790–1830
Marble
H. 5" W. 17¼" D. 37½"
Collection of the Shaker Museum and Library,
Old Chatham, New York

IMPROVISED

Many Shaker-made objects provided answers to a need rather than being carefully thought-out combinations of aesthetic and religious concerns. Improvisation could produce designs even less conventional than was normal in the Shaker world as they took part in the "Yankee ingenuity" that combined quick solutions with thrift. In the 1970s, Roger Bacon, a Maine dealer in early rural material, made popular the term "made-dos" for those things that were patched together or altered to serve a new purpose. The Shakers throve on such endeavors, for, like other practical Americans, they enjoyed developing ingenious solutions to everyday problems.

120. BROOM-MAKING TABLE
New Lebanon, New York, North Family
1810–50
Maple and pine colored dark red; metal; leather
H. 45" L. 72⅝" D. 30¾"
Collection of the Shaker Museum and Library,
Old Chatham, New York

121. BROOMCORN SORTING BIN
Watervliet, New York, West Family broom shop
1825–75
Pine and maple colored dark red; numbers in
black paint
H. 37¼" L. corner to corner 75"
The 13 divider pegs are modern replacements
Collection of the Shaker Museum and Library,
Old Chatham, New York

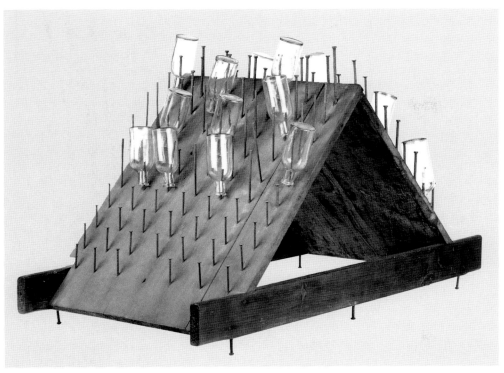

122. BOTTLE-DRYING RACK
New Lebanon, New York, Medicine Department,
Church Family
1870–90
Pine painted red; three sizes of steel nails, one in
a lower row missing
H. 20¾" W. 17¾" D. 40"

Bottles
New Lebanon, New York,
purchased from the world for the Medicine
Department, Church Family
1870–90
Glass
H. 5¾" Diam. 2¼"
H. 5½" Diam. 2"
H. 4¾" Diam. 1⅞"
Collection of the Shaker Museum and Library,
Old Chatham, New York

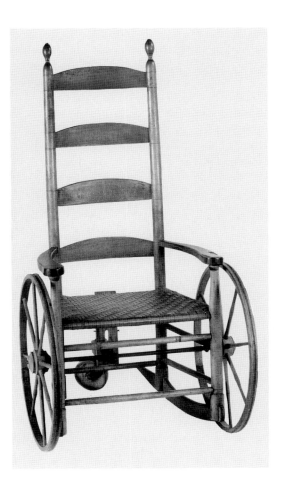

Far left:
123. CHAIR WITH "BOOTS"
Pleasant Hill, Kentucky
Chair: 1835–45; boots probably later
Maple and hickory; pewter collars on top of boots
H. 44½" W. 20" D. of seat 14¼"
Collection of the Shaker Village of Pleasant Hill,
Harrodsburg, Kentucky

Left:
124. ROCKING ARMCHAIR ADAPTED
TO BECOME A WHEELCHAIR
Chair: New Lebanon, or Watervliet, New York;
purchased at Hancock, Massachusetts
Chair: 1800–20
Maple and oak colored brown; splint seat; metal
H. 47½ W. 26 D. 31¾"
Collection of the Shaker Museum and Library,
Old Chatham, New York

Equipment used by the Shakers in their businesses was usually artistically pleasing, even when improvised. The broom-making table (figure 120) from New Lebanon was fairly carefully planned, while the Watervliet broomcorn sorter (figure 121) was a more spontaneous solution to a need. The former joins a horizontal bench top, two vertical broom clamps, and four angled round-turned legs. The legs raking toward the clamps were sheared off at an angle and nailed to the inside of the stationary, vertical planks of the clamps. (More standard square, or rectangular, in-cross-section legs would have been easier to join to the verticals.) Thus the piece has practicality while including a form of leg the Shakers enjoyed making throughout the nineteenth century. (Perhaps the piece started as just a bench with four legs and later the vices were added. Either way the use of taper-turned legs is pleasing and characteristically Shaker.) The more spontaneously designed sorter has numbered compartments for broomcorn of different sizes, and a cutting arm at the left. It seems that after it was built it was found to be too low for convenience; a block was added under the left end, and the right end was raised by nailing on a plank. The visual play between the thin and thick parts, and the curved and straight sections make it a delight to observe.

The bottle-drying rack in figure 122 is from the medicine department of the New Lebanon Church Family. To produce a serviceable object, wide boards, into which large nails had been driven, were nailed together at the top and held at the base by strips of wood. These are recessed into, and project about 2½ inches beyond, the main boards. The projecting parts served as carrying handles, and their corners were rounded. (The nail holes along the top edges show that they were formerly used for some other purpose.) Six long round-headed screws serve as feet. Areas have different sized nails for different sized bottles. At first this may seem a dismissable object, too minor to be of aesthetic interest, but it speaks clearly of a pragmatic, forceful life that can bang together a solution and incorporate in its rudimentary presence an innate sense of integrated forms. Had it not been found visually pleasing, as well as practical, it could easily have been replaced by a more carefully considered object. But, a more consciously designed object may not have had a better balance of parts. This piece has the immediate presence of the most rugged and exciting "folk art."

Adding "boots" to a chair to make its seat higher is clearly within the "make-do" tradition. Those on the Pleasant Hill chair in figure 123 have pewter collars to keep them from splitting. The red-painted wheelchair in figure 124 is an early Watervliet or New Lebanon rocking armchair to which three wheels were added. The large ones have grooves in their outer faces that once held leather or some other gripping material. An early date of 1800–20 for the chair is suggested by the thickness of the posts and their increased size where they hold the rockers. The vertical position of the small rear wheel is adjustable. The resulting adaption is a delightful tangle of straight lines, gentle curves, and circles.

It was logical for the Shakers to convert a rocking chair because they had made few armchairs without rockers. A similar Shaker wheelchair, also adapted from a rocking slat-back, is at Pleasant Hill. Its large wheels have been lost. Adapting armchairs into wheelchairs was not confined to Shaker hands: an ingenious Englishman, J. Alderman, "Inventor, Patentee and Manufacturer" of 16 Soho Square, London, and active about 1830, added two large and one small wheel to an armchair with baluster-turned front legs, and an upholstered back and cushioned seat.[73] The Maine State Museum has a worldly example that results from wheels being added to the seat, back, and arms of a "Boston Rocker." The seat never had legs attached. To make the Shaker wheelchair in figure 124, an iron bar was bolted below the top side stretchers; it holds the large wheels.

The red-painted cupboard with a yellow-painted interior (figure 125) stood in the Office of the Second Family at Alfred; it held the best china used for visitors. The three strongly raised panels confirm an early date of 1800–20. There is a round molding, like the beaded edge of peg rails, on the inner edges of the boards that surround the top and sides of the door. This finished edge was standard on architectural doorways in the world, and easily moved onto Shaker-made buildings and furniture. The simple projecting top bespeaks the cupboard's Shaker origin. What is surprising about this piece is the nature of the glazed door: it is an eight-pane window sash turned on end. That is why, against all worldly practices at this date, the panes run horizontally rather than vertically. (The sash in the cupboard door was larger than, but similar to, the eight-pane sash in the window next to it.) The edges of the window sash within the door frame are visible from the front. Since window sashes are thicker than cupboard doors, the sash projects into the cupboard beyond the inner surface of the door. Like many other rectilinear grids that speak with a Shaker accent, this piece has a wonderful play of slightly surprising rectangles.

Opposite:
125. DISH CUPBOARD USING A WINDOW SASH
Alfred, Maine, Second Family Office
1800–20
Pine; exterior painted red; interior area seen through glass painted yellow
H. 85½" W. 35¼" D. 14¼"
Metal door latch missing
The United Society of Shakers, Sabbathday Lake, Maine

Chapter VII
COLOR AND VARNISH: HISTORY AND
WORLDLY PRACTICES, AND SHAKER USE

The purpose of this chapter is to provide an understanding of how and why the Shakers used the colors they employed. Since they have recorded limited information on the subject, it is necessary to review the role of colors before 1790, and then to see how the world around the Shakers used them. With this understanding it is possible to see more clearly what the Shakers borrowed from the world, and the ways and the reasons they chose to be different.

HISTORY

At least since the time of ancient Egypt, color has played a dramatic role in architecture and art. The objects found in the tomb of Tutankhamen used precious and semiprecious materials, or employed paint to simulate them; white paint, for example, suggested ivory. England's late medieval rural culture provided the inspiration for much of the New World's seventeenth-century visual imagery. It was a bright world with strongly colored textiles, pieces of furniture, and house woodwork. During much of the eighteenth century, while higher styled furniture tended to show the natural tones of walnut and then mahogany, the accompanying textiles and woodwork remained colorful and the vernacular furniture of the period was usually painted. The Enlightenment's appropriation of classical colors during the last decades of the century brought the tones of ancient Greece and Rome into general circulation. White was also given a key role, which happened to be historically incorrect. Its use was encouraged by a new love for white marble statues; the fact that these had been painted by the Greeks and Romans was overlooked. Even when the ancient statues were made of bronze, the lips and nipples might be of copper, and the teeth of silver, to suggest a more realistic image. Time and cleaning had changed the marbles, and their whiteness seemed to suggest the virtuous purity popularized during the Enlightenment.[1] From his travels in Italy (1754–58), Robert Adam, like others of his time, brought back to England the antique world's bright cool palette, and applied it everywhere: to walls, ceilings, curtains, rugs, and furniture. Adam placed in his confections both cleaned ancient and new white statues. Clothing fashions of the time changed to allow the female body, and the lower half of the male, to be nearly as discernible as those of naked statues. The women wore dresses of thin, white cloth, which clung to the body as it moved or sat in suggestive positions. Men began wearing tight, revealing trousers.

Colored furniture was again part of the high-style mode, and became an accepted alternative to the newly-in-vogue light-colored woods: satinwood, maple, or birch, under a clear finish. New types of furniture were developed, such as sideboards and sectional dining tables for the new fashion of having a dining room. Earlier forms of furniture were adjusted to agree with the new tight-form aesthetic: for example, the chest with drawers in figure 19 continues a traditional practical form developed in the late seventeenth century. But it incorporates new circular-cut-out bracket feet, and wooden knobs of flat appearance that echo the shape of fashionable brass pulls.

Varnish and Paint
Painted surfaces can be made more vivid in color and easier to clean with a finishing coat of varnish. The problem with varnish, as restorers of paintings have long realized, is that it darkens over time, and pieces that are brightly painted can appear very dark. There are two kinds of varnish. Oil-resin varnish is a solution of natural plant resins in oil. For this a resin—often a fossilized plant exudation, such as copal, or amber—is dissolved (usually by cooking), commonly in linseed

oil or walnut oil, and this is diluted with a volatile solvent such as turpentine. Spirit varnish is normally made of alcohol-soluble resins such as shellac, dissolved in a volatile solvent such as alcohol.

There have long been recipes for making paints and varnishes and how to combine them for smooth, easily cleaned surfaces. William Salmon in the seventeenth century gave two volumes of advice on the subject in his 1675 *Polygraphice: or, The Arts of Drawing, Engraving, Etching, Limning, Painting, Vernishing, Japaning, Gilding, &c.*[2] George Hepplewhite in *The Cabinet-Maker and Upholsterer's Guide* (1788), included: "For chairs, a new and very elegant fashion has arisen within these few years, of finishing them with painted or japanned [painted and then varnished] work, which gives a rich and splendid appearance to the minuter parts of the [painted] ornaments, which are generally thrown in by the painter . . . and by affording the prevailing colour to the furniture and light of the room, affords opportunity, by the variety of grounds which may be introduced, to make the whole accōrd in harmony, with a pleasing and striking effect to the eye. Japanned chairs should have cane bottoms [seats] . . . ."[3] In his *The Cabinet Dictionary* (1803), Thomas Sheraton wrote "Of Japanning Window Cornices" that after the board of the cornice is smooth, it should be painted and then "give it a clear varnish before the ornament is painted upon the ground." After the decorative details were added, "give the work at least two coats of white hard varnish."[4]

In nineteenth-century America it became standard to finish the painted surface of furniture and interior architectural wood with a varnish. The 1812 painter's manual printed in New Haven, *Directions For House And Ship Painting,* by Hezekiah Reynolds, is a helpful avenue to understanding both the composition and manner of applying paint, and when it might be covered with varnish. "Designed for the use of learners," it carefully details each step. Fortunately it was republished in full in 1978. For slate, a color the Shakers mention often: "To equal quantities of white Lead and Spanish White; add lampblack . . . the shade may be varied at the discretion of the painter."[5] In Shaker communities, the discretion would rest with the Ministry. The publication ends with a description of how to make floor- and oilcloths.

Andrew Jackson Downing's influential book, *The Architecture of Country Houses* (1850), discusses furnishings as well as buildings, and he grades interior surfaces: the most satisfactory are "the native woods" where the house is built "[of] such as maple, birch, ash, black-walnut, or oak. This requires no painting, simply a coat or two of varnish, and the effect is excellent." As a substitute he suggests "either grained, in imitation of these woods, or, in the cheapest cottages, *stained,* to have the same effect . . . . The grained [and stained] surface . . . being made smooth by varnishing, does not readily become soiled, and when it does, a moment's application of a damp cloth will make all clean and bright." Downing did not like an unvarnished painted surface for it "is always somewhat rough, and catches dirt readily."[6] He recommended that decorated painted furniture always be finished with a coat of varnish.

Freemasonry; Colors and Symbols

There is a similarity between how the Masons and the Shakers used color, and a correspondence between Masonic symbols and those appearing on Shaker gift drawings. Much of what the Shakers wrote about color echoes what the Masons believed about color, and many of the symbols on Shaker gift drawings cease to be so mysterious when they are seen as regular features in Masonic art. There may have been no direct borrowing of the meaning of colors or of symbols by the Shakers from the Masons; perhaps both participated separately in generally known ideas, particularly those derived from the Bible. But a linkage seems certain. The late-eighteenth-century Masonic hall rife with Masonic symbols shown in figure 55 is only a few miles from New Lebanon and Hancock. Many Masons who became Shakers took Masonic documents that display Masonic symbols into Shaker communities. Masonic symbols were widely recognized and part of various religious discussions in the early years of the nineteenth century. For example, in 1830 an early Mormon preacher, Parley P. Pratt, addressed the Shakers at New Lebanon and afterwards saw in cloud formations a Masonic square and compass that he interpreted as a "marvelous . . . sign of the coming of the Son of Man."[7] Even if there was no conscious borrowing from the Masons' visual vocabulary, which seems unlikely, the closeness of the two show how in tune the Shakers were with the world around them.

Probably Ann Lee was aware of the power of Freemasonry and how its vow of silence could conflict with opening a heart during confession: In the 1828 account of his time with the Shakers, the apostate William Haskett reported a confrontation between Ann Lee and her brother William about his knowledge of Freemasonry, adding that Ann Lee was well aware of its mysteries. Haskett may have stressed this in order to discredit both Ann and William.[8] Mary Dyer, who lost her children and her husband Joseph to the Shakers, included in her denunciation of the sect a testimony by one Robert Crain that involved a Mason's loyalty to Masonic secrets. He wrote that Joseph Dyer had said to him about 1814, "I have known what it was to give up my wife and children, which were as dear to me as yours are to you, and signed the covenant, and sacrificed all [i.e., give up his property] to God; and one thing more I have done, harder than all the rest, and which you will never have to pass through, and that was divulging the secrets of Masonry."[9] He had received the degree of Entering Apprentice on September 29, 1798.[10] Richard McNemar, one of the first converts in the West, and eventually an important leader—the land he donated became part of Union Village—is also reported to have been a Mason.[11]

Freemasonry had developed into an influential and publicly recognized organization by the eighteenth century, and members in America included leaders such as George Washington, Benjamin Franklin, and Paul Revere, and a great number of the middle class. After the Revolution the appeal of secret knowledge and symbols combined with the fraternity's function as a civic organization to draw membership from throughout bourgeois America; between 1790 and 1830 perhaps a hundred thousand men joined Masonic lodges. During the anti-Masonic period of the 1830s and '40s the membership became less visible, and many lodges closed. During those years, for example, four-fifths of the New York State lodges turned in their charters; most of the remaining lodges were in New York City.

It is impossible to generalize and still accurately represent the many Masonic rites, for even when they use the same title they differ significantly from one lodge to another even within countries. And, even though the written ritual of a given rite is supposed to be identical throughout Freemasonry's component organizations, individual interpretations of the text produce variations in the rituals of each group. The York Rite fraternity has long had a wide membership in America. It consists of four groups organized around a progressive set of degrees: Master Masons, the Royal Arch Chapter, the Council of Royal and Select Masters, and the Commandery of Knights Templar. The organization of Master Masons is also known as the Craft Masonic Lodge, the Blue Lodge, and the Symbolic Lodge. To this lodge, blue symbolized immortality and fidelity.

Masonic writers once believed that Masonry originated with Solomon's Temple and the majority of the symbols of Freemasonry are associated with that structure. For example, Masonic lodge rooms are traditionally based on the design of the Temple and face east. When using a normal room for Masonic rites during the years the society's membership was secret, the temple design with all its symbolic features was drawn on the floor with chalk, charcoal, or clay—which was easily removed so non-Masons would not know a meeting had occurred. By the early eighteenth century there were "tracing-boards": cloths painted with the floor designs formerly drawn temporarily to convert a room into a temple plan. Placed on the floor, the tracing boards signaled the significant stages of the ritual.[12] Later, as in figure 162, such schemes became wall decorations.

Myths and legends connected with the Temple, although now known not to be literally true, are accepted as symbolically true. The pillars of the porch of the Temple are of great significance, and the two pillars appear in countless Masonic images. The one the Masons pictured at the left is called Jachin, a name associated with foundations or establishments; it signifies Jehovah. That on the right is called Boaz, a name that means strength. In Masonic rituals members first pass through the pair of pillars and go up "steps" painted on the floor, which symbolize stages, or degrees of membership. In 1776 a "Plan of the Drawing on the floor at the making of a Mason," was published in London, in *Jachin and Boaz*, a guide to understanding Freemasonry. The book was published in the United States in 1801. On the plan the first "step" is inscribed: "1st deg. or entered Apprentice's step, kneel with the left Knee." The second "step" reads: "2d deg or Fellow Craft's step, Kneel with the Right Knee." The last "step" is titled: "3d or Master's step Kneel with both Knees."[13] Beyond the steps there is usually a Masonic pavement of white and black squares representing life, which is made up of good and evil.

In some Masonic images, there are three columns, which imply wisdom, strength, and beauty, and symbolize the natural law, nature, and creation. They exemplify the three classic orders: Doric, Ionic, and Corinthian, which represent the Master, the Senior Warden, and the Junior Warden. Sets of paired columns, three columns (sometimes seen as a triple branch candleholder), steps, and the Masonic pavement also appear on some Shaker gift drawings.

The Masonic lodge room in the Gilbert House (figure 55) is just three and a half miles from the Lebanon community. Unfortunately it was restored about 1898 and many of the symbols painted on its walls and ceiling are lost. But many of the fifty remaining, and a few others that were recorded before the restoration removed them, are the same the Shakers used. The ceiling was once painted with an all-seeing eye surrounded by heavenly stars. The all-seeing eye is central to Masonic imagery; it symbolizes the Deity, and by analogy His omnipresence. Among the symbols remaining in the room that relate to Shaker images are: steps, the Masonic pavement, paired pillars, the sun, stars, the moon, a circle, a single feather, books, candlesticks, a three-branch candleholder, hearts, a dove with an olive branch, an ark in a ship, keys, a trumpet, swords, a rainbow, ladders, and a royal arch decorated on one side with a Masonic pavement. Ladders, for both the Masons and the Shakers, symbolize Jacob's ladder, the means to heaven. Masonic ladders usually have three rungs for faith, hope, and charity, the progressive steps upward, although some use many more rungs. Both Shaker and Masonic imagery featured clocks. Those in Masonic work have only one hand, pointing to the figure 12. This image comes from the frontispiece in Batty and Thomas Langley's *The Builder's Jewell: or, the Youth's Instructor, and Workman's Remembrances,* first published in London in 1741. Shaker and Masonic painted lines and borders are often decorated with a tessellated zigzag or chevron pattern (see the line around the checkerboard in figure 164). The gift drawing in figure 163 has an all-seeing eye, moons, and stars, above a checkerboard flanked by pillars. The drawing in figure 168 is capped by rainbows. At the center of the lower edge of figure 165, steps lead up to the door of heaven. They are flanked by a pair of trees. Above the door is an all-seeing eye over a cross. The full correspondence between Mason and Shaker symbols could provide an extensive list.

The Masons and Colors

Because of the multifarious nature of Masonry, a variety of meanings have been assigned to Masonic colors, depending on when, where, and by whom they were given. A few mentions of color significances suggest the many meanings and roles they have played for the Masons. White is found in all the ancient mysteries and is part of the investiture of a Masonic candidate. White was also one of the colors of the curtains of the tabernacle of Solomon's Temple, where it symbolized the element of earth, and also purity. It is the basic color of the Masons' apron, which has been the symbol of honorable labor back to the early history of Israel. An added colored edge designates the degree, or level, of the member wearing it.

Blue is the most important Masonic color. It is the color of the first three degrees, which are the most ancient, and the only one, except white, traditionally used in a Master's Lodge. It symbolizes immortality, fidelity, eternity, chastity, and universal brotherhood. Blue also reaches back into antiquity: "and thou shalt make the tabernacle *with* ten curtains of fine twined linen, and blue, and purple, and scarlet" (Exodus 26:1). The robes of the high priest's ephod (a richly embroidered outer vestment), and the ribbon for his breastplate, used blue; men were to wear a blue ribbon above the fringe of their garments. It was the color of the biblical "blue vault of heaven" and the "starry-decked canopy." Pale blue represented prudence and probity.

Yellow refers to the brass of which compasses were made, and the blue to the blue steel of their points. Yellow by itself seems the least important color in Masonic symbolism. Red, scarlet, or crimson are the colors of divine love and the elevated Masonic degree of the Royal Arch. In the higher degrees of Masonry red is as predominating a color as blue is in the lower three degrees.

Green is the emblematic color of a Knight of the Red Cross, and the degree of Perfect Master. It symbolizes the moral resurrection of the candidate, teaching him to be dead to vice in order to be revived in virtue. Some Masons see green as a sign of victory and as a symbol of truth. For others it is a sign of a new creation, and of a moral and physical resurrection. From antiquity black has been a sign of sorrow, grief, and mourning. It is assigned to only a few Masonic degrees. Purple combines the blue craft degree and the scarlet of the Royal Arch. It represents the purple veil between the first blue veil and third scarlet veil of the Temple. Purple is the color of the Royal Arch Council, and members of Grand Lodges wear purple collars and purple-edged aprons.[14]

PAINTED FURNITURE: THE STRIPPED VERSUS THE UNTOUCHED

Painted Shaker and worldly wood suffered equally during the first half of this century as collectors took off original paints. But there was much more worldly material to outlast the vigor of those who preferred things in natural woods, and collectors of the worldly stopped damaging their objects nearly a decade before most Shaker collectors became aware of the aesthetic and monetary value of original surfaces. Fortunately, there have always been a few who understood that the finishing surfaces were the final statements of the makers. Antiquarian collectors of worldly vernacular, such as Nina Fletcher Little, who began to buy pieces in the 1920s, prized equally the paint and the wood under it, for both had belonged to earlier people. (She owned a small group of Shaker pieces; figure 17 was one of them.) For collectors like Little, wear or changes were records of cultural and of art historical developments. A few early collectors of Shaker material, such as Dr. J. J. Gerald McCue and Erhart Muller, understood both the historic and aesthetic value of pieces with original Shaker surfaces. Recently Gerald McCue told me that at an early point he tried to educate other collectors to buy only untouched objects, but he soon found that communicating his understanding made it more difficult to acquire a bargain at auctions.

The appreciation for original surfaces on worldly objects grew in the 1960s in part because of the new aesthetic for worn and scumbled surfaces in the work of such artists as Jasper Johns and Robert Rauschenberg. They had learned from the Abstract Expressionists the excitement of a dialogue between painterly gestures and the visibility of the supporting material. In those 1960s paintings, the play of paint on canvas is very like the aesthetic of worn paint against worn wood.

As the prices for untouched worldly pieces gradually grew during the late 1960s the custom of stripping surfaces diminished. Although not instantly popular, Dean A. Fales's 1972 *American Painted Furniture, 1660–1880* helped make old paint respectable by featuring painted furniture that fit neatly into the "country" or folk art tradition. A major change in collecting habits was signaled by the results of the 1974 Huntington sale. Christopher Huntington of Mount Vernon, Maine, was one of the few dealers to champion the untouched, and the very high prices brought during the sale of his stock surprised nearly everyone. *Maine Antiques Digest* (established the year before) disseminated the surprising prices and the excitement they caused. The fallout was that many, particularly some younger dealers, who loved the untouched but feared to invest money in it, felt inspired to reevaluate what they bought and sold.

In 1975 I included in my book, *The Impecunious Collector's Guide to American Antiques,* a chapter titled "Buy It Ratty and Leave It Alone." That publication made the untouched, the grungy surface, acceptable, even desired. "A Kirk surface" became a term to describe the condition of an object among dealers, collectors, and conservators. Unfortunately Shaker material was still treated as a separate category. In Fales's book only four of the more than five hundred objects shown are Shaker. Two were pictured in black and white, and a blue table, and the yellow chair seen here as figure 142, were in color. It would be nearly 1980 before most Shaker collectors joined the collectors of worldly artifacts in prizing original surfaces.

Gerald McCue developed one of the great collections of untouched Shaker artifacts. He purchased his first piece from the dealers Edward and Faith Andrews in 1946 and continued to collect until about 1960. He reports that in their early years as dealers, the Andrewses regularly refinished their Shaker material, noting that at least three of the pieces in their book *Shaker Furniture* (1937) had been structurally altered or stripped by them. (The trestle table in Plate 3 was shortened, and sanded; the sideboard in plate 28 was cleaned down; the double chest of drawers in plate 42 had its red paint removed.) However, by the time McCue bought his initial piece, the Andrewses were emphasizing original surfaces. After McCue wrote them his first check, Faith Andrews said to him, "Now you own it, but please promise me not to change it for a year," feeling that by then he would understand the importance of the totally old. The Andrewses also encouraged McCue to visit William Lassiter, Curator of History and Art at the New York State Museum in Albany, to learn more about the Shakers. The museum owns a large collection of Shaker artifacts, many of them acquired directly from the Shakers. When McCue went to see Lassiter sometime between 1947 and 1949, Lassiter was sanding a New Lebanon piece. He said to McCue, "I hate Shaker finishes."

In the late 1960s the standard look for usable Shaker funiture was still that which had been stripped. When the George and Gladys Jordan collection of refinished Shaker objects was sold in 1968, prices were so high that the press reported a new interest by collectors and museum curators in Shaker materials. But by the time of the sale of William Lassiter's personal collection at Sotheby's on November 13, 1981 (he had died in 1977), a revolution had occurred; Lassiter's stripped Shaker pieces brought so little that Sotheby's lost money because they had guaranteed a greater amount. (The printed material and small items he had not touched brought high prices. Contributing to the new understanding of why Shaker things should not be refinished was the display next to the Lassiter objects of the Howard and Jean Lipman collection of folk art and painted funiture. It was to be sold the next day. The colorful and beautifully worn Lipman pieces made the Shaker furniture look raw.) A sale held the previous June by Ed Casazza in Portland, Maine, included a number of untouched Shaker pieces, and their prices left Sam Pennington, the editor of *Maine Antiques Digest,* gasping when he reported the auction in August, 1981. "[The] Maine Shaker auction was not for the faint of heart. A single rocking chair in chrome yellow paint sold for $8,000, an oval four-fingered box, probably painted with paint from the same can, made a record $1,550 . . . ." Later in the piece Pennington noted: "It does seem a curious and contradictory fact of Shaker collecting that while buyers will occasionally pay a premium for old paint . . . they generally seem to prefer major pieces refinished. One dealer explained that this was because the premier collection, that of Edward and Faith Andrews, was primarily refinished, as were most of the Shaker pieces pictured [in their books]. This led to collectors preferring to buy just what they saw in books."[15]

THE SHAKERS' USE OF COLOR

Eighteenth-century Shaker objects used the strong colors of the third quarter of the eighteenth century, but by 1810 many were painted with the lighter, brighter colors of the new era. In Shaker hands, color provided clarity, and some variation in what were standard forms that had been developed for reproductive convenience and theological unity. Blue, yellow, red, sometimes patterned surfaces, and very occasionally green, played against consciously marble-smooth white walls, colored woodwork, and painted floors with colorful rugs. Through such rooms moved Believers in colorful clothing, and crisp, white or modestly colored curtains hung at the windows.

It is now hard to visualize how colorful the Shakers' world was throughout most of the nineteenth century. On many of the untouched pieces the varnish put over paint to make it easy to clean has darkened. But the greatest alteration occurred because so much of what they made in wood has been stripped of its final finish of paint or stain. The color began to disappear from all American furniture at the end of the nineteenth century for several reasons: the arts and crafts movement emphasized natural materials, and the colonial revival encouraged the use of uncolored wood in early American homes. These stylistic emphases joined the concurrent moral cry for cleanliness as a virtue, in encouraging many users of old pieces to strip them to expose the wood. Echoing these new ideas, most reproductions of earlier painted work were produced without a colored finish.

The wholesale stripping of old objects, and the dissemination of reproductions without color, so falsified our understanding of the past that by 1900 America's early years were recalled as drab. The newly cleaned furniture and house woodwork seemed to support that belief. As the colonial revival moved into the twentieth century, it assumed many guises, and joined the "frontier aesthetic" of glistening knotty pine and shining maple popularized in endless cowboy movies.

Shaker color was stripped away for two reasons: Shaker material was seen in light of the revised colonial aesthetic, and various scholars touted it as a precurser of modernism, a movement that valued the visibility of the basic materials. In Chapter X, Edward Deming Andrews, and other arbiters of the "correct" Shaker look, will be seen as natural products of their time. Here it is sufficient to mention that in his first article, published in *Antiques* in 1928, Andrews seems perplexed about how to handle Shaker color: "The vogue for finishing furniture 'in the wood' was anticipated by the Shakers a century ago," was his main point, even though he wrote briefly about the Shakers' use of color.[16]

The Meaning of Colors to the Shakers
The 1845 Millennial Laws listed colors, but not their intentions or meanings. They reaffirmed the central icons, the meetinghouses, as white, with blue and white inside. As before, buildings were to be increasingly darker as they were further from the public eye (see figure 126). Economics did not play a major role in this gradation, for lighter colors were not necessarily more expensive than darker ones. White, made of white lead and a filler, was not an expensive paint. Prussian blue, chrome green, and chrome yellow were costly.

A manuscript booklet entitled "Explanation of the Holy City" accompanied the *Holy City* plan given as a gift on March 16, 1843 (see figure 48). The manuscript defines the role or meaning of a number of colors, and gives them a variety of contexts in heaven. Since New Lebanon, called by then by its spiritual name, the Holy Mount, was to become like heaven, the colors are helpful in understanding how Believers thought about them. The entries have been arranged here by color. Each entry begins with the number assigned it in the booklet. It corresponds to the number on the drawing.

Blue

1. The blue without the walls shows the waters of life, spreading thro'out the whole earth for the healing of the Nations.

9. Spring of the eternal love;—Its waters are blue.

24. The Saints Spring of Love.—Its waters are blue.

28. Spring of love belonging to the outer court.—Its waters are blue.

36. Mothers Spring of joy. Its waters are blue.

37. The Saviors Spring of Love. Its waters are blue.

53. Fountain of the holy waters of life.—This fountain is fed by seven springs . . . . their waters are clear as christial, and of a blewish cast.

Dark Color
[Black]

1. The dark color roundabout the circular wall, shows that all is darkness without. [The four edges of the drawing were colored with the same watercolor black.]

Gold and Yellow
[all the streets within the large square are yellow]

10. . . . [A]nd the golden street on either side [of the river] was 30 feet broad.

10. . . . [U]pon the pleasant green[i.e., lawns] & golden quays. . . .

54. The square around about the pillars & fountain, is the meeting ground paved with gold.

54. The gardens and orchards round about the Holy Fountain and golden meeting ground are very large and beautiful.

67. There are alters, paved around about with gold . . . . These pillars are bright gold built in a manner to reflect light to an astonishing degree . . . .

68. The four yellow bars are gold shining bars of justice or judgment. The three yellow circles are three seats of gold.—The middle and largest is for the angel of Judgment. The one on the right, as facing the center of the temple, is for the recording angel, & the one on the left, is for the witnessing angel.

Green
[On the drawing, the dominating walls are green, the color of jasper stone as designated in Revelations]

1. The green shows the walls of the City.

10. . . .[U]pon the pleasant greens [i.e., lawns].

29. Spring of charity belonging to the outer court.—Its waters are light green.

67. The circle of green is a wall around about the four and twenty pillars of light.

68. The circle of green is a wall around about the temple of judgment.

Purple

38. The Saviors Spring of peace. Its waters are purple.

Red, Crimson, Pink

1. The red shows the streets of the suburbs.

9. Spring of eternal Blessing.—Its waters are pink color.

11. Spring of eternal power.—Its waters are a light crimson color.

25. The Saints Spring of Comfort.—Its waters are dark crimson or pink.

68. The red circle is the place for the spirit that is brot to judgment.

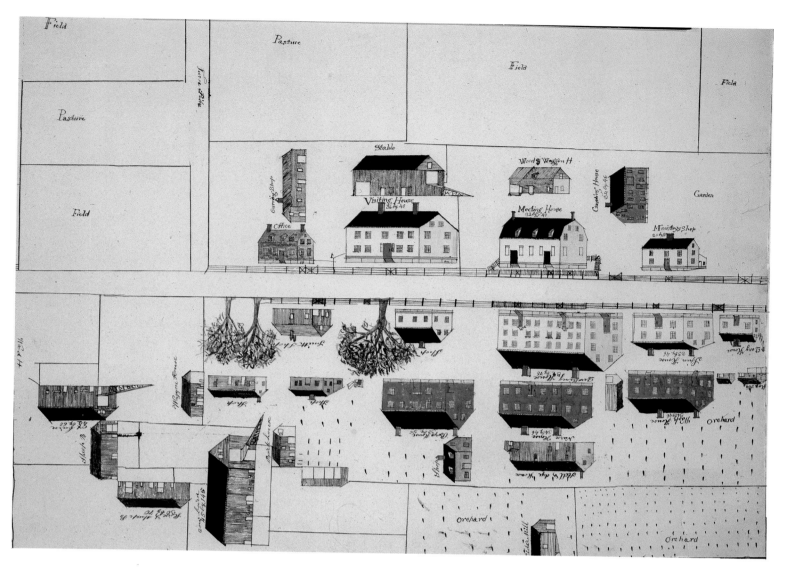

68. The place of the soul brot to judgment is a red circle and a white floor within.—This circle being small and red shows that the soul is encircled with a wall of tribulation, that it can turn neither to the right or to the left.

White

2. They who are redeemed from among men, continually worship God their Father, having his name written in their foreheads & being clad in beautiful white garments; these are Saints of the most high God . . . .

10. . . . [T]he snow white lambs are dancing & jumping about in mery glee.

12. Spring of eternal Wisdom.—Its waters are white.

39. Mother Spring of Union. Its waters are white.

68. The white floor [under a red circle—see red] shows that purity is the result of honestly and thankfully coming to judgment.[17]

Calvin Green, one of the few Shakers to write about the meaning of color to Believers, left two helpful documents. The first includes:

I will here state that I have ever observed Green *color, in vision, to be a sign of an increase. All things in a growing state are green.* Red, *always denotes sufferings—tribulation.* White, *represents clean; purified from the stains of sin—accepted.* Blue, *represents heavenly.* Azure blue, *or peach blow color represents Love.* Gold, *denotes pure—rich in goodness.* Silver, *when spiritually seen, represents Union, for it is common currency.—Every color has its peculiar meaning, & to such as understand, all such appearances are instructive.*[18]

126. "A PLAN OF ALFRED MAINE" (DETAIL)
By Joshua H. Bussell
August 28, 1845
Ink and watercolor on paper
Full sheet: H. 21⅝" W. 39⅜"
Library of Congress, Washington, D.C., Geography and Map Division

In another writing Calvin Green reflected Isaac Newton's understanding of color:

[T]here are seven original colors in nature, namely Red, Orange, Yellow, Green, Blue, Indigo and Violet. All other colors originate from these seven: all the various shades of colors are certain mixtures and modifications of these as has been proved to a demonstration. However, black is considered as a destitution of all colors. Hence, as colors are the glory of the natural world, and are the reflecting rays of light, therefore black is put to represent a destitution of all light and glory both in a natural and spiritual sense. And pure white is taken to represent the light and highest glory of heavenly objects, because white is a certain mixture of the glory of all colors. Hence heavenly beings are represented so frequently as arrayed in "garments clean and white" &c., and clouds of brightnes are put to represent the glory of God. This purity and glory of the seven heavenly colors are the shining forth of the glory and brightness of "the seven / lamps of fire, which are the seven spirits of God." By the shining of the Sun thro' a proper medium, that is, thro' a prism or glass vessel having three equal sides, so as to be reflected into seven principles the seven natural colors are produced. This prism is a lively representation of the three universal principles by which all things are brought into existence; namely the generator, the bearer and the substance brought into being. But there is nothing in nature that has any real color of itself on earth but things are being put in a certain position, and having certain qualities which attract the rays of light so as to produce the peculiar reflection, is that which produces the colors of each kind. These beautiful colors that decorate the natural creation, are an emanation from and a representation of the shining of the eternal sun of all glory and its operation upon the "seven lamps of fire," by and thro' which the orders and proportion of Divine glory are reflected and manifested "throughout all the earth" according to the natural order of things.

And as colors and beauty in the natural world are caused by the arrangement and qualities of all things that attract the rays of light and show forth beauty and glory to their order and qualities; so all Divine glory is seen in all things, and in all things according to their order, and those qualities which attract the rays of "the Divine sun or righteousness." Therefore we see that all glory emanates from the Divine elements; and that the glory of all beings here and hereafter, must be in exact proportion to the right order and principles which they have gained so as to attract the Divine light, for by its reflecting rays their glory according to its degree will be declared.[19]

A small elongated octagonal gift drawing in the library at Sabbathday Lake is inscribed: "Written with blue ink on yellow paper. Blue signifies peace Gold signifies Glory earned." The ink is black and the paper white. Either this was a preparatory drawing for a more colorful work, or the paper and the ink have changed colors.[20] When I discussed colors with Brother Arnold Hadd at Sabbathday Lake in 1988 he said that according to a New England tradition, blue is the color the devil hates; blue and white signify heaven; yellow and brown suggest the earth; and red means tribulation. He also referred to the Elder Calvin Green material quoted above.

Colors were so much a part of Shaker life that a mode-ometer (a device used to set the tempo while practising songs; during worship the songs set the tempo of the dances.) had its speeds designated by colors. The stick—$6\frac{5}{8}$ inches long, $1\frac{3}{4}$ inches wide, and $\frac{3}{8}$ inches thick—is painted in blocks of color, and a movable stop could be slid along the stick and fixed at a particular one. From the stop, a weighted string swung like a metronome, and set the desired tempo.[21]

The Meaning of Colors in Shaker Textiles

During the years of the Era of Manifestations, gift drawings regularly depicted the shapes and colors of heavenly objects. On New Year's Day, 1842, the Ministry at Hancock received the gift of the "heavenly costume":

[For the Brothers there would be] a pair of beautiful fine Trousers, as white as snow; these resemble a garment of purity, with many shining stars thereon. The buttons of a sky blue color and the appearance of them like glass. A jacket of a sky blue color also, with gold buttons thereon; and on these are wrought in fine needlework, many elegant and pretty flowers of different colors.

A fine white silk handkerchief, bordered with gold, to tie about the neck; this resembles a band of Holy Love; and Heavenly union. O then let these heavenly graces shine.

The beautiful jacket resembles a garment of meekness, and sincerity, peace and goodwill.

A coat of heavenly brightness, of twelve different colors, which cannot be compared to any natural beauties, for no mortal eye hath ever seen the glory of my holiness; saith Eternal Wisdom.

A pair of heavenly shoes, perfectly white . . . . These are a preparation of peace and a mark of humility, and that ye may walk softly before your God are ye shod with these.

A fine fur hat, of a silver color, which is to shine upon your heads, even as your holy faith in your Mother's work, doth cause you to shine.

For both Brethren, and Sisters, is a white pocket handkerchief of fine linen, these are tokens of honesty, simplicity, love, peace, and purity. Upon these are printed each one's names, and under this, is a seal of approbation and love, in the forms of a little star.

. . . Now the Sister's garments are these . . .

A gown of heavenly brightness, even like that of the Brethren's coats which have twelve very beautiful colors and do shine exceedingly, these are the emblems of holiness, virtue, and purity. A pair of Silver colored Shoes, resembling true innocence, and are for way marks to guide your feet in your Mother's lovely path.

A fine muslin cap with beautiful trimmings, also a pretty Color [i.e., collar] and handkerchief for the neck.

On these are many stars and Diamonds, and your names are also written thereon. These are garments of meekness, simplicity, freedom, gospel love, and heavenly Union towards each other.

A Bonnet of silver color, trimmed with white ribbons, also a pair of blue silk gloves. These denote holy faith, and true honesty, and cheerful cross bearing.[22]

As Beverly Gordon reports: "Believers were told they might use any color they could dye themselves, and Shaker dyebooks, mostly dating between 1830 and 1840, included recipes for shades of red and scarlet, orange, brown, beige, rust, blue, gray, slate, yellow, lavender, and purple."[23] Another list adds black, lead or mouse color, salmon, pink, green, drab, brown, crimson, buff, and blue-black.[24] Of all these colors only yellow, orange, and gold were limited in early Shaker clothing. The feelings against drab became so great that about 1847 drab overcoats were abandoned and dark gray was adopted.[25] After the advent of aniline, or synthetic, dyes in 1856, the Shakers embraced the stronger colors they made possible.

Silk neckerchiefs, and later berthas (figure 127) added striking color. On New Year's Day, 1832, every Sister at South Union, Kentucky, wore a silk neckerchief made from the silkworms

127 A–F. FOUR NECKERCHIEFS AND TWO BERTHAS

A: (bottom of stack) Kentucky; 1835–65; rose and white iridescent silk with self-stripe border; H. 36½" W. 35"

B: Kentucky; 1835–65; green and rose iridescent silk with green and white borders; H. 36" W. 35"; small initial "S" in middle

C: Kentucky; 1835–65; light tan and rose producing gold iridescent silk; H. 33½" W. 32"

D: Kentucky; 1835–65; purchased from Canterbury Church Family; pink with light and dark blue borders and red fringe; H. 38" W. 36¼"

E: Purchased from Mount Lebanon; 1870–90; probably Shaker-made tan iridescent silk producing areas of blue; black lace; four blue glass buttons; H. 14¹/₁₆" W. 19¼"

F: Purchased from Mount Lebanon; 1870–90; probably Shaker-made red iridescent silk producing areas of purple; black lace; white lace; five purple glass buttons; H. 14½" W. 19⁵/₁₆"

Collection of the Shaker Museum and Library, Old Chatham, New York

their members cultivated. A year later the Brothers, who had been envious of the neckerchiefs, received silk neckbands and ties.[26] On October, 13, 1833, the *Albany Evening Journal* reported "The Shakers, near Lexington, Ky. have commenced the raising of silk-worms, and the preparing and manufacture of silk."[27] Gordon reports Shaker silk-dying recipes for scarlet, blood red, orange, slate color, and yellow.[28] Andrews lists dyes for orange, slate, brown, red, crimson, blue, green, black, and purple silk.[29] Silk neckerchiefs were traded and sold to the world and to other Shaker communities. In the 1850s David Parker traveled to South Union and bought many for the Sisters at Canterbury,[30] even though the 1845 Millennial Laws had sought to outlaw "gay silk handkerchiefs."[31]

An account from Watervliet gives directions for dying cotton madder red, catechu brown, fancy blue, London brown, copperas, orange, yellow, green, and slate; wool could be black, orange, fancy blue, yellow, green, scarlet, lavendar, madder red, and drab.[32] In 1845 the Shakers "colour 3 runs of yellow yarn for the office," and in May of 1850 an Englishman named John Robins came from Tyringham to New Lebanon to teach bleaching and coloring. Of the "33 receipts [recorded] from his own mouth," he covered blue, yellow, purple, and orange, for silk, wool, and cotton. In September, among other colors, they dyed wool yellow for carpet binding.[33] (Textiles are further discussed under specific colors later in this chapter, particularly under blue.)

Early textiles and gift drawings that have not been exposed to sunlight are now a good means to correct our understanding of colors used on wood, or other easily damaged surfaces, for during any given period, colors tend to be similar on everything. (Susan Buck has found that the pigments used in paints for the furniture and gift drawings paints were often the same, although those used for the drawings would have been bound in gum arabic.) The color of painted wood, even when left alone, usually fades somewhat from exposure to sunlight, but surviving textiles and drawings are often treasured pieces preserved in chests and cupboards where they are protected from damaging light. Beverly Gordon, writing in *Shaker Textile Arts* in 1980, expressed surprise that the colors of Shaker and worldly textiles are more alike than the colors of Shaker and worldly furniture and architecture.[34] She was able to make this observation because the visual closeness of Shaker and worldly textiles is easy to see; but many painted wood products had been coated with varnish, which has darkened, or have had their paint removed. When Gordon published her book, many collectors were still stripping the paint from their Shaker furniture.

Shaker Finishes on Wood

How the Shakers finished their furniture is one of the most intriguing interlacings of philosophy and practicality in the history of design. It involves raw wood, paint without varnish over it, paint covered with varnish, and, eventually, varnish on unpainted wood. The 1821 Millennial Laws do not mention color except for an injunction against soiling the outside of a painted building: "No kind of liquid matter may be emptied out the windows of our painted buildings."[35] There are cautions against wearing out the surfaces of walls, beds, rungs of chairs, and furniture in general.[36]

In 1841 Brother Philemon Stewart received by inspiration from the spirit of Joseph Meacham a list of what could be stained, painted, and varnished, and what could not be varnished over.[37] (Many of the ideas were already being acted upon.) This listing was developed further in the 1845 Millennial Laws where color and/or varnish is included in fifteen laws distributed in four sections of parts II and III. The most extensive list occurs in Part III section IX; Law 3 acknowledges a gradation of colors: the meetinghouse is white outside with "a bluish shade" inside on the walls. Houses and shops should be uniform in color, but the shops should be a darker shade than the dwelling house. This hierarchy of light to dark was both visual—putting the focus on a community's place of worship—and to a degree economic, for clay-based pigments—raw sienna, burnt sienna, raw umber, and burnt umber—were cheap. But both red lead and white lead were also comparatively inexpensive. Downing in 1850 agrees with this color gradation: "Browns and dark grays are suitable for barns, stables, and outbuildings, which it is desirable to render inconspicuous—but for dwellings, unless very light shades of these latter colors are used, they are apt to give a dull and heavy effect in the country."[38]

Law 4 has the floors of the dwelling houses, if stained at all, a reddish yellow, the shop floors, a yellowish red. Law 5 asks that the wooden buildings facing the street be a lightish hue and not red, brown, or black. Law 6 again says that only the meetinghouse may be white, although various Shaker-made views of Shaker communities show all the buildings belonging to a Church Family as white (see figure 126). By this time, for some in the world, white was found too bright for the eyes. Downing wrote: "white is a color which we think should never be used except upon buildings a good deal surrounded by trees, so as to prevent its glare, we should make it [the white paint] fawn or drab color before using it."[39]

Law 7 again asks that barns and back buildings, such as houses for storing wood, if painted at all, should be dark: red, brown, or lead color, or something of the kind, unless they front on the road or are easily seen. Then they should be of a medium color. (The 1860 "Rules and Orders," concerning paint colors inside and outside buildings, are discussed in Chapter IX, under "Relaxing the Rules," p.193).

Law 8 lists what may not be painted or oiled: cart or ox wagon bodies, lumber wagons, sleigh boxes, sleds or sleighs (unless they are the ones used at the office for trips where they will be seen by the world), wheelbarrows, hand-cart bodies, hand sleds used for rough works, hoe handles, fork stales (used for manure), rake stales, broom and mop handles not to be sold, plough beams, milking stools, and all such articles used heavily, whether indoors or outside.

Law 9 lists what may be painted: all cart and wagon wheels and gearing or working parts, carriages and sleighs for "nice use," wheelbarrows, hand carts, and hand sleds used exclusively for "nice use." Things that may be stained or oiled are ox yokes and snow shovels. The frames of carts, wagons and gates may be put together with paint in the joints (where the parts touch), to stop rot, but they may not be completely painted.

Law 10 details what may be varnished. (As had been traditional for centuries, and as Downing pointed out in 1850, varnishing over anything made it easier to clean.) Varnish, if used in a dwelling house, may be applied only to the movables such as tables, stands, bureaus, cases of drawers, desks, boxes, drawer faces, chests, and chairs. Carriages used exclusively for riding or "nice use," banisters, and hand rails might also be varnished. Oval or "nice" boxes may be stained reddish or yellow but not varnished.

Drawer pulls made of hard woods, and usually not painted or varnished, were so favored over brass pulls that in 1833 Henry DeWitt of New Lebanon could note with pride the turning of two hundred "drawer buttons" in two days.[40] In 1840 some brass knobs were removed, as we have seen, and replaced by wooden knobs, but not all Shaker pieces were so changed. The earliest dated piece owned by the Shaker Museum and Library is a chest dated 1798, and it had an interior drawer, below a till, with a brass knob.[41] As mentioned, a chest of drawers made at Union Village about 1836 has round brass pulls (figure 38); and in 1869 the guests from South Union saw small white and brass knobs on "little drawers of boxes, tables &c." at Mount Lebanon. Later in the century, in a reverse action, some wooden knobs were taken off drawers in Hancock's 1830 Brick Dwelling House and patterned pottery knobs installed.

The role of knobs on worldly furniture is equally varied over time. The first pulls used in America were much like early Shaker-made wooden knobs. About 1680 brass pulls became fashionable, and from then on higher style furniture had bright brasses, which played a role in enriching and organizing facades. Wood pulls always remained an alternative on vernacular pieces (see figure 21), and when broad, flat, round brass pulls became fashionable about 1820, the wooden knobs usually took on their form (see figure 20). When writing about chests of drawers in his 1839 *An Encyclopaedia of Cottage, Farm, and Villa Architecture and Furniture,* John Claudius Loudon stressed the value of wooden knobs over brass ones: "Knobs of the same wood as the furniture . . . are now generally substituted, as in most other pieces of furniture, for brass. They harmonize better and do not tarnish; besides, the fashion is, at present, comparatively new in London, and this confers on them a certain degree of factitious elegance, viz., that of novelty and fashion."[42]

The Shakers, very conscious of what would show wear during the Millennium, generally used unpainted hard-wood knobs on otherwise painted pieces during the early years. The drawer faces were painted, usually without an overcoat of varnish; since careful handling was expected, it was thought that they would not show wear. (There are at least two early chests with drawers made in the Canterbury Community that have their only coat of paint continuing over their wooden knobs. One is in a private collection, the other was given to Canterbury by Helen Upton.) The assumption that Believers would not touch the drawer fronts did not prove true, and the 1845 Laws included under what may be varnished: "drawer fronts." From about 1860 the carcasses of many pieces were painted, sometimes under varnish, but every surface likely to be touched was varnished with no paint under it. The worktable in figure 203 has been varnished directly on the wood of the door, drawers, and slide; the carcass, including the back, is painted red. A similar attention to painted and unpainted areas occurred on a few worldly pieces: some eighteenth-century Windsor chairs, which were invariably painted and often varnished over, had unpainted but varnished mahogany or walnut arms, since the dark arms would not show wear. (This contrast occurred also on a few higher-styled painted worldly armchairs of the same date.)[43] In the nineteenth century, armchairs, such as those now grouped under the heading of "Boston rockers," had unpainted, varnished, dark-wood arms.

Wood that is not painted generally needs its grain filled before varnishing. In 1880 Elder Giles Avery of Mount Lebanon wrote: "To prepare hard woods to varnish use—*Filling varnish*—prepared on purpose to rub off and rub down. *Or use beeswax* dissolved in Turpentine, rubbed on with a rag."[44] It has recently been discovered that the Shakers on occasion use gum size under paint as a means of filling the wood grain; producing a smooth surface, the size saved paint by making thinner or fewer coats sufficient. (See discussion of figure 132.)

Varnish, with or without color under it, could change color quickly. In a journal entry in November 1816, Isaac Newton Youngs noted: "Made two timepieces . . . . Put on to these faces a last coat of copal varnish, but I find it to be a poor way, it turns yellow etc."[45] Varnish could also make things seem too slick. In 1861 Isaac Youngs wrote: "There is great *proclivity* in this, our day, for fixing up matters very nice, & the varnish has to go on to the cup-boards, drawers &c.& the paint on to the floors, everything has to be so slick that a fly will slip up on it!"[46]

The question of when to varnish and when not to varnish continued to intrude on the joint concerns of practicality and housekeeping. On May 23, 1865, Daniel Boler of the Mount Lebanon Ministry wrote from Watervliet, where he was temporarily in residence, to Orren Haskin, at Mount Lebanon:

At [a meeting] it was unanimously agreed that Tables, Stands, Cases of drawers with Cupboards attached, (& such like wooden furniture which might be termed movable appendages to our dwelling or retiring rooms,) might receive a coat of Varnish—Since that time there has been several quite prominent deviations from that decision—The practice of papering some of our plastered walls has been one means of promoting the use of Varnish, and a desire to look very nice indeed, another—It is quite possible that the time has arriven to have another general council held on the same subject— "The world has moved" since that time—What the Deacons may say about dollars and cents, can be repeated as occasion may require, or opportunity offer in the future—In the present case as touching the use of Varnish on the wood work of our dwellings in the Sanctuary [Ministrys' quarters in the meetinghouse] at the Mount, we have unitedly decided to have what varnish is used, put into the last coat of paint—Yet some of our members are inclined to feel some like the old Indian who did not want or like much pudding in his rum, and finally concluded he did not care about any—however, on the present occasion, I rather believe I guess we had better have some pudding for union and for example sake—[47]

The question of what to varnish and over what kind of undercoat was a prime concern of the Shakers for it mixed theology, practicality, and cost, the three aspects of their life they always discussed at length. In an undated letter (probably during the 1860s) Freegift Wells at Watervliet wrote concerning these matters to Mount Lebanon:

In answer to Brother Gile's [Avery] suggestions concerning the use of paints & varnish—my judgment in the matter &c—I will say, that previous to my residence in the Western country, I had but little knowledge concerning the utility of varnish, but while there I found it was considerable used on various articles of furniture, such as desks—drawcases, clock cases—tables—stands—chests—chairs & the like.

They prepared their varnish themselves, & as I understood, it cost but little more than paint, yet they thought it much more valuable on account of the hard glossy surface which it formed wherever it was used on furniture & made it much easier to clean than that which was painted or stained, as nothing more was necessary than to wipe it of[f] with a wet or damp cloth &c—and I thought it would save much labor in cleaning if the inside work of dwelling houses were varnished, & that the extra expense would be but trifling.

I have seen furniture made of curled maple & varnished over without any kind of stain, & it would remain of the same complexion as when first planed, yet as smooth as glass, & as impenetrable with ink, or any such stain. But as there did not seem to be much liberty for using it here [Watervliet] I have not said much about it, but being called on for my judgement concerning it I must say that I consider it a valuable article for the uses above named, & perhaps many more. Yet I do not think it ought to be brought into common use unles[s] believers learn to make it themselves, & even then it ought to be kept under the same restrictions as paint, otherwise the imprudent & wasteful will make an extravagant use of it.

Question 2nd Is it deemed proper to paint wheelbarrows and hand sleds &c?—My judgment is, that, were two wheelbarrows or handsleds made of exactly one material, & one left in its original state & the other well painted, & both put to one use, with equal exposure to the sun, storms and hardship, I should imagine that there would be but very little if any difference in their duration, because the first failure from rot or decay takes place in the joints where no paint reaches them unless they are put together in paint, which is seldom the case. But such articles well painted are almost always taken better care of & sheltered more from the rains & hot sun, & in this way they will do double the service that those will that are continually exposed to the weather as those not painted are too apt to be, & in this way paint does much good in preserving them & I think may be considered a real benefit, & saving of property, I should therefore recommend the practice.

Question 3rd Is it advisable to stain mop or broom handles for home use? I should without hesitation answer Nay, for it neither adds to their strength or duribility. When the Sisters have a good broom or mop, that performs well, they are apt to be careful of it, whether the handle is painted or not; but if the article is poor, a stained or painted handle will not make them feel very choice of it, & it generally does but little service.

The above impressions have been imbibed from past experiences & observations.

Freegift Wells.

One thing more. It is my impression that it is a wrong practice to paint the inside to tubs—pails— or any kind of wash dishes because the water or milk which stands in such vessels will partake in some degree of the poison contained in the paint; & there has been many stomachs & eyes very much injured by drinking, & washing in water which stood in such vessels. Besides this, hot water & soap suds which it is difficult to always keep from such vessels will soon ruin the paint. Thus I consider that all paint used in that way is worse than lost. Slop pails excepted.[48]

The Shakers recorded many formulas for making paint and varnish. An extensive list is found in a "Receipt Book" probably developed by Elder David Austin Buckingham of Watervliet. (He later passed it on to Rosetta Hendrickson with whom it is often associated, but she seems not to have added to it.) Dated entries range from 1844 to 1857.[49] It included recipes for the stains, paints, and varnishes that follow:

Stains:
Tere-de-Sena, to give a mahogany color "especially when under a coat of Varnish"
For wood and ivory: yellow, red, black
Red stain for wood, leather, paper, etc.

Varnishes, etc.:
Flat copal varnish
Black varnish
Mastic varnish
How to repair varnish
Gum Shelack dissolved in Water
lacker

Paints:
Mahogany color
Paris green for the window blinds, Meeting House, Church Family, Watervliet, 1849
Canterbury Green
Outside Green for New Meeting House [Watervliet]
Blue
Sky blue for New Meetinghouse, Church Family, Watervliet, 1849
White, with Blue Shade [Ministry probably painting both ceilings of living quarters, Watervliet]
To Whiten Hard-finished Walls White wash
Superior Whitewash
Cream color
Cream color "for Meetinghouse fence, & 2d. Order's New Farmer's Shop and Joiners Shop. 1849"
    [Watervliet]

Cream color, New Lebanon Church Family
Cream color, Watervliet Church Family
Cream color, Watervliet Second Family
Ivory
Stone color as used at USA arsenal at West Troy
Gray or stone color
Lead color
Dead color for blackboard
Black
Black for iron
Red for Meetinghouse shed, 1849 [Watervliet]
For removing paint [using a handful of soda in a quart of water: it was applied to doors and drawer
  faces, and "whatever also required and desired"]
Painted cloth for table covers[50]

Shaker documents give recipes for making colors and varnishes, including copal varnish, and common varnish, and suggest what colors to varnish: red, blue, green, yellow, and purple surfaces. "To colour Blue wood" and, "To Colour Pink or red on Wood" are followed by "when dry varnish." There is a recipe employing turpentine, warm water, skim milk, and soap for the cleaning of painted woodwork. The concoction left a beautiful gloss wherever it was used, and removed all stains.[51] Many of the formulas are for outside colors, the surfaces most seen by non-Believers. In 1836 Isaac Newton Youngs recorded painting the expanded Church Family dwelling at New Lebanon using a mix of white lead, French yellow, and chrome yellow.[52]

In her research on Shaker paints and varnishes Susan Buck has found that the recipes in Shaker notebooks, journals, letters, and so forth, were often copied directly from worldly sources, even to using the same punctuation. Following recipes she found in Shaker sources, she made the board of samples in figure 128. The top half was sized before the paint or stain was applied; the lower half was left raw wood. None of the colors have been varnished over. There are no Shaker

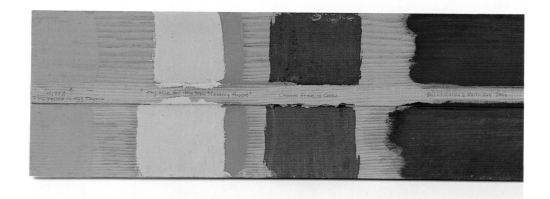

128. MODERN COLORS USING SHAKER RECIPES
Made by Susan Buck, April 12, 1994
The top half sized; colors from left: zinc yellow in egg tempera; "Sky blue for New Meetinghouse," Watervliet; a darker blue made by adding more Prussian blue; chrome green in casein; burnt sienna and vermillion stain
Private collection

recipes for egg tempera, but the physical evidence on two yellow-painted objects (a carpenter's cupboard and a washstand) suggests egg tempera was occasionally used. This type of paint uses egg yolks as the binding medium, but the number of yolks needed to do a large body of work, and the inconvenience of employing it, probably limited its use. A few of the formulas are for paints that use milk as the medium, but these were confined to architectural painting. Most of the paints suspend the pigments in (usually linseed) oil. After 1900, however, the Shakers generally purchased their paint. Despite the presently-held view that the Shakers preferred thinly painted surfaces, Susan Buck has found that although about half the objects that she has studied exhibit thin, almost stain-like coloring, the other half are thickly coated. Her research has not as yet made it clear if there were a category of objects that received stain rather than paint. Although recipes for shellac appear earlier in Shaker records, she has not found it used on furniture before 1870.

The poem "The Shakers' Race" was written by a non-Shaker and published in 1876. It humorously records the sect's practice of allowing the public the most fashionable and expensive paint, while keeping the lesser for themselves. Part of it reads:

The Shakers had a famous fence—
It talked, and talked with common sense:
". . . This fickle climate to endure,
I must be painted—that is sure;
And, as I am no common fence,
And quite a trifle more expense,
Will paint a fashionable white
My front, the most exposed to sight;

My rear, where strangers seldom come,
With ochre colors may be done."
The farmer-deacon, sore afraid,
In haste the miracle obeyed.
He gave the front a coat of white,
With yellow ochre out of sight.
The traitor-fence proclaimed aloud:
"The Shakers are becoming proud!"[53]

Regional Differences

As with the design and construction features discussed in Chapter III, Shaker communities tended to use those colors employed in the world around them. Worldly Maine furniture, for example, generally used brighter colors than that of the rest of New England, and Shaker furniture made in Maine is often more vivid than Shaker pieces made elsewhere. Writing about early Maine Shaker furniture in 1983, Brother Theodore Johnson of Sabbathday Lake noted: "Primitive Maine Shaker furniture may be characterized as substantial, perhaps even heavy, yet vigorous and eminently practical. It bears all the marks of the Maine soil to which its creators' lives were so firmly attached. Pieces of the [early] period are, as we might expect, most commonly made of pine or of maple. Obviously Maine joiners of the period saw little beauty in the natural wood itself, for virtually all pieces from the period are painted or color-stained. An indigo-based blue, mustard yellow, a dark forest green, and a variety of shades of red are the predominant colors."[54] (It is now known that little of the blue Shaker furniture used indigo for its color.)

COLORS

White and Blue

Thomas Sheraton, conscious like Calvin Green of Isaac Newton's ideas on colors, put under the heading "Blue" in his 1803 Dictionary: "Blue and white, blue and black, very light blues and yellow, will harmonize."[55]

Blue and white held a special place in Shaker thinking, and despite the Laws, white was not limited to the meetinghouse. Seven of the Church Family buildings depicted in Joshua H. Bussell's 1845 drawing of Alfred, Maine, are white (see figure 126, and the jacket of this book). On the east side of the road: the "Visiting House," "Meeting House," and "Ministry Shop," on the other side the "Dary House," "Spin House," "Dwelling House," and "Shop." All but the meetinghouse have a blue stripe around them just above the blue-gray foundation. The "Office" is green and has a red roof. The same coloring appears on Bussell's plan of about 1848, except there the meetinghouse also has a blue band, and the green office has a blue band and a black roof.[56]

A basic combination of the American costume of about 1800 was blue and white,[57] and in parts of the world blue has remained the worker's costume. One only has to think of a trip through modern France to realize blue's lingering role in society. Blue became a basic color for Shaker men and women because they were creating heaven on earth, and because the indigo plant, which supplied much of the blue for textiles, was a reliable dyestuff. Blue and white were the dominant colors at Sunday meetings. The first Sabbathday costume for men was a white shirt with blue worsted sleeve ties fastened just above the elbow, a blue waistcoat, and a long blue wool coat. Their breeches, extending just below the knee, were black or blue. (After 1805 breeches were mostly replaced by trousers or pantaloons, a tight form of trousers.) Originally the men wore white socks on the Sabbath and blue ones on other days. After 1806 blue was used less, but by the 1850s it again became so popular that many pieces in other colors were redyed blue. By midcentury the color dominated worship services, intensifying their visual excitement.[58]

When Benson John Lossing visited New Lebanon in 1856 the men were wearing "pantaloons of blue linen, with a fine white stripe in it; vests of a much deeper blue, and plain, made of linsey-woolsey . . . . stout calf-skin shoes and gray stockings . . . . The women wear, on Sunday, some a pure white dress, and others a white dress with a delicate blue stripe in it. Over their necks and bosoms were pure white kerchiefs, and over the left arm of each was carried a large white pocket-handkerchief. Their heads were covered with lawn caps . . . . Their shoes, sharp-toed and high-heeled, according to the fashion of the day when the Society was formed, were made of prunella, of a brilliant ultramarine blue."[59] (See his drawing of the scene, figure 135.)

129. PEG BOARD

New Lebanon, New York, Second Meetinghouse
1822–24
Pine board, maple pegs, painted blue; pegs
secured into the rail by screw-threads
H. 2¾" L. 78½" D. 3"
Private collection

Blue

Blue was one of the most striking of the neoclassical colors, and the Shakers embraced it and imbued it with theological meaning. Prussian blue was first synthesized in Berlin, Germany, in 1704, and became the basic blue pigment used on wood by the world and the Shakers. Indigo was only occasionally employed there. The peg board shown as figure 129 comes from the second meetinghouse at New Lebanon, where it made a line through plaster walls painted light blue (shown in figure 53). The religious significance of blue increased during the Era of Manifestations, from 1837 to 1850. Not only was it used in meetinghouses and religious dress, but it was also discovered to be the color of the home of heavenly Native-American spirits who come from the "Blue City" to unite with living Shakers during worship.[60]

Blue furniture was standard in early nineteenth-century New England, where countless wooden objects were painted various shades of Prussian blue. The set of oval New England boxes in figure 130 displays the typical blue of the first half of the nineteenth century. These boxes differ from the Shaker-made oval boxes in figure 131 in the formation of their overlaps and their tacks. The Shaker boxes have graceful "swallowtails"[61] secured with copper tacks, while the worldly boxes normally use a single, or at least fewer, points, which are held with iron tacks. (Dividing a side into many long swallowtails helps prevent cracking when shrinking occurs.) The use of oval boxes was a very conscious part of Shaker life. In 1819 Ruth Farrington of Union Village, Ohio, sent to the New Lebanon Church Family "a pretty ovel box fil[l]ed with maple shugar." Lucy Wright supervised all the Brothers and Sisters as they shared the treat straight from the box, but with two spoons.[62]

The light blue sample in figure 128 follows the recipe in Buckingham's Receipt Book for "Sky Blue, for New Meetinghouse, Ch[urc]h [Family], Watervliet, 1849: Inside Wash, To 10 #s White Lead, put 1# Prussian Blue, Mixed in Linseed Oil and drying Materials. For the Meetingroom Doors &c. a little Varnish was added."[63] Just to the right of the light sample is the same mix, but with more Prussian blue added. The addition of even more Prussian blue would have brought

130. SET OF NON-SHAKER OVAL BOXES

New England
1810–40
Maple and pine; iron tacks; painted blue
H. 2⅞" L. 6⅛" D. 4½"
H. 2¼" L. 5⅝" D. 4⅛"
H. 2½" L. 4" D. 3"
Private collection

131. SET OF SHAKER OVAL BOXES

New Lebanon, New York
1840–60
Maple and pine; copper tacks; painted blue
H. 4" L. 7⅜" D. 10⅜"
H. 3½" L. 6⅛" D. 9"
H. 3" L. 5" D. 7⅜"
Hancock Shaker Village, Pittsfield, Massachusetts

the color to the intensity seen on the Canterbury counter in figure 132. The pigment, although expensive, was not hard to make, for it was synthesized from iron. (In 1831 a manufacturer in New Bedford, Massachusetts, produced ten thousand pounds of it.) The pigment was not used in milk paints, for it is incompatible with the casein base. Cobalt blue, discovered in 1802, was a very expensive pigment.

The extraordinary tailor's counter in figure 132 reflects social and aesthetic issues that faced the Shakers early in the nineteenth century. It was installed in the third floor of Canterbury's meetinghouse, and located in the south room, the side of the dwelling area used by the Eldresses.[64] Tailoring was an activity suited to the Ministry, for it could easily be stopped for brief periods when community business required attention, or for longer stretches when the Ministry was in residence in the other communities in their Bishopric. The counter is made of pine. There is gum size under the paint to fill the grain and make the wood less absorbent of paint.[65] The base is painted Prussian blue while the top and the interior of the cupboard are a bright orange. The top is varnished although the rest of the counter is not; the knobs are unpainted cherry. The front of the piece is broken into an unbalanced design with two stacks of same-height drawers flanked on the left by a cupboard.

When the counter was made is uncertain. For what is now seen as one of the major pieces of Shaker furniture this may seem surprising, but in Shaker communities changes were constant.[66] The Canterbury meetinghouse was completed in 1792, and from then it has been reworked many times. Pertinent to this counter is that in 1815 the chimneys were rebuilt as stoves replaced fireplaces, the inside stairs were removed and one put in a new addition on the east side, and the inside received its first coat of paint. On December 30, 1872, the members decided not to build a new meetinghouse, and from 1874, meetings were held elsewhere in a larger room. In 1878 the inside woodwork was painted a lighter blue, and the Ministry moved out of the upstairs rooms.[67]

The counter does not date from when the meetinghouse was completed in 1792: it does not have a raised panel in the cupboard door, as found in eighteenth-century Shaker work (see figure 7); it is made with machine-headed cut nails available from about 1815 to the 1830s. When the counter was painted in place, small areas of the paint applied to the room's woodwork in 1815 were covered over. It seems likely, but it is not certain, that the counter was installed shortly after the meetinghouse was renovated in 1815, perhaps as part of that work, but after the walls and other woodwork were painted. Elder Henry Blinn in 1892 wrote in an account of the 1815 alterations to the building: "The color [put on] was dark blue throughout the whole house," and "this coating of paint remained without any additional painting until the year 1878 when the meeting room was repainted with a much lighter and brighter shade . . . . The upper rooms of the building still remain as they were when first painted."[68]

The woodwork of the room in which the counter was used is painted the same blue as the counter, but it covers two or three earlier finishes. Susan Buck reports the first finish on the room's woodwork was a thin, deep red over a gray primer. The second appearance of the woodwork was of a red glaze over a thick coat of deep red. Above these is a layer of plant resin varnish, which could have been a finishing coat for stage two, or perhaps a third stage. Finally, in 1815, the blue

132. TAILOR'S COUNTER
Canterbury, New Hampshire, from the Eldresses' room, south side of third floor in Meetinghouse
About 1815
Pine; cherry knobs; glue size under paint; case painted blue, top and inside of cupboard painted orange; top finished with varnish
H. 38³/₄" W. 104³/₈" D. 25¹/₂"
Collection of the Shaker Museum and Library, Old Chatham, New York

133. BOX

Mount Lebanon, New York, Church Family
1860–80
Printed label reading "Tabitha Lapsly" on one
end; she lived at Lebanon from 1834 to her death
in 1900
Heavy cardboard finished with blue paper
H. 13¾" L. 19½" D. 14"
The Sisters' caps shown as figure 106 were found
in this box.
Collection of the Shaker Museum and Library,
Old Chatham, New York

that matches the counter was applied. On the east wall of the room there are clear indications of where the counter was built in: one of the iron brackets that held it is still attached to the wall, and there are corresponding holes in the counter; there are also lines of orange and blue paint on the wall, and a line of blue on the floor that match the shape of the outer edge of the base molding, from when the piece was painted in place. (There is also a thin line of yellow on the counter's bottom molding from when the floor was painted yellow *after* the counter was installed.) To install the piece, workmen cut away portions of the chair rail and baseboard *after* they were painted blue, and some orange paint from the counter can be seen over these cuts. The sequence, then, is: meetinghouse finished 1792; interior blue paint applied 1815; chair rail and baseboard cut to receive the piece; piece installed; piece painted; floor painted. Is the piece much later than 1815? The blue of the room's woodwork matches the blue of the counter. The shallow neoclassical proportions of the piece suggest that a date of about 1815 is likely; later pieces tend to be built deeper.

It seems surprising that there are so few pieces of blue Shaker furniture, since the color was theologically so important. Blue was ubiquitous in Shaker textiles, standard in their gift drawings, and common in worldly pieces. There are a few blue Shaker wood-boxes, square and oval boxes, and pails. Some chairs were painted blue early in the nineteenth century at Pleasant Hill, Kentucky.[69] Blue Shaker chairs were made for sale: on March 7, 1814, "one set of blue chairs" made by Richard McNemar of Union Village, Ohio, was sold into the world for $5.50.[70] The blue heavy cardboard domed box in figure 133 held the bonnets of Tabitha Lapsly, who died at Mount Lebanon in 1900. (Four bonnets found in the box are shown in figure 106). In the box they were supported on paper forms. Tabitha Lapsly's name appears in letterpress printing on a label at one end.

Benson John Lossing made a composite watercolor of his separate sketches of Shaker dress (figure 134). He also painted a view of "The March" (figure 135). The Brother at the left of the first, in "Worship Costume," has a blue vest, as do the Brothers in "The March." In Lossing's watercolors the Sisters wore blue shoes, although now the color is somewhat faded. The 1840s or 1850s worshipper's wool vest in figure 136 was purchased at Hancock. Both the dark blue outside, and the glazed light blue inside, have pockets and there are two "tails" at the back. The blue prunella-covered shoes from Canterbury in figure 137 are of the same date as the vest. The New Lebanon "comfortable," a soft, probably down-filled, quilt (figure 138) is blue on one side and butternut on the other and tied-and-knotted with green yarn. On one corner of the brown side is an inscription in faded ink: "MINISTRY 1857." The blue cloth Canterbury Sisters' gloves in figure 139 are lined with muskrat fur, and were probably made early in this century.

134. SHAKER DRESS SEEN AT
NEW LEBANON, NEW YORK

By Benson John Lossing, combining various
drawings of individual members
August, 1856
Pencil and watercolor on paper
H. 5" W. 8"
The Huntington Library, San Marino, California

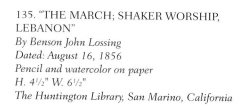

135. "THE MARCH; SHAKER WORSHIP,
LEBANON"
By Benson John Lossing
Dated: August 16, 1856
Pencil and watercolor on paper
H. 4¹/₂" W. 6¹/₂"
The Huntington Library, San Marino, California

136. VEST
Probably New Lebanon, New York, or Hancock,
Massachusetts
Initials "E.M." stitched on inside
1840–60
Dark blue wool; thin light blue glazed lining,
linen or cotton
H. 26" W. 20" D. 1¹/₂"
Collection of the Shaker Museum and Library,
Old Chatham, New York

137. PAIR OF SISTERS' SHOES
Canterbury, New Hampshire
1840–60
Leather and blue prunella
Each: H. 5" W. 3¹/₈" L. 10"
Collection of the Shaker Museum and Library,
Old Chatham, New York

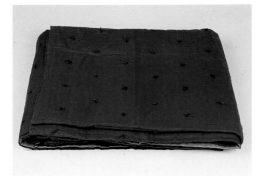

Right:
138. COMFORTABLE
New Lebanon, New York
Ink inscription on underside: "MINISTRY 1857"
Cotton; top blue, bottom brown, green ties; goose down filling
L. 81" W. 32⅞" D. 3"
Collection of the Shaker Museum and Library, Old Chatham, New York

Far right:
139. PAIR OF GLOVES
Canterbury, New Hampshire
Early twentieth century
Wool dyed blue; muskrat fur
L. 13¼" W. 5⅜" D. 4"
Collection of the Shaker Museum and Library, Old Chatham, New York

The Shakers mixed their much-loved blue wool with wool of other shades to make desired degrees of bluish material. In 1837, overcoat material was to be "⅘ blue. ⅔ of this should be colored dark as you have patience too." The best dresses were half blue but the work dresses were two-thirds blue.[71] Around 1870 Brother David Parker, Trustee at Canterbury, originated the "Parker mixed," which joined ninety percent of the unspun wool dyed dark blue with ten percent that remained white.[72] The mid-nineteenth-century lightweight wool dress material from the Church Families at New Lebanon and Canterbury (figure 226), mixes red and blue to produce a strong iridescent pink glow. Blue was at times used as a lining for other cloth, and an early nineteenth-century red-brown wool skirt at Sabbathday Lake is lined with a vivid blue linen. The expense of the imported indigo plant used in all this coloring—even to the cost of the tubs and kettles—was recouped by selling blue-dyed cloth to the world.[73]

Yellow

Yellow suited the neoclassical taste for brightness and clarity. Thomas Sheraton in his 1803 *Dictionary* suggested light blues would harmonize with yellow on walls of service areas. Back halls, kitchens, and stables of various English country houses were painted with the upper two-thirds light blue and the lower third deep yellow.[74] It now seems surprising that yellow was often used with blue in ways that allowed the yellow part to receive the most abuse. In the meeting room of the Sabbathday Lake meetinghouse, painted inside in 1839, there is bright yellow below the built-in seats, where feet can hit it, and deep blue on the seats and backs of the benches. The dovetailed box in figure 140 is slightly larger than its mate, also at Canterbury, which has a hand

140. BOX
Canterbury, New Hampshire
Similar to smaller box inscribed on paper label on bottom: "Canterbury Infirmary"
1830–60
Pine; painted yellow outside; inside of lid painted blue; inside surface of box (sides and bottom) papered blue; iron carrying handles painted black; hinges attached to top of box and back edge of lid
H. 9⅛" W. 24⅜" D. 9⅞"
Box dovetailed
Canterbury Shaker Village, Canterbury, New Hampshire

written label "Canterbury Infirmary." Outside it is painted yellow, with black-painted iron carrying handles. To protect the bottles, the inside of the box has blue paper; the inside of the lid is painted blue.

Loudon in his 1839 London publication gives recipes for staining wood yellow.[75] Various American nineteenth-century advice books, such as Eliza Leslie's *The House Book: or a Manual of Domestic Economy for Town and Country* (1841), recommend for painting the floor "yellow ochre being the cheapest but Slate color the Best."[76] Yellow appears on many pieces of nineteenth-century worldly furniture, but as the ground for decoration, on which fruit, flowers, and painted lines abound. Yellow bamboo-turned Windsor chairs generally had their bamboo lines painted in a contrasting color. Although it is rare to find in the world a plain, yellow-painted piece, countless nineteenth-century picture and mirror frames have gold leaf on their fronts, but yellow paint on their sides. The gold, a fashionable color, had the additional property of reflecting light onto the picture or looking glass. Painting the edges yellow made them fit in without the expense of gold leaf.

The Shakers made many pieces of yellow furniture. In the meeting room of the 1830 Hancock Brick Dwelling House, as described in the long quotation in Chapter VI (p. 89), the woodwork was stained with "a bright orange color," and the inside of the room's cupboard doors are bright yellow. The interiors of the cupboards themselves were left unpainted. John Ott has suggested that the yellow on the inside of the doors was intended to reflect light into the deep cupboards. This does indeed occur when light from the nearby windows strikes the doors.[77] According to the 1845 Millennial Laws: "Floors in dwelling houses, if stained at all, should be of a reddish yellow, and shop floors should be of a yellowish red." A September 5, 1816 entry in a visitor's diary notes seeing at New Lebanon yellow floors and "floor cloths—made at home & painted the color of the floor."[78]

Yellow is a color associated with gold, and the Shakers look forward to gold in heaven. The main street of the Holy City in heaven (figure 48) was shown as yellow, and described as "golden." Shortly before her death Ann Lee had a vision of her brother, who had recently died, coming to take her: "I see Brother William coming, in a Golden Chariot, to take me home."[79] She is in her gold chariot at the lower right of the gift drawing in figure 165. At center bottom of that drawing, a pair of gold steps in profile lead up to two doors with iron latches in profile. Through these, Brothers and Sisters entered heaven. The center right of the drawing shows a Greek revival style chair, a form not employed by the Shakers while on earth. In heaven it is made of gold.

The Bible has hundreds of references to gold. I Kings 6:21 established the role of gold chains as both protective and uniting: "So Solomon overlaid the house [Temple] within with pure gold: and he made a partition by the chains of gold before the oracle; and he overlaid it with gold." Lucy Wright's last words, spoken about fifteen days before her death in 1821, were:

To my sense Believers are held together in union by a golden Chain. This chain is composed of the gifts and orders of God and every order is a link in the chain; and if you break any of these orders, you break this chain and are exposed to be led astray, But while you are careful to keep the gifts and orders of God, you are surrounded with this golden chain, and are secure from evil. You are on safe ground, and nothing can injure you unless by disobedience you break a link in the chain, and so expose yourselves to the enemy without, for the enemy cannot come within to injure any one.[80]

A copy of this statement was included in a revision of the 1845 Millennial Laws.[81] Those Laws describe the Central Ministry's communication with other Societies as the "golden chain of love and union."[82] Various visions during the Era of Manifestations included gold: Phoebe Smith at New Lebanon received "gold chains, rings, diamonds, pearls, jewels, beautiful white robes of the virtues of the gospel."[83] Golden crowns were brought to Believers, and one of the spirit gifts was "a little gold oval box with a diamond in it from blessed Mother Ann."[84] Another Believer "Received an oval box about six inches long and four in width. It was made of solid gold and had four balls about the size of a large grape two of which were attached to each end of the box about an inch apart."[85] For another gift "A necklace of gold beads was placed about the neck."[86]

In 1841 a "large GOLDEN CROSS " was given to each Shaker instrument (the person receiving the spirit, or the spiritual gift); an angel placed one "upon each and every one of your breasts . . . and from the ends of this cross, is extended a shining band of silver over your shoulders and back under your arms, to the cross again; and on the cross is written 'GOOD AND FAITHFUL CHILDREN, AND FAITHFUL INSTRUMENTS IN THE HANDS OF YOUR

141. CASE OF DRAWERS
New Lebanon, New York, Church Family
1830–40
Pine painted yellow; pine and basswood; cherry knobs
H. 73" W. 43" D. 18¹/₂"
Collection of the Shaker Museum and Library, Old Chatham, New York

MOTHER AND HEAVENLY PARENTS.' "[87] Yellow is one of the main colors in gift drawings. Gold-linked rings cross the middle of one executed by the instrument Elder Joseph Wicker of Hancock in 1844. The center of each is inscribed with a virtue, such as Love, Hope, Humility, Meekness, and Thankfulness.[88]

Gold and yellow could play a negative role in visions, or in Shaker dreams. Garrett K. Lawrence, botanist and promoter of the medical herb industry at New Lebanon, had a dream in 1818 in which these colors symbolized lustful pleasure. In the dream he was "viewing a very beautiful Partridge. It was all over spotted with a beautiful yellow which glittered like gold, especially in its tail which was larger than its whole body, as it fluttered around." In interpreting the dream Lawrence saw the large phallic golden tail as representing sensual pleasures dominating his body. He

142. CHAIR
New Lebanon, New York
1830–50
Maple, painted yellow; original tape seat
H. 36¾" W. 18" D. of seat 13½"
Collection of the Shaker Museum and Library,
Old Chatham, New York

despaired of ever controlling lust: "I saw that the nature of the flesh, or of man, was wild, and never could be tamed. And as the tail of the Partridge, was larger than the whole body, & seemed to steer & govern it, so it was with man."[89] Whether the color yellow on furniture, floors, and the exteriors of buildings was a conscious symbol of future heavenly rewards is not recorded. Its ubiquity in Shaker hands may result from the light color it adds to a room. Yellow ochre, a clay-based pigment known since antiquity, was inexpensive; chrome yellow, not in commercial production until 1818, was expensive, as was zinc yellow, available after 1850.

It is hard to visualize just how bright the yellow furniture first appeared; a fresh mix of chrome yellow pigment in oil, which served as the basis for much Shaker yellow furniture, is as strong a yellow as on a lemon. A small single rectangular sheet, a "token" or "card of love," inscribed, "A Beautiful Present From my ever blessed & loving Mother Ann, Brought by her little Angel, Jan 1st 1843, A Pretty Little Crown which the Angel placed on my head, Two beautiful Little Gold Crosses, one on each sholder, & a Kiss from the little Angel. Mary Hazzard," is a similar bright yellow.[90] The yellow sample in figure 128 is zinc-yellow in egg tempera.

The pine New Lebanon Church Family case of drawers in figure 141 is just over six feet high and is coated with a thin yellow paint. The knobs are unpainted cherry. In what seems a rather conventional use of drawer size there is great variation: the drawers vary as much as ¼ inch in length from those of a similar size; they diminish in height as they mount upward, but not in an exact progression. Starting at the bottom, their heights are, in inches: 8⅜, 8⅜, 7⅞, 7¾, 7⅞, 7⅞, 7⅜, 7. Paint splashed on the sides of the drawers, and thus protected from change, is a bright lemon yellow. Various similar pieces were painted red.

143. OVAL CARRIER
Canterbury, New Hampshire
1850–60
Maple, pine, and ash; copper tacks; painted
yellow
H. 7³/₄" H. of box 4" L. 11" D. 8¹/₄"
Collection of Dr. and Mrs. M. Stephen Miller

Right:
144. LAPBOARD
Purchased at Hancock, Massachusetts
Two holes held a hanging cord
1830–50
Pine painted yellow over red
H. 18" W. 11⁷/₈" D. ³/₈"
Collection of the Shaker Museum and Library,
Old Chatham, New York

Far right:
145. *A HOLY, SACRED AND DIVINE ROLL
AND BOOK; FROM THE LORD GOD OF
HEAVEN . . . . IN TWO PARTS. PART I*
Author: Philemon Stewart
Published: Canterbury, New Hampshire
1843
Labeled on cover by Irving E. Greenwood,
Canterbury, in 1936 or 1937: "SHAKER
LIBRARY, No. 30, Section Reference," and on
first page facing cover by Henry Blinn about
1880.
H. 8³/₈" W. 5³/₈" D. ³/₄"
Collection of the Shaker Museum and Library,
Old Chatham, New York

Opposite:
146. BUILT-IN CUPBOARD OVER
DRAWERS
Hancock, Massachusetts, Brick Dwelling House,
third floor
1830–31
Pine; butternut drawer fronts; cherry knobs; for
colors see text
H. 94⁵/₈" W. 41³/₄"
Hancock Shaker Village, Pittsfield, Massachusetts

Some scholars have asked how the drawers of these pieces were divided among the inhabitants of a given retiring room, whether it was standard for each person to have the same number of short and long drawers, for example. The variation in numbers of short and long drawers in many pieces of similar size suggests that there was no standard arrangement, however.

The yellow New Lebanon chair with tilters and original seat tape in figure 142 was purchased from Hancock. The Church leadership and most of the community goods moved there when Mount Lebanon sold off its last property in 1947. The oval carrier in figure 143 is from New Hampshire. Jerry Grant has found that boxes made there had the top edges of their rims machine-rounded before they were bent; the heads of the copper tacks show evidence of having been smoothed in place by a slightly coarse file. Boxes from New Lebanon have flat top edges, and the tacks have a smoother surface, as though smoothed by sandpaper. The wonderfully early pine lapboard with rounded edges in figure 144 was purchased at Hancock, but it may have been brought there from another community. It first had a red coat, and later it was painted yellow. The two holes at one end once held a hanging cord or thong.

Yellow, Red, and Orange

The 1843 *A Holy, Sacred and Divine Roll and Book; From the Lord God of Heaven, to the Inhabitants of Earth* was by heavenly direction to be "bound in yellow paper with red backs; edges yellow also" (figure 145). The yellow used for the cover and edges is as bright as forsythia in full bloom. The binding was bright red before it faded.

The cupboard over drawers (figure 146) is built into a third floor room of the 1830 Brick Dwelling House at Hancock, where the woodwork was described in 1832 as orange. The butternut drawer fronts are red-orange. The wood between them, the cupboard area, the moldings, and the enclosing board to the left and at the top, are yellow on pine. (The yellow on the top board does not continue all the way to the end at the right: the red of the board between the built-in and the large walk-in cupboard door, continues up onto the right few inches of the top board. This makes a unified yellow rectangle of the upper part of the top of the built-in.) The orange color on the butternut drawer fronts has remained intense; the same paint on the pine woodwork to the right is now a less intense tone. The yellow on the pine wood has, in a similar way, become rather dim. The orange color on the top and in the cupboard interior of the Eldresses' counter (figure 132) has remained bright. Susan Buck reports that the first generation of paints on the 1793 Church Family Dwelling House at Canterbury were yellow moldings, red baseboards, and bright white walls.

Many Shaker buildings combine yellow exterior walls under red roofs, and many near-similar

147. CHEST OVER TWO DRAWERS
New Lebanon, New York
1820–40
Pine painted yellow; maple knobs
H. 36¹/₄" W. 42¹/₈" D. 18³/₈"
Collection of the Shaker Museum and Library,
Old Chatham, New York

pieces of Shaker furniture differ only significantly in whether they are painted yellow or red. The two New Lebanon chests, each with two drawers (figures 147 and 20), both made 1820–40, should be compared, for they demonstrate how variety was achieved in rather standard forms, most dramatically by varying inexpensive paints. It is not known if any Shaker retiring room had all yellow or red furniture. From the seventeenth century, rooms with one dominating color were standard in the world: all green or all red, for example. There the fabrics might not be the same, but the color was: a red room might combine red wool, silk, cotton, and leather. But the newly recognized early Shaker combining of red and yellow woodwork in a room strongly suggests an early mixing of red and yellow furniture.

Although immediately similar in basic stance, the red and yellow pieces in figures 147 and 20 differ in almost every measurement, and in the shape and wood of their drawer knobs. The mahogany knobs on the red chest echo the shape of contemporary brass knobs. The maple ones on the yellow piece continue a traditional form. The end cleats on the tops of both have a molded lip that projects down over the sides of the chest. Both have slightly rounded lipped drawers. A comparison of measurement shows the variations:

	Yellow	Red
Height	36¹/₄"	37¹/₄"
Width	42¹/₈"	43¹/₄"
Depth	18³/₈"	19¹/₂"
Height of top front board	14"	14 ³/₈"
Height of top drawer	5³/₁₆"	5¹¹/₁₆"
Height of bottom drawer	10¹/₈"	10¹/₈"

Both paints are thin, and there seems to be no finishing coat of varnish. The colors were once much brighter: on the yellow piece, the front of the drawer sides, over the dovetails, are lemon bright.

Red

Red was the basic eighteenth- and nineteenth-century paint. It was cheaply made of various combinations, for example, with red ochre in oil with some filler; with red lead, lamp black, and burnt umber; or with red lead, red ochre, and any number of blacks. Sometimes a little of the more

148. SISTERS' CLOAK
New Lebanon, New York, Church Family
Mid-nineteenth century
Dark red wool; thin light green glazed lining,
probably linen or cotton
H. nape of neck to hem 61½"
Collection of the Shaker Museum and Library,
Old Chatham, New York

expensive vermilion was added to make a stronger red. In the long letter from William Deming describing the 1830 Hancock Brick Dwelling House he noted that "The outside [the brick] of the house is painted with four coats of a beautiful red." On eighteenth-century worldly vernacular furniture red could suggest walnut, mahogany, or cherry. In the nineteenth century it gave the appearance of mahogany, or with dark streaks over it, rosewood. In 1839, the English author John Claudius Loudon gave a recipe for red, and noted that it was commonly used on Windsor chairs made in the neighborhood of London. He also gave a formula "for Rosewood Pink."[91] Some Shaker furniture is painted pink, particularly that from the New Lebanon Community.

Red stain was used to intensify the red color of cherry, and indeed, red fingerprints appear inside the drawers of the counter in figure 83. Susan Buck made the red color visible in figure 128 by following a recipe in David Austin Buckingham's Receipt Book for "making and applying the Tere-de-Sena Stain" that could give wood "a kind of Mahogany color." This stain, like the reconstructed yellow and green paints in the same illustration, produced a stronger color when applied to the sized upper half of the wood than the raw lower part.

Red could be seen by the Shakers as too fancy. The 1845 Millennial Laws state: "No writing with red ink, may be done for ornament, and none at all without liberty from the Elders."[92] But despite this admonition, a mid-century Shaker recipe for red stain mentions ink: "Red stain for wood, leather, paaper &c. Take 1½ oz Brazill dust, put it in one pint of alcohol—warm it a little in a water bath, or on a stove—say half an hour—then put in, say about one tea spoon full of Bookbinder's acid, which will turn it to a beautiful red. This will made *red ink*, only use good strong vinegar instead of alcahol, and purple, by using Logwood. Logwood makes a beautiful stain with alcohol. The Ink will need a litle Gum Arabic."[93]

Red appears regularly in gift drawings and there are many recipes for dying textiles shades of red. The Sister's wool cloak in figure 148, from the Church Family, New Lebanon, is of a strong dark red, and is lined with a bright jade-green. The dyeing of red material for horse blankets was strenuous and "long before we got cleaned up we promised ourselves never to do so again."[94] Red became a dramatic color when combined with black borders for plush chair cushions made after the Civil War, and could be combined with red and black chairs (see figures 190 and 195). The very popular butternut color was a vibrant reddish brown, and Shaker children were sometimes dressed in a muted red cloth that had been dyed along with binding material for carpets.[95] Throughout the nineteenth century many Shaker roofs, including those on meetinghouses, were painted red.[96]

149. CHAIR
Enfield, New Hampshire
Back of top slat stenciled in black: "12"
1840–60
Birch painted red; cane seat
H. 40⅞" W. 18½" D. of seat 13½"
Collection of Dr. and Mrs. M. Stephen Miller

150. OVAL CARRIER
New Lebanon, New York
Inscribed on bottom: "SW/S Warren/ 1845/ 1826/ 29 Third St./ J M Warren 1879/Troy NY"; one side inscribed: "JM Warren/Troy NY" 1832–45 (planning marks between swallowtails from machine used at New Lebanon after 1832)
Maple, pine, and ash; copper tacks; painted salmon pink
H. 9⅜" H. of box 3⅜" L. 14¾" D. 11⅛"
Fruitlands Museums, Harvard, Massachusetts

On chairs, as on other furniture forms, red, often in tones leaning toward brown, was the most popular color. The fine red chair with tillers in figure 149 exhibits the style of finials, slenderness of parts, and caned seat used in Enfield, New Hampshire, between 1840 and 1860. There is a figure 12 stenciled in black on the back of the top slat. The oval carrier in figure 150 is painted with the pink color associated with New Lebanon, and it has planing marks between the swallowtails left by a machine used there after 1832. It bears inscriptions with dates.

Green

Gift drawings are rife with green—as vegetation or lines denoting the earth, architectural and decorative details, and organizing or framing lines. In Shaker hands, green is rarely used on furniture and buildings, or in textiles. Historically the color green has been associated with verdure—vigorous and flourishing conditions—and increase. To the ancient Egyptians, for example, green was the color of vegetation, and the skin area of some mummy masks was colored green to signal rebirth. For many non-Shakers green has implied procreation, but to Calvin Green, the color signified increase in membership.[97] For the Masons it suggests virtue, truth, resurrection, and immortality.

A.F.M. Willich in his *Domestic Encyclopaedia,* published in Philadelphia in 1801, reported: "The only simple green of a tolerable degree of brightness, is *verdigrease* [an acetate of copper], or its different preparations: though far from being durable, it may be rendered more so, as a watercolour, by dissolving it in the pure tartarous acid. A green colour may be made by compounding Prussian or other blue, with yellow: but it is by no means fixed, and much inferior to common verdigrease."[98]

Although the Shakers used verdigris, their green was generally made by mixing blue and yellow—such as Prussian blue and yellow ochre or Prussian blue and chrome yellow. Black added to yellow can produce an acceptable olive green; adding lampblack to yellow ochre makes a very cheap green. When blue was used, it was generally Prussian blue, a fairly permanent color when exposed to light and air. When blue is used on paper, light may soon make it pale or turn it brown. (Much of what is now brown ink on blue paper may once have been blue ink on blue paper.) Some yellows are also fugitive; therefore, a green, depending on its composition, might change over the years. Perhaps some of the formerly green furniture now appears blue or black. Chrome green is the most stable of the green pigments, and was frequently used on beds and other wooden objects painted after it came into general use in 1850.

The intensive Millennial Laws of 1845 decreed, "Bedsteads should be painted green."[99] Why, for the Shakers, green was to be applied to celibate beds is not known. Perhaps, as in Calvin Green's words, it was a sign of increase in membership. Brother Arnold Hadd at Sabbathday Lake, discussing how the Maine communities ignored the 1845 Laws, cited the fact that beds were not painted green in Maine. When writing about beds, Edward Deming Andrews suggested that there was "in one community at least, a dark shade for the common members, and a brighter, lighter green for the ministry."[100] Susan Buck found varnish in the top layer of two of the green beds she examined, and a recipe for putting varnish in all three layers, with more added to the top one. The presence of varnish would make the paint slicker and darker, and perhaps that is what Andrews observed. Or, one or more beds may have faded. She has also found that two early beds now at Hancock Shaker Village were once painted orange and later made green. Perhaps they were repainted to bring them into accord with the new laws. One of the two beds was later made dark blue.

The scarcity of green Shaker furniture has been intensified by the paint-strippers. In 1978 Robert Emlen discovered an early green-painted turned-leg stand at Enfield, New Hampshire, "being used as a plant stand in the bedroom of one of the religious sisters connected with the then-owners, the Missionaries of the Lady of La Salette . . . . Ten days later I learned it had been stripped."[101] Emlen's slides taken before it was stripped show a dark green coat that goes over the broad, turned drawer knob. This suggests that it was a later coat of paint. One well known green chair, made at Enfield, Connecticut, about 1840 had the green coat applied after a thickly padded seat was installed. (The removal of the padded seat, to install a cloth tape seat, left areas without the green on the legs around the seat rails.)[102] Jerry Grant has suggested that the green on the chair, and other repainted green pieces, may be left over from the paint used on house trim—doors, shutters, and so on.[103] Some collectors of Shaker material spurn objects that have later paint, as though that makes them less Shaker. But if it was Shaker-applied, then it is the result of a Shaker decision. Richard Candee, who has worked extensively to understand New England ver-

151. CLOSE-CHAIR
New Lebanon, New York
1850–60
Marked on bottom of seat: "JAS. X.
SMITH/NEW-LEBANON/N.Y"
Sycamore, yellow poplar, cherry, maple, birch
stained red under clear finish; tin plated iron can
painted green; seat tape tacked on to bottom of
seat to form a circle against which the can is
pressed by a foot lever
H. 24" W. across arms 21¼" Cir. across seat 16"
Collection of Dr. and Mrs. M. Stephen Miller

nacular architecture, reports that green was used widely in the world for machinery because it was a "very forgiving" color: it did not show wear.[104]

The Windsor close-chair shown as figure 151 was made about 1850–60 and marked "JAS. X. SMITH/NEW-LEBANON/N.Y." on the bottom of its lathe-turned sycamore seat. That surface also has decorative lathe-turned rings and a circle of green and gold seat tape near the edging of the opening. The green-painted tinned can, which has a bail handle with a wooden carrying part, can be pushed up against the tape by a foot-operated mechanism under it. The thin seat lid is yellow poplar; the spokes of the back are cherry; the legs and stretchers mix maple, cherry, and birch; all were covered and united by a red stain under varnish.

Recipes for "Paris" green (also known as Emerald green) for window blinds, "Canterbury Green," and "Outside Green," for the second Watervliet meetinghouse completed in 1848 appear in the list of Shaker stains, paints, and varnish given earlier (pp. 137–8). Doors painted green on the outside are mentioned in the long quotation about the new 1830 Hancock Brick Dwelling House (p. 89). A letter of October 19, 1858, from Abraham Perkins at Canterbury to Austin Bronson of Enfield, New Hampshire, noted: "In reply to the subject of painting doors. I admit that I spoke in favor of painting them green. This was on account of the custom; not that there is any particular order for or against. If you can get a handsome slate color and it is cheaper and as durable as green, and your Elders are united with it we certainly have no objection to it."[105] On two town plans of Alfred, Maine, drawn and colored by Joshua H. Bussell in 1845 and about 1848, the "Office" was colored green. On the first plan (figure 126) it had a red roof; on the second plan, the roof is black.[106]

Black

Black is a rare color in Shaker hands, except as clothing, and there it is limited. In 1824 an English visitor was shown a black silk handkerchief by a Brother "of their own making, which he was wearing around his neck . . . . Some of the longer established societies, he said, made silk of a very superior description."[107] In carpets black can appear alone or as one color integrated with another as a darkening agent. Some architectural ironwork was painted black, as the list of paints included earlier records (p. 138). Black also appears on the iron parts of many buckets and pails, and on the iron additions to the box in figure 140. Late in the nineteenth century black paint, or a black stain, appeared on production chairs. There, when put under a varnish, it was called ebony (see figure 195). For black pigment the Shakers might use charred wood or bones, or lampblack, which although greasy, was easily collected from lamp chimneys. According to David Austin Buckingham's Receipt Book, "A strong solution of Nitric Acid on Wood or Ivory will make a black."

152. CHAIR
New Lebanon, New York, probably Second Family
About 1852
Figured maple; pewter tilters patented in 1852, balls secured by leather thongs; cane seat
H. 41⁷/₈" W. 18¹/₂" D. of seat 13³/₈"
Collection of the Shaker Museum and Library, Old Chatham, New York

153. OVAL BOX
New Lebanon, or Watervliet, New York
1800–20
Maple and pine; wooden pegs; copper tacks; grain-painted red-brown over yellow
H. 4¹/₂" W. 13¹/₂" D. 10"
Collection of Jerry Grant

154. DOMED CHEST
New Lebanon, New York, Church Family
1830–40
Pine; grain-painted black-brown on red; iron
carrying handles painted black
H. 15¼" L. 36" D. 17⅛"
Collection of the Shaker Museum and Library,
Old Chatham, New York

Patterned Surfaces

The Shakers used patterned surfaces, either employing solid woods or veneers, or as painted versions of natural grains. Some Believers did decry such fanciness, but there are many surviving examples of the taste. The New Lebanon chair shown in figure 152 delights in its figured maple. Its rear legs end in a pewter ferrule and ball foot that the Shakers patented in 1852. (For another chair with a patterned grain see figure 46.) Edward Deming Andrews published a description of a looking glass veneered in curly maple,[108] and Jerry Grant cites veneering in an 1860 quotation from Alfred Merrick Collier of Harvard, Massachusetts: on February 13, "I . . . began a little trunk for myself," and the next day "veneered the two ends of it."[109] Several Sisters' worktables, made of hickory and oak at Enfield, Connecticut, in the 1880s, possibly by Thomas Fisher, have veneered drawer fronts.[110]

Painted versions of elaborate wood appeared early, and the practice persisted throughout the nineteenth century. The 1800–1820 oval box in figure 153 was finished with intricate graining at New Lebanon or Watervliet. It was constructed in a special way: instead of using copper tacks to secure the swallowtails, their ends tuck into slots cut into the box. The Shaker Museum and Library owns an early grain-painted domed chest (figure 154) and a late grained stool. An early cupboard over drawers with later nineteenth-century graining is shown as figure 228. A similar resurfacing of an early piece is seen in figure 199. When the meeting room in the Dwelling House at Sabbathday Lake was built in 1884 the doors, probably made of pine, were grained by an outsider, Ezekiel Gam, uncle of one of the members. The painted pattern matched the beautiful grain of the ash wood used for the rest of the woodwork.[111] In the 1870s and 1880s the Shakers grained hundreds of their seed boxes. About the same time they used paint to imitate the grain of oak, often over older surfaces. About 1900, for example, a white-painted north door of the Church Family Sisters' Shop at Canterbury was oak-grained over the white.

Complex patterns could be seen throughout the Shaker communities. During the 1830s Henry DeWitt recorded marbling the outside of leather bookcovers at New Lebanon:

1836 feb 6:	*Daniel Sizer came over here to learn how to marble books. I marble a lot for Miles & 2 for him . . . .*
1836 feb 2:	*I finish said quarto book I began yesterday. it is for Perter [Peter] Long. Brand & letter this said book; & marble a couple.*
1836 may 13:	A.M. *I branded a couple of quarto books 1 for miles 1 for (b.c.)* PM *I marbled books. 7 hymn books 4 Anthem books & 4 verse books.*
1836 dec 31:	*I went to the North house to show them how to marble books.*
1837 jul 18:	*Marbled said books and finished them—19 of them all.*[112]

Certain colors were symbolic for the Shakers, and a great variety played active roles in their environments. If we could see the original, unfaded colors of the furnished rooms that the Shakers actually lived in during the second quarter of the nineteenth century, our concept of these people as retiring and quiet would be greatly changed. It would also be corrective if we saw the original colors on reproductions of early Shaker things. Having them produced, as is now the practice, without paint or painted with purposely "faded" tones, reinforces the misunderstanding of these lively people.

Chapter VIII

ERA OF MANIFESTATIONS, 1837–1850: ANGELS, PURGES, GIFT DRAWINGS, THE NARROW PATH, AND SEXUALITY

The Era of Manifestations, 1837–1850, is the name given to more than a decade of an unusual number of visits to the Shakers by heavenly spirits. They appeared personally to deliver gifts such as songs, dances, and visions. Sometimes what they brought was recorded as drawings, but more generally a written description was made, such as a gift of "a white marble Box."[1] The purpose was to deliver immediate knowledge of heaven and those who dwell there, and to instruct how Believers should act and believe. This was the aspect of Shaker belief that most pushed against the strict patterning of life the Society had accepted when it came into Gospel Order. Now designated the Era of Manifestations, the time is also known as Mother Ann's Work, for she was one of the principal spirits active in the communications. It was a special time for the Shakers, but the countrysides around them were also experiencing spiritual activity, and the Western world in general was undergoing a time of more emotional living than had been known during the previous period. In many ways there was a general move from thinking to feeling.

In 1837 Victoria became queen of Great Britain and Ireland. Her reign, which lasted until 1901, was to coincide with, and to some degree condition, an unbridled proliferation of artistic styles, many of them ardently eclectic. Neoclassicism's noble simplicity and calm grandeur, which had stressed rationally conceived ideals, gave way to a romanticism that sought to express the mystery of the unintelligible. In a reaction to static conformity, the romantic artist, essentially a passionate individualist, sought to convey ideals thought to be beyond logical discourse. Innate sensibility and the authenticity of personal emotions took precedence over other concerns. In music this was the age of Berlioz, Chopin, and Schumann; the Italian violin virtuoso Niccolo Paganini played freakishly difficult music and wrote compositions so demanding only he could perform them. In 1838 the "Swedish Nightingale," Jenny Lind, was wildly successful in Weber's 1820 *Der Freischutz*. America was replete with major writers: Emerson, Hawthorne, Longfellow, Poe, Thoreau, and Melville. In 1836 Emerson published *Nature*, an essay that outlined the tenets of the Transcendentalist movement; in 1845 Thoreau moved into nature at Walden Pond.

The American painter Washington Allston wrote: "Be industrious and trust to your own genius; *listen to the voice within you,* and sooner or later she will make herself understood, not only to you, but she will enable you to translate her language to the world, and this it is which forms *the only real merit of any work of art.* An artist must give the impress of his own mind to his works or they will never interest, however academically correct they may be."[2] Allston praised Paganini's ability to let his soul govern his performance, and wrote that those who heard him play "think it hardly extravagant to say, [he] seemed almost to embody silence."[3] In 1827 Allston sent a friend some advice to pass on to Thomas Cole, a young American artist who had emigrated from England with his family when he was seventeen, and was about to visit Europe: "You say that [Thomas Cole] is a passionate admirer of nature. Let him never lose his love of her . . . . [T]he young artist should study nature and pictures together . . . . [I]n their best works [the old masters] express the highest truth, such as nature reveals only to a gifted few. Their effect may be called the poetical moods of nature . . . ."[4] In 1836 Thomas Cole painted his *Course of Empire* series, canvases that take viewers from the savage state of the world to arcadia, then a classical empire, and, finally, destruction and desolation.

In 1830 Joseph Smith published the *Book of Mormon* given to him on gold plates by the Angel Moroni in 1827. Because of persecution, Smith's new Church of Jesus Christ of the Latter-Day

Saints moved westward: to Ohio, then Missouri, and at last Utah. In the 1830s religious revivals were powerfully affecting established rural churches. Many people postponed decisions or improvements, believing that the end of the world was near. In February 1840, for example, a Mary Pease of East Boston wrote to Pliny Freeman at Sturbridge, Massachusetts, whom she later married: "If you should have any call to Boston I should be happy to have you call over to East Boston. I have not purchased any spectacles at present for there is rumor that the world is coming to an end in 1843 and I did not think it was worth a while to spend my money useless."[5] In 1790 there were fourteen American religious newspapers; there were more than six hundred by 1830. From 1826 the American Temperance Society promoted moderate drinking, but soon sanctioned total abstinence. By 1831 the Society claimed 170,000 members.[6]

THE SHAKERS

A list of the major buildings the Shakers constructed between 1822 and 1837 demonstrates the sense of permanence the Believers in most communities felt during the 1820s and early 1830s.

1822–24	second meetinghouse, New Lebanon
1824–34	limestone Centre Family Dwelling, Pleasant Hill
1826	round stone barn, Hancock
1830	Brick Dwelling House, Hancock
1831	expanded Church Family Great House, New Lebanon (between April and December)
1834–37	white granite, Church Family, Stone Dwelling House, Enfield, New Hampshire

Out of this sense of security arose a challenge to the Society. The early years of the religion involved spiritual, psychological, and physical struggles during which the faithful were propelled by the excitement of joining the Shakers and overcoming evil, the world, and basic human nature. The 1827 *Testimonies Concerning the Character and Ministry of Mother Ann Lee and the First Witnesses of the Gospel of Christ's Second Appearing* recorded the testimonies of thirty-one Believers who joined during Ann Lee's lifetime. Although nearly all had been religious before joining, they found happiness only in the Shaker faith. (Only one was not religious before joining and only two had not been church members.)[7] They had created a theology that included celibacy, confession, and a female messiah, and fought the world that disliked the peculiar sect. By 1800 the Shakers lived in an interlocking structure that organized people into Families, Families into Communities, Communities into Bishoprics, and placed all this under the rule of a handful of self-perpetuating leaders.

By the 1830s the situation had changed. There was now a generation of young people who had spent most of their lives in the communities and who had not experienced the costly choice of leaving the world. Upon reaching the age of twenty-one, when they could sign the covenant and become members of a Family, many questioned the need for the institutional constraints the leaders imposed. Also, many recent converts had joined because they saw the communities as rational, organized, and successful situations in which to live. Since neither group knew or understood the personal cost Believers had experienced in the early Church under blind obedience to authority, they wanted the Ministry to relax the restrictions and to give them more say in how things were managed. Isaac Newton Youngs, working as the official scribe for the Central Ministry, wrote about 1842:

Thus the state of things became very different from that in the year 1800. Many of the rising generation, and such as had been lately gathered in, had embibed much of the spirit of the world, and would hardly restrain themselves from adopting its manners and customs; they disregarded, as matters of importance, the wholesome laws and orders which had been established by Father Joseph and Mother Lucy, and by this means many lost their protection and fell back to the beggarly elements of the world.

And tho' a good portion who were honest hearted retained their integrity, & kept on good gospel ground, yet all, both Lead [i.e., leaders] and people, were forced to feel the darkening influence of the cloud that hung over the whole body.

These things were clearly seen and known by the faithful, they bro't much tribulation upon the Ministry & Elders, and upon the faithful first born of our heavenly Parents, who embraced the gospel in the days of mother Ann's Ministration.[8]

The resulting confrontation between older, established Believers and these questioning members led to a decade of intense spiritual activity, the purging of the weak in commitment, and the writing of the most restrictive laws the Shakers were to know. The leaders' move to take firm control of the wild spirituality included closing the worship services to outsiders from 1842 to 1845. (They had previously closed worship meetings to outsiders from 1792 to 1798.) Hundreds of gift drawings and thousands of gift songs were brought by angels. The greater isolation caused the "classic Shaker" look to continue longer than would otherwise have been possible.

Gifts "Showered Down upon This People"[9]

There had been a quickening of spiritual activity before the Era of Manifestations. On February 21, 1836, Rufus Bishop recorded, "Repentance increases to a wonderful degree, many abase themselves in the dust. Even C.G. [Calvin Green?] cried earnestly for charity mercy and forgiveness. This afternoon we [the Ministry?] all visited at the Second Order & attended their meeting, in which there were great manifestations of the power of God, which followed the gift of repentance particularly among the youth & children, who were operated upon in a marvelous manner, from the oldest youth to the youngest boy."[10] On January 4, 1837, James Smith at Watervliet had a "Remarkable Vision." Subsequent public meetings were unusually "full of demonstrations of power, in diverse operations & gifts of the Spirit." On August 12, Gidion Kibbee saw a "company of heavenly host" with Ann Lee in the lead marching through the community three to four feet off the ground.[11] On the sixteenth of August, during a meeting for worship at Watervliet, three girls between the ages of ten and fourteen were suddenly possessed and began to shake and whirl and speak and sing in unknown tongues. When they recovered they described in detail a journey to heaven.

Girls and young women, like the young Joan of Arc, had often been instruments through which spirits communicated, a phenomenon that has continued into modern times.[12] As the excitement spread to other communities, the common pattern was for the young in the Families furthest from the center of community power to receive the initial experience. From there, the fervor moved toward the Center Family.[13] As has been noted, in 1838 Horace Greeley, a visitor at Watervliet, observed at the end of a meeting, "what was a measured dance becomes a wild, discordant frenzy; all apparent design or regulation is lost; and grave manhood and gentler girlhood are whirling round and round, two or three in company, then each for him or herself, in all the attitudes of a decapitated hen, or expiring top."[14] The apostate David R. Lamson published in 1848 the wood engraving "The Whirling Gift" (figure 155), in his *Two Years' Experience Among the Shakers*.

The Central Ministry at New Lebanon, who served also as the Bishopric Ministry over New Lebanon, Watervliet, and Groveland, had a double responsibility to see what was happening at Watervliet. In 1838 Isaac Newton Youngs recorded the first stages of the experiences of the three girls mentioned above. In part it reads:

155. "THE WHIRLING GIFT"
Published in David R. Lamson's, Two Year's Experience Among the Shakers, *1848, p. 85*
Wood engraving
H. 2⅜" W. 3⅛"
Collection of the Shaker Museum and Library, Old Chatham, New York

The first external appearance of the late extraordinary manifestations of God, occurred at Watervliet . . . in one of the out families, at the place now spiritually called Wisdom's Valley.

It was first noticed in the forepart of August, in the year 1837, among the female youth and children, residing at what is called the South family, or gathering order, who had practised more or less to assemble on sabbaths, for the purpose of learning to sing and exercise in the worship of God. In these meetings some of them were taken with powerful exercises of body, such as turning, shaking, and such like operations.

On the 16th: of August, three of these youths were taken under external exercises of the power of God; in the evening their senses appeared withdrawn from the scenes of time, and absorbed as in a trance:—they were laid on beds. In that position one of them began to sing these words, "Where the pretty angels dwell, Heaven! where the pretty angels dwell forever."

Many of the family went to view this now [i.e. new?] and wonderful scene. As soon as they entered the door, the children sprang from their beds & began to turn, and some of those who came to see them, joined in with them, and such a scene cannot be described by mortals, of turning, bowing, shaking, &c.

. . . One of them was asked what she saw; she answered, "The first I knew Mother Ann came to me, and she asked me if I knew her, I said nay; She said, "Did you ever hear of Mother Ann? I said yea; She said, My name is Mother Ann."

. . . The account of this was written and signed by more than a dozen of the family. [15]

The Ministry could not deny the spiritual value of the visions and approved them as genuinely from God; indeed, the revelations revived excitement, giving new and old members an involvement similar to what the first Church had known. But not all Believers liked what was happening; for example, in May 1838, Calvin Green was forced to publicly confess that he was wrong to speak against the manifestations.[16]

The Shakers had in the previous decades experienced times of quickening religious activity. And, at least on one occasion, the ecstatic delights had threatened the Shakers' furniture: in 1810, some new members at Pleasant Hill, Kentucky, fell into complex behavior. Some wallowed in mud until completely covered, others pounded on furniture until "their hands were so sore & swollen that they could not use them."[17] But this new activity in 1837 was beyond what had occurred since Ann Lee and the Church had awakened seekers in the eighteenth century. What had become patterned worship gave way to bedlam. Children took center stage, and through them, angels instructed the Elders. Those Believers who had long acted as mediums were busy, but scores of new instruments were possessed by angels, many of them departed Shaker saints: Ann Lee, Joseph Meacham, and Lucy Wright were regular visitors. Beside departed Shakers, Old Testament prophets and New Testament saints appeared in great numbers. Important personages arrived, among them George Washington, Lafayette, and Napoleon. Eskimos, Hottentots, Chinese, and Native Americans visited. The latter came in greater numbers after the meetings were closed to outsiders, and over a long period brought new native dances and songs. The Shakers converted many of these non-Shaker visitors to the Shaker religion, including Washington and Lafayette, making it possible for them to be with the saved for eternity. Ann Lee, like other religious leaders before her, had claimed the power to convert the dead, including Native Americans; how else could those who had not had the opportunity to be saved by the True Church receive life everlasting? Many Believers saw the spirits and their gifts as tangible realities, while others perceived them as symbolic and coded with meaning.

A Holy, Sacred and Divine Roll and Book; From The Lord God of Heaven to the Inhabitants of Earth, published in 1843, records revelations, and the testimonies of the truth of those visions. It was communicated in a revelation that five hundred copies were to be printed, and they were to be in Shaker yellow and red (figure 145.) One of the now most famous of the testimonies was by Adah Zillah Potter, who received a vision communicated by the angel Ma'ne me'rah vak'na si'na Jah'. An angel, in a dream in 1841, gave directions to build an ark to hold sacred writings at Hancock:

I dreamed that a Spirit or an Angel came into the meeting house where I was in bed, & asked me if I believed the Book of Holy Laws . . . . It is to have a place built in the meeting house, to keep all these sacred writings in, where they will be safe & secure. It is to be made in the following form.

It is to be square on the base, 4 feet each way, & 6 feet in height. The top shall be mitered in form. One side shall stand against the wall, & the other three shall have each a door, wide enough for a per-

son to enter. The doors shall be single panelled—one above & one below, & on each door shall be a lock. The wood on the outside, shall be of the color of the inside of the house, but the inside shall be white. I[n] the center shall be a stone table 2 feet square, placed on a wooden frame. In the middle, & raised some inches above the table, shall be a rectangular stone of the size each way, of the Book of Holy Laws. On one side of the table shall be placed the records of visions that are to be preserved, & on the other side, are to be all the spiritual letters & communications.

When ye enter to take any of these, ye shall enter by the side on which each lays, respectively . . . . Upon this holy ark or tabernacle is an Angel placed to guard & protect these holy & sacred gifts. One has been selected & appointed to do this work at New Lebanon. In this meeting house Brother Grove is to do it. And as it is made in this meeting house & the meeting house at Lebanon, so shall it be done in all meeting houses of the Zion of God upon earth.

At the end of an 1886 copy of this writing, the scribe notes: "I believe . . . that it was never executed. Certainly not in N. Lebanon, tho' I know not of any objection to it."[18]

At first these exotic experiences seemed to overturn the authority of the leaders, for they were not having the visions. To stop the chaos created by spirits who did not recognize the established line of Shaker authority, the Ministry pushed forward established charismatic instruments (mediums who were proficient at receiving spiritual visitors), for they were not likely to introduce gifts that threatened established patterns. The leaders also took control of all gifts by requiring that before they were given to the community, they had to be presented to the Elders, and written down. This allowed the Ministry to sort the God-sent from the evil-inspired, and to be the source from which gifts were introduced. Real spiritual activity was to be valued if it was God-sent, but it had to be properly handled if it was to generate finer religious lives. But as with the order brought by Meacham and Wright after the chaotic time just before Ann Lee's death, the Ministry had made themselves arbiters of both thought and behavior. Like Lucy Wright, they realized the value of allowing the sensual delight of participating in repetitive and slightly bizarre behavior within parameters created and controlled by themselves.

To share the new wealth of religious excitement, instruments approved by one Ministry were sent to other communities to provoke spiritual activity. There they were again judged by that community's leaders before they began to distribute messages. Hervey Elkins grew up at Enfield, New Hampshire. In his 1853 narrative of his time as a Shaker he includes an account of two instruments from Canterbury, New Hampshire, who were permitted to judge the religious condition of the assembled members of Enfield after the Ministry had judged the instruments.[19] He wrote with deep sentiment of his own experiences during this time, and noted how the Elders were guiding spirit visitations when they asked him to take on an Indian, a Norwegian, and an Arabian spirit. Although he tried to oblige, he found these possessions less satisfactory than when unsought spirits came to him:

During the revival I became sincerely converted. I, for a time, by reason of prejudice and distrust, resisted the effect of the impressions, which, at length, overwhelmed me in a flood of tears, shed for joy and gladness, as I more and more turned my thoughts to the Infinite. At last, a halo of heavenly glory seemed to surround me. I drank deep of the cup of the waters of life, and was lifted in mind and purpose from this world of sorrow and sin. I soared in thought to God and enjoyed Him in His attributes of purity and love. I was wafted, by angels, safely above the ocean of sensual enjoyment which buries so many millions, but into which I had never fallen . . . .

Two years thus passed, in which my highest enjoyments and pleasures were an inward contemplation of the beauty, love and holiness of God, and in the ecstatic impressions that I was in the hollow if His hand, and owned and blessed of Him . . . . Though instruments or mediums were multiplied around me, dancing in imitation of the spirits of all nations, singing and conversing in unknown tongues, some evincing a truly barbarian attitude and manners, I stood in mute thanksgiving and prayer. At times I was asked by the elders if I could not unite and take upon me an Indian, a Norwegian or an Arabian spirit? I would then strive to be impressed with their feelings, and act in conformity thereto. But such inspiration, I found, was not the revelation of the Holy Ghost. It was not that which elevated and kept me from all trials and temptations. But my inward spontaneous devotion was the kind I needed. I informed the elders of my opinion, and they concurred in it . . . .[20]

Elkins included information about a young Shaker called Henry, and shows how group activities had moments in which sensuality and spiritual bondage were united:

Henry, for that was the name of the youth who was so zealous in his aspersions, united awkwardly and derisively in these exercises. Amidst so many arms, legs and bodies, revolving, oscillating, staggering and tripping, it is not remarkable that a few should be thrown prostrate (not violently however) upon the floor. One evening, in a boy's meeting at a time of great excitement, when the spirits of some of our companions were reported to be in spiritual spheres, and other departed spirits were careering their mortal ladies in the graceful undulations of a celestial dance, Henry and many others, among whom I was seen, were whirling, staggering, and rolling, striving, in vain, by all the humility we could assume, to be also admitted into the regions of spiritual recognition, Henry suddenly tripped and fell. One of his visionary companions instantly sprang, passed his hands with great rapidity over him as though binding him with invisible cords, and then returned to his graceful employment. The clairvoyant's eyes were closed, as indeed were the eyes of all while in that condition. In vain Henry struggled to rise, to turn or hardly to move. He was fettered, bound fast by invisible manacles. The brethren were summoned to witness the sight. In the space of perhaps half an hour the clairvoyant returned, loosened his fetters and he arose mortified and confounded.

In time Henry grew too skeptical of the spirits and he was expelled from the Society.[21]

Cleansing Gift; Mountain Meetings

Together the Central Ministry and their instruments established structured rituals for the commentaries as dramatic as the former free-wheeling religious services they now controlled. The first was the "cleansing gift," which began in December 1841, just before the anticipated visit of Holy Mother Wisdom on Christmas Day. The cleansing gift began with prayer and fasting followed by extraordinary cleaning. Shaker communities had long been known for their order and cleanness, and this only intensified their visual purity: a small group of instruments and singers led the community in a pantomime and actual sweeping, scrubbing, and dusting of everything, both inside and outside the buildings. The ritual, called "Mother Ann's Sweeping Gift," occurred annually for eight years.[22] The peak of excitement was achieved in 1841 when, after advance announcements, Holy Mother Wisdom came to restore order and harmony, and distributed admonitions to some and encouragements to others. (Her first spiritual visit in April was of short duration.) On the eleventh of November she dictated through an instrument a pamphlet-length set of advice and rules and explained herself as "I am Infinite Wisdom. I dwell with Eternal Father, and have known all things and transactions of both good and evil spirits on the earth and in the heavens, ever since the beginning and creation thereof."[23] Since Holy Mother Wisdom was the female part of the Godhead, she could dictate with authority. Her communication was written down on the fourteenth of November, and published in 1842 as *The Youth's Guide in Zion, and Holy Mother's Promises*. Since her injunctions were given to and distributed by the Ministry, they and God were in accord. On her second visit, begun Christmas Day, she was accompanied by three instruments when she visited with the Ministry during the morning. In the afternoon she began a series of visits to Brothers, Sisters, and Trustees in various Families. This stay lasted several days.

The organized extravagances called "Mountain Meetings" began in 1842 and continued twice a year, in May and December, until 1854, when a spiritual message announced their discontinuation. For these a "feast ground" on elevated land overlooking a community was cleared for outdoor worship. The events began with an evening of purification: fasting, prayer, confession, and the distribution of "Spiritual Garments." The following day, at the feast ground, instruments, under the guidance of the Ministry, led the Believers in "figurative" activities: anointing with oil, washing feet, sowing and watering spiritual seeds, eating from a spiritual "bowl of love and union," and consuming sumptuous feasts while drinking "Mother's wine," which caused some Believers to stagger about in figurative inebriation.[24] (The 1854 gift drawing *A Bower of Mulberry Trees*, figure 166, provided a visual record of a wonderful heavenly meal.)

In New England the great spiritual activity began to ebb in the late 1840s, but placing dates on the beginning and end of events in Shaker history requires loose generalizations, for each community was to some degree separate in things of the spirit as in things temporal. For example, the greatest number of spirit manifestations at South Union, Kentucky, occurred in the 1860s, a decade after the communities in the Northeast had returned to quieter living.[25]

THE DRAWINGS

Today the best known gifts brought during the Era of Manifestations are the visions recorded on paper. Most of the about 200 known drawings were made between 1839 and 1859, and the vast majority were executed at New Lebanon and Hancock; a few were made at other New England communities, and in Ohio and Kentucky.[26] One of the first drawings specified that its purpose was to allow instruments to see the form of heaven, as can be seen clearly in the drawing shown as figure 48. Other instruments would soon record the same purpose.[27] In Kentucky early in the nineteenth century, the Shakers had learned to convey spiritual and theological information through the words of new songs. Their even greater creation of written records during the same years fixed the Shakers' past and made firm their present. Gift drawings incorporated some Shaker history, but more importantly they provided visual evidence of the rewards Believers would receive for the difficult Shaker experience on earth.

Many of the drawings were first established in pencil and then painted in colored inks or watercolors; some combined the two. A few used tempera, an opaque paint thicker than watercolor. Most were executed by women; only a few were by men. At the time watercolor was mostly a women's medium, for during the first years of the nineteenth century this technique of painting was taught regularly in girls' academies and womens' seminaries. While the gift drawings, which recorded heavenly realities, were mostly by women, the town views that described earthly places were invariably by men. (Susan Buck has found that while the gift drawings make use of the same pigments as are found on furniture, at least some of the town plans employ more fugitive watercolor materials. The plans were also varnished, to make them more durable when being unrolled and rolled during times of display.)

Painting a vision became a conscious option for instruments and sometimes what they saw was beyond reproduction. In 1843 Sophia F. Mace of Maine wrote that she could not paint what she had seen:

On the morning of the eighteenth of September, eighteen hundred and forty two, as I was busily engaged in my usual occupation, I heard a sudden noise like that of a strong wind, and rain beating powerfully upon the house. I quickly arose and passed along toward the window, and observed that the natural elements were all calm and still; but I cannot describe or paint on paper that which I saw and felt. The heavenly music which I heard, and the bright Angels which I saw, took every natural thing from my view, and my soul was swallowed up in adoration and love to God. [28]

It is now difficult to know how these works were viewed. Were they seen only by the medium, the artist who may also have been the medium, and the Ministry who approved them, or, more probably, were they enjoyed by a larger audience? How they were used and who knew about them have been obscured by conflicting reports of their "discovery" in this century. Olive Hayden Austin, who grew up at Hancock and later left the Society, recorded their discovery: "It wasn't until about the year 1925 when we young folks were doing our spring cleaning in the attic that Sister Alice [Smith] found a couple of them in the very top most cupboard where no one had bothered to clean for ages. We all dropped our dust cloths and mops just to study them, they were so beautiful. Sister Alice took them to her room and we never saw them again." Mrs. Austin recalled a second group of drawings being discovered early in the 1930s, when Sister Alice was showing the Andrewses around the village. The meetinghouse had been closed for years, and upstairs, in the Ministry Sisters' retiring room, in one of the topmost cupboards, they found, she said, most of the extant drawings.[29]

But Alonzo Hollister at Mount Lebanon gave Shaker material, including gift drawings, to the Berkshire Athenaeum before his death in 1911, and the practice was continued by Catherine Allen, Eldress at Mount Lebanon. Beginning in 1912 Catherine Allen sent a variety of Shaker material to Wallace H. Cathcart at the Western Reserve Historical Society for safekeeping, and gift drawings were part of what went west during the first and subsequent years. In 1917 she gave the American Society for Psychical Research twenty-two "detached brief manuscripts . . . including several drawings."[30] She gave Clara Endicott Sears the gift drawing shown in figure 156 for her growing Shaker collection in 1918. In a letter of November 18, 1918, she offered the drawing and asked it not be displayed publicly:

Now I will just whisper *something to you which I would like to have you hold apart from the mis-understanding public. Among the literature of the "Manifestations period["] of our people—1837–47 are some charts made by one of the Sisters, of visions received and communications given by spirit messengers.*

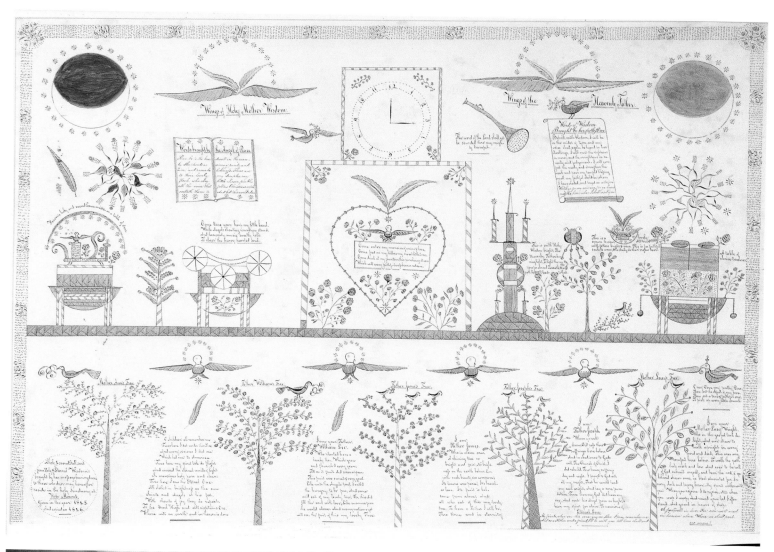

These I found among Ministrys' things. It was deemed unwise after those manifestations ceased to have either the records or charts open to those who had no knowledge of that the spiritual work then experienced and so these "gifts" were all brought to the Ministry for safe keeping.

As you proved capable of understanding much of the spirit and meaning of that time—and hold a thought so reverent, I feel that it will not be out of place for me to place one of these under your personal care to exhibit only to those whom in your judgment are capable of feeling as well as seeing with outward vision. It will be sent in a roll, and marked—"Miss C.E. Sears—personal.["] As many of our people have never seen this collection would prefer that nothing ever be written or spoken about . . . the chart [to] them. [31]

A photograph, taken before 1929, shows the drawing hanging on the wall of the Shaker building Sears moved to Fruitlands Museums in 1920 (figure 157; Mother Ann's chair is in the foreground).

Andrews, who encouraged the idea that he initiated Shaker studies, wrote that the first Shaker gift drawing he saw was in the 1930s when he was shown one by Sister Alice, who, according to Andrews, told him that she had rescued it with others as a child as they were about to be used to light a fire in the kitchen and she "took the bundle to her own room." [32]

Marks from wear and handling on the ends of the large maps of communities—which can measure up to 6 feet in length—attest that they were often stored rolled up. (A detail of one is shown in figure 126.) Written descriptions record that at least some were carried between communities to convey information. On July 5, 1834, Isaac Newton Youngs of New Lebanon unrolled a view of his home community on a table in Union Village, Ohio, and later recorded in his journal: "We went in to see the sisters, about 20 of them. Pretty sociable;—My map of New Lebanon . . . must be brot on to the table, which makes up quite a dish of discourse." [33]

It has become traditional to believe that the Shakers never displayed gift drawings. However, the gift drawing in figure 48 had a cove molding tacked on at the top and a rod tacked onto the base. The top molding was fitted with tape at its center that probably held the drawing closed when it was rolled around the rod. Like early maps it could be unrolled and displayed, and this plan of heaven was undoubtedly shown to numerous groups of Believers, much as earthly community plans were shared. [34] The photographs of Shaker interiors made from the 1870s show pictures, charts, and maps in considerable number. A postcard image of a Church Family room at Mount Lebanon, probably made between 1913 and 1917 (figure 158), shows Eldress Miriam Offord who moved there from Enfield, Connecticut, on May 6, 1913; she died there on June 18, 1917. On the wall behind her is the gift drawing shown here as figure 73. Perhaps at first most of the gift drawings were kept rather private, since mid-century feelings would have encouraged that, and later, many were tucked away and forgotten.

Shaker scholars anxiously avoid calling all these works on paper art. This is because most of

158. PHOTOGRAPH OF DISPLAYED GIFT DRAWING
Miriam Offord at Mount Lebanon, New York
1913–17
H. 3 1/2" W. 5 1/2 "
Collection of the Shaker Museum and Library, Old Chatham, New York

the gift drawings were made between 1843 and 1847, and the 1845 Millennial Laws read: "No maps, Charts, and no pictures or paintings, shall ever be hung up in your dwelling-rooms, shops, or Office. And no pictures or paintings set in frames, with glass before them shall ever be among you. But modest advertisements may be put up in the Trustees Office when necessary."[35] No such injunction exists in the earlier 1821 Laws. (Frames were disliked because they gathered dust, and the Shaker tradition of cleanliness had turned into a ritual of sweeping and dusting.) The emotional nature of these injunctions suggests Shaker walls had images on them at that date; they certainly did by the time of the print shown as figure 114. But art need not be framed or hung.

In his book *Shaker Village Views* Robert Emlen dismisses the town plans as art because they were not made to be hung. He sees them as mere diagrams or historic records. But even if they are classified as maps they need not be excluded from the category of conscious artistic statements: maps are collected by art museums. Further, these works that show numbered and colored buildings regularly introduce decorative features that go beyond the recording of roads, buildings, fences, trees, and other structural facts: for example, birds carry ribbons inscribed with the title of the work, and the arrows that indicate north are typically very elaborate. Clearly the artists delighted in such details and on occasion included wagons, carriages with horses and drivers, and pedestrians. In one drawing, balloons that come from the heads of two Brothers contain the words being spoken. In another, foreground figures add charm as they establish a sense of depth. In a drawing probably by Joshua H. Bussell, the artist borrowed the layout of the town and the foreground figures from a commercially produced wood engraving of 1835 (figures 159 and 160). Showing the selective mind of an artist, he eliminated some sheep, moved the two he used, added a horse, a sun, a very decorative north-pointing arrow, and in the sky the title, "Shaker Village. Canterbury. N.H."

There are periodic attempts to place Shaker artistic statements under the term *folk art*. This is never a happy fit, particularly when everything Believers made is lumped together as one kind of art. In fact, much of what they produced followed long established rural traditions in both design and manner of execution. Many of the makers were trained in those traditions while still in the world; others spent a conventional six or seven years learning a trade from skilled Shakers. The Shakers also often hired workers from the world. The gift drawings, however, are by untrained artists and more neatly fit the traditional folk designation.

LOOKING AT THE DRAWINGS

Many of the better known drawings provide the name of the spirit delivering the vision, the name of the person to whom it was sent, the instrument who received it, and the person who transformed it into a painted image (the receiver and the recorder may be different people). A drawing may have both the date it was delivered and the date when it was recorded. The name of the community in which it was experienced may be included. Often the community's spiritual name is used: Holy Mount for New Lebanon, for example. Often there is one or several texts in paragraph form. The depictions of heavenly spirits, plantings, and furnishings may be named, and their significance given: for example, lamps as Christ's guidance; harps for joyful worship; drums denoting soldiers of God; swords signifying power; ladders recording a means to pass between earth and heaven; birds or heads with outstretched wings representing departed saints; and wings alone to signify the "wings of Holy Wisdom" and "Wings of Heavenly Father." Many of the meanings found in Shaker work are the same, or close to, those for similar emblems used by worldly groups, sects, denominations, and religions. Winged heads were so common that they easily appeared in such fanciful watercolors as "Angels are now hovering around us," by Mary Ann Willson of Greenville, Green County, New York, made in 1800–1825 (figure 161). In it young women wearing hats and earrings appear on wings colored red, yellow, and blue; the palette is the same as that which the Shakers adapted at the same date from neoclassical coloring.

161. THREE ANGEL HEADS
By Mary Ann Willson, Greenville, Green County, New York
Inscribed: "Angels now are hovering round us . . . ."
1800–25
Ink and watercolor on paper
H. 16" W. 13"
M. and M. Karolik Collection, Museum of Fine Arts, Boston

The parallels between the Shaker and Masonic colors and emblems were noted in Chapter VII. The Bible is the standard source for the images and their meanings refer mainly to objects in Solomon's Temple and those delineated in Revelation: candlesticks, gold chains, gates, paired columns, winged angels, trumpets, swords, books, trees of life, paths of gold, precious jewels, and pearls. Other biblical sources provide such images as Jacob's ladder as a means between heaven and earth. The Masonic tracing board (a layout of the stages of the ritual) in figure 162 was painted and gold leafed by the Masonic Brother Jonas Prentiss of West Cambridge, Massachusetts, in 1818. He was a member of the Hiram Lodge located in what is now Arlington. Upon entering it visually, the viewer "passes" various Masonic emblems that include a ladder marked for faith, hope, and charity, and the Bible, while passing through the pillars Jachin and Boaz (see p. 126). Then the viewer "climbs" the three steps to the Masonic pavement representing the porch of King Solomon's Temple. The squares there are centered by a star and are enclosed in a tessellated border. Beyond this is the Temple itself. There are winged heads in the pediment, and above the celestial arch, the sun, the moon with the Masons' standard seven stars, and an all-seeing eye. In other Masonic works, the Temple is shown as a very large and architecturally complex building. A few Masonic designs show a very simple building, only slightly more grand than the one in the Shaker drawing in figure 163. In the Shaker image the viewer "climbs" steps placed between a checkerboard-enriched wall that fronts a porch. The outer corners of the porch have decorative columns, as do the corners of the building. The Shaker-paired doors are flanked by columns that rise to curve in and hold globes or lights. (During the first decade of the nineteenth century, in Masonic images, the celestial and the terrestrial globes that had rested on the checkered floor, moved up onto the main paired pillars. They are symbolized by the round balls on top of the large pillars in figure 162.) To people used to looking at Masonic images, the roof in figure 163 is shaped like a baldachino, or cloth canopy, placed over an altar or throne. Just below its lower central arch is an all-seeing eye.

Many of the symbols, as drawn by the Shakers, take the form of objects the Shakers used and prized on earth, but with a decorative surface added for use in life-everlasting: recognizable Shaker chairs and tables become fancier, normally through more complex coloring. The central icon of the faith, the 1822–24 New Lebanon meetinghouse, appears with recognizable tightness of form and barrel-shaped roof, but the surface is suitably decorated, as seen in the lower left of figure 164. That drawing also uses symbols significant to Freemasonry: the all-seeing eye, stars, moons, a checkerboard pattern enclosed in a tessellated line, winged angels, an ark, and a pair of

162. MASONIC TRACING BOARD
By Jonas Prentiss, West Cambridge, Massachusetts
February 18, 1818
Oil and gold leaf on canvas
H. 72" W. 48"
Museum of Our National Heritage, Lexington, Massachusetts; gift of Hiram Lodge

163. "A PRESENT FROM MOTHER LUCY TO ELIZA ANN TAYLOR"
By Polly Reed, New Lebanon, New York, Church Family
April 8, 1849
Blue ink and watercolor on pale blue paper
H. 14" W. 16³⁄₈"
Hancock Shaker Village, Pittsfield, Massachusetts

164. UNTITLED GIFT DRAWING
Attributed to Sarah Bates
New Lebanon, New York
1840s
Ink and watercolor on paper
H. 15" W. 20¾"
Philadelphia Museum of Art, Philadelphia,
Pennsylvania; gift of Mr. and Mrs. Julius Zieget

columns. Worldly forms not easily allowed into Shaker spaces are regularly part of their heavenly furnishings. For example, there is a gold Greek revival, saber-leg chair and what looks like a puffed stool in figure 165, with four curved saber-form legs. The latter is labeled "Father Josephs Desk." (In many mid-eighteenth- and nineteenth-century depictions of Masonic rituals the Bible, which is the focal point of the arrangement, sits on a saber-leg table; many of these were drawn long before the Greek revival style made the shape fashionable.)[36]

The text of the drawing attributed to Miranda Barber in figure 165 includes: "So, Come sit down in the Mansion of the blessed to go no more out." Four angels blow the four horns of Revelations, while a horse, bull, sheep, and Mother Ann in her golden chariot decorate the lower edge. Brothers and Sister's doors, marked between them "Come Thou Blessed," are reached by way of a left and right flight of golden stairs. (These recall the similar Masonic use of steps that signal the entrance to the Masonic commitment and Solomon's Temple.) Above each flight, a door has a rendering of an iron, Shaker-design door latch in profile.[37]

The drawing "Seen and painted in the City of Peace [Hancock] by Hannah Cohoon," on September 13, 1854 (figure 166), records that "I saw a beautiful great bower four square on the ground, the trees met together overhead as you will perceive by the representation; it was painted upon a large white sheet and held up over the brothrens heads, I saw it very distinctly . . . . The long white table standing under the bower . . . with cakes knives etc. upon it . . . . The ground was cover'd with beautiful short green grass . . . ." (The text cites biblical references to mulberry trees: II Samuel 5:24 and I Chronicles 14:14, 15.)

The drawing is unusual in having its entire surface, inside the strong blue edge, covered with an opaque white. This follows in the literal manner characteristic of the Shakers, the vision being "painted upon a large white sheet." The table was depicted in "Shaker Yellow," although the vision asked for a white table, probably so that it can be seen against the white ground. Most real Shaker tables were not of either color. Above the bottom blue edge is short green grass. This record of a heavenly repast coincided with the last year of the Mountain Meetings, begun in 1842, where Believers figuratively consumed sumptuous feasts.

From Holy Mother Wisdom. To Elder Ebenezer Bishop.

Thou art sealed with eternal life; a Priest of the Most High God and shalt reign with Him Forever. Thou hast found thy salvation through pain and sufferings and now thou shalt have thy reward. So Come and sit down in the Mansion of the blessed to go no more out. Come with Wisdom for thy mansion is prepared, and the feast made ready; here in my holy Court in thy robe and crown. Come, for thy joy will be full, in my Love.

165. "FROM HOLY MOTHER WISDOM.
TO ELDER EBENEZER BISHOP."
*Attributed to Miranda Barber, New Lebanon,
New York, Church Family
1840s
Ink and watercolor on paper
H. 11³/₈" W. 14½"
Philadelphia Museum of Art, Philadelphia,
Pennsylvania; gift of Mr. and Mrs. Julius Zieget*

166. "A BOWER OF MULBERRY TREES"
*By Hannah Cohoon, Hancock, Massachusetts
September 13, 1854
Ink, watercolor and tempera on paper
H. 18¹/₈" W. 23¹/₁₆"
Hancock Shaker Village, Pittsfield, Massachusetts*

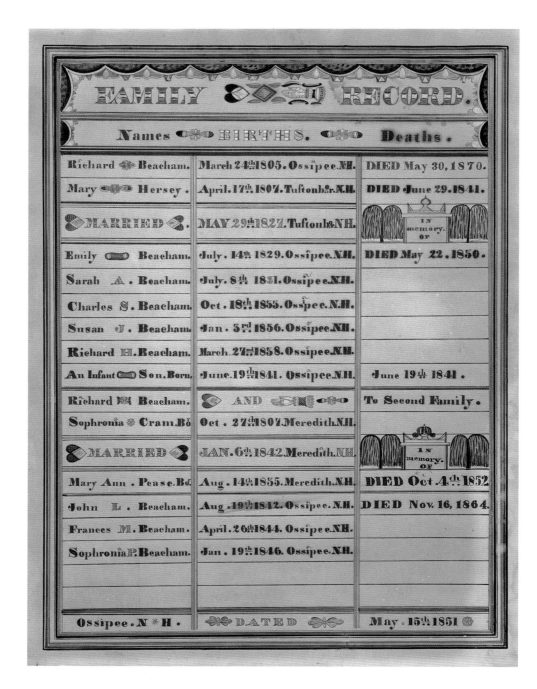

167. BEACHMAN FAMILY RECORD
Probably by Mary Hall
Ossipee, New Hampshire
May 15, 1851
Ink and watercolor on paper
H. 14¹¹/₁₆" W. 10¹⁵/₁₆"
M. and M. Karolik Collection, Museum of Fine Arts, Boston

Opposite:
168. "AN EMBLEM OF THE HEAVENLY SPHERE"
By Polly Collins, Hancock, Massachusetts
January, 1854
Blue and black ink and watercolor on paper
H. 23³/₄" W. 18⁵/₈"
Hancock Shaker Village, Pittsfield, Massachusetts

The shapes of the emblems, and how they were arranged on a sheet of paper, were influenced by images both at-hand and remembered. The primary but not exclusive sources were: gravestone iconography (which used an ordered text and often showed winged heads), appliqué quilts, embroideries such as bedcovers and samplers, printed textiles, decorated ceramic plates, decorated tinware, books, and other printed matter. The similarities between gift drawings that are basically grids and calendar quilts were discussed with figures 72 through 74. Worldly family records on paper or textiles were often in grids of parallel lines, as in figure 167. They are similar to the hierarchical arranged drawings of Shaker saints in figure 168.

In the extraordinary drawing, "An Emblem of the Heavenly Sphere . . . A Present from Mother Ann, given Jan. 1854. Dictated by the Prophet[es?]s Deborah." (figure 168), Polly Collins produced a family tree of Shaker saints. It is edged by a blue line that is set out slightly where it flanks the text in the upper fourth of the drawing. Vertical lines of squares flank images of Shaker saints stacked hierarchically, twelve high and four across. They are crowned by rainbows. In the top tier, from left to right, are Ann Lee, James Whittaker, William Lee, and Christopher Columbus, who is honored for finding America where the Shaker faith prospered. Jesus is below Ann Lee, and to his right is Saint Paul. Most of the outer squares contain heavenly trees or flowers. In two labeled "Bower of Love" and "Bower of Peace," there are yellow benches. "Treasure Table" appears in the square below the left bench. In the lower left square, "Writing Room Guardian Angel," there is a

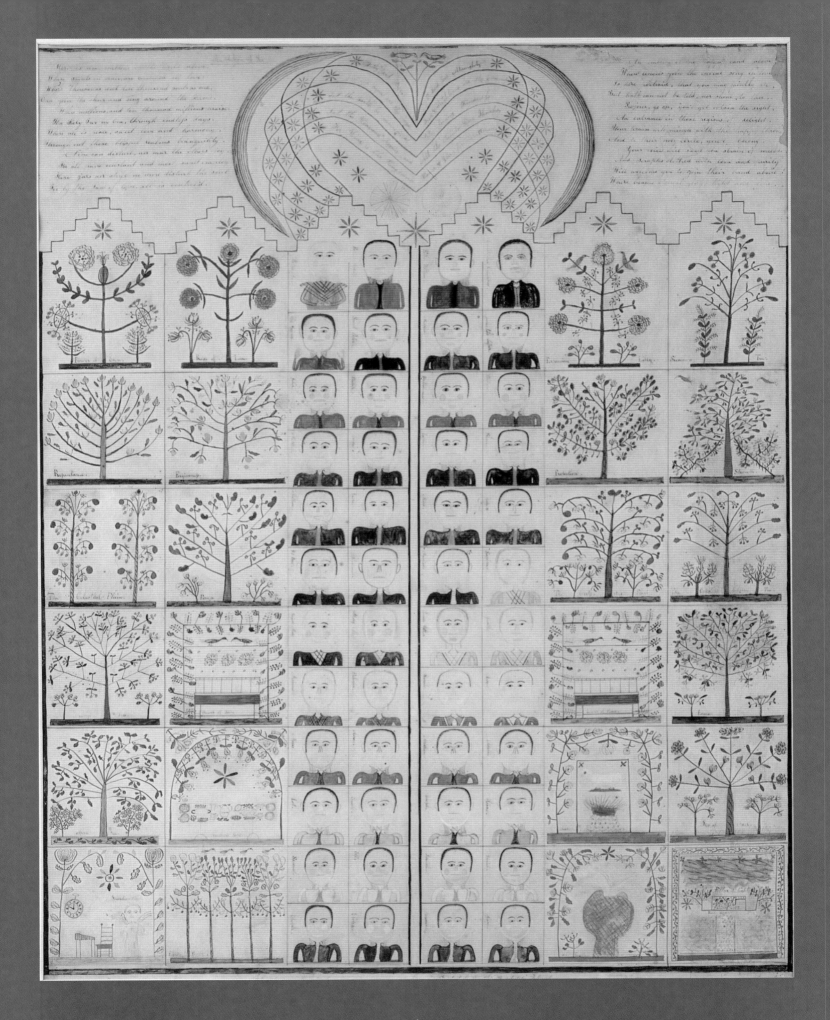

In the image, handwritten on the drawing:
love, *joy*, *peace*, *temperance*, *mechanist*, *kindness*, *virtue*, *charity*, *faith*, *hope*, *patience*, *purity*

*To cultivate the youthful mind
In knowledge useful and refined
Has been your teachers ardent care
And stamp impressions deep & fair*

*Elizabeth view her interest here
And humbly claim a saving share
By true repentance faith & love
And be prepared for joys above*

Tree   Life

*Presented to Miss Elizabeth Perry for her delegence
improvement and good behaviour while at School
Rebecca Bliss*

169. REWARD OF MERIT "PRESENTED
TO MISS ELIZABETH PERRY"
By Rebecca Bliss, teacher
Probably New England
1820–40
Pencil, ink, and watercolor on paper
H. 9½" W. 8"
Private collection

yellow desk and a red slat-back chair. As in all great Shaker thoughts and images there is a rich play between this physical object and the spirit world. Such gifts record expected heavenly bliss, where the saved will one day use rather exotic versions of day-to-day objects, as well as more fanciful ones not allowed in Shaker communities on earth. Many such drawings also show angels. They were not thought of as something in the future, however, for the Shakers experienced heavenly spirits as normal events.

Many worldly forms of trees of life on textile or paper are close to those painted by Shaker hands. Often the worldly ones have the fruit inscribed with a name, if it is a family tree, or a word or phrase, as in the award of merit, figure 169. This drawing was made by Rebecca Bliss for her student Elizabeth Perry, probably in New England. (There were Bliss and Perry families in Rehoboth, Massachusetts.) Many of the yellow fruits are titled with virtues. Some of the worldly trees have, like Shaker images, an earth mound or an area of grass holding the tree. The green and red leaves and fruits of the Shaker tree of life in figure 170 are enriched with embroidery-like markings. Since the drawing was made at Hancock, where the 1830 Brick Dwelling House had four coats of red paint on the bricks and exterior green doors, the artist may have been acknowledging the building's colors. In another drawing by the same artist the leaves have dashes around their edges as though they were bits of textile sewn in place (figure 171). A general neoclassical sense of placement and detailing found on many embroidered pieces is reflected in many gift

170. "THE TREE OF LIFE"
By Hannah Cohoon, Hancock, Massachusetts
July 3, 1854
Pencil, ink, and watercolor or tempera on paper
H. 18⅛" W. 23⁵⁄₁₆"
Hancock Shaker Village, Pittsfield, Massachusetts

171. "THE TREE OF LIGHT OR BLAZING TREE"
By Hannah Cohoon, Hancock, Massachusetts
October 9, 1845
Ink and watercolor on paper
H. 18⅛" W. 22⁹⁄₃₂"
Hancock Shaker Village, Pittsfield, Massachusetts

drawings. The Connecticut embroidery piece in figure 172 uses a lean design, and like many Shaker works, was laid out with the aid of a compass or circular patterns. This textile made in Windsor, Connecticut, about 1813, has figures, birds, flowers, and shrubs dotted about, as do some Shaker drawings. Many Shaker drawings emphasize circular designs, and they may incorporate flowers. These, too, are like designs found on textiles, and circular designs are one of the basic arrangements used on hand-decorated "folk" pottery. There, borders surround and enclose a central pattern; a gift drawing with a similar arrangement is shown as figure 173.

Many of the gift drawings are less popular today because they lack bright colors, and many have indecipherable lines that now seem mysterious. As with the example shown as figure 174, most are unsigned. Most are also undated. But if studied, these are visually exciting and intellectually informative: they depict places, arranged in an orderly manner, with regimentated forms and lines, and thus express Shaker concerns of spiritual, personal, and community order. They

172. BEDCOVER
By Mary Beebe Strong, Windsor, Connecticut
About 1813
Embroidered linen
L. 86¼" W. 78¾"
Courtesy of America Hurrah Antiques, New York,
New York

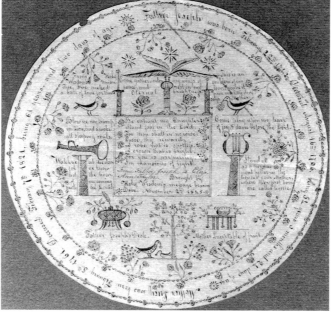

**173. "FROM FATHER JOSEPH, TO ELIZA-
ANN TAYLOR"**
By Sarah Bates, New Lebanon, New York
November 2, 1845
Ink on paper
Diam. 6"
Western Reserve Historical Society Library,
Cleveland, Ohio

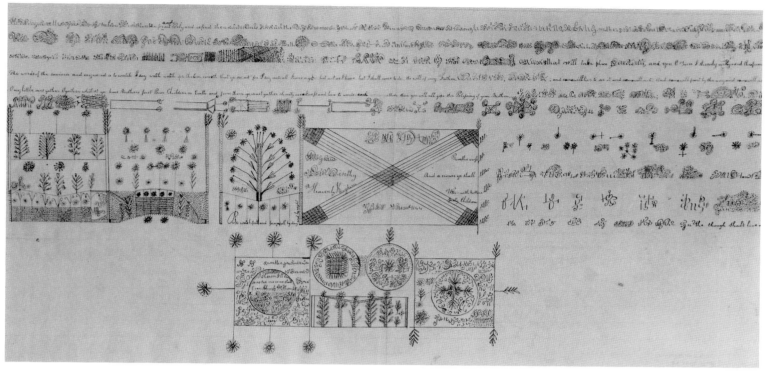

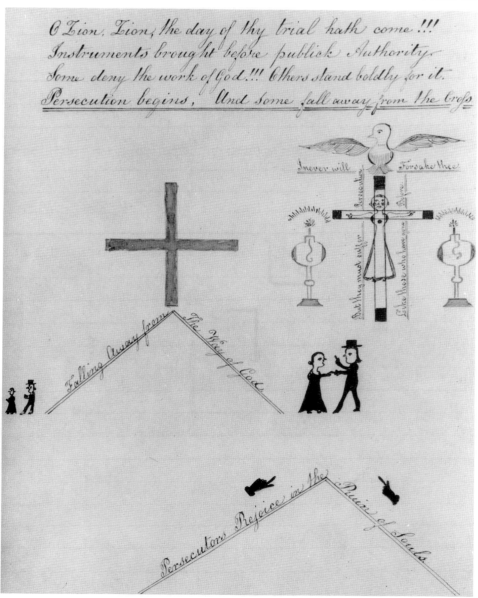

174. "WORD OF THE SAVIOUR"
New Lebanon, New York
Inscribed in pencil: "Seen June 9, 1843 Copied
June 14 Word of the Saviour"; in the picture the
date 1850 is given in ink
Blue ink on paper; two sided drawing, on separate
sheets glued back to back
H. 16" W. 31¾"
Collection of the Shaker Museum and Library,
Old Chatham, New York

175. ANN LEE'S CROSS
Attributed to Miranda Barber and Polly Reed
New Lebanon, New York
June 1848
Ink and watercolor on paper; in a manuscript
book of inspired writings and drawings
H. 8½" W. 6 ½"
Western Reserve Historical Society Library,
Cleveland, Ohio

resemble the grids of Shaker towns, fields, and working and living spaces. They also echo objects of daily Shaker habit: regimented walls of doors and drawers, lines of peg rails, and long halls. At the same time the indecipherable marks on the drawings are full of the energy of visiting spirits. These drawings, therefore, combine two aspects of the Shaker life: order, and an openness to spirit possession that disrupts order.

Many gift drawings included crosses. Some of these were Christian in form, with a long vertical, as on the right in figure 175. There Mother Ann is repeating Christ's redemptive act, and she is enclosed in words: "I never will forsake thee," "But they must suffer," "Like those who have gone Before." She is flanked by paired lamps, rather than two thieves. Many of the crosses were in the Greek cross form, with arms of equal length. These were either vertical and horizontal in orientation, as at the left in figure 175, or tipped, as in figure 176. The latter was one of two large inscribed wooden crosses used at New Lebanon to warn off outsiders when, in 1842, the worship services were closed to the public.[38]

DEPICTING THE STRUGGLE

Many of the less picturesque drawings deal with the psychological and physical work the Shakers undertook on earth to know God. They describe the suffering and mortification the earthly struggle could entail.

Many Shakers have found it hard to carry the crosses of celibacy and obedience to heavenly and earthly leaders. The apostate Reuben Rathbun wrote in 1800 that the "First Ministers" had taught Believers to destroy "the nature of generation, both as to the inclination of the spirit and the natural faculties of the body."[39] In 1812 Thomas Brown wrote: "They told me that some had had gifts of mortification, to bark like a dog, and crow like a cock, make a noise like a squirrel, and mew like a cat. Also, that many have had the gifts to rejoice by laughing, &c."[40] "They now pressed forward in the work of mortification and suffering with cheerfulness and resolution, and endeavoured by every possible means to root out and destroy this inherent propensity [desire for sex] . . . . They often danced with vehemence through the greatest part of the night, and then

176. MEETINGHOUSE CROSS
New Lebanon, New York
1842
Paint on wood
Crossed boards: L. of boards 36⅛" D. 1⅞"
Hancock Shaker Village, Pittsfield, Massachusetts

instead of reposing their wearied bodies upon a bed, they would, by way of further penance, lie down upon the floor on chains, ropes, sticks, in every humiliating and mortifying posture they could devise."[41] Brown reported some early Believers whipping themselves to mortify the flesh.[42] About 1793 three girls were made to strip and whip themselves and each other as a means of mortification for watching two flies having sex.[43] As Isaac Newton Youngs reported, "The prevailing motto and theme was *mortification,* crucifixion of pride and self, in spirit, which was sought for thro' mortification of the body." [44]

In a letter to Youngs, working at Watervliet, of April 3, 1826, his friend Garret K. Lawrence discussed the prospects of a husband and wife actually joining the Society, and whether the husband would survive what he would be put through:

Joseph Babe with his wife & 4 children came here from Boston, either since you left here or before. Joseph appears quite tender *[open to commitment], but his wife is quite* tough; *and means to consider long enough, before she starts for the kingdom. I am told the man has opened his mind [confessed], but I observe he still puts his hands in the fashionable pockets, steps across the floor and says, good morning with quite a Boston air. I apprehend this babe would like very well to rock in the cradle of gospel liberty, and hang upon the tree of life, till his debts are all paid, but should the wind of mortification blow, I fear down would come cradle, ba—be and all.*[45]

Hervey Elkins recorded extended use of humiliation by the leaders as a means of testing the more advanced Believers to see if they qualified for a governing role: "It is common for the leaders to crowd down, by humiliation, and withdraw patronage and attention from those whom they intend to ultimately promote to an official station. That such may learn how it seems to be slighted and humiliated, and how to stand upon their own basis, work spiritually for their own food without being dandled upon the soft lap of affection, or fed with the milk designed for babes."[46] With the quickening of religious activity of the 1830s and 1840s there was again an earnestness of commitment, and an emphasis on mortifying the flesh. About 1847 Enoch Jacobs left the Ohio Shakers, saying he would rather "go to hell with Electra his wife than live among the Shakers without her."[47]

The suffering entailed was recorded in both gift drawings and gift songs. One of the more picturesque drawings attributed to Miranda Barber, an instrument for Holy Mother Wisdom during her visits to New Lebanon, was from "Holy Mother Wisdom," and sent "To elder Ebenezer Bishop" (figure 165). It is undated, but seems to fall in the mid-1840s. The first line of the inscription is gentle: "Thou art sealed with eternal life; a Priest of the Most High God and shall reign with Him Forever." The second line is about how this state was achieved: "Thou hast found thy Salvation through pain and suffering and now thou shalt have thy reward." Another gift drawing attributed to Barber,[48] figure 177, is a rectangle with each corner filled by a near-square with five prison bars. The remaining area forms a cross and on this are two doves and two scourges. At the top is written, "Some scourged and cast into Prison for their faith." This recalled for the Shakers Ann Lee and others in prison—both in England and America. Still another drawing attributed to Barber (figure 178) and drawn in 1843, depicts the cataclysm that will be visited on the unrepentant: "And there will be terrible winds in the earth and fire and hail, and dreadful earthquakes." The images are titled "Hail," "Earthquakes," "Fire," and "Wind," symbols linked together in Revelations, as punishments. These are not gentle ideas and were not meant to be easy or soothing; they recorded that the move into the love of God, and remaining there, was demanding.

THE NARROW PATH

The Turning Shuffle (p. 77) had been introduced about 1790, when Joseph Meacham sought to increase the strenuous character of the dance. Members were to "labor down into mortification & into as deep and heavy bearing for the loss of man, as any body of people was able to endure, even deeper than any would ever hereafter be required to descend."[49] An 1815 letter records the noise of such concentration: "the Sound is like mighty thunderings, Some a Stamping with all their might and Roaring out against the nasty stinking beast . . . . Others turning with great Power and warring against the flesh, and at the same time a number Speaking with new tongues with Such Majestic Signs and motions that it makes the powers of Darkness tremble . . . ." [50]

In 1840, a new dance, "Walking the Narrow Path," helped purge those weak in commitment. The gift of this ritual was from the spirits of Ann Lee, William Lee, and James Whittaker. The sec-

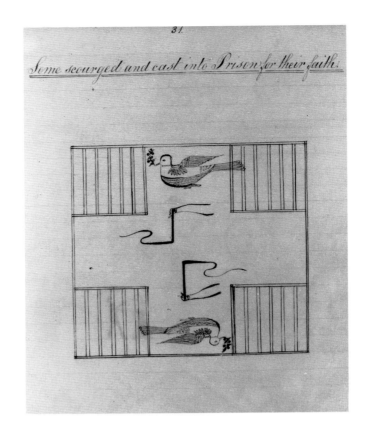

177. "SOME SCOURGED AND CAST INTO
PRISON FOR THEIR FAITH."
Attributed to Miranda Barber, New Lebanon,
New York, Church Family
June, 1843
Blue and brown ink on paper; page 31 in an
untitled manuscript book of inspired writings and
drawings
H. 8½" W. 7"
Shown in color as figure 268
Western Reserve Historical Society Library,
Cleveland, Ohio

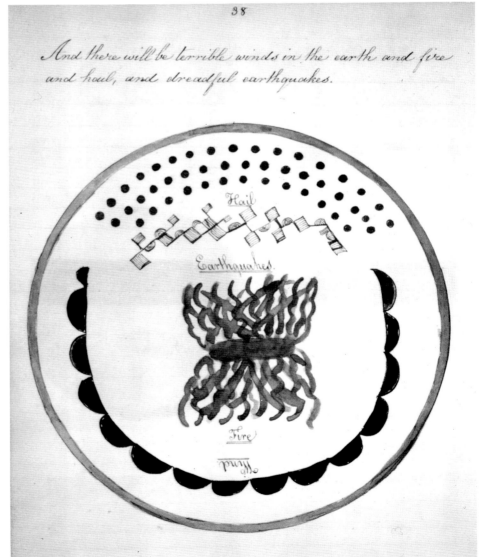

178. "AND THERE WILL BE TERRIBLE
WINDS IN THE EARTH . . . ."
Attributed to Miranda Barber, New Lebanon,
New York, Church Family
June, 1843
Blue ink and watercolor on paper; page 38 in an
untitled book of inspired writings and drawings
H. 8½" W. 7"
Western Reserve Historical Society Library,
Cleveland, Ohio

ond of these had been one of the greatest experiencers of ecstatic behavior among the first Believers; the third was perhaps the most determined among the early Church to mortify the flesh. The March had been introduced by Lucy Wright in 1817 as "a figure of marching the heavenly road, and walking the streets of the New Jerusalem,"[51] but this Narrow Path gift was something new. It involves a slow heel-to-toe walking on the cracks of the meetinghouse floor. It strengthened the strong and exposed the weak:

November [1], 1840
Right after Union meeting those between 60 & 30 were called together.—The elders spake, that Fr Wm [Father William Lee] had made known the mind of our heavenly parents, concerning those of us now called together.—Fr Wm had brot for each of us a strait & narrow path to walk, it was strait as straitness, no turning to the right nor left. And he desired we would each of us devote 10 minutes everyday to walk in this path. Daniel [Boler] & Betsey [Betsy Bates] showed how we were to walk placing one foot just before the other—walk in solemn meditation, & and in the fear of God—This doing daily, until our heavenly parents should meet with us, which would be in their own time. After this F. James [Whittaker] spake to us . . . . He said when we walked this narrow path let it be in perfect silence, in prayer & the fear of God . . . She [Mother Ann Lee] then asked Betsy if she would walk with her in her strait path, yea—then Betsy & the instrument [person speaking for Mother Ann Lee] walked the line of the floor thro the alley [empty space between the brothers' and sisters' ranks in the meeting house] to the foot [far end] slowly, placing one foot right before the other . . . After this E. Br [Elder Brother David Meacham] proposed for Mother's class to walk in the strait path. We walked some time, on the joints of the floor,—& the rest stood by.[52]

Three days later Father James brought a song "to walk the strait narrow path in," on the cracks between the floorboards[53] (see music and song, figure 179).

179. GIFT SONG FOR WALKING THE NARROW PATH
1840
From Daniel W. Patterson's, The Shaker Spiritual, *p. 363*

The use of a penitential path is not unique to the Shakers, for example, some medieval monastic churches have penitential paths of one color of stone, or brick, imbedded in a different color stone. Various early monks, and other spiritual seekers, wrote of the narrow path to salvation. Peter Damian wrote to Stephen, a fellow monk in 1057, "this road [the eremitic life], moreover, is both wide and narrow, but in such a way that whoever follows it possessed of a desire of Heaven, is not harmfully impeded because of its narrowness, nor diverted from the straight line of virtue because of its width."[54] The Shakers' narrow path has a parallel in the Buddhist tradition.[55]

The gift drawing in figure 180, executed by Emily Babcock about 1843, was about 8½ feet long. It depicts walking the narrow path. At one end of the ruled lines are the fruit tree and brick walls of Zion hovered over by angels. Along the path leading to this goal are instruments of mortification that seekers could experience. Believers could use the tools for self-inflicted pain to further themselves on the way to salvation, or evil people (or Satan) could use them to cause Believers pain and disruption. Surviving the struggle produced martyrs and saints. The eight sheets that comprise the drawing vary in length, from 12³/₁₆ inches to 12⅞ inches, and are approximately 4 inches wide. Although they are now separate, they were once attached to each other by

Overleaf:
180. THE NARROW PATH TO ZION (8 SHEETS FORMERLY ATTACHED IN A LINE)
Attributed to Emily Babcock (1823–apostatized 1846), New Lebanon, New York, Second Family Possibly 1843
W. most sheets 4" L. total length 8'5³/₈"; seven sheets varying in length from 12³/₈" to 12⅞" with black ink; final "Walls of Zion" sheet, 12³/₁₆", with blue and black ink
Shaker Collection. Ms. 106, Rare Books and Manuscript Division, The New York Public Library. Astor, Lenox and Tilden Foundation, New York, New York.

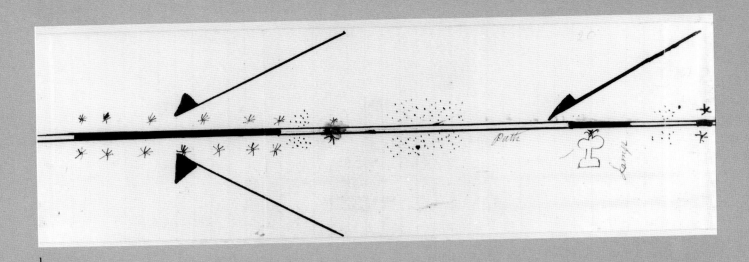

1

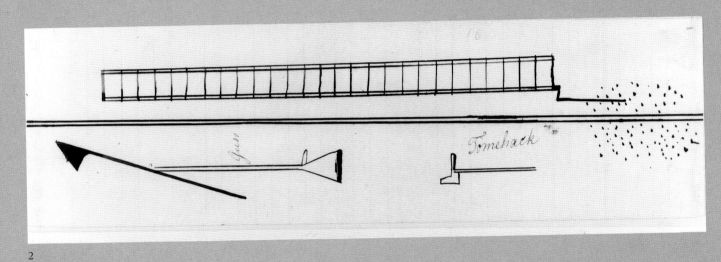

Path *Lamp*

2

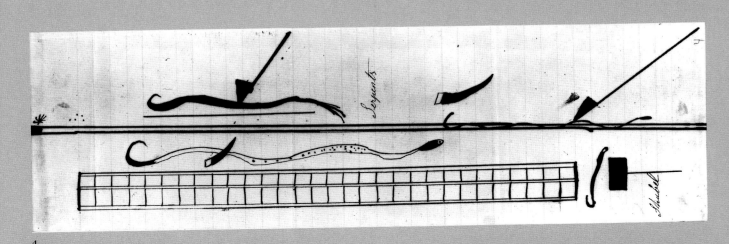

Gun *Tomehack*

3

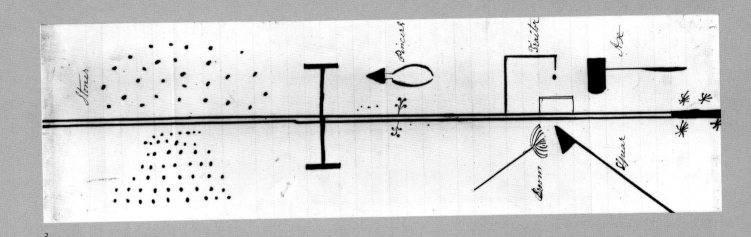

Stones *Pincers* *Smelt* *Ax* *Sword* *Spear*

4

Serpents

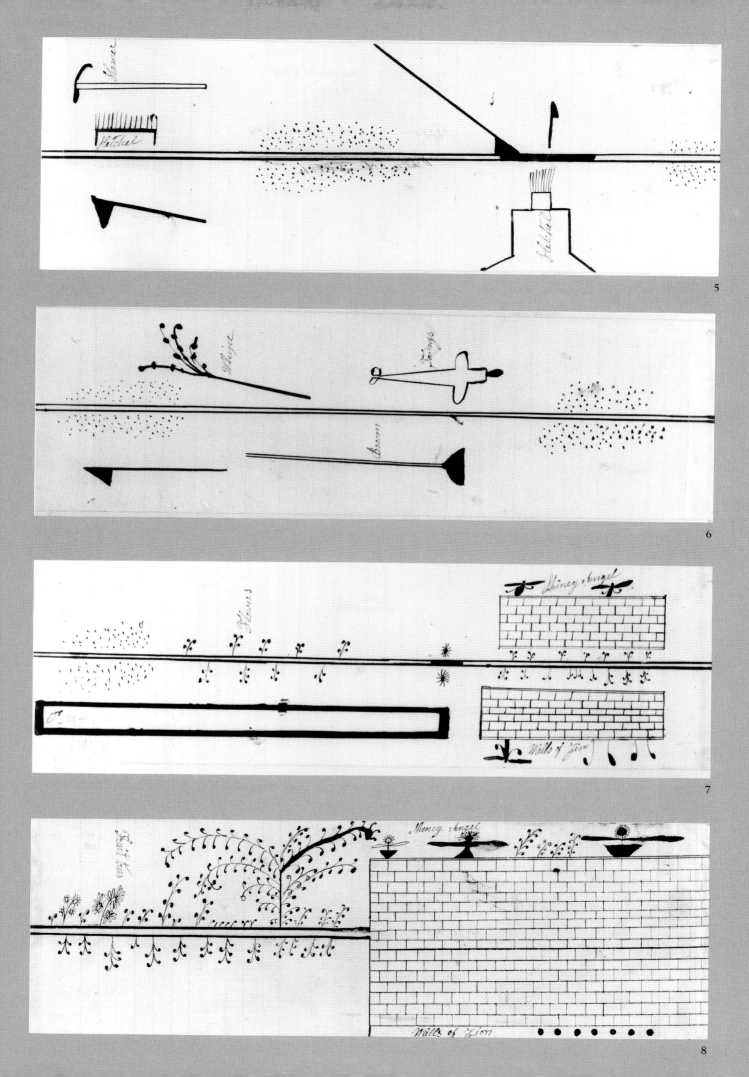

5

6

7

8

narrow strips of glued paper. Some sense of their original order can be obtained by studying the central pair of ruled lines, which were adjusted to match the ends of other pairs. Some of the edges of the sheets have been trimmed to meet with abutting edges. Their original order still remains uncertain, and there may have been more sheets in the group. All but the last are in black ink. The sheet depicting Zion, the goal of the path, is in blue ink—except for the three inscriptions, which are black. This sheet is the only one with words—"fruit trees"—facing back toward the beginning, but this is probably not significant. A ruler was used to make the lines of the path and the horizontals of the brick walls. The verticals on the walls were done freehand. The artist depicted a lamp to see by and the following tools: a Gun, a "Tomehack," Stones, Pincers, a Broom, a gallows (titled "Traitor"), a Spear, an Ax, Serpents, a "Shubel" [shovel], a Hetchel [used for breaking flax], a Hammer, a Whip, and Tongs. All these objects symbolize the stages or times of hardship in a Shaker's spiritual path. One scholar writing about this drawing speculated: "Either the artist was making an idiosyncratic interpretation of the ritual or she was hard pressed to think of objects that would adequately symbolize inward threats like pride, anger, lust, sloth, gluttony, and unbelief."[56] I would argue that she depicted the flesh-tearing quality of mortifying oneself as necessary to achieve the perfection required for sainthood.

In 1844 a seventeen-foot-long scroll was unrolled on benches during worship in the Watervliet meetinghouse. It had been "written by Inspiration, & in hiragliphics about a year since."[57] The use of a narrow path in life was not new in the 1840s, for as noted in Chapter VI, Charles Nordhoff saw at Pleasant Hill, and elsewhere, walks connecting buildings so narrow two persons could not walk abreast.

Christian literature is replete with instances of finding the struggle to salvation demanding, sometimes beyond toleration. In the 1730s Jonathan Edwards's uncle became so obsessed with his own sinfulness that he cut his throat. As the news of his suicide spread "multitudes in this and other towns seemed to have it strongly suggested to 'em, and pressed upon 'em, to do as this person had done."[58] Shaker writings record suicides among Believers, but none seem to have an awareness of sin as the cause.[59] There are in Shaker literature instances of total subjugation of the body during religious ecstasy. Many of the groups of seekers to which the Ministry sent missionaries were already disposed to welcome the frenzy that the Shakers could induce. In Maine they found converts among those who had been excited in 1781 by a Freewill Baptist evangelist. Some became so rowdy and bizarre that it was necessary "to take them out and fasten them with ropes to a tree."[60] In the height of religious passion, an overlay of obedience and self-inflicted ascetic deprivation can provide periods of ecstasy that require physical restraints, often mixing the ascetic with the sensual. Hervey Elkins reported times when possession among the Shakers became so extreme that restraints were necessary. Instruments normally conveyed good spirits, but they could be filled with bad spirits—often the spirits of apostates—and the mediums might then writhe about in anguish.[61] In one instance the possessed one came to himself after being bound with a "surcingle," or strap.[62]

SEXUALITY

Sexuality is implicit in these references. The role of frenzied worshipers, dancing for extended periods of time, or emotional spirit-led activities inside or outside of formal worship, surely helped deplete the need, or substituted for, sexual activity. Slow marching and other rituals of mortification permitted exhaustion to overcome interest. In Chapter II it was seen how some struggled under the watchful and demanding eye of Joseph Meacham to eliminate even the natural emission of semen, and when they failed, gave up the attempt.

The Shakers have been frank about acknowledging the cost of bearing the cross of celibacy; many have seen it as the hardest part of the Shaker life. Others, such as Lucy Wright, felt "I hate my old natural disposition and I find need of the cross."[63] Any personal contact between the sexes was carefully prevented. The 1845 Laws include many protective rules, ranging from the general to the specific: "Brethren and sisters may not pass each other on the stairs"; "Sisters must not mend, nor set buttons on brethren's clothes, while they have them on." Perhaps as a protection against a cross-dressing interest they add: "Brethren and sisters must not wear each other's clothes, nor be trying them on, on any occasion whatever."[64] The Shakers have been wary about how sex and celibacy among the Shakers are discussed by outsiders. In 1984, the Tenth Annual Shaker Conference sponsored by Elmira College and Berkshire Community College was based at

Mount Lebanon. The announcement of the conference listed a visit to the Shaker Museum where a lecture titled "Sex and the Single Shaker" was to be given by Richard E. Williams. When the Shakers at Sabbathday Lake saw the program they strongly protested this talk. It seems they disliked the title for it suggested to them a flippant handling of one of the most difficult crosses of the faith. It is not known if sex in general or a specific kind of sex was the issue. By the time the final program was printed, the title had been changed to "Perfectionistic Movements and Celibacy." Williams now feels it was the word "sex" in the original title that most offended. What he was addressing were the theological bases of a variety of religious practices. He investigated the relationship of spiritual and sexual ecstasy; he pointed out that the same biblical text had been used by groups to justify behavior as widely different as celibacy and polygamy; he did not address homosexuality.[65]

Clearly the many references to emotional ecstasy—hooting, running about naked, crying, laughing, rolling about together, restraints and binding—suggest sexual expression, and often Believers were carried away in same-sex groupings. Even during patterned religious dances, kissing Believers of the same sex was part of the ritual. Throughout the years (in 1782, 1827, and 1855, for example), it was recorded that the "gift of love" closed the service: women embraced women, and men embraced men. Elizabeth Lovegrove wrote in 1827, "we finished our meeting in hugging in loving and blessing each other in sincerity and truth."[66] Another manuscript of the same period records: "Elder Brother said let us arise from our knees and greet each other with a kiss of charity . . . so we all went to hugging and kissing in good earnest, and loved a heap."[67] A writer who spent three months as a Believer (probably in the 1840s), described what was for him distasteful kissing, distasteful because of the physical state of the other men: Services grew in excitement through marching, dancing, gesticulations, and singing until he was reminded of "whirling Dervishes of the East. For suddenly the whole company broke from their ranks into a wild whirl, traversing and retraversing the room in all directions, and each two, on meeting, kissing each other with no slight *impressment*. (Of course it must be understood that men only kissed men, as did women, women, for any other proceeding would have horrified the 'Believers.') For myself, I found the operation very little to my taste, since the men were mostly, both stolid in aspect, and extremely *rough-faced,* from the fact that shaving above twice a week was interdicted by law."[68] An engraving of 1870 shows Sisters kissing on the cheek during a circle dance.[69] Images, such as the one in figure 69, showing two Brothers facing each other in a room with beds, would today be read as conveying at least an emotional, if not a homoerotic, exchange.

Many of the descriptions of commitment to the Church, and love between members, employ cords and chains: "May we ever be bound together by the Silken cords of Love, as children of one Mother." Chains, whether gold or not, are regularly mentioned. David Austin Buckingham received from the spiritual world "a Basket made of flowers, in which were chains—one to bind him to the ministry one to bind him to the elders, the third to bind him to the brethren and sisters, & a 4th to bind & encircle him to the 2d order—this was done by Br. Eliab. The remainder were to be carried by 4 angels to Watervliet, and these to bind him to the whole church."[70]

Sexual interest between anyone is not acceptable in Shaker life, but possibly realizing the naturalness of the issue for those looking in from outside, homoerotic interest among Believers has been denied since the Shakers began explaining the faith in the eighteenth century. In the 1785 letter to his parents in England, James Whittaker wrote about "redemption from the bondage of corruption; which is that sordid propensity to, or ardent desire of copulation with women." As a protection against a criticism for not having children, he included that he had "begotten many thousands of children" by conversions to the faith. Then he twice dealt with the possibility of homosexuality. He used the contemporary word "effeminate," which may mean either homosexuality or the receptive partner. "Think ye that I will look toward you, while you live after the flesh, defiling yourselves with effeminate desires, and profaning the command of God for a cover?" And, "being separated from all effeminate desires and sensual pleasures." Thomas Brown, in his 1812 account of the Shakers, wrote: "The apostle Paul gives us an account of several characters that shall not inherit the kingdom of God; one of whom is the *effeminate*." Brown cited I Corinthians 6:9: "Be not deceived: neither fornicators, nor idolaters, not adulterers, nor effeminate, nor abusers of themselves with mankind." Later in his book Brown recorded from the writings of Reuben Rathbun (who was, during the 1790s, before he left the sect, an Elder at Hancock): "I have never had any unlawful connection with any woman; and from the time I first knew the Shakers to this time, I never defiled myself with what is called among you effeminacy."[71]

During the discussion of gay and lesbian rights in the military during the early 1990s, many members of the armed forces, who remained closeted and non-practicing sexually while in uniform, spoke of their comfort in all-male or all-female environments. It was not the possibility of sexual partners that attracted them, but the enjoyment and naturalness of being with the same sex. Future studies investigating both the comforts and the problems of cloistered, celibate, same-sex groupings will find the Shakers an important area of research. We do have some easily accessible evidence of same-sex bonding among the Shakers that goes beyond the general nineteenth-century practice of expressing love, even lavish and tender expressions of love, for those who are on the same religious journey.

Part of the difficulty in understanding sexuality in the nineteenth century is that before the last decade of the century, and the introduction of scientific categorization, terms for sexual behavior outside the heterosexual norm existed for men but not for women. Throughout history it has been recognized that a minority of men found beauty and pleasure in other males. At times they had a legitimate place in society and during others they have been ruled outsiders.[72] Writing about Walt Whitman, David S. Reynolds describes his freedom during the middle of the century to participate in and write about same-sex passions, which were seen as natural in America for "sexual types had not yet solidified." Both men and women felt sex to be fluid and could move freely between heterosexual and homosexual experiences. "The lack of clear sexual categories (homo-, hetero-, bi-) made same-sex affections unselfconscious and widespread." In the 1880s Whitman began to adjust his poems to suit a changing attitude toward sexually explicit poems, but it was his heterosexual poems that were getting him into trouble. As Reynolds points out, same-sex affection would remain "normal and acceptable in wide areas of American culture until the 1930s," but by 1900 the new categories began to diminish tolerance and Whitman, like others, became less open about his loves.[73]

Recently scholars have begun to deal with pre-categorized relationships between women: "Until the late nineteenth century, British and American men defined women's relations in platonic and romantic terms. Indeed, for centuries, within Western societies women's love for one another was considered to be one of women's noblest characteristics. Both men and women praised women's lifelong friendships, and their passionate declarations of love for other women. Although such loving relationships have existed in every century, the first two-thirds of the nineteenth century enveloped them with an aura of intense romanticism."[74] Alfred Kinsey's statistics showed that 12 percent of women in his sample who were born in the nineteenth century had had lesbian contacts to orgasm.[75] Since these relationships were not seen as deviant, and many of those involved did not think of them as sex, such friendships did not generally prevent the women from marrying. During the last decades of the nineteenth century such researchers as Havelock Ellis began to categorize male sexual behavior, and they felt a need to balance their work by defining the behavior of women. Then, for the first time, what had been seen as a natural relationship between women was isolated and acknowledged as a separate pattern of behavior, and female homosexuals stood in the same relationship to society as their male counterparts.[76]

Another factor clouding our understanding of women's behavior and their own understanding of it has been that until recently studies seeking to understand an earlier time have been carried out by men and from their perspective. New feminist studies have begun to explore the woman's point of view. New research on women during the Second Great Awakening, the worldly revivalist frenzy that just preceded the Shaker Era of Manifestations, is informative when considering the submission of women to the Shaker life. "The submission required of those who were to be saved was consistent with female socialization, but this submission was also an act of initiation and assertion of strength by female converts. Conversion set up a direct relation to God's authority that allowed female converts to denigrate or bypass man's authority—to defy man—for God."[77] There must have been an increase in conscious and unconscious satisfaction when submitting to female authority in a sect that made God male and female, and placed Ann Lee side by side with Jesus. Since personal writings such as journals and letters were read by the Ministry, or someone they designated, any recording of any physical interest is rare.

Rebecca Jackson

An example of female bonding was recorded in the many writings of Rebecca Cox Jackson, a free African-American woman born near Philadelphia in 1795, and her longtime companion Rebecca Perot. Rebecca Cox married Samuel S. Jackson and they almost certainly did not have children. A seamstress, she was a visionary who had elaborate spiritual dreams and out-of-the-body experiences while awake. She became a Methodist preacher, and in 1831 experienced a revelation that "destroyed the lust of my flesh, and made me to hate it . . . . Of all things it seemed the most filthy in the sight of God, both in the married and unmarried, it all seemed alike."[78] After extended disputes with her husband, including physical violence against her, she became celibate in 1836.[79] That year, during a preaching trip to Albany, she went to Watervliet, where she met Shakers for the first time. Upon seeing an elderly Believer, she wrote:

My spirit ran to him and embraced him in my arms as a father. I loved him as I loved nobody on earth. And it was said to me "These are my people" . . . . When they came in [to meeting], the power of God came upon me like the waves of the sea, and caused me to move back and forth under the mighty waters. It was as much as I could do to keep my seat. . . . They all were dressed alike. They all looked alike. They all seemed to look as if they were looking into the spiritual world. For the first time I saw a people sitting and looking like people that had come into a place prepared for the solemn worship of the true and living God . . . .[80]

Rebecca Jackson was separated from her husband when in the late 1830s she began a thirty-five-year attachment to an African-American disciple, Rebecca Perot who was about eighteen years her junior.[81] By 1840 they were associated with a group of Perfectionists, most of them Caucasian, living near Albany. They and the other members of the Perfectionists' group visited at Watervliet in the winter of 1842–43, and Jackson and Perot joined the South Family in 1847; "the two Rebeccas" shared a room, probably with one or two other sisters. Jackson's confession of all her sins, as necessary for membership, did not satisfy the Shaker leaders or herself. Rebecca Jackson always had trouble submitting to the authority of others, and in 1851 the two Rebeccas left Watervliet without permission to encourage faith mostly among African Americans in Philadelphia. An entry for July 12, 1851, in the Watervliet Church Family Diary by David A. Buckingham records: "We understand that Rebecca Jackson and the other colored woman that came with her, have started out, in their own gift [i.e., without permission] some time last week, on a mission to convert her nation, or under that pretence, perhaps consciously, but I should say, rather delusively."[82] The Shakers had acknowledged her visions as important and recognized the power of her preaching, although it was rare for a Shaker woman to preach. But there remained a tension between the Shakers and this gifted woman, who had long experienced the freedom of independent judgment and actions. Jackson felt the Shakers did not fully embrace her because of her race. Jackson and Perot lived for six years in Philadelphia, where Jackson had elaborate dreams about her relationship to the Watervliet Shakers. In September 1857 Jackson and Perot returned for one year to Watervliet, where Jackson was ill for nearly half the stay. In October 1858 Jackson and Perot again left Watervliet for Philadelphia, but this time with official Shaker blessing. There Jackson held her first meeting as a Shaker Eldress in April 1859. Throughout the Civil War Jackson and Perot held meetings and visited the sick, and Jackson continued to have visions and revelations.

Jackson was conscious of the parallels between herself and Ann Lee: working-class background, married, pushed to prominence by ecstatic experiences, and the ability to convert others. Both understood celibacy as a means of reaching a close relationship with God. (In her extensive writings Jackson placed her belief in celibacy before any knowledge of the Shakers.) Both lived a public life under the stress of being different. In Philadelphia Jackson was called Mother Rebecca. Perhaps the title came from her early affiliation with Methodists, who used it widely. (The Shakers had ceased using the title in 1826.)[83] The Philadelphia Shaker family survived Jackson's death in 1871 by nearly forty years. For much of this time it was led by Perot, who took the name "Mother Rebecca Jackson" (figure 181, taken in Philadelphia in the 1880s).[84] For a Shaker to take the name of an honored member was not too unusual. Lucy Smith, when appointed to the Ministry at Pleasant Hill early in the nineteenth century, had adopted the name Lucy to honor Lucy Wright, for example.[85]

The Philadelphia Family fluctuated between about twelve and twenty women, including some white members. A few men were associated with the Family in the 1870s. During the years, visits of two or three weeks were made to the Philadelphia Shakers by Watervliet and New Lebanon leaders. In 1896 Rebecca Perot and three other elderly Philadelphia Shaker Sisters moved to Watervliet, where at least two Believers from Philadelphia had already settled. Rebecca Perot died there in 1901. The Shaker community in Philadelphia probably survived until at least 1908.[86]

There is no evidence in Jackson's writings that the bonding of Jackson and Perot went beyond an emotional dependence. In her introduction to the extensive writings of Rebecca Jackson, Jean

McMahon Humez notes: "[These texts] offer very little direct evidence either to support or to contradict the theory that there was an acknowledged sexual component in her relationship with her lifelong disciple and companion, Rebecca Perot. That the love they felt for each other helped make heterosexual relationships unnecessary for either seems very clear, but both also subscribed to an antisexual ideology."[87] Within the communities of the faithful there must have been many instances of deep love and emotional commitment, although the requirement of celibacy, and the practice of confession, made explicit sexual activity rare.

Isaac Newton Youngs

A group of letters connected with Isaac Newton Youngs, of New Lebanon, has puzzled scholars of Shaker material because the "gutsy" and "flowery" language used seems "un-Shaker." Indeed, the heightened sense of sexuality in the letters is unusual in Shaker writings. During the years they span, Youngs was the designated scribe for the Ministry's correspondence, and this may have protected his writings from the scrutiny others experienced. More than once Youngs notes that the recipient of his letters should be careful with them, because of the freedom with which he wrote: "N.B. Keep this scroll to yourself, & not let even your left hand see it";[88] "Excuse my airy freedom"; and again, "You may do what you have a mind to with that part burn it up, or something. It is well, you know, to be cautious,—'Goose quill chats' are more dangerous than common chats, because it stands in black & white."[89]

In 1826 the nine-year-old Benjamin Gates, who normally worked with Youngs in the New Lebanon tailoring shop, wrote to Youngs, who was temporarily at Watervliet and not feeling well: "Beloved Brother Isaac, I want to see you so very much that I am in hopes if you get any better you will come home and see me so that I can stroke your head and kiss you once more as I used to."[90]

On April 3, 1826, Garrett K. Lawrence, who was brought up in the faith with Isaac Youngs at New Lebanon, wrote from there to Youngs at Watervliet with sexual innuendos:

Beloved Brother;
. . . Now dear Brother, I suppose that the sun shines bright, the sky looks blue, and the water runs clear with you; and, that every now and then you receive a kiss of charity; while with a fair wind, smooth sea, flowing sails and streaming colours, you are sweetly and swiftly sailing for the celestial Land. While poor me is a beating the briny billows against wind and tide, enveloped in fog and rowing for life. But I am not discouraged at all. If you will take up your spying glass and look away back, and listen with both ears, you may perhaps hear the splash of my oar as I tug at the midnight hour, and perhaps see the surge beat upon the bow of my little bark, while I perseveringly stem the tide of nature. I shall fetch it by and by. I have a good compass firmly placed in the binnacle, and the needle has lately been touched with the heavenly magnet, and feels the invisible attraction of gospel love; and though it may some time vary, when passing over extensive beds of natural & attracting ore, yet in the main it points to the true polar star . . . .[91]

Garrett Lawrence became the physician at New Lebanon and, until his death in 1837, remained Youngs's closest friend. Youngs wrote an unusually extended obituary for Lawrence in the "Domestic Journal," and attended and described his autopsy (the body was filled with strange tumors). Lawrence was the only friend Youngs mentioned in his autobiography, and he did so in verse.[92] Garret Lawrence's spirit appeared often, as Youngs noted in June 1838: "He has been seen here, at Canterbury, & at Harvard &c Should think 40 times. He frequently appears in a like dress, having a golden chain across his shoulders, coming down passing around his waist & crossing before, as I understand it."[93]

Late in the summer of 1826 Youngs met Andrew C. Houston, who was accompanying a Union Village Elder to New Lebanon. In August of 1827, Youngs sent Houston a letter contrived to be a conversation in which each spoke to the other. It included Houston saying: " 'Dearly beloved and respected brother,' . . . 'I have kept safe my little measure of the gospel, and am laboring for an increase of the same'[.] . . . let me be honest; I am not disappointed; for I looked 'for a good deal of freedom from you,' & I find you are free."

In his own parts of the conversation Youngs writes: ". . . my beloved friend & brother: often have I thot of you, & how do you do? . . . 'It gives me the greatest satisfaction to hear from you' & more especially to feel you, & realize your love . . . . I can be so with the more ease where I am in free company, for I am so made that I must be like my company, or feel uncomfortable." "You

181. PHOTOGRAPH OF REBECCA PEROT,
CALLED MOTHER REBECCA JACKSON
AFTER 1871
By P. E. Chillman, 914 Arch Street,
Philadelphia, Pennsylvania, 1880s
Chillman moved his studio to this address in
1880
Western Reserve Historical Society Library,
Cleveland, Ohio

know last year we were building a new shop . . . . and the old one where you and I took our last hug, is torn down." "So now beloved I must soon draw to a close & shall compres[s] all my good wishes to you, in these few words viz. My beloved brother Andrew, may all virtue & the blessing of heaven be your everlasting portion."[94]

On July 29, 1828, Youngs wrote to Andrew Houston, "My much beloved Brother Andrew, . . . Your memory still glows with warmth in my breast. Never, I trust, will be untied that knot of love, which we tied together, in the summer of 1826: never will be cut asunder those silken cords of union which grew with our first acquaintance, & have strengthened with succeeding communications." He signed himself, "From your lover, Isaac N. Youngs."[95]

On June 4, 1829, Houston wrote to Youngs, acknowledging the letter contrived as a conversation; in his reply Houston mixed love, memories of being physical with Youngs, and commitment to the cross of Shaker faith. His letter reveals his personal struggle between love and faith but he signs himself "from your friend and lover." "My Dearly Beloved Brother Isaac, I am yet alive, well & hearty, and standing up as snugly under the cross as I know how . . . . But O my beloved brother you have almost superabounded in your kind notices of me (one of the least of the thousands of Israel) your most comforting & chearing epistle of August 18th 1827 written by way of a conversation; I confess, interested me very much, and when ever I look over it, streams of love & warm sensations are the consequence . . . ."[96]

On September 1, 1829, Isaac Youngs answered a letter from Andrew Houston and in it Youngs appears to accept faith over personal love. Sexual innuendo is absent but the love such as between Jonathan and David is mentioned:

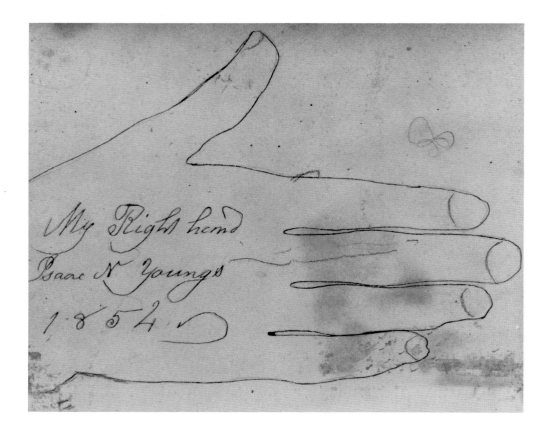

**182. DRAWING OF RIGHT HAND OF
ISAAC NEWTON YOUNGS**
New Lebanon, New York
1854
Right and left hand traced onto the inside of
the front and back of a journal he kept between
1839 and 1858
Ink on paper
Western Reserve Historical Society Library,
Cleveland, Ohio

My dearly Beloved brother Andrew,
The greatest consolation that I feel in the thots of my existance, is that it is to be eternal! without end!
even so, the thots of my union to my spiritual relation, give me the greatest consolation, on reflecting
that it is to be unceasing & endless. So I feel, while entering once more into discourse with you, con-
serning our union & love to each other. I read your last communication to me/of June 4th with much
satisfaction. Joy, I dare say sparkled in my eyes, & cheering glows flushed over my countenance, as I
traced the feeling of my distant friend . . . .

I must beg you not to think me guilty of willing neglect; for as true as Jonathan ever loved David,
I would go to the extent of my abilities to do any friend a favor, & you in particular—I can say no
more . . .

So in confirmation of all my past good wishes, love & to you, I again bid you farewell
—Isaac N. Youngs[97]

In a letter written to Houston in 1836 and addressed "Beloved, ah, much beloved," Youngs discusses a personal friendship between himself, Garrett Lawrence, and Houston.[98]

Emotional language with modest sexual overtones is fairly standard in nineteenth-century
writing. For example, when in 1857 the cabinetmaker Alfred Collier of the Harvard Community
lost his eighteen-year-old apprentice and nephew Charles Collier to the world he wrote, "with
pain and grief I record the exit from this place of Charles Henry Collier . . . . O! I love him! I love
him! I love him!"[99] Such an emotional signaling of loss of a loved one suggests a sexual intensity
of feeling, but it may be the recording in contemporary language of deep sadness. Some of the
Youngs-related letters seem to record sexual activity in their use of phallic and other sexual
images. Youngs was an intelligent and creative Shaker the Ministry used repeatedly for special
tasks. He may not have been elevated to the Ministry because he remained unpredictable and
somewhat unconventional for a Shaker, as when he kept a journal and wrote part of it in a personal code, and when he traced his left and right hands inside of the front and back of the journal kept between 1839 and 1858 (see figure 182).

Seen from Outside
Through all the upheavals that began in 1837, the communities continued to produce the "Classic Shaker" artifacts that employed aspects that began to be standard about 1810, and spoke of
order and constraints. The Shakers lived in communities worldly people admired. Despite the
prejudiced words of Charles Dickens and Nathaniel Hawthorne discussed in Chapter IV, visitors

generally saw value in what they were allowed to see: communities functioning as successful towns. There were exceptions, particularly unhappy apostates who lost the land they had given and could not get it back, or those who wanted to be paid for labor performed while with the Shakers. Others were furious at having wives, husbands, or children "stolen." But what impressed many observers was the way the communities functioned as commercial and agrarian units, and the good health and obvious prosperity of the people. In 1838 the Englishman James S. Buckingham visited Watervliet and wrote:

> . . . no one can doubt who has watched the progressive advancement which this society has made in the augmentation, as well as improvement, of its possessions, and in the neatness, order & perfection by which every thing they do or make is characterized; this is so much the case, that over all the United States, the seeds, plants, fruits, grain, cattle, & manufactures furnished by a settlement of Shakers bears a premium in the market above the ordinary price of similar articles from other establishments. There being no idleness among them, all are productive. There being no intemperance among them, none are destructive. There being no misers among them, nothing is hoarded, or made to perish from want of use; so that while production and improvement are at their maximum, and waste and destruction at their minimum, the society must go on increasing the extent and value of its temporal possessions, and thus increase its means of doing good, first within, and then beyond its own circle. [100]

In 1856, when the frenzy had been quiet for nearly a decade, Benson John Lossing visited New Lebanon for his piece in *Harper's* and wrote: "I had come to visit the people in the quiet Shaker village upon the mountain terrace . . . ." and he felt "how beautiful!" as he watched "four or five hundred worshipers marching and countermarching in perfect time."[101]

AFTER 1860: "VERY MUCH LIKE THE INHABITANTS OF THE SECTION OF THE COUNTRY WHERE THEY RESIDE."

A CHANGING SOCIETY

As the second half of the nineteenth century unfolded, and the twentieth century dawned, the Shakers experienced so many changes that the events seemed to tumble over themselves. They moved so close to the world in ideas and behavior that in 1897 the Canterbury Church Family Elder Henry C. Blinn was able to write with pride in the Shakers' periodical, *The Manifesto*: "The Shakers are very much like the inhabitants of the section of the country where they reside."[1]

At midcentury contentment similar to what the Shakers had known during the 1820s returned to most communities, and the abatement of vigorous religious activity coincided with major changes throughout the nation. Religion had less control over daily life, and more choices were made from a secular perspective. A wave of industrialization transformed the rural agricultural economy to an urban industrial base; men and unmarried or widowed women easily found employment. Great areas of land in the Mid- and Far West became available for settlement. Railroads sprawled out to link the Midwest to Washington, Oregon, and California, and between 1865 and 1900 the amount of track increased five times. After the Civil War the resurgence of hope and energy sent thousands westward on a tide of demand for the American dream of success through personal achievement. In 1876 William Dean Howells, writer and editor of the *Atlantic Monthly,* observed: "There are several reasons for the present decrease [in Shaker membership], besides that decrease of the whole rural population . . . . The impulse of the age is towards a scientific, a sensuous, an aesthetic life. Men no longer remain on the lonely farms, or in the little towns where they were born, brooding upon the ways of God to man; if they think of God, it is too often to despair of knowing him; while the age calls upon them to learn this, that, and the other, to get gain and live at ease, to buy pianos and pictures, and take books out of the circulating library."[2]

The Philadelphia Centennial Exposition of 1876 showed the nation and the world America's new industrial strength by displaying a great array of machinery—including the giant Corliss engine. The New Lebanon Shakers participated in the Exposition to show their chairs, plush floor rugs, and fancy articles under the supervision of Robert Wagan. In another booth, Canterbury, New Hampshire, showed a washing machine.[3]

At this time in the arts, the romantic Hudson River School of painting was challenged by an increasing demand for European art. There was a fresh commitment to studying, and perhaps remaining, abroad. James Abbott McNeill Whistler, living first in Paris and then London, became a controversial figure in the international art world throughout the 1860s and 1870s. Mary Cassatt settled in Paris in 1873 and joined the artistic revolution initiated by the French Impressionists. John Singer Sargent, another America expatriate, rose to worldly success in the 1880s, living in Paris and then in London. Henry James moved permanently to England in 1876 and wrote about cosmopolitan Americans in many of his novels. At home, Winslow Homer, a leading illustrator before and during the Civil War, became our best-loved painter of scenes from everyday life and bold poetic landscapes of the Northeast.

CHARLES NORDHOFF

As mentioned in Chapter IV, one of the best and most extensive accounts of the Shakers during the 1870s was written by Charles Nordhoff, an important journalist known for his probity and ability to look clearly at the subjects he researched. In 1874 he visited the best-known communistic societies in America to see if their internal affiliation could suggest a possible solution to the growing labor unrest. The increasing demands of the trade unions unnerved him, for tensions between owner and worker seemed inevitable and without solution. While keeping an active role for capitalism, he hoped to find an alternative to labor's dependence upon it. "Hitherto, in the United States, our cheap and fertile lands have acted as an important safety-valve for the enterprise and discontent of our non-capitalist population." In 1875 Nordhoff published a record of over a dozen American societies in *The Communistic Societies of the United States*. He found in all a remarkable business ability—many had begun poor but were now wealthy; all had overcome idleness, selfishness, and "unthrift" in individuals; some lived in common in dwellings, but others had separate households; some were celibate, while others permitted marriage. He gave his greatest attention to the Shakers, but also wrote extensively on the Amana Society of Iowa; the Harmony Society in Pennsylvania; the Perfectionists of Oneida and Brooklyn, New York, and Wallingford, Connecticut.

Most of the communities Nordhoff visited were based in religion and dealt with sexual relations in special ways. The Amana community permitted marriage but kept the sexes separated as much as possible. For example, although families lived with children, each in its own house, they ate communally and the women sat separated from the men.[4] The Harmony Society, then of Economy, Pennsylvania, had been developed by George Rapp, who permitted marriage until 1807 when, during the "Great revival of religion," the younger members convinced everyone to accept celibacy as a higher and holier spiritual state.[5] The Separatists at Zoar, Ohio, were at first celibate, but in 1828 or 1830 began permitting marriage, while stressing that sexual relations should be for the procreation of children.[6] The Perfectionists or Oneida communities followed the teaching of John Humphrey Noyes, who held that everything, including people, should be in common; communal sex made marriage unnecessary, or "as they put it, 'complex marriage takes the place of simple'";[7] all the men and women married each other. Noyes affirmed "an ideal marriage, may exist between two hundred as well as two; while the guarantees for women and children are much greater in the Community than they can be in any private family."[8] Noyes was very conscious of the suffering childbirth and too many children could cause women. The men practiced male continence or *coitus reservatus*.

Nordhoff began his section on the Shakers: "The Shakers have the oldest existing communistic societies on this continent. They are also the most thoroughly organized, and in some respects the most successful and flourishing."[9] He reported eighteen Shaker societies—he visited all but four of them—scattered over seven states, a total of fifty-eight families, and a membership of 2,415 souls on about one hundred thousand acres, of which nearly fifty thousand were home farms.

A DECLINING SOCIETY

At the time Nordhoff visited the Shakers a sharp decline in membership was underway. The demographics developed by Priscilla J. Brewer for the eleven eastern communities show a nearly equal number of males and females in 1790; the peak years were during the fervent late 1830s and early 1840s; after the Civil War both the men and women found other opportunities more rewarding.[10]

Decades	Men	Women	Total
1790	244	294	538
1800	562	811	1,373
1810	651	900	1,551
1820	821	1,135	1,956
1830	974	1,342	2,316
1840	1,016	1,411	2,427
1850	942	1,307	2,249
1860	812	1,248	2,060
1870	540	904	1,444
1880	382	796	1,178
1900	153	492	645

The Shakers knew their membership was falling, but they could not envision that the decline would continue: the New Lebanon Elder Frederick W. Evans acknowledged to Nordhoff that membership was decreasing but said, "they expected large accessions in the course of the next few years, having prophecies among themselves to that effect . . . . 'You will be surprised to know that we lost most seriously during the [Civil] war. A great many of our younger people went into the army; many who fought through the war have since applied to come back to us . . . .'"[11] At Enfield, New Hampshire, Nordhoff was informed: "They lost some members during the war of the Rebellion, young men who became soldiers, and some others who were drawn away by the general feeling of unrest which pervaded the country."[12]

William Dean Howells assigned the decline in membership to lethargy and wishful thinking. He found among the Shakers a sense that seekers should find them, and so they instituted no active outreach. Visitors still came in great numbers to see the drama of religious services, and to purchase Shaker-made goods, but not to join. What visitors found, at least on Sundays, was the worship crowded by sightseers, so much so that at times not all the Shakers could find room to attend. Visiting Canterbury in June, 1876, William Alfred Hinds reported a mob scene:

> At the meeting here yesterday there were at least two hundred strangers and visitors present. I am informed that during the summer months this number is sometimes doubled, compelling most of the Shaker brothers and sisters to absent themselves; and that those who are present are often crowded into such close quarters that their "goings forth in the dance" are necessarily omitted. The meetings here are indeed wonderfully attractive. Thirty-seven carriages came yesterday from the towns near and distant, and many people on foot. Probably the greater number attended the meetings from mere curiosity; but some doubtless find in them spiritual nutriment.[13]

Many of those who joined did so only for the winter months: "For some years they have neither increased nor diminished, except by the coming and going of 'winter Shakers,' and 'we sift pretty carefully,' they told me," reported Nordhoff.[14] In the November 1872 edition of the Society's publication *The Shaker,* a growing resentment was expressed: "Our Society is not a public establishment—a free hotel, or boarding house, for curiosity-seekers. Nor for city people seeking 'an out in the country,' at little expense to themselves. It is our home."[15]

The Shakers readily took paying guests and divided visiting couples into separate rooms: "In summer they entertain visitors at a set price, and have rooms fitted for this purpose. In the visitors' dining-room I saw this printed notice: 'At the table we wish all to be as free as at home, but we dislike the wasteful habit of leaving food on the plate. No vice is with us the less ridiculous for being fashionable.' 'Married persons tarrying with us overnight are respectfully notified that each sex occupy separate sleeping apartments while they remain.'"[16]

An 1873 publication for the Novitiate Order defined the process of joining, and it lacks any sense of energetic immediacy to make a commitment: after paying all debts seekers are neither accepted or rejected, "we *admit* them, leaving the Spirit of Goodness to decide as to their sincerity . . . . After becoming thoroughly acquainted with our principles, we ask individuals to give evidence of their sincerity, if really sick of sin, by an honest confession of every improper transaction or sin that lies within the reach of their memory . . . . It often takes years for individuals to complete this work of *thorough confession and repentance* . . . ."[17]

ORPHANS AND CHILDREN FROM THE WORLD

Orphans, or children with perhaps one parent and in need of a home, had previously been taken in large numbers with the hope that those brought up experiencing the advantages of the faith would join. Nordhoff spent much of his time at Mount Lebanon in the company of Elder Frederick W. Evans, who spoke of why the practice was no longer advantageous: "They had changed their policy in regard to taking children, for experience had proved that when they grew up they were often discontented, anxious to gain property for themselves, curious to see the world and therefore left the society."[18] At Harvard an Eldress said, " 'Yes, we like to take children—but we don't like to take monkeys'; and, in general, the Shakers have discovered that 'blood will tell,' and that they can do much better with the children of religious parents . . . ." At Shirley, Nordhoff found, "of the children they adopt and bring up, not one in ten becomes a Shaker." After the Civil War the Elders at South Union, Kentucky, "sought out twenty orphans in Tennessee, whom they adopted," and tried to get fifty from Memphis when it suffered from yellow fever, "but were unsuccessful."[19]

In the mid-1930s Sister Sadie Neale said to a visitor at Mount Lebanon: "You see, we used to add to our members by adopting orphan children. But when the state and denominational orphan asylums became more numerous, the children who were offered to us frequently turned out to be more suited to reform schools than to our way of life."[20] The Shakers at Sabbathday Lake took a variety of children into the 1960s.

RELAXING THE RULES

Evidence of a changing Society is seen in the new governing restrictions of 1860 and those that supplanted them in 1887. No longer called Laws, the first were called "Rules and Orders," the second, "Orders." The "Rules and Orders for the Church of God or Christ's Second Appearing" removed many of the stultifying features of those formulated in 1845, and had only nine "Rules" and six "Conditional Orders." In them the look of rooms remains a concern: Part II, Section VII, "Orders Concerning the Furniture of the Retiring Rooms." Rule 4. "The furniture of the dwelling rooms, among Believers, should be plain in style, and unembellished by stamps, flowers, paintings and gilding of any kind: And looking glasses ought not to be purchased by Believers, exceeding about 12 by 20 inches." Part III covers temporal economy, and Section V, concerning "Buildings, Painting &c," reviews details on furniture and buildings: "[1.] Beadings, mouldings and cornices, which are merely for fancy, may not be made by Believers. 2. Odd, or fanciful styles of architecture, may not be used among Believers; neither should they deviate widely from the common styles of buildings, without the union of the Ministry and Elders." Under "Counsels": "[1.] It is advisable, to paint meeting houses white, without, and of a bluish shade within for the sake of uniformity. Dwellings should also be as near uniform in color as consistent and shops in like manner should be uniform as far as practicable, and a little darker than dwellings. 2. For uniformity, it is advised for dwelling house floors, if stained at all, to be of a reddish yellow. 3. Back buildings, as barns, wood houses, etc., if painted at all should be of a darker hue, than dwellings or shops, as Red, Brown, Umber, Lead color, Chocolate or some such modest color; but when such buildings front the streets, or command a sightly aspect, they should be painted like shops. 4. It is imprudent, and unadvisable, to paint such articles as come to ready wear, so as to wear out before they rot out [in some manuscripts it says "rust" out]."[21]

The 1887 "Orders for the Church of Christ's Second Appearing" had only six "Rules" and five "Conditional Orders." Previously only the retiring rooms had been mentioned; now all the rooms in a dwelling house were lumped together and given a simple requirement: "The furniature of dwelling rooms should be plain in style." Restrictions against seeing people from the world were far less severe: "Visiting between the world and Believers should be done at the office [the most public building] as far as possibly consistent." "Brethren and Sisters should avoid thronging the office late in the evening to visit guests." The look of clothing and purchased goods was less restricted, but the Ministry still hoped for control: "No new fashions concerning clothing or important wares of any kind may be introduced into the Society of Believers without the approval of the Ministry of the society." But Believers could purchase modest things on their own: "Members should not purchase articles of considerable value for themselves, without the union of Deacons & Deaconnesses, each sex in its own order." Burials remained plain in style. "The Corpse should not be dressed in costly garments." "Coffins for burial should be cheap and plain, unembellished with needless ornaments."[22]

AN OPENNESS TO CHANGE

Within the disciplined context of Shaker life, change was expected, and after 1850 it came rapidly. In 1874 Nordhoff was told at Union Village, Ohio, "Celibacy and the confession of sins are vital; but in all else we ought to be changeable, and may modify our practices; and we feel that we must do something to make home more pleasant for our young people—they want more music and more books, and shall have them . . . ."[23] Not all Believers welcomed the new openness. At a business meeting at Union Village, Nordhoff heard "some of the sisters say that one matter which had occupied their thoughts was the too great monotony of their own lives—they desired greater variety, and thought women might do some other things besides cooking. One thought it would be an improvement to abolish the caps, and let the hair have its natural growth and appearance—but I am afraid she might be called a radical."[24]

A sense of outward peace and contentment is projected by the image of Daniel Crosman, Elder of the Church Family at Mount Lebanon, calmly overlooking the second meetinghouse and

183. PHOTOGRAPH: CHURCH FAMILY
ELDER DANIEL CROSMAN
OVERLOOKING MOUNT LEBANON
Published by O. B. Buell, Pittsfield,
Massachusetts
Taken about 1870
Half of a stereoscopic view; full card: H. 3⁷/₁₆"
W. 6¹⁵/₁₆"
Collection of Jerry Grant

the other Church Family buildings at Mount Lebanon about 1870 (figure 183). (He is the oval box maker who provided a group of spit boxes for the new Dwelling House after fires devastated his community in 1875; see figure 68.) When Nordhoff provided the weekly schedule of events and meetings, it clearly demonstrated a slowed-down sense of time.[25]

MUSICAL INSTRUMENTS

Previously outlawed, instruments now appeared in many of the communities. Some members disapproved, but during Nordhoff's visits there was a piano in the Sisters' sewing room at Canterbury, and a young Sister taking a music lesson; the schoolhouse had a melodeon and a special music room.[26] At Enfield, New Hampshire, there was a large music room in a separate building.[27] Enfield, Connecticut, had a cabinet-organ in their music room and held a weekly singing-school for the young people.[28] Union Village, Ohio, had two cabinet-organs; South Union, Kentucky, had just purchased a piano, and had a Brother from Canterbury, New Hampshire, to instruct some of the Sisters.[29] One of the engravings of Shaker interiors published by Nordhoff was of a "Shaker Music-Hall" replete with movable benches and a piano, an organ, and post–Civil War Greek revival rocking chairs (figure 184); it was probably based on a photograph taken in the early 1870s.[30] In figure 105, the 1880s photograph shows a Sister at the left holding a concertina. The view of the library at Mount Lebanon taken early in the twentieth century (figure 185) shows a piano under a print of Jean-François Millet's *The Angelus* (1854–59), a French painting that had been commissioned by a Boston collector. An Eastlake style organ appears in figure 218.

CLOSING COMMUNITIES

The adjustment to allow many new practices and objects into the Society, and the greater freedom to enjoy travel into the world, may have slowed the slide to near extinction. Nevertheless, the

184. "SHAKER MUSIC-HALL"
Enfield, New Hampshire
Published in Charles Nordhoff's, The
Communistic Societies of the United States,
1875, facing p. 214
Engraving
H. 3" W. 3¾"
The benches have backs like those made in
Canterbury, and Enfield, New Hampshire
Collection of the Shaker Museum and Library,
Old Chatham, New York

185. PHOTOGRAPH: "IN THE LIBRARY"
Mount Lebanon, New York; Sisters Catherine
Allen, Leila Taylor, and Mazella Gallup
After 1904, when Mazella Gallup joined
H. 5¼" W. 8½"
Collection of the Shaker Museum and Library,
Old Chatham, New York

last three decades of the nineteenth century and the first years of this century saw a continuing decrease in membership in the sect, and the closing of most of the communities. Three closed between 1875 and 1895: Tyringham, Massachusetts in 1875; North Union, Ohio in 1889; and Groveland, New York in 1895.

After 1900 most of the remaining communities closed on an almost regular basis, moving the Central Ministry's home community twice, as follows:

1907 *Whitewater, Ohio*
1908 *Shirley, Massachusetts*
1910 *Pleasant Hill, Kentucky, and Watervliet, Ohio*
1912 *Union Village, Ohio*
1917 *Enfield, Connecticut*
1918 *Harvard, Massachusetts*
1922 *South Union, Kentucky (the last of the western group)*
1923 *Enfield, New Hampshire*
1931 *Alfred, Maine*
1938 *Watervliet, New York*
1947 *Mount Lebanon, New York (The Central Ministry moved to Hancock)*
1960 *Hancock, Massachusetts (The Central Ministry moved to Canterbury in 1957)*
1992 *Canterbury, New Hampshire, was incorporated as Canterbury Shaker Village in 1969. The last Shaker to live there died in 1992.*

Sabbathday Lake, Maine, remains an active community.

SHAKER-MADE AND SHAKER-USED OBJECTS

Shaker Industries

Home industries could no longer easily compete with modernized worldly factories, and many of the Shakers' small businesses collapsed. The Shaker seed business experienced a slump during the early 1860s, but it recovered in the middle of that decade in part because of the new use of brightly colored advertisements and labels placed on many Shaker-made products. These were generic, worldly images, over which any company could place its name (see figures 186 and 187). But by the middle of the 1870s the seed business faced overwhelming competition, and in 1876 Brother John Vance of Alfred wrote: "The Garden Seed and Herb businesses were destroyed in consequence of the great competition of extensive establishments in the West who flooded our State with Seeds."[31]

186. CAN LABEL FOR ANDREW CROSWELL'S FRESH-APPLES
About 1890
Multi-color letterpress, ink on coated paper
H. 6¹⁄₂" W. 20⁷⁄₈"
Collection of Dr. and Mrs. M. Stephen Miller

187. CAN LABEL FOR MOUNT LEBANON FRESH APPLES
About 1890
Multi-color letterpress, ink on coated paper
H. 6¹⁄₄" W. 19¹⁄₄"
Although it appears to be very close to the preceding worldly ad, most of the areas are slightly smaller
Collection of Dr. and Mrs. M. Stephen Miller

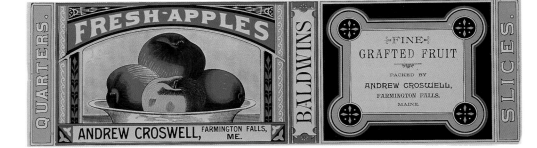

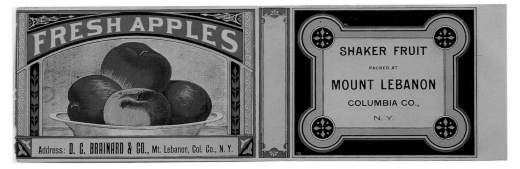

The Shakers continued to have a few small industries: "Some of the families make brooms, others dry sweet corn, raise and put up garden seeds, make medicinal extracts; make mops, blankets, chairs . . . . the range is not great."[32] At South Union (and elsewhere) Nordhoff was told they had cattle, hogs, sheep, and chickens for sale,[33] and land "let to tenants, among whom I found several colored families . . . ."[34]

The Chair Business; Decorative Finishes

In general, after 1860 the Brothers' businesses became less important while those of the Sisters grew. The main exception was the making of chairs. The Shakers had been selling chairs to the world since the 1790s. Now, one family exploited the Shakers' reputation for good traditional work. In the 1860s the Second Family of New Lebanon divided into two Families and part became the South Family. Under the guidance of Brother Robert M. Wagan they became major chair producers. Their products were successful because they were backed by sound business practices and an advertising campaign that exploited the tradition of Shaker craftsmanship. In 1872 the South Family built a new chair factory and standardized production. They assigned numbers to indicate size and type—0 being the smallest and 7 the largest—rather than traditional terms such as small chair or large rocker. Working with worldly printers' firms they circulated chair catalogues (see figures 188 and 189). In 1875, for example, Weed, Parson and Company of Albany, New York, was paid $32.43 for woodcuts and stereotypes and $67.85 for printing them.[35] The Mount Lebanon chair display at the Philadelphia Centennial Exposition of 1876 received a Certificate of Award from the United States Centennial Commission, and large commercial out-

188 AND 189. CHAIR CATALOGUE
Mount Lebanon, New York
About 1880
On cover: "Illustrated Catalogue and Price List of Shakers' Chairs Manufactured by
the Society of Shakers. R.M. Wagan & Co.,
Mount Lebanon, N.Y." On title page: "Catalogue
and Price List of Shakers' Chairs. Press of Geo T.
Denny, Pittsfield, Mass."
H. 5⅝" W. 3"
Collection of the Shaker Museum and Library,
Old Chatham, New York

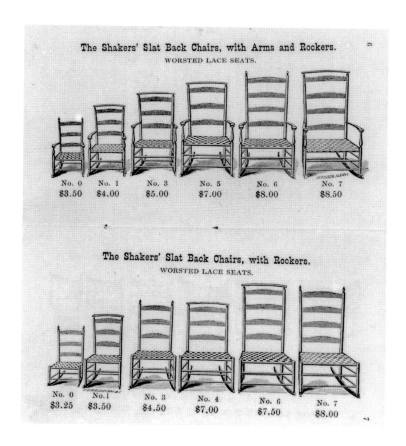

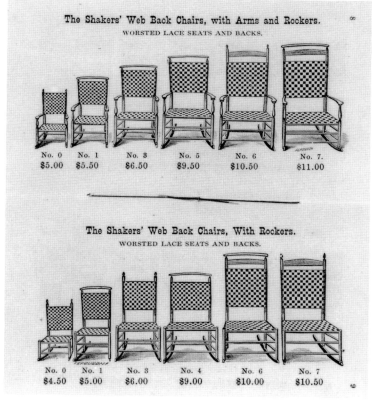

lets began to carry Shaker-made chairs. The chairs became even further standardized because of the use of new specialized machinery. For example, boring machines produced mechanically guided holes for rungs and slats; this eliminated the need for scribe marks to guide handwork. The products became ever simpler: arms that previously graduated from thinner at the rear to heavier at the front became one easily produced thickness. The rockers and the turnings became simpler in shape, and by the 1880s side and rear stretchers, or rounds, were made of purchased dowels that did not swell gracefully to a thicker central area; the front ones continued a swelling shape. The New Lebanon Shakers were producing chairs by the thousands, and in 1885, 40,500 chair rounds were purchased.[36] Cushions for backs and seats could be ordered as extras.

The chairs were a success because they were folksy, well made, comfortable, and worked well

190. NUMBER 7 PRODUCTION ROCKING
ARM CHAIR, AND PLUSH CUSHIONS
Mount Lebanon, New York
Chair purchased November 10, 1873
Maple, stained a dark mahogany color
H. 40¾" W. 24½" D. 29"
Cushions made for a number 6 chair
Pile: wool; warp and weft: cotton or linen
Collection of the Shaker Museum and Library,
Old Chatham, New York

in a number of different aesthetic contexts: simple domestic situations, nostalgic colonial revival settings, and elaborate, eclectic arrangements. In the 1870s, the painter Frederick Church built Olana, a splendiferous house perched above the Hudson River near Greenport, New York; he added a wing in the late 1880s. There Shaker rockers were mixed in with Eastern carpets, objets d'art, southwestern artifacts, caned bentwood chairs, assorted highly finished furniture, and paintings in gilded frames. The result was a high Victorian eclectic masterpiece.

The mahoganized rocking armchair in figure 190 is an early Mount Lebanon Number 7 mass-production chair purchased from the Shakers on November 10, 1873, with red and black cushions, for $17.00.[37] In 1878 Walter L. Palmer painted a view of the library of Arbor Hill, Albany, New York, that included this chair with a fringed antimacasser covering the upper half of the back cushion (figure 191). The painting shows the chair standing in high Victorian splendor on overlapping Oriental rugs. The rooms have gas chandeliers, large columns with Ionic capitals, and gilt-enriched striped wallpaper. (The red and black cushions now on the chair in figure 190 display the colors shown in the painting, but they are not the ones sold with the chair, which was given to the museum without cushions. Those on the chair are too narrow for this example, and came

191. LIBRARY OF ARBOR HILL, ALBANY, NEW YORK
By Walter L. Palmer of Thomas W. Olcott sitting in his library. The rocker seen in figure 190 and the red and black plush cushions had been purchased by his daughter on November 10, 1873, from Robert Wagan at Mount Lebanon. (The cushions now on the chair are not those she purchased)
1878
Oil on canvas
H. 25¼" W. 20"
Collection of the Albany Institute of History and Art, Albany, New York. Gift of the Heirs of the Estate of Robert Olcott

192. PHOTOGRAPH: MOUNT LEBANON, NEW YORK; SISTER CLARISSA JACOBS, SECOND FAMILY
1880s
H. 4½" W. 7½"
Collection of the Shaker Museum and Library, Old Chatham, New York

from a Number 6 chair.) The Shakers used such chairs and cushions, often with a handworked white cover (see figure 192).

The idea of adding warmth and comfort to slat-back or other simple chairs had a long tradition. Seventeenth-century turned chairs normally had a turned top rail over which a cloth could be hung. Some slat-back chairs made in the eighteenth century had a turned rail above the top slat

193. PORTRAIT OF MOSES BROWN,
PROVIDENCE, RHODE ISLAND
1839
Engraving by W. J. Harris
H. 12" W. 9"
The Rhode Island Historical Society, Providence,
Rhode Island

over which a shawl or other cloth could be draped to give comfort and protect against drafts.[38] The image of Moses Brown of Rhode Island in figure 193 shows him in the 1830s, seated in a Philadelphia green-painted Windsor armchair, which has been fitted with a green baize cover with only the scrolled ears of the chair's crest rail showing. (The chair is at the Rhode Island Historical Society. It was given with the baize covering, but a former director of the institution threw out the covering because "It was full of holes"!) As in the Moses Brown chair, some Shaker-used chairs of this period had their arms padded (see figure 192).

Chair cushions were made by Shaker Sisters as early as 1834.[39] By 1860 they were being described as having a "very rich velvet appearance."[40] The 1876 Centennial catalogue for the Mount Lebanon Shaker chairs says: "We have all the most desirable and pretty colors represented in our cushions, and they can be all one color, or have different colored border or with different colored stripes running across the cushion."[41] These late nineteenth-century plush cushions were not made by the Sisters but in Shaker buildings by immigrant laborers. In 1873, Henry Blinn noted that the plush could not be made by machine, and he saw two old hired men working hand looms. They made three to four yards a day, worked ten hours a day, and received fifty cents a yard.[42]

The chairs fit into worldly interiors in part because they were painted with worldly colors. Henry Blinn noted only two sizes being made: "They are all stained in a hot logwood dye which forces the color into the wood. When varnished they are bright red. Already they have orders for more than they can finish."[43] Just after the date of the 1873 chair in figure 190, a catalogue noted that frames could be colored "Mahogany, Ebony, or White finish—that is the natural color of the maple wood, for either styles the price is the same."[44] Another catalogue of about the same time lists for colors: "Cherry, Ebony, Mahogany, or White [clear varnish] finish."[45] In a perhaps slightly later catalogue the wooden part could be "white, or the natural color of the wood [just varnish], ebony, black, and red or cherry color."[46] (Ebony probably differed from black in having a coat of varnish over the black paint or stain.) In 1874 the Shakers inserted a colored page in their catalogue and one of the three colored items was a red and black cushioned chair.[47] The use of red and black was fashionable and based on Asian red and black lacquered work. An example of the

194. BEDROOM, CHATEAU-SUR-MER,
NEWPORT, RHODE ISLAND
*Designed by Seth Bradford, 1851–52; remodeled
by Richard Morris Hunt, 1871–78, for George
Peabody Wetmore*
*The Preservation Society of Newport County,
Newport, Rhode Island*

striking look these colors could produce is seen in the bedroom in Château-sur-Mer, Newport, Rhode Island (figure 194). The building had been designed in 1851–52, but this picture is of the room after it was remodeled by Richard Morris Hunt between 1871 and 1878, the date of the chair in figure 190.

The red and black work chair in figure 195 was made for Shaker use between 1880 and 1920. It is a Number 4 chair with the upper side stretchers cut out after the chair was made, but before it was painted, to allow the installation of a pair of drawers to hold handwork. (Or, the legs may have been drilled for stretchers but the holes filled in as soon as it was decided to add drawers.) Both drawers have metal stops to prevent their being pulled out too far and spilling the contents. The sitter's right-hand drawer has three compartments. The bottoms of the drawers use a kind of plywood: its core is formed by strips of wood about 1 inch wide; these are faced above and below with heavy paper. The top rail, front side and rear stretchers, and the rockers are painted red over black. The faded original tape was once black with two tan stripes. When fresh, it was a very dashing object.

Various worldly chairmakers sought to benefit from the Shakers' prestige as chairmakers and sold their own chairs as Shaker-made. In their 1874 catalogue the Shakers began warning against such frauds: "Beware of imitation chairs which are sold for our make, and which are called Shakers' chairs. Read, and remember where you can send for the Shakers' chairs and get the genuine." Between the printing of the 1874 and 1875 catalogues, the Shakers developed a trademark: "All Chairs of our make will have a Gold Transfer Trade Mark attached to them and none others are Shakers' Chairs."[48]

The chair business remained successful into the twentieth century, although there were even

195. ARMLESS ROCKING NUMBER 4
WORK CHAIR
Mount Lebanon, New York, South Family
1880–1920
Maple painted black and red; original black and
tan seat and back tape; drawer bottoms: heavy
paper either side of strips of wood
H. 33³/₄" W. 22" D. 28⁷/₈"
Collection of the Shaker Museum and Library,
Old Chatham, New York

fewer people to produce them and put on the webbing. The factory burned in 1923, and much of the machinery was lost. The business was reestablished in another building and the chairs incorporated more pre-turned stock. By the 1930s the posts, as well as the rounds, were purchased already made, and on them the Shakers turned pommels, or finials (see figure 196). To make a tall-back chair, separately turned pommels were added to the top of the pre-turned back posts. They were held in place by round tenons that extended down from the pommels. William Perkins was the last Shaker man to make chairs. After he died in 1934, the sole maker was Lillian Barlow, who appears in figure 196. She produced chairs until her death in 1942. Sarah Collins had long added the webbing (figure 197), which had always been Sisters' work, and she continued working on chairs until her death in 1947. She had a "large business in reseating and refinishing old chairs, for they were so well made that they never wear out, and with a new seat, and perhaps a coat of shellac, they are as good as new."[49]

The structural characteristics of oval boxes changed very little between the early 1830s and 1880, but after 1870 some were given newly fashionable colors and surface patterns. There are oval boxes that join red and black. Most have a black, or very dark green, box and lid, with the band of the lid painted red over the black or green paint. A few of these show the black—or green from which the yellow pigment has faded—applied as sponge-decoration (figure 198). (Scarcer

196. PHOTOGRAPH: LILLIAN BARLOW AT
A LATHE
By N.E. Baldwin
Mount Lebanon, New York, Second Family Chair
Factory
About 1939
H. 4¹/₂" W. 6¹/₂"
New York State Museum, Albany, New York

197. PHOTOGRAPH: ELDRESS SARAH
COLLINS
By William F. Winter, Jr.
Mount Lebanon, New York, South Family
1923–30
H. 10" W. 8"
Private collection

are red boxes with a black lid band.)[50] The Shakers continually repainted or revarnished pieces, often adding a fashionable, or preferred color or pattern. The early Sabbathday Lake chest of drawers in figure 199 was grained with what appears to be a red-brown varnish at about the same time as the oval box was sponge-decorated. (The piece in figure 228 was similarly brought up to date.)

Moving Ever Closer to Worldly Design

The closing of the Society to outsiders during the Era of Manifestations diminished the contact between the Shakers and the outside world. Members of the Ministries, and others, still traveled, and business contacts continued, but they were more carefully monitored. For example, in addition to closing the worship service between 1842 and 1845, the Trustees' Office at Groveland, New York (located in the center of the community), was closed for three months in 1842. Business was conducted at the Gathering Family, also known as the West Family, at the edge of the community.[51] By 1850, when the Shakers began greater contact with the world, non-Shaker designers had passed through the Greek and Gothic revivals, and were well into the rococo revival taste. It was not until about 1860 that the Shakers were ready to consciously reflect new worldly

198. OVAL BOX
Mount Lebanon, New York
1870–80
Maple and pine painted dark green, with black
sponge decoration; rim painted over with red;
covered with a clear finish
H. 4¹¹/₁₆" L. 12¹/₁₆" D. 8⁷/₁₆"
Collection of Suzanne Courcier and Robert W.
Wilkins

designs, something they had not done since about 1810. With the new openness, the pieces the Shakers made or purchased echoed the post–Civil War versions of the Renaissance, Greek, and rococo styling, and, when they came along, the Arts and Crafts, Eastlake, and colonial revival attitudes.

The Shakers' ability to produce sound, simple chairs that recalled the past and suggest the handmade, paralleled the development in England of the concerns that initiated the Arts and

199. CHEST OF DRAWERS
Sabbathday Lake, Maine
1810–30
Pine; maple pulls; grained with red-brown
varnish (it goes over breaks in the drawer lips)
probably 1870–90
H. 46¹/₄" W. 40¹/₄" D. 17³/₄"
Base dovetailed at front corners
The United Society of Shakers, Sabbathday Lake,
Maine

Crafts Movement. There, many designers turned away from the cheap ornamental effects machine production ushered in, and these reformers sought ways to keep craftsmen from being eliminated by new industrial practices. William Morris joined others in the fight to have early rural pieces made of local materials provide inspiration for new designs. In the 1880s England saw the founding of a variety of art-workers guilds, and in 1888 the Arts and Crafts Exhibition Society held its first exhibition. The English ash chair of about 1888 shown in figure 200 was designed by Ernest Gimson, and is typical of the movement's reworking of rural ideas and practices. These concerns and ideas came readily to America, but it was not until 1897 that an American Society of Arts and Crafts was founded, first in Boston, then in Chicago, New York, Minneapolis, and Detroit. By the end of the nineteenth century the desire for simple, sturdy pieces that expressed handwork produced manufacturers such as Gustav Stickley. After visiting Europe to observe various arts and crafts shops, Stickley began his own Craftsmen enterprises in 1900. Between 1901 and 1916 he published the magazine *Craftsman,* which helped popularize the look. What the Shakers were producing for sale was useful in such settings for they shared a similar design philosophy.

200. ARMCHAIR
Designed by Ernest Gimson, England
About 1888
Ash; rush seat
H. 49½" W. 22"
Victoria & Albert Museum, London, England

Help from Outside: Tenants and Paid Workers
In Shaker communities farming remained careful and slowly paced. More outsiders were hired to work the land, particularly those pieces not attached to the home communities. At Mount Lebanon Charles Nordhoff was told "a farmer who is in the employ of the Shakers is considered a fortunate man, as they are kind and liberal in their dealings. Every where they have the reputation of being strictly honest and fair in all their transactions with the world's people."[52] At Pleasant Hill, Nordhoff found between fifteen and twenty African Americans employed in farming, and "they had two colored women and a little boy in the 'office' kitchen, hired to help the sisters; and this is the only place where I saw this done."[53]

At least since the building of the second meetinghouse at New Lebanon, the Shakers had employed outside workers to help when they needed extra people or special skills. With the aging of the membership and the smaller percentage of men, more of the men's work was done by women or hired men, or purchased from the world. Isaac Newton Youngs, who had made so many clocks and other pieces of furniture, was able by 1857 to write about the carpenters and cabinetmakers: "for many years such work was all done within the Ch[urc]h . . . . Of late years, however, from necessity there had been much hiring in of the world, to do jobs of woodwork . . . ."[54] In 1876 William Dean Howells, after his visit to Shirley, Massachusetts, noted: "The Shakers used to spin and weave all the stuff they wore, but to do this now would be a waste of time; they buy the alpaca and linen which both sexes wear in summer, and their substantial woolens for the winter . . . . There are no longer carpenters, blacksmiths, and shoemakers among the Shakers at Shirley, because their work can be more cheaply performed by the world-outside, and the shops once devoted to these trades now stand empty."[55]

Things from Outside
In 1875 two fires about a week apart, and probably set by an arsonist, burned eight buildings at Mount Lebanon, including the Church Family's Great House. George Wickerham and Giles Avery were the architects responsible for designing the new one. For that building the Shakers purchased objects they would once have built: they did buy Shaker-made chairs from the South Family, but from the world came marble top tables, cases for the Brothers and Sisters, and long beds for the Brothers, which were borrowed temporarily by the Sisters until their shorter ones arrived, as daybooks record:

January 2, 1877, Attention is now being paid to getting the rooms ready. B.[enjamin]G.[ates] left this morning with a hired man for Albany to get the New Bedsteads.[56]
January 11, 1877, The New Bedsteads 25 in No. arrive. 12 of them are lent to Sisters, as these are all measured to Brethren.[57]
February 9, 1877, A week since the Cases ['A thing composed of cupboard & drawers'[58]]for Br use being built at Pittsfield commenced to be brought home. 6 have arrived and Brethren are gradually moving in![59]
March 2, 1877, The last of the cases arrive. 17 are in using among the Br. being the No. of Brethren now in the House. 13 are among the Sisters.[60]
March 8, 1877, The springs for [the short] Bed steads come in. We have now received 25 long ones 6½ feet and 19 6 feet—in all 44.[61]

March 16, 1877, We have long anticipated our fit out of Marble tables in the Dining Room—Today they are erected and 8 in number, seating if we had them 64 people; as it is they are not filled at the first sitting, 11wanting of Br and 8 Sisters.[62]
December 13, 1877 Ministry Sisters go to South Family to Select some chairs for our home.[63]
January 27, 1877 Have rec'd 62 new chairs from the South Family, for house.[64]
March 17, 1877 Received the last of our chairs, every Br & Sister in the family has one Min[istry] included.[65]

The South Family-made chairs were probably used in the retiring rooms, while the worldly chairs were used at the marble-top dining room tables, and in some work areas. They had the saber legs and reverse-curve backs of Greek-influenced chairs of the post-Civil War era. They are seen in a view of a sewing room at Mount Lebanon (figure 201). The room edges toward the complex interiors found in many Shaker rooms from at least the 1880s. The clock is beautifully stark, but the wallpaper is striped. While choosing these inexpensive but fashioned worldly chairs, the Believers hired carpenters to make a group of round tables for the new dwelling house.[66]

While the latest style furniture was of the plain and inexpensive variety, the china they eventually bought for this new home was more lively: floral and fern designs danced around their boldly stated name. On October 12, 1886, the Mount Lebanon Church Family Trustee Benjamin Gates, Deaconess Cornelia French, and Mary Hazzard went to New York City "on business concerning dishes for table use; to be made by Order." On February 20, 1887, an entry in a Sister's diary in the Church Family says: "We have a set of new dishes on our table [this] morning, marked Shakers MT Lebanon, they are pretty and costly we know." Another Sister's diary reads: "We have a surprise of great value, on our breakfast table; a set of new dishes. Porcelain ware marked for us Shakers &c . . . . We hope it may be long ere we need another set." The extant pieces, a few seen in figure 202, have three different floral patterns. They were made by Union Porcelain Works in

Greenpoint, now part of Brooklyn, the first American firm to have lasting success producing porcelain. Some of the pieces are dated on their bases [18]86 and others [18]87. The company began to produce porcelain in the mid-1860s, and had shown their wares at the Philadelphia Centennial Exposition of 1876, where the Mount Lebanon Shakers exhibited chairs and other products. It is possible the Shakers became aware of this china factory at the Exposition.[67]

Rules for Furniture

In acknowledging that hands would dirty and wear the paint of the surface around the knobs, the Millennial Laws of 1845 allowed drawer faces to be varnished over the paint. By 1860 the varnish often appeared on drawer fronts without any paint below. The workstand of the 1880s from Canterbury in figure 203 has red paint on the carcass, including the back. The wooden knobs and all the movable parts—figured butternut drawer fronts, door, and work slide—have only a clear finish. This form of furniture was made as work units for Sisters. Several are signed, dated, and inscribed to a particular Sister by the maker, suggesting they were often personal acknowledgments by a Brother of a Sister. The inscription on the bottom of the drawer on one of a pair made by Henry Blinn in the 1870s is lovingly personal: "These two Sewing desks were made from Mother Hannah's Butternut trees, grown South of Ministries Shop. Were cared for by her when saplings."[68] A piece of the same form by Eli Kidder is inscribed "Work Stand" and dated 1861. As both Brothers lived at Canterbury, the two terms for the form must have been interchangeable.[69]

The form probably derives from small worldly desks made since the end of the previous century and popular throughout much of the nineteenth century. A typical example, shown as figure 204, has a stepped-back top, many useful drawers, small lathe-turned legs, and a work surface that opens.

Mostly Shaker-Made

Most new Shaker-made pieces, even when they continued some traditional features, usually introduced new ideas. Henry Green of Alfred, Maine, a schoolteacher and business agent for the community, moved through the world as he sold Shaker fancy goods at resort hotels in Maine and

205. TAILOR'S COUNTER
By Henry Green, Alfred, Maine
About 1875
Pine top and back; maple frame; butternut
drawer fronts and side panels; cherry pulls; top
and frame cleaned of red paint
H. 35¼" L. 71" D. 34"
The United Society of Shakers, Sabbathday Lake,
Maine

New Hampshire (see figure 221). He eventually became an Elder at the Alfred Church Family in 1896.[70] The counter he made about 1875 (figure 205) continues the asymmetry, rectilinear grid, and round legs of the earlier period, while introducing newer, worldly features: broad flat knobs and horizontally paneled ends. Originally the maple frame around the butternut drawer fronts and end panels and the pine top were painted red; the butternut received a clear finish. The red paint is gone because the Shakers at Sabbathday Lake proceeded to strip the color from many of their pieces after they received thirty-one truckloads of household goods on the closing of the Alfred Community in 1931. They did this to pieces they intended to use, and to encourage the sale of the rest. The view taken about 1903 of a sewing room, with a probably Shaker-made cabinet for the sewing machine (figure 206), shows how such counters were often employed as ironing surfaces.

206. PHOTOGRAPH: SEWING ROOM
By James E. West, Hoosick Falls, New York
Mount Lebanon, New York
About 1900; the woman and child were non-Shaker visitors
H. 5½" W. 8½"
The sewing machine cabinet is probably Shaker-made
Collection of the Shaker Museum and Library,
Old Chatham, New York

About 1860 arched panels, which had been popular in the second quarter of the nineteenth century (as seen in Loudon's 1839 designs, figure 82), were again in vogue, and Henry Green—who could work in the older or the newer styles—employed them with fashionable glass rather than wooden panels in an 1880s cabinet and the desk and bookcase seen in figure 207. It reflects the world's emphasis on arched, glazed panels, vertically oriented wooden panels, and a slanting fall-front desk area (see the worldly piece in figure 214). This piece adds the Shakers' traditional sense of a strong grid of rectangles; here they are oriented vertically.

The stereoscopic view of a retiring room in the Stone Dwelling House at Enfield, New Hampshire (figure 208), was made about 1873. In it early chairs mix with a purchased Renaissance revival bed, a purchased chest of drawers (at the left), colonial revival white-painted drawers, and a patterned rug on a patterned linoleum-covered floor. The beds may have been bought in some quantity, because the form appears in a different Enfield room in another stereoscopic view.[71] The Shaker-made Renaissance revival-style bed in figure 209 was probably made in the

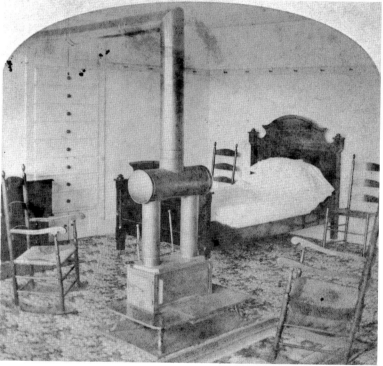

207. DESK AND BOOKCASE
By Henry Green, Alfred, Maine
About 1882
Butternut and maple
H. 83" W. 40½" D. 20"
The United Society of Shakers, Sabbathday Lake, Maine

208. PHOTOGRAPH: RETIRING ROOM, STONE DWELLING HOUSE, ENFIELD, NEW HAMPSHIRE
By W. G. C. Kimball, Concord, New Hampshire
About 1873
Half of a stereoscopic view; full card: H. 3⁷/₁₆"
W. 6¹⁵/₁₆"
Collection of the Shaker Museum and Library, Old Chatham, New York

1880s at Enfield, New Hampshire, by Franklin Young. In the world contrasting woods were now a regular feature, and often in Shaker-made pieces dark areas stood out against a light color wood. The bed's light-colored panels are enriched and enclosed by dark walnut. The legs continue a traditional Shaker turned form.

The chest of drawers with a Renaissance revival pediment in figure 210 was probably made by Thomas Fisher of Enfield, Connecticut, about 1890. The chestnut chest has a cherry top. The side panels are vertical in orientation and have raised centers, as found during the previous century, but now they are machine-made thin.[72] It resembles the washstand form found in countless worldly bedroom sets. Those were usually of a painted soft wood covered with painted decoration.

Early in the 1880s Henry Green of the Alfred Community accepted the role of the jigsaw and certain post–Civil War Renaissance-style elements—such as the shaped drop attached under the lower front rail of the desk in figure 211. It is one of more than a dozen of this form Green made as Sisters' writing desks. In contrast, he could make the quieter piece seen as figure 212. Its vertical panels play against the strong horizontals of the drawers, base, and top shelf. The two pitched top boards are like those on figures 210 and 214. The cherry and pine desk made by Delmer C. Wilson of the Sabbathday Lake Community, begun in 1895 and presented as a gift in

209. BED
Probably by Franklin Youngs (similar to a bed
he made for his own use)
Enfield, New Hampshire
Probably the 1880s
Ash, cherry, and walnut
H. 51¼" W. 42" L. 67¼"
Canterbury Shaker Village, Canterbury, New
Hampshire

210. CHEST OF DRAWERS
Attributed to Thomas Fisher
Enfield, Connecticut
About 1890
Inscribed in pencil on the bottom of fifth drawer:
"Made in Shaker Village/THOMAS FISHER
[caps in different hand]/Enfield, Conn/Sister
Lillian Philps." Inscribed on back: "Mt. Lebanon"
Chestnut, cherry, white pine, oak, and ash; cast-
iron pulls
H. 42" W. 40" D. 21⅛"
Canterbury Shaker Village, Canterbury, New
Hampshire

1896 (figure 213), is like the worldly piece seen as figure 214 in its form, its use of panels and circular bosses, and its jigsaw shaping. Thomas Fisher of Enfield, Connecticut, could also adopt to different worldly styles: he probably made figure 210, and the rococo-influenced table seen as figure 215. The cheeks (or raised part of the legs) and the molding on the rails below the top board of the table, which are of cherry, provide the fashionable contrast of colors.

The English architect-turned-journalist Charles Eastlake reworked two articles, and in 1868 published *Hints on Household Taste*. The book became widely successful, and by 1881 had appeared in six editions, influencing everything from chairs to buildings. In it, Eastlake showed an eclectic medieval styling that featured panels, brackets, groups of thin horizontal lines (to suggest the decoration produced by molding planes), recessed concave circles—filled with flowers or a circular pattern—and small areas of incised carved lines forming floral or geometric patterns. The turned posts and balusters on the pieces he designed had many groups of horizontal lines. The Union Village, Ohio, Trustees Office, built in 1810, was remodeled under the influence of this style between 1892 and 1895 (figures 216 and 217). Because of the use of seven kinds of marble for the floors (seen in figure 217), it became known as Marble Hall. The 1920s Mount Lebanon postcard in figure 218 shows Sarah Collins at an Eastlake-influenced organ purchased from the world. The door latch in figure 219 shows influences from the Eastlake style, and is easily seen as enjoying the wild eclecticism and complexity of the aesthetic movement.

It was perfectly natural that the Shakers would join in the fad to make crazy quilts when they

became fashionable at the end of the century. The Shakers loved color and pattern, and they longed to save and use, or reuse, everything they found acceptable. The world began piecing together bright textiles, and covering the surface with rickrack, spider web, and various aesthetic-movement stitched enrichments around 1880. At least two Shaker-made examples were made between 1890 and 1900 (see figure 220, which was sold into the world). It is typical of the Shakers that they would wait before embracing something new, for although they might want it, they did not want to appear to themselves, or the world, as though they were reaching after fashion.

Fancy Goods

By the 1860s various groups and individuals were making small, colorful, easy to carry, and often amusing "fancy" goods for sale to the ever increasing tourist trade staying at the grand hotels that dotted the New England landscape. Native Americans sold various items, but were especially known for their baskets, for example. Fancy goods were produced in various Shaker communities, and most families had shops to sell them to their many visitors. They were also peddled beyond the communities, first by wagon (see figure 221), and then by car to resort hotels and vacation spots. Those made by the Shakers always had some practical application. Before the Civil War the Brothers' woodenware—buckets, tubs, pails, boxes, firkins, measures, flax wheels, wool wheels, and winders—had been profitable. After the war the Sisters made delightful, colorful, items useful to women. The Shakers also became famous for their applesauce, maple syrup and maple sugar.

Above, left:
211. DESK AND BOOKSTAND
By Henry Green, Alfred, Maine
About 1883
Butternut, cherry, and pine
H. 62" W. 32" D. 16"
The United Society of Shakers, Sabbathday Lake, Maine

Above, right:
212. DESK AND BOOKSTAND
By Henry Green, Alfred, Maine
About 1905
Butternut, birch, and pine; later stain accents the grain of the butternut
An early photograph shows it in use in the Second Family, Alfred. It was given to the farmhand Otis Wallingford, probably in lieu of wages, when the Second Family broke up in 1918
H. 65" W. 38½" D. 17⅜"
The United Society of Shakers, Sabbathday Lake, Maine

About 1880 the Shakers developed the Dorothy cloak, designed by Eldress Dorothy Durgin of Canterbury. Made of wool, it was full-length without arm slits and had a shoulder cape and hood. The lining and interior pockets were made of silk and long silk ribbons tied under the chin. An advertisement for it says it was "made in all popular shades of broadcloth, for auto, street or ocean travel, or in pastel shades for evening wear." It also came in "Harvard red," "Dartmouth green," "Navy blue," gray, black, and white.[73] Grover Cleveland's future wife wore one to the president's inauguration in 1885. Although the Shakers did not wear Dorothy cloaks themselves, they knew their market, and because of their popularity, about 1900 they trademarked the design. Cloaks appear for sale on the back wall in figure 223. During the last quarter of the nineteenth century, and through to the 1940s, the Shakers produced brightly colored and practical children's cloaks. Although there were now few children in Shaker communities, the cloaks were widely sold in the

217. PHOTOGRAPH: CHURCH FAMILY
TRUSTEES' OFFICE, UNION VILLAGE,
OHIO, SHOWING MARBLE FLOOR
*Called: "Marble Hall"; built 1810, rebuilt
1892–95*
Album inscribed: "Wm. C. Ayers" on front
Photograph: 1895–1900
H. 4⅝" W. 6½"
*Collection of the Shaker Museum and Library,
Old Chatham, New York*

world. The Shakers bought a machine to knit heavy crew-neck sweaters, and well into the 1930s sold them in considerable numbers to Dartmouth, Harvard, Yale, and other eastern colleges where "letter" sweaters were fashionable. A view of the North Family Mount Lebanon store with Sister Martha Burger seated in a late slat-back chair is typical of how fancy goods were displayed in communities about 1895 (figure 222). The 1920s view in figure 223 is of the sales room at Canterbury. A list of about sixty types of items sold from the Enfield, Connecticut, store in 1910 shows it was natural for the Shakers to mix previously used objects with newly produced goods.[74]

218. PHOTOGRAPH: SARAH COLLINS
PLAYING ORGAN
Mount Lebanon, New York
1900–1905
H. 3¼" W. 5¼"
*Collection of the Shaker Museum and Library,
Old Chatham, New York*

219. DOOR LATCH
*Sabbathday Lake, Maine
Purchased for the north
door of the 1883
Dwelling House by its
builder George Brock
of Portland, Maine
About 1883
Brass; plate made
in two pieces
H. 14¾" W. of plate 2½"
The United Society of
Shakers, Sabbathday
Lake, Maine*

Figures 224 and 225 show Shaker goods made for their personal use or for sale from the 1840s to 1950. Early in the 1860s Sisters in various communities began to produce fancy boxes by pasting richly colored or patterned papers over cardboard or wooden boxes (figure 224). (Tabitha Lapsly's blue box in figure 133 is a large example of this practice.) Sometimes one or more sides of a small box were made of glass. Some lids had velvet padding inside. The Canterbury red circular box at right front predates this development. It was made by drying the skin of an orange, then covering it with red paper; the bottom and domed inside of the lid have blue paper; in 1847 the Canterbury Shakers made seventy-two orange peel boxes for sale to the world.[75] The lid of

Right:
220. CRAZY QUILT
Made at Mount Lebanon, New York
Made about 1890 from pieces brought to the
Shakers by a Dr. McCord or his mother
Silk patches; silk stitches; red silk-plush edges
L. 70¼" W. 69½"
Collection of the Shaker Museum and Library,
Old Chatham, New York

Below:
221. PHOTOGRAPH: HENRY GREEN ON
SALES TRIP TO THE WHITE MOUNTAINS
FROM ALFRED
Inscription on mat: "Compliments of Jean Paul
Gelinger/Studio 711 Boylston St. Boston, Mass."
1896
H. 6¼" W. 8⅜"
The United Society of Shakers, Sabbathday Lake,
Maine

222. PHOTOGRAPH: MARTHA BURGER IN MOUNT LEBANON, NORTH FAMILY STORE
By James E. West, Hoosick Falls, New York
About 1895
H. 5¼" W. 8½"
Collection of the Shaker Museum and Library, Old Chatham, New York

223. PHOTOGRAPH: FANCY GOODS FOR SALE
Canterbury, New Hampshire
1920s
H. 10" W. 8"
Collection of the Shaker Museum and Library, Old Chatham, New York

the circular cardboard box at the left bears the initials "E. F."; the bottom has a pencil inscription, "From A. Russell, 1850." The box holds a tiny spool rack for embroidery silks. The central, turned handle is two inches tall; twelve pegs hold twenty-six tiny spools. An inscription on its base reads, "Made by Ednah F. Fitts, 1864." The miniature Canterbury chest of drawers, of about 1860 to 1870, is made of wood and was covered inside and out with brightly colored papers. The exterior paper now appears in tones of brown because sunlight has faded it. The two rectangular boxes, and the blue and orange box and lid at the center, also came from Canterbury and were made around 1900.

Throughout the nineteenth century, oval boxes and carriers were popular sales items. The two sewing carriers at the top left of figure 225 were made by Delmer Wilson in the second quarter of this century. They have a Sabbathday Lake trademark on their bottoms. The larger one is lined with a rosebud-patterned cloth, the smaller one with blue silk. In the second quarter of the twentieth century the Shakers in several communities purchased round boxes, added handles, varnished them, lined them with bright materials, added sewing equipment, and sold them in place of those previously made by Shaker Brothers. The pincushion and spool holder at the right was made about 1920 to 1930 and probably comes from Mount Lebanon. The sewing basket in the center with blue ribbon bows and hinges is covered with a Shaker-made cloth that employs very thin strips of yellow poplar as the weft. It was produced at Mount Lebanon about 1900 to 1910.

Many of the things the Sisters made for sale were inexpensive to produce and could delight tourists wanting something cheap and light as a memento of a visit. The pine cone of about 1920

Opposite:
224. MINIATURE CHEST OF DRAWERS; PAPER COVERED AND ORANGE PEEL BOXES; AND MINIATURE SPOOL HOLDER
Various communities, see text
1840s to about 1900
Collection of the Shaker Museum and Library, Old Chatham, New York

Above:
225. FANCY GOODS
Various communities, see text
1900–50
Collection of the Shaker Museum and Library, Old Chatham, New York

is painted gold and carries a ribbon reading "From the Home of the Lebanon Shakers, N.Y." The three ribbons at the front were for securing bunches of asparagus about 1920; they read "I Grew at the Home"—"Of the Lebanon Shakers." The felt-skirted doll penwipers at front right were made at Mount Lebanon from about 1890 to 1920. Five of the objects in figure 225 were made by the Canterbury Shakers in the 1950s. Although they are like what the Shakers sold in their own shop, these were provided for sale in the Shaker Museum's store in Old Chatham. They are a white crocheted dog, with shoe button eyes and a bell on a red ribbon; a bean-bag frog, with white button eyes with black "slit" lines; a blue crocheted squirrel teapot holder, with shoe button eyes; two crocheted chicken egg cozies; and a cat made from a yellow washcloth (the legs are the rolled ends of the cloth, the ears pipe cleaners, the eyes and whiskers sewn on black yarn and thread).

THE SHAKERS MARKET THEIR PAST

The Shakers were cautious about impostors selling non-Shaker chairs as Shaker-made, but were pleased to utilize the public's image of the Shakers. Some of the items the Sisters made not only borrowed images from their past, but many incorporated early Shaker materials. Their rooms, closets, and chests were full of old things, and logically, they mined this surplus. Among the early reused items, the Sisters turned Shaker-made silk scarves into fancy aprons,[76] and they cut up early nineteenth-century wool textiles to dress dolls they imported from Germany. Martha Burger has some of these dolls displayed on the table in figure 222. They appear for sale in boxes in the upper left corner of a photograph of the shop at Canterbury (figure 223). The 1840–50 light-weight wool dress material from two Church Families in figure 226 mixes blue and red yarn to produce a glowing pink-purple. The piece in the foreground of figure 226 is marked "CHH2" which could mean the Church Family, Second Order, the second piece of this type made, or something else. The German doll was dressed in similar nineteenth-century material about 1950. It wears a straw bonnet, striped stockings, black rubber shoes, and a complete set of underclothes.

226. EARLY DRESS MATERIAL AND MID- TWENTIETH-CENTURY DOLL
Textiles: front piece, New Lebanon, New York, Church Family; marked: "CHH2"; L. 72½" W. 32". Left piece, Canterbury, New Hampshire, Church Family; L. 81" W. 37". Both mix red and blue wool threads.
1840–50

Doll: German; Bisque Head Marked: "Made in Germany #168.9½"; Dressed by Jennie Wells about 1950 at Hancock, Massachusetts; H. 22¾"
Collection of the Shaker Museum and Library, Old Chatham, New York

The easiest way to profit financially from the past was to sell early objects without changing them, and by the end of the nineteenth century the Shakers were giving away or selling their growing surplus of things. The china shown in figure 202 was ordered in 1886, and we know that there were sixty-eight members of the Church Family in 1885. It is not known how many place settings were purchased, but in the group of twenty-eight pieces now at the Shaker Museum and Library, there are three patterns. There may have been three complete sets—each big enough for all the members to have the same design—but more likely such a large order necessitated the use of three variations to provide one place-setting each. Such material was sold as novelties, or mementos, in the Shaker shops to antique dealers, collectors, and the curious. (There is china for sale on the shelves in figure 222.) The twenty-eight pieces now together came from seven donors and two purchases.[77]

To raise money, the Shakers sold objects at public auction. In 1918, for example, the Church Family at Enfield, New Hampshire, had a sale of new and old objects nearly five years before they closed the community and the last members moved to Canterbury:

The Church Family Shakers have for some weeks been having a sale of furniture and other house-hold goods, chairs, tables, chests and drawers of various sizes and quality. They have still many things to dispose of as they contemplate selling the place later on. They have some large pieces like cases of drawers 6 or 8 feet tall, one good roll top desk good as new, two or three tall old style desks or secretaries. Most of these articles were made on the place when there was lumber of a value which we do not have today. Several old clocks quite valuable to one who values old things, and a few more modern clocks. If interested in buying please come and look it over as we shall close the house as the weather gets colder.[78]

In 1922 there was a sale on site of Shaker material used by the West Family at Pleasant Hill before it closed in 1910. The broadside advertising the sale made clear that there was a growing interest in things Shaker. "This collection is the best settler's furniture extant. It was all manufactured by the Shakers . . . and has never been out of their possession." The sale included: "about 27 beds, 6 children's beds, about 40 cherry chests, about 10 chests of drawers, a number of chairs, a number of tables an candle stands, several stoves, a number of spinning and flax wheels, a number of rugs, 2 corner cupboards, several clocks, a number of other small articles manufactured and used by the Shakers."[79]

The Shakers have always been generous to those in need, and they have often sent material or money to help during emergencies. In 1919 they made a donation to a farm for boys: "A truck from Berkshire Industrial Farm will take away many things suited to their interests. Also furniture and other things helpful in their efforts to double the number of boys now under their care. Among the things presented is a good strong-toned organ."[80]

Being up to date, the Shakers participated in the colonial revival as they painted earlier wood-work white and turned pieces into unpainted objects for their own use and for sale. For commer-

227. PHOTOGRAPH: ENFIELD, CONNECTICUT
For the community where each object was made, see text
1906–13
H. 3¼" W. 5½"
Collection of the Shaker Museum and Library, Old Chatham, New York

228. CASE WITH CUPBOARDS AND
DRAWERS, NEW LEBANON, NEW YORK,
SOUTH FAMILY
Case: 1800–20; originally a built-in
Pine; remaining grain-painting probably
1870–90
H. 80⁵⁄₁₆" W. 37⁵⁄₈" D. 12¹⁄₂"
Shafts of drawer knobs do not go all the way
through the drawer fronts. Cupboard originally
had six pegs spaced across the inside of the back;
only the shafts in back board remain. Peg
projecting from the right side is not original: it is
in a new hole. Left rear corner has a three-quarter
round molding.
Collection of the Shaker Museum and Library,
Old Chatham, New York

cial reasons, they linked themselves to the colonial craze. For example, in various images Sisters posed with spinning wheels—the requisite symbol of America's past, and the women's role (see figure 227). This 1906–13 photograph shows Eldress Miriam Offord at Enfield, Connecticut, standing, and Sister Eliza Brown with a Canterbury stove; a New Lebanon spinning wheel stamped on the end DM; a New Lebanon yarn winder; an Enfield, Connecticut, Sisters' work-table; and a striped pail (in front of the window) probably from Hancock or Lebanon.[81] To capture the "early" furniture market Shaker Sisters scraped early pieces with broken glass to get off the old finish and offered them for sale. The high chest of drawers with a cupboard (figure 228) is from the South Family, New Lebanon. An early date of about 1800–20 is suggested by the strongly raised panel in the cupboard door. At first it was built-in; later it was freestanding, and a cornice and base were added. Perhaps when that was done, probably in the late nineteenth century, grain-decoration was added. (The decoration is not original, because it goes over some broken areas of the drawer lips.) Now there is only graining on the drawers, for when a collector first saw the piece and immediately purchased it, the drawers were out and Sisters were removing the paint from the carcass. Many times, the income from any sale was helpful; during the Depression years, the Shakers sold what they could, and at times that meant the chicken, quart of milk, loaves of bread, or vegetables from the Family larder.[82]

THE LOOK OF SHAKER ROOMS: THE WRITTEN RECORD

Many modern scholars have repeatedly stated that the Shakers took the design ideas of about 1800, and continued them to the end of the century, but that was not possible. Change always creeps in if there is any openness to new ideas. Even in more restricted sects, such as the Amish, new ideas, new technologies, and new materials invariably appear, and in a group that prides itself on an openness to change, it was inevitable and often welcomed. The Shakers' successful chair industry, and growing trade in fancy goods, played on quaintness, usefulness, and the virtues of the handmade. Also the Shakers turned the once stringent leanness of form and sparse placement of objects into an iconic look. Unlike Williamsburg, and other twentieth-century re-creations that made up a past that never really quite existed, the Shakers kept alive and exploited an image of a real past while living differently in the present.

It is difficult to deal with the disparity between the written record, which speaks of plainness, and the pictorial record, which shows ever more complicated room arrangements, without accepting that two kinds of Shaker spaces coexisted: one, the public areas used to connote true belief, the other, where the Shakers dwelled. A review of writings by outsiders of the rooms they were permitted to see shows consistent plainness well into the twentieth century. In 1869 William Hepworth Dixon, editor of the *Athenaeum*, described his room at the North Family, Mount Lebanon:

My room is painfully bright and clean. No Haarlem vrouw [housewife] ever scraped her floor into such perfect neatness as my floor; nor could the wood, of which it is made, be matched in purity except in the heart of an uncut forest pine. A bed stands in the corner, with sheets and pillows of spotless white. A table on which lie an English Bible, some few Shaker tracts, an inkstand, a paper-knife; four cane chairs, arranged in angles; a piece of carpet by the bedside; a spittoon in one corner, completes the furniture. A closet on one side of the room contains a second bed, a washstand, a jug of water, towels; and the whole apartment is light and airy, even for a frame house . . . .[83]

Nordhoff visited Mount Lebanon in 1874 and his experience was of plain rooms:

We passed through a hall in which I saw numerous bonnets, cloaks, and shawls hung up on pegs, and passed an empty dining-hall, and out of a door into the back yard, crossing which, we entered another house, and, opening a door, my guide welcomed me to the "visitors' room." "This," said he, "is where you will stay. . . .

I found myself in a comfortable low-ceiled room, warmed by an air-tight stove, and furnished with a cot-bed, half a dozen chairs, a large wooden spittoon filled with saw-dust, a looking-glass, and a table. The floor was covered with strips of rag carpet, very neat and of a pretty, quiet color, loosely laid down. Against the wall, near the stove, hung a dust-pan, shovel, dusting-brush, and small broom. A door opened into an inner room, which contained another bed and conveniences for washing. A closet in the wall held matches, soap, and other articles. Every thing was scrupulously neat and clean. On the table were laid a number of Shaker books and newspapers. In one corner of the room was a bell, used, as I afterward discovered, to summon the visitor to his meals. As I looked out of a window, I perceived that the sash was fitted with screws, by means of which the windows could be so secured as not to rattle in stormy weather; while the lower sash of one window was raised three or four inches, and a strip of neatly fitting plank was inserted in the opening—this allowed ventilation between the upper and lower sashes, thus preventing a direct draught, while securing fresh air.

The dress of the men is remarkable from a very broad, stiff-brimmed, white or gray felt hat, and a long coat of light blue. The women wear gowns with many plaits in the skirt; and a singular head-dress or cap of light material, which so completely hides the hair, as so encroaches upon the face, that a stranger is at first unable to distinguish the old from the young. Out of doors they wear the deep sun-bonnet known in this country commonly as a Shaker bonnet. They do not profess to adhere to a uniform; but have adopted what they find to be a convenient style of dress, and will not change it until they find something better.[84]

What is new in this description is the narrow cot-bed, for until the 1860s the Shakers used double beds (except for hired men, and in the infirmary). Narrow late Brothers' beds appear in the print shown as figure 69. Dining tables were now covered with oilcloth.[85] There was a lack of hurry: "Shakers do not toil severely. They are not in haste to be rich; and they have found that for their support, economically as they live, it is not necessary to make labor painful."[86]

In his 1876 article in the *Atlantic Monthly* William Dean Howells described Shirley as clean, and he saw plain communal rooms, those "that one could see":

In each village is an edifice known as the Dwelling-House, which is separate from the office and the other buildings. In this are the rooms of the brothers and sisters, the kitchen and dining-room, and a large room for family meetings. The first impression of all is cleanliness, with a suggestion of bareness which is not inconsistent, however, with comfort, and which comes chiefly from the aspect of the unpapered walls, the scrubbed floors hidden only by rugs and strips of carpeting, and the plain, flat finish of the wood-work. Each chamber accommodates two brothers or two sisters, and is appointed with two beds, two rocking-chairs, two wash-stands, and a wood-stove, with abundance of rugs . . . . There were few tokens of personal taste in the arrangements of rooms . . . .

The dining-room was provided with two large tables, at one of which the brothers sat, and at the other the sisters. The monastic rule of silence at meals is observed, because, as we were told, the confusion would be too great if all talked together. In the kitchen was an immense cook-stove, with every housekeeping convenience; and everywhere opened pantry and store-room doors, with capacious cellars underneath—all scoured and scrubbed to the last degree of neatness.[87]

For an article for *Granite Monthly* in 1877, Amanda B. Harris went to Canterbury and justified liking what she saw:

If one's preconceived idea about the rooms is that they are unattractive, by reason of the austerity in furnishing, and the general primness—that is altogether a mistake. There is an esthetic, as well as a very practical side. But it is by no means certain that it is not the latter which most readily takes the eye of the visitor who has ever had a house of her own. To such, there is refreshment in the absolute cleanliness and tidiness, and order. It is the one kind of household life where the rule of having "a place for everything, and everything in its place," is always carried out. The consummate result has there been reached. Everything runs smoothly. Evidently those who planned the domestic arrangements, while they had in view handiness and compactness, did not overlook the fact that there might be a great saving of noise and labor in the construction of furniture; and so, as far as practicable, they had presses and heavy benches built into the wall, instead of movable fixtures.[88]

Decades later, in 1934, Homer Eaton Keyes, editor of *The Magazine Antiques*, visited Hancock and in his magazine he continued the reporting of plain rooms:

Here I was permitted to view one of the least ostentatious but yet most singularly appealing rooms that I have ever entered. White as moonlight I remember its walls, white and plain linen curtains at the window, and against this pure background a few pieces of warm-toned nutwood furniture, soberly demure, yet without a hint of severity. On a bed in the corner a blue homespun coverlet of wool was neatly spread; braided rugs patterned the floor with ovals of soft color. Near the centre of the room a chair stood beside a small round table, on which a single candle shone like the eye of innocence.[89]

In 1947, as residents were about to close the community and move to Hancock, the British writer E. M. Forster visited Mount Lebanon with some companions who were to write about the community for *The New Yorker*. There his perceptive eye found the clutter and a slight craziness many others missed:

Each [Believers] had plenty of room in the vast building . . . it was like an almshouse where the inmates are not crowded and need not quarrel, and they seemed happy. I had a touching talk with the Eldress, now ninety-one, who had come from England . . . . She did not regret the days when Mount Lebanon had eighty inmates. "It is much better like this," she said. Her room was full of mess and mementos, all of which she misdescribed as Shaker-made. It was nothing of the mess in the apartment of Sisters Ada and Maime, who kept kneeling without obvious room on the carpet and cracking toilet paper at the parrot to make him dance. On their wall ticked a clock which had the face of a cat, and a cat's tail for pendulum . . . we saw the dining-room, where a place was laid, a little humorously, for Christ. We saw the communal meeting-room. Did they—er—shake ever? No—nobody shook now. Did they—er—meet here for prayer? No, said the Eldress complacently. We used to meet once a month. Now we never meet. They are in fact bone idle and did not know it . . . .[90]

Forster met Brother Curtis White and was shown the other half of the building where White lived alone. Later the writer reflected on his visit: "My companions were moved by them [the Shakers] to a degree which I could not share; they were a symbol of something America supposes herself to have missed, they were the dream that got bogged [down]."[91]

The writer for *The New Yorker,* Berton Roueché, returned the next day and talked with Sister Jennie Wells who said, " 'I'm trying to think where to begin,' she said. 'Most of our visitors these days are antique collectors, and all they're interested in is buying up what little fine old handmade Shaker furniture we have left. Why, those people would grab the chairs right out from under us if we'd let them. Our furniture is very fashionable all of a sudden, you know. I understand it's called modernistic . . . .' "[92] She wanted to make clear that there was a strict division of the sexes: that men and women had different halves of the dwelling house. (In the previous century it had been common to live on different sides of the same corridor.) " 'I want you to see the rest of the place. Then we'll come back to the dwelling house . . . . There are only seven of us left in the North Family, and our house has eighty-one rooms . . . . The men lived in the left half and the women in the right. My stars, I hope you didn't think that we actually *lived* together!' "[93] Sister Jennie showed Roueché her room. It was crowded with furniture, and some chairs hung from pegs on the wall. She said happily: " 'There isn't a thing in the room that I'd let one of those greedy antique collectors lay a finger on, except over my dead body.' "[94] The constant pestering by dealers may have caused some members to crowd their rooms to preserve their past.

During the third quarter of the twentieth century, Mildred Wells, who lived at Canterbury but did not sign the covenant, went about the village, often at night, and took things from various buildings to sequester them in Enfield House, where she lived alone. Since she kept everyone else out, the thousands of items she saved were not known until her death in 1987. During these years she was known rather negatively as shy and reclusive, but her persistent acquisitiveness saved an important cross-section of Canterbury Shaker life.

THE LOOK OF SHAKER ROOMS; THE VISUAL RECORD

The pictures of interiors from the 1870s onward show the Shakers were living in complexity, yet showing visitors simplicity; Nordhoff noted that when they took people as visitors, they "have rooms fitted for this purpose."[95] Like making stage sets, the Shakers with ever greater consciousness arranged an idealized and pretty past that may never have existed in quite the way it was shown. (The idea of following inventories and other historic information for room displays would not arrive until the 1970s.) By talking about and showing plain rooms, the Shakers were exhibiting pride in what and who they had been, which justified what they were. As with adver-

229. PHOTOGRAPH: ROOM 7, STONE DWELLING HOUSE, ENFIELD, NEW HAMPSHIRE
By W. G. C. Kimball, Concord, New Hampshire
About 1873
Half of a stereoscopic view: full card: H. 3⁷/₁₆"
W. 6¹⁵/₁₆"
Collection of Shaker Museum and Library, Old Chatham, New York

tising their chairs and fancy goods as full of traditional values, they were continuing a long practice of presenting to the public an admirable, visual purity: the cleanliness written into earlier Laws. By living in more up-to-date rooms, at least some of the Shakers were being consciously modern.

Following a sequence of images here will show how Shaker rooms grew even more complex as the floors and walls were enriched with patterned linoleum, carpets, and wallpaper, and the walls were hung with maps and framed and unframed pictures. When Nordhoff visited Enfield, New Hampshire, in 1874, the Music-Hall, with Canterbury or Enfield, New Hampshire, benches, had up-to-date musical instruments and chairs (figure 184). Likewise, a view of an Enfield, New Hampshire, retiring room, made about 1873, shows an array of things on the floor, including a purchased Renaissance revival bed (figure 208). The walls remain plain, although the woodwork has been painted "colonial white." The view of Sisters working with herb extracts, figure 114, was drawn in 1884 (and published as a print a year later). It shows walls covered with images. The stereoscopic view of room 7 in the Enfield, New Hampshire, Stone Dwelling House, in figure 229, was made about 1873. It includes a grouping of worldly pieces, and only two that are discernibly Shaker-made: the cushioned chair in front of the window, and the center table. The worldly desk is similar to that in figure 214. In the 1880s "Our Home" photograph (figure 192) there is a complex, purchased table, and the chairs have fancy handwork covers. The photograph of about 1900, with a piano and print of a Millet painting (figure 185), is full of richly detailed objects. The chair-up-on-pegs photograph of the 1880s (figure 105) is not quite as complex, but the right and far walls have pictures. The picture of a sewing room in figure 206, taken about 1905, shows many objects on the walls, and four kinds of patterns on the floor.

Public spaces were plainer: The photograph shown as figure 230 was taken about 1890. The room, a space used for public meetings, is relatively plain. The ceiling is divided by moldings into areas of contrasting colors. The organ and seating pieces mix a variety of styles, but the walls are without pictures or other decoration. In fact, the room is very like a worldly public room of the same date. The Church Family dining room at Canterbury, about 1900, is festooned with paper garlands in figure 231, and is like other contemporary large eating areas during a festive moment, except that other institutions might use table covers.

Prints from a period are not as trustworthy as photographs as evidence, for more than photographs, they can incorporate a prevailing attitude that may color what is depicted. For example, the view of the North Family, Mount Lebanon, dining room in figure 232 first appeared in *Frank Leslie's Illustrated Newspaper* in 1873, and shows three long tables with Sisters on benches (the one at the right continuing improbably beyond the table). At the left, four Brothers sit on chairs at part of a table. Photographs of dining rooms at this date (except when with paper chains as seen in figure 231) show they retained a quiet plainness, possibly because this was one of the spaces visitors could use, or because it was one of the ritualized spaces of the Believers. Certainly, as presented by *Leslie's,* it is a harsh place. It has the same bleak and oppressive atmosphere one sees in many contemporary illustrations that purport to show how seventeenth-century Puritans lived. The sense of rawness surrounding the clock on the wall recalls Charles Dickens's cry about "a grim clock, which uttered every tick with a kind of struggle." This is more a colonial revival presentation than an accurate depiction of a room used by late nineteenth-century people.

CONSERVATIVES AND PROGRESSIVES

It is possible that the reason some photographs of richly furnished rooms with complex purchased furniture exist is because some of the Shakers made sure photographers recorded the sect as progressive and modern. In the late nineteenth century there was a battle developing between the progressive part of the Society and the traditionalist wing. The progressive members wanted reform and reconciliation with the world. The traditionalists, led by such Believers as Harvey Eads and Alonzo Hollister, wanted to keep the Society closed.

Elder Giles Avery, a conservative member of the Central Ministry, in his "Circular concerning the dress of Believers," of about 1866, exhibits an attitude that continued among this faction. He hoped for a continuation of a uniformity in dress: "There are very strong reasons in favor of uniformity, both in style, or pattern of dress, and color and quality of dress fabrics; each one, and all of these subjects, effects, materially the welfare and prosperity of Believers, both spiritually, socially and financially. Spiritually, because, uniformity in style, or pattern in dress, between members, contributes to peace and union in spirit, in as much as the ends of justice are answered, and righteousness and justice are necessary companions."[96]

230. PHOTOGRAPH: MEETING ROOM
MOUNT LEBANON, NEW YORK,
CHURCH FAMILY DWELLING
About 1890
H. 5¼" W. 8⅜"
Collection of the Shaker Museum and Library,
Old Chatham, New York

231. PHOTOGRAPH: CHURCH FAMILY
DINING ROOM, CANTERBURY, NEW
HAMPSHIRE
By W. G. C. Kimball, Concord, New Hampshire
About 1900
H. 4⁵⁄₁₆" W. 6¹¹⁄₁₆"
Collection of the Shaker Museum and Library,
Old Chatham, New York

232. "DINING-ROOM OF THE NORTH
FAMILY"
Mount Lebanon, New York
Drawn for this wood engraving by Joseph Becker
First published: Frank Leslie's Illustrated
Newspaper 36 *(September, 1873), p. 13*
H. 4⅞" W. 9½"
Collection of the Shaker Museum and Library,
Old Chatham, New York

233. PHOTOGRAPH: PHEBE AND
CATHERINE VAN HOUTEN, TWIN
SISTERS, OF MOUNT LEBANON, NEW
YORK
1880s
Frame: H. 28½" W. 24¼" D. 2¾"
Collection of the Shaker Museum and Library,
Old Chatham, New York

234. PHOTOGRAPH: ELIZA ANN TAYLOR
OF MOUNT LEBANON, NEW YORK
1880s
Frame: H. 29¼" W. 25¼" D. 1½"
Collection of the Shaker Museum and Library,
Old Chatham, New York

Much of the reformist attitude came from the North Family at Mount Lebanon. In their role as the Novitiate Order, they were responsible for bringing in new members, and sought ways to open up the Society. The Church Family, in conservative contrast, seemed more like an old-folks home.[97] The North Family Elder Frederick Evans championed the revisionist faction. He wanted the Society, and America as a whole, to change for the better. He worked against such things as processed flour, meat, liquor, tea, coffee, impure air and water, perpetual land tenure, poverty, slavery, masculine domination, and the perversion of spiritualism. Catherine Allen gave away spirit drawings and other Shaker material to be sure Shaker history was preserved. She sought radical social and political changes, including women's rights. In 1891 she had organized a Self-Improvement Society to improve the "habits and manners" of young Sisters of the North Family and develop their appreciation of "substantial, interesting and beautiful things."[98]

In 1889 the non-Shaker Charles F. Wingate affirmed the Society's insistence on advancing with the times in *The Shaker Manifesto:* "The Shakers are a progressive people and are always experimenting with new devices. When the farmers in the vicinity want to buy new implements or machinery they usually call and see what the Shakers are using, and what they think will serve best for the purpose."[99]

Increasingly during the second half of the twentieth century the Shakers, and those who have written about them, have affirmed to the public that they are actively part of the modern world. "Shakers were among the first to acquire electricity and automobiles, and their use of the camera itself manifested their continuing interest in technical innovation . . . . In the economic realm, as in their physical and social dimensions, the Shaker photographers present a fascinating and unique combination of the traditional and the modern."[100]

STUDIO PHOTOGRAPHS

In keeping with the fashion of the 1880s and 1890s, many Shakers had themselves photographed in professional studios where they sat in or stood beside studio props. The images were placed in contemporary worldly frames. A few show a concern for what must have been thought a traditional look. The twin sisters Phebe and Catherine Van Houten (1817–1895 and 1817–1896, respectively) in the 1880s photograph seen as figure 233, lived at Mount Lebanon. Possibly they felt a contained pose and the use of an oak frame, with only a thin gold inner edge, an appropriate expression of traditional Shaker modesty. Sister Eliza Ann Taylor (born in Manchester, England, in 1811, and died at Mount Lebanon in 1897), felt it proper to have a fashionable pierced gold rococo-edged frame on her portrait (figure 234). Brother Robert Valentine, who died in 1910 at Mount Lebanon at the age of 88, looks like a successful contemporary businessman of

Above, left:
235. PHOTOGRAPH: ROBERT VALENTINE
OF MOUNT LEBANON, NEW YORK
1880s
Frame: H. 25½" W. 21½" D. 2¼"
Collection of the Shaker Museum and Library,
Old Chatham, New York

Above, right:
236. PHOTOGRAPH: ELIZABETH
CANTRELL OF MOUNT LEBANON, NEW
YORK
About 1890
Photograph tinted with colors
Frame: H. 30¾" W. 27" D. 2½"
Collection of the Shaker Museum and Library,
Old Chatham, New York

237. PHOTOGRAPH: ELDRESS LIZZIE
NOYES OF SABBATHDAY LAKE, MAINE
Shown at Chicago World's Fair, 1893
Mat signed: "Rieber"; frame labeled by V. J.
Wagner, established 1886, "Manufacturer of
Picture Frames and Mirrors, Importer of Religious
Articles . . . Phila"
Frame: H. 27¼" W. 20¼"
The United Society of Shakers, Sabbathday Lake,
Maine

the 1880s in figure 235; his photograph has a standard post-Civil War gold rococo revival frame. He made the two short brooms in figure 95. The pose of Sister Elizabeth Cantrell in figure 236, taken about 1890, is similar to that of contemporary worldly sitters in photographs and charcoal drawings. Figure 237 shows a photograph of Eldress Lizzie Noyes, in which she takes the pose of Whistler's mother in his celebrated portrait of 1871. This photograph was shown at the Chicago World's Fair in 1893. The grain-painted frame came from Philadelphia.

238. PHOTOGRAPH: EASTER PAGEANT
AT CANTERBURY, NEW HAMPSHIRE
Sister Marguerite Frost as Jesus
1932
H. 4¹/₂" W. 2¹/₂"
Canterbury Shaker Village, Canterbury, New Hampshire

Photography of Individuals

Despite all the evidence of a more liberal Society, and the seeming ubiquity of professionally taken portraits, the Central Ministry was still trying to prevent too great a display of worldly images in Shaker rooms. In a circular of 1876 the Ministry wrote: "We have our order, which, we believe, wisely prohibits among Believers the use of these things [i.e., photographs, and other pictures], except the photographs of landscapes, villages, &c. The pictures of individuals, as the persons of our Brethern and Sisters, or our Friends or relatives in outside society, are inadmissible to be kept by Believers, and the Leading Authority of New Lebanon, never have given their union and approbation to have any such pictures taken." Possibly the Ministry's main concern was the cost of collecting pictures, and the albums needed to hold them in: "Then, having many pictures, an Album would be wanted to keep them in. To purchase these pictures @ from 15 to 25 cts each, and Albums @ from $1.00, to $3.00 each, would cost from $1.00, to $4.00, to the individual pr year . . . ." "The Spiritual corruption, pride, worldly vanity, envy, jealousy, and discussion, in consequence of individual *preferments* or *rejections* and neglects, would be appalling!"[101]

In the 1920s the Shakers began to rely less on their own traditions and attended worldly religious services, or sometimes asked outside ministers to give sermons in their communities. The members at Hancock, Canterbury, and probably Mount Lebanon, took in more religious aids from the world. They purchased from religious supply houses prepackaged materials for special celebrations; for example, backdrop scenery accompanied by scripts and dress-up clothing. The 1932 photograph in figure 238 shows two unidentified Sisters, and Marguerite Frost as Jesus, during an Easter pageant at Canterbury.

As the Shakers' fame as a curious but likeable sect has grown, they have been featured ever more frequently in newspaper and magazine articles, and eventually television shows. In these they have spoken of traditional Shaker beliefs while being careful to record that they have always been progressive. In the photographs taken for these articles they are seen among traditional objects doing modern things. In figure 239, taken for a 1949 spread in *Life Magazine*, Cora Sarle is seen painting a picture in her Church Family room at Canterbury, which mixes the old and the new.

SHAKER ANONYMITY

From the early years of the nineteenth century the Shakers have kept excellent written records in many areas, but they have handed on much of their knowledge through oral communication.

239. PHOTOGRAPH: CORA SARLE,
CANTERBURY, NEW HAMPSHIRE
Taken by Nina Leen for Life Magazine *in 1949
for article "The Shakers," March 21, 1949. This
picture was not included.*

During the early years this proved a useful means of transferring ideas and developing a theology, for it allowed changes to be absorbed gradually, and it helped keep information private. The Shakers have always sought public anonymity in all aspects of their life. Shaker chairs were sold as "Shaker" and not the product of individuals, although among themselves they knew who had made them. The 1845 Laws required that pieces not be signed, and the elimination of most names helped solidify the groups while maintaining the line of authority. It also gave the world a unified Shaker image. As the number of Shakers declined, and the amount of information about authorship multiplied, the degree to which such information was preserved declined. Where once most members could tell who made a particular item, most are now anonymous, and this new circumstance fits the traditional effacing of individual members. In the 1930s Carl Carmer, a writer interested in New York folk history, visited Mount Lebanon to gather information for a book he published in 1936. Near the end of the visit he said: "And now I'd like to take a picture of you two with my Kodak if I may." Emma Neale, one of the two Sisters remaining in that community, reacted to his inquiry: "I am sorry to have to refuse you, I suppose it's all right but our religion never approved of the singling out of any members. What work we did, we did for the whole Family and no one ever claimed individual credit. I feel that a picture might be considered vanity."[102] Effacement of the individual was affirmed when in the twentieth century many Shaker communities removed individual gravestones and installed one general marker for all the deceased community members.

Chapter X
THE TWENTIETH CENTURY: MYTH MAKERS, REVISIONISTS, AND A COMPARATIVE AWARENESS OF PERFECTION

This chapter discusses those who co-opted the Shakers and their artifacts for personal, political, financial, or art historical agendas. It would be inappropriate, and lacking in historical perspective, to rant against previously skewed understandings, for everyone is of her or his own time and full of personal motives. But, it has been a constant fact at least since Charles Dickens's mid-nineteenth-century sniping against the Shakers, that Shaker-made and Shaker-used artifacts have been summarily pulled out of their historic context and treated in isolation from the theological and physical conditions that made them possible. We now have a set of myths about the Shakers that satisfy some and upset others. One of the prevalent myths about the Shakers sees their serene objects as products of a tranquil people; Chapters I and II of this book show that this is a naive oversimplification.

The greatest thrusts to mythologize the Shakers' past occurred when America was seeking to adjust its relationship to Europe. Without realizing that early Shaker designs were part of rural neoclassical styling, historians since the 1910s have used the Shakers' artistic expressions as evidence that the Shakers, and by extension other Americans, anticipated the tight, functional, stripped forms of the German Bauhaus. In a related way the artist Charles Sheeler used Shaker objects in his modernistic paintings and photographs of the late 1920s and the 1930s, to help his drive to make a modern American art that seemed independent of European precedents. By the 1940s Shaker art, particularly the furniture, was one of the American factors evoked to confront the foreign fascist threat, as it was admired for having no basis in a European artistic traditon.

From the Shakers' first years in America the curious have gone to see them. During the second half of the nineteenth century a growing number of intellectuals and writers visited them to experience the unusual, and to augment their understanding of a variation from the general, or to find cultural or religious evidence to prove their assumptions. Even government dignitaries, beginning with Lafayette in the late 1780s, went to wonder and learn. Beginning in the late eighteenth century the Shakers have been idolized or disparaged in books, plays, music, dance, and reproductions of what they made. Nor have the inquisitive been limited to these shores. For example, for a few years in the early 1890s at least two Mount Lebanon leaders, Frederick Evans of the North Family and Alonzo Hollister of the Church Family, corresponded with Leo Tolstoy about issues they had in common: Christianity, property in common, celibacy, and women's rights. Along with letters, the Shakers sent Shaker books and tracts. In a letter of December 6, 1890, Evans, as a reformer, answered Tolstoy's expression of being "pained" about the early ideas of "Ann Lee, & spirit intercourse," by stating that the Shakers had outgrown their understanding of Jesus and Ann Lee as the two Christs: "What [our beliefs] *were,* when the 'Millennial Church' was written, leave to the people of those times. Paul says, 'When I was a child, I thought & spake as a child . . . .' " Tolstoy also wondered how the Shakers, as pacifists, could defend their property, even if it were communal, against outsiders, if they should want to take it from the Shakers. Evans, parsing layers of theological, philosophical, and political theories, wrote that the command was to become perfect, but "That is the *end* of our Christian travail," and even as "Jesus was not yet perfected" until after his death, "We hold and defend our Communial property under Civil Laws of the New Earth."[1] The Shakers had changed from when Ann Lee and Jesus were the two manifestations of Christ, and when, with raw energy, the leaders brought the Church into Gospel Order.

Since the nineteenth century there have been a growing number of international scholars of folk patterns who sought out the Shakers. In the twentieth century, as colonial nostalgia became ever more popular, the curious were joined by the avaricious who wanted to own, or to resell, Shaker artifacts. Because the Shakers had lots to dispose of, for a while they delighted in the attention and income they received.

COLLECTING SHAKER MATERIALS

For the first half of the twentieth century the collecting of Shaker things fell outside the general parameters of collecting Americana for two reasons: the artifacts were from the then unpopular nineteenth century, and the Shakers were seen as a marginal cult. The first collectors of Americana, particularly those most linked to European taste, were interested in discovering evidence of an aesthetically powerful American past that paralleled America's new industrial strength. In the 1920s John D. Rockefeller began at Williamsburg, Virginia, to sweep aside the nineteenth century and to fill some old—and many reconstructed—buildings with New England artifacts (particularly furniture) and European furniture, silver, glass, ceramics, paintings, and prints. Most of the carpets came from even further afield. Thus he produced beautiful images of an idealized early America, in which he and others of his class could feel comfortable. Similarly, Henry Francis du Pont created Winterthur, near Wilmington, Delaware, first as his home (he had been born there in 1889) and then as a public museum in 1951. In it he consciously reflected the grandeur of English country houses, acknowledging: "I want things kept as they are because in fifty years nobody will know what a country place was."[2] He, like many collectors, began by ignoring Shaker material, seeing it as far outside the European-based eighteenth-century American objects he loved.

The wealthy Americans who formed most of the large collections of Americana had grown unhappy with industrialized America, from which they had benefited. They saw as threatening the new monied elite that had sprung from the wave of immigrants from southern and central Europe. It was natural for those from the Anglo-Saxon tradition, who thought of themselves as preservers of America's greatness, to focus on those materials most easily associated with preindustrial Anglo-American culture.[3]

Some of the more recently established rich American families purchased American artifacts as a way to join the financially and socially secure; others did so to thank this country for the opportunities they now enjoyed. Francis Patrick Garvan, whose father had come from Ireland without money and sent his sons to Yale, collected Americana for both these reasons. In 1930, after he had become important and wealthy, Garvan began to give his alma mater what would grow to become a collection of ten thousand examples of American decorative arts, paintings, prints, and sculpture. He made the gift to thank America for his family's rise to prominence within two generations, and to give Yale students the opportunity to understand America's greatness by seeing its art. Garvan also hoped some of the pieces would be copied, so that Americans would have access to good designs. He gave no Shaker items, perhaps because his interests did not extend to the nineteenth century in the decorative arts, although he embraced that century's paintings and prints.

Between 1951 and 1959 *The Magazine Antiques* focused a single issue on each of seven museums oriented toward American art and artifacts: Colonial Williamsburg, Winterthur, Old Sturbridge Village, the Henry Ford Museum and Greenfield Village, the New York State Historical Association, Old Deerfield, and the Shelburne Museum. The only Shaker artifact shown in any of the magazine's issues was a counter owned by the New York State Historical Association. Displaying a similar attitude, collectors considered "Victorian" too late and too un-colonial, and the cut-off-date of about 1810–30 remained operable. That, they felt, was the end of the great handmade object, and the beginning of the unacceptable imposition of machines. The magazine's issues included only one mid-century piece: a Belter-type sofa. Late in their lives many of these collectors added material from the second quarter of the nineteenth century, for by then the timeframe of the permissible had been extended. Between 1960 and 1962, under the guidance of Faith Andrews and Edward Deming Andrews, du Pont added Shaker rooms, which he had in storage, to the Winterthur display. (The woodwork is from Enfield, New Hampshire. As was often his practice, du Pont reworked it to fit available spaces.)

There was another kind of collector, more antiquarian in nature, who sought out regional, vernacular work, and from about 1900 an increasing number of these included Shaker items in their collections. A few collectors began to focus specifically on Shaker materials. For example, in 1905, the Ohio bookseller John Patterson MacLean compiled A *Bibliography of Shaker Literature*, which contained 523 items. By 1911 Wallace H. Cathcart, director of the Western Reserve Historical Society, Ohio, had found most of the books mentioned by MacLean and others, and by 1920 that Cleveland institution was the leading repository of Shaker books and manuscripts. Cathcart did not purchase non-library Shaker artifacts except those small enough to be carried home in his car. Those he displayed in curiosity cases. MacLean saw the Shakers he knew in Ohio as surrounded by the comforts of life, with no restraints placed upon their opinions, and that they had no creed, but experienced a wide latitude in religious beliefs. He felt that the distress and hardship endured by so many non-Shakers should make the Shaker communities a haven. Although his readings made him realize that "their discipline is of a different stamp," his general perception was of a gentle-appearing people with a strong inner fiber developed by discipline. This view of the Shakers, and Shaker life, has spread to the general public. Those who have understood the early demanding aspects of early Shaker life have usually set it aside in favor of admiring the quieter, model-citizen Shakers and their beautiful objects.

Clara Endicott Sears

The Shakers made the first Shaker museums as they created rooms different than those in which they lived. As the Shakers were swept up in the colonial revival's interest in their past, they hoped that the ever increasing appreciation for their objects would lead people to understand Shaker values; it also brought them an even greater understanding of their own history. Sister Josephine Jilson may have created the first display of Shaker artifacts not contemplated as a period room. After she moved from the just sold Harvard Community to the North Family at Mount Lebanon in 1918, she set up a display of Shaker material for the edification of visitors.

In 1920 Clara Endicott Sears created the first Shaker museum not developed by the Shakers. She was a "seeker," sympathetic to spiritual rituals, and curious about such groups as the Shakers, Native Americans, and the Transcendentalists. She had developed a friendship with the Shakers at Harvard and was allowed to read journals and other writings that the Shakers had held private. In 1916 she published extracts from these in *Gleanings from Old Shaker Journals,* which has remained an important source of information about Shaker life. In 1920 she moved a 1790s office from Harvard to her growing Fruitlands Museums, which she founded in 1914 on her estate just west of Harvard. The building was furnished with Shaker material, much of it obtained from her Harvard Shaker friends. In 1922 Sears wrote a novel with a Shaker thread, *The Romance of Fiddler's Green,* which included ideas for a Shaker garden. Miss Sears became so close to the Harvard Shakers that she, like many other outsiders involved in Shaker communities, saw a Shaker spirit.[4] In general, Miss Sears seems to have been faithful to the trust placed in her by the Harvard Shakers, even though she did hang a gift drawing in a public place after Eldress Catherine Allen, who had given it to her, asked her to keep it private (see figure 157).

Charles Sheeler

From the second decade of this century many American artists have sought to develop a style of painting that would side-step European influences and establish a purely American approach to art. One of these, Charles Sheeler, collected Shaker materials and depicted them in his art. Just before his death in 1965, he sold fifteen pieces of Shaker furniture to Hancock, which had become a museum in 1960. Sheeler had included most of them in a group of paintings and photographs, and lent them to an important exhibition of Shaker objects. Sheeler as much as anyone, except Edward Deming Andrews and William F. Winter, Jr., set the tone of how this material and its makers are now viewed. His handling of the material is revealing of how the Shakers were understood and their objects exploited during the first part of this century.

Charles Sheeler was born in Philadelphia in 1883, and he entered the Pennsylvania Academy of Fine Arts in 1903. There he became friends with Morton L. Schamberg, and the two artists developed in parallel, first as painters and then as photographers. After graduation they shared a studio and about 1910 rented a small eighteenth-century stone house in Doylestown, Bucks County, Pennsylvania, where they painted and photographed on weekends and holidays. They had learned of the house from Henry C. Mercer, a lawyer turned archaeologist and collector of early American artifacts, whose property joined that on which the house stood. Sheeler and Schamberg, through trips to Europe, first under the tutelage of William Merritt Chase, and later, on their own, discovered the work of Cézanne, Picasso, Braque, Matisse, and other avant-garde artists. In Paris they saw modern art displayed with much earlier artifacts in the homes of such American-born collectors as Michael and Sarah Stein, where it was not unusual to place early modern paintings, from Impressionism to Cubism, in gilt rococo-revival frames over antique furniture. Perhaps the most familiar juxtaposition of the old and the modern are the photographs of the rooms of Leo and Gertrude Stein, the younger siblings of Michael Stein. In their Paris home, paintings by Cézanne, Braque, Picasso, and Matisse hung over heavy seventeenth-century furniture that featured rectilinear forms made of dark woods. The same eclectic mixing of the new and the old persisted when Gertrude Stein lived there with Alice B. Toklas. Collectors like the Steins intuitively established a balance between the powerful new art and the direct shapes of earlier furniture.

From about 1910 Sheeler steeped himself in the work of Cézanne, whose use of broken forms and patterned shapes was to remain a feature of the American artist's imagery. In 1913 Sheeler and Schamberg were included in the Armory Show, America's first large-scale exhibition of modern art. Soon after, they met the New York collectors and supporters of artists and avant-garde publications, Walter and Louise Arensberg. Sheeler described the Arensbergs as "the top people, because they . . . had that great ability, radar eye."[5] Their apartment on West 67th Street was a meeting place for artists and poets, many of them just fresh from escaping the growing conflicts in Europe. Among the most influential of the regular guests of the Arensbergs were the French exiles Marcel Duchamp, Albert Gleizes, and Francis Picabia. Sheeler and Schamberg joined the circle with other American artists, such as Charles Demuth, Man Ray, and Joseph Stella. It was Duchamp, with his wild originality, who created most of the excitement. In the mid-1910s Sheeler began to collect early American objects, and he often went antiquing with the Arensbergs and helped them acquire early American materials.

240. *DOYLESTOWN HOUSE—
DOWNSTAIRS WINDOW*
By Charles Sheeler
Photograph, 1917
H. 10" W. 7⁷⁄₈"
*The Lane Collection, Museum of Fine Arts,
Boston*

Sheeler, Juliana Force, and the Arensbergs

About 1914 Sheeler met Juliana Force. From 1907 Force had worked with Gertrude Vanderbilt Whitney to sponsor institutions celebrating and promoting American art. Beginning with an artist-centered club, they moved to ever more professional museum situations until they created the Whitney Museum of American Art. One of Juliana Force's responsibilities was to distribute Whitney money as stipends to needy artists, and to support interesting American-related art projects. In 1914 she and her husband bought Barley Sheaf Farm in the Pennsylvania village of Holicong, just a few miles from Doylestown.[6] She knew Sheeler from the New York art world, and understood the beauty of the Doylestown home he shared with Schamberg. She, like Sheeler, had a passion for early American things, and included a few Shaker pieces among the many antiques in her new country house. She and Sheeler liked each other, and for some years she saw that Sheeler received a steady flow of financial support. By the 1920s he had many connections with the Whitney enterprises, as its photographer, sometime art reviewer and exhibition curator, and as an artist shown in Whitney galleries.[7] In 1914–16, Sheeler reached his mature style as he developed a modern vision that layered spaces and objects in a formal abstract manner. Among his best-known photographs are those he took in the Doylestown house where the architectural verticals and horizontals are exploited in vivid lights and darks (see figure 240). In 1916–17 Sheeler began photographing and drawing barns. Most of the images show the barn as a three-dimensional shape; but among the best are those that exhibit flat patterns, some using Whistlerian whites, while others feature blacks. In these photographs, Sheeler's sense of design is most Shaker-like in

241. *LIVING ROOM OF NEW YORK
APARTMENT OF LOUISE AND WALTER
ARENSBERG (SOUTHEAST CORNER)*
By Charles Sheeler
Photograph, about 1918
H. 7⁹⁄₁₆" W. 9⁵⁄₈"
*Collection of the Whitney Museum of American
Art, New York; gift of James Maroney and
Suzanne Fredericks. 80.30.1*

242. SOUTH SALEM, LIVING ROOM
By Charles Sheeler
Photograph, 1929
H. 7³/₁₆" W. 9⁹/₁₆"
The Lane Collection, Museum of Fine Arts,
Boston

243. TABLE
Probably by Abner Allen
Enfield, Connecticut
1845–55
Maple, figured maple, and pine
H. 29" W. 130³/₄" D. 32¹/₂"
Belonged to Charles Sheeler
Drawers under projecting ends added later
Hancock Shaker Village, Pittsfield, Massachusetts

exploiting patterns of quiet and purposeful verticals, horizontals, and rectangles. About 1918 Sheeler photographed the Arensberg apartment, and five of his negatives were produced as finished works.[8] In one, seen as figure 241, Sheeler's drawing of a barn hangs at the lower right of the facing wall. In this apartment hung Duchamp's *Nude Descending a Staircase,* the painting that had caused such outrage when it was exhibited at the Armory Show. Critics thought it degraded the tradition of nude studies, and that it looked "like an explosion in a shingle factory." As with many European art collections, the room is filled with early furnishings, but here they are eighteenth- and early nineteenth-century American vernacular pieces.

In 1918 Schamberg died of pneumonia. The grief-stricken Sheeler wrote to the photographer and dealer Alfred Stieglitz: "This is the first moment that I have had the strength of spirit or body to tell you—that Schamberg died Sunday night . . . . Knowing both of us as well as you did makes it unnecessary for me to tell you what it means for the one who remains."[9] The following year Sheeler moved to New York City and after that he used the Doylestown house less, although he continued to rent it until 1926. In 1921 Sheeler married Katherine Baird Shaffer, "a stout, vivacious woman two years his senior."[10] They spent the summer in the Arensbergs' Manhattan apartment.

Forbes Watson was the first critic to publish a profile on Sheeler's work, in *The Arts,* May 1923. Watson saw Sheeler's realism as reflecting his American heritage, "the native flavor in his art." He found parallels between Sheeler's work and early American furniture, with its "clear-cut fineness, the cool austerity, the complete distrust of superfluities." He believed Sheeler's "ultimate literalness" and "extremely simplified realism" to be essentially American.[11]

In the early 1900s a group of artists had begun championing the concept of an artistic tradition that grew out of America's native soil. The main energy for that endeavor came from Robert

244. *HOME, SWEET HOME*
By Charles Sheeler
1931
Oil on canvas
H. 36" W. 29"
The Detroit Institute of Art, gift of Robert H.
Tannahill, Detroit, Michigan

245. *AMERICANA*
By Charles Sheeler
1931
Oil on canvas
H. 48" W. 36"
Metropolitan Museum of Art, New York. Edith
and Milton Lowenthal Collection, bequest of
Edith Abrahamson Lowenthal, 1992 (1992.24.8)

235

Henri, and those who followed his lead, such as William Glackens, John Sloan, George Luks, and Rockwell Kent. They did not like Duchamp's *Nude Descending a Staircase* and other art not based in American reality. In 1916 Sheeler had been included in the New York Forum Exhibition, which featured seventeen artists who had been selected principally by Stieglitz, Henri, and Willard Huntington Wright. For the Henri group, Sheeler's art was at the time too near European modernism, but it was seen as growing closer to American themes.

Sheeler's Use of Shaker Artifacts in his Art

About 1926 the Sheelers moved to South Salem, New York. In 1928 Juliana Force bought a house in South Salem, just a few miles from where the Sheelers were living, and named it Shaker Hollow. There she installed her growing collection of Shaker objects.[12] In 1932 the Sheelers moved to Ridgefield, Connecticut. In the South Salem and Ridgefield houses, between 1926 and 1934, Sheeler made seven finished photographs (there are more images in negative and contact sheet form) and seven related paintings that link him permanently to Shaker studies. The photograph in figure 242, *South Salem, Living Room,* is typical of the group of images Sheeler made. In it are possibly five Shaker objects. The Hancock or New Lebanon bench is one of a pair Sheeler owned; in paintings it is seen to have a coat of red paint. The large table was made at Enfield, Connecticut, probably by Abner Allen, 1845–55. It has three original drawers with tapered sides, as in figure 36, and two drawers added later under the wonderful overhangs (see figure 243).[13] The small table in figure 242 with an applied edge and square-tapered legs, in the lower left corner, is probably from New Lebanon or Hancock. It has lost its paint. The possibly Shaker bed, also without paint, may be one of those the Shakers purchased from Albany in 1877, as listed in the "Things from Outside" section of Chapter IX. The oval box on the large table is probably Shaker, but with its telling overlapping side hidden, that is not certain. In paintings it lacks color, so if it is Shaker-made the date is post–Civil War; if earlier, it has been stripped. The other objects in the photograph are generic vernacular, and most of the furniture has lost its paint: the large, four-door step-back cupboard seems to revel in knots, which its maker would not have left visible. The stripped splay-leg table to the right of the cupboard changes locations in a number of Sheeler views. At the end of the large table is an English slat-back chair. It is not known if Sheeler knew he had an English piece, for many chairs of this type were being imported and sold to the American market without admission of their origin. It now seems surprising that Sheeler would have featured a chair with so many curves, but it may have appealed to the sensibility that caused him to produce rather cluttered rooms with lots of visual action. (Sheeler sat in an English vernacular "Chippendale"-style chair when in 1943 he painted himself painting a landscape, in *The Artist Looks at Nature.*) Other views of the Sheelers' rooms include such non-Shaker items as a Pennsylvania paint-decorated chest, spool-turned bed and bench, and a variety of Windsor and slat-back chairs. In Sheeler's images, a great variety of patterned textiles—patchwork quilts and hooked rugs in particular—adds complexity.

Sheeler was creating a self-consciously American series of works, and the paintings made at the same time he shot these photographs were titled to announce a delight in America and security within a home. In Sheeler's painting *Home, Sweet Home,* he showed in the lower right corner a bit of the bench and the large table, but in the center, as the main image, he placed a generic slat-back armchair next to a modern, smooth-sided stove (figure 244). It sits in front of a closed-in fireplace and thus joins the old and the new. In Sheeler's *Americana,* shown as figure 245, the large table, viewed from above, is flanked by two benches. The angled furniture and hooked rugs provide a Cézanne- and Cubist-derived breaking of space and forms, while giving a lived-in, informal appearance to the room. The sleek top of the table looks like the machine finish on the modern room heater in *Home, Sweet Home.* These remind us that at times much of Sheeler's income was derived from photographs he took for use in advertisements of smooth-surface objects as diverse as typewriters, silverware, and the machinery in Henry Ford's automobile plant.

Sheeler also photographed and painted views of Shaker buildings. His interior view of the Mount Lebanon meetinghouse taken about 1934 (figure 246) shows from the Ministry's side one of four slatted windows they added in 1851, so they could watch the public meetings unobserved.[14] (All but one were removed when the meeting room became a library.)

Sheeler talked to his first biographer freely about how he saw Shaker objects. For him they were symbolic of part of America. He did not seek to isolate them from other American things, and perhaps because such concerns developed years later, he neither cared about their original context, nor does it seem that he took much interest in their original surfaces.

246. MEETING HALL WINDOW, MT. LEBANON SHAKER VILLAGE
By Charles Sheeler
Photograph, about 1934
H. 6" W. 8¼"
The Lane Collection, Museum of Fine Arts, Boston

Sheeler's Chest of Drawers and a Dubious Surface Treatment

The tall chest of drawers seen in figure 247 belonged to Sheeler and is now at Hancock. Glued inside the case is a paper label that reads: "This Case of Drawers were made by Elder Grove [Wright] and Brother Thomas [Damon] and placed here thursday, January 13th, 1853. It was the day our Ministry expected to return to the City of Peace [Hancock], but were detained on account of the snow storm which occurred on that day."[15] These men worked in the three communities of the Hancock Bishopric—Hancock and Tyringham, Massachusetts, and Enfield, Connecticut—and the piece has the tapered drawer sides found in work from Hancock and Enfield (see figure 36). The case and the interior parts of the drawers are made of pine. The drawer fronts, the front ¼ inch of the sides, and the drawer dividers are of butternut. The cornice, even at the front, is of pine. The pulls are walnut. It was once a strong red, and traces of that color remain in the end grain of many of the drawer lips. In 1962, it was one of the fifteen pieces Sheeler lent to an exhibition of Shaker material at the Philadelphia Museum of Art. Only a handful of the over 250 objects were illustrated in the *Philadelphia Museum Bulletin* (Spring 1962) that served as the catalogue. The tall chest of drawers is shown in a black and white photograph. In 1966 Edward Deming Andrews and Faith Andrews included room views of that exhibition in their *Religion in Wood*.[16] One shows this piece and the large table and the benches shown in figures 242, 244, and 245.

The fifteen pieces Sheeler had lent to Philadelphia went directly from there to Hancock, and the museum purchased them in 1964, a year before his death. In both the Philadelphia catalogue and *Religion in Wood,* the black and white photographs show the surface of the tall chest of drawers as worn. But now that surface is a matte, saddle-brown, for it was subjected to what was until recently considered an acceptable practice of treating furniture with a three-part solution: one-third each of linseed oil, vinegar, and turpentine. The purpose was to restore luster to a clear finish, or rejuvenate a painted surface. That unfortunate "conservation" practice has damaged thousands of objects it was meant to help: the oil that penetrated the wood has darkened, and what has remained on the surface has turned to a chewing-gum-like layer. During the 1970s and 1980s Hancock, like countless dealers, collectors, and museums, regularly used the three-part solution on their furniture. The resulting nut-brown look allowed such altered pieces to fit easily into the then-prevailing Americana aesthetic.

Constance Rourke and Sheeler

In 1938 Constance Rourke wrote the first extensive biography of Sheeler: *Charles Sheeler, Artist in the American Tradition.* As the title suggested, and her introductory note affirmed, Sheeler was about to be made an "All American" product, and his interest in Shaker artifacts would be seen as one of his attributes. The opening note includes: "The work of Charles Sheeler has been noticed for its fresh and original use of the American subject; and still further for the imprint it shows of forms which strongly and essentially belong to us."[17] She continued: "Sheeler discounts alto-

247. CASE OF DRAWERS
By Grove Wright and Thomas Damon
Before 1853, see text
Pine and butternut; walnut knobs; cleaned of
original red paint and oiled, see text
Belonged to Charles Sheeler
H. 84" W. 40¾" D. 19"
Hancock Shaker Village, Pittsfield, Massachusetts

gether the brief phase of his own painting in which he used cubist forms and pure abstraction . . . ."[18] Sheeler "was tapping main [American] sources by his use of architectural forms of Bucks County and likewise by his more or less conscious study of the handicrafts which he found thereabouts."[19] Where Picasso had been influenced by "primitive Negro sculpture," Sheeler had widened the view and looked "toward other primitive forms." By the time Rourke gets to Sheeler's own words, and his use of Shaker forms, it would have been difficult for him not to cast aside European art, which so strongly conditioned his work. He spoke lovingly about Shaker objects, seeing them all to be of an amazingly high quality.[20]

Perhaps Sheeler did not realize Shaker objects varied in both quality of design and manufacture; that the Central Ministry could expect finer things; and that the look and construction of pieces used by the general membership depended on when they were made, who made them, and in what community they were produced. It was perhaps easy for Sheeler (who *did* know lean, rectilinear worldly pieces, because his rooms were full of them) to miss the emergence of Shaker styles out of worldly objects, because no one was stressing the logic of that evolution. A few collectors such as Andrews did know how close the worldly material could be, but most, including Andrews, wanted to believe otherwise. For some, it was simply not allowing the linkage to emerge in their minds; for others, who had a vested interest in keeping Shaker and worldly separate, it was better to present Shakers work as a unique and indigenous American expression without roots. Without the linkage to worldly objects, Sheeler was able to place the Shakers, and by extension himself, as progenitors of modernism:

It is interesting to note in some of their cabinet work the anticipation, by a hundred years or more, of the tendencies of some of our contemporary designers toward economy and what we call the functional in design . . . .

Seeing the Shaker meetinghouse at New Lebanon recently showed the difference in emotional response to the thing which is of one's own lineage from that which is not. It has a final assurance and is sufficient of itself to make one rejoice in having derived from the soil that brought it into being.[21]

In a flight of praising the present where he was a potent force of the American new, and forgetting his much loved house in Doylestown and wide collection of Americana, Sheeler finishes his statement about the Shakers: "I don't like these things because they are old but in spite of it. I'd like them still better if they were made yesterday because then they would afford proof that the same kind of creative power is continuing."[22]

Rourke and the Shakers as "Folk"

In 1942, four years after her book on Sheeler, Rourke, in *The Roots of American Culture*, sought to see the Shakers as a folk, a group that formed its own pattern. She felt the Shakers could be seen as part of the folk tradition because what they made was unplanned and the result of habits and beliefs; their objects were not designed, but resulted from a folk unity that came from imagination and communal customs and language.[23] Rourke had the strong urge, still persistent in many who look at Shaker work, to think that the Shakers were so isolated that they had a "lack of familiarity with the language of ornament." She did not realize that the Shakers were following the Western world's stress on lean, tight, neoclassical forms, that much of their work was produced by the normal shop practices of small businesses, and that they often employed hired laborers. Rourke wanted to place the Shakers within a broader context by considering them as part of a general New England folk pattern, which necessitated cutting New England from England as a source of design ideas. (She did recognize the Shakers', and New England's, historic link to England, but not in the arts.) She wrote that, unlike most of continental Europe, neither New England nor England developed a decorative arts or folk tradition. Her ignorance of the English decorative arts tradition is not surprising for the English had not yet acknowledged their own vernacular and folk traditions.

Edward Deming Andrews; Faith Andrews

In *Fruits of the Shaker Tree of Life,* published after her husband's death by Faith Andrews in 1975, she and Edward Deming Andrews summarized a series of myths that they had created about themselves and the beginnings of Shaker studies. For example, the book says that they made their first visit to the Shakers in 1923.[24] But the Andrewses knew the Shakers, and their objects, long before 1923. Hugh Howard's research into the lives of the Andrewses has established that both grew up near Hancock, and that Faith Andrews's mother attended Shaker services. In 1919 Edward Deming Andrews was stationed at Fort Devens, Massachusetts, only two miles from the Harvard and Shirley communities, and it is certain he walked over and saw Shirley. Further, while stationed there, Andrews saw inside the house of the early collector of Shaker material, Frank Lawton, who had bought things from the Shirley Community.[25]

It would be impossible not to honor the work of the Andrewses for it saved Shaker materials and made known Shaker theology, history, and art. Furthermore, they became the premier scholars and dealers in Shaker materials, and helped form major collections. In the early 1960s, for example, they encouraged and helped Henry Francis du Pont to add Shaker rooms to Winterthur, and they were the major source of Shaker rooms and furnishings for the Metropolitan Museum of Art, and the American Museum in Bath, England. They did not, however, discover the Shakers nor originate the collecting of Shaker things. Others, for at least two decades before them, had collected the Society's artifacts, and the Shakers themselves knew much of their own history through an active oral tradition, their own considerable written works (which were read extensively by members), and their archives.

The Andrewses' first article on the Shakers was encouraged by Homer Eaton Keyes, editor of *The Magazine Antiques.*[26] It appeared in August 1928, with an introductory note by Keyes, which comprised one-fifth of the text and explained Shaker history. The Andrewses were conversant with the closeness of Shaker expressions to worldly furniture, for they had collected worldly objects long before they purchased Shaker ones. The link between the two was one of the main subjects of the article: "A study of the characteristic forms of Shaker furniture suggests the hypothesis that the early craftsmen adapted to their own designs existing Colonial models before them." The Andrewses discussed the relationship of Shaker and worldly chairs, trestle tables, stands, drop-leaf tables, chests of drawers, beds, and stools that "suggest an undeniable affinity to early forms." Then they listed other "Plainly borrowed" forms.[27] It is a good, well-rounded short article that explains Shaker originality within an historical context. In the Andrewses' second article in *Antiques,* published eight months later in April 1929, they firmly parted the Shakers from the world, tucking influences from "Colonial" patterns into two captions. The focus of that article was on Shaker uniqueness, and it discussed slight variations within similar Shaker products. After only eight months the Andrewses saw the financial value of Shakers as an isolated development. In eight books and more than fifty articles, they stressed Shaker separateness and the glory of Shaker design as a uniquely American phenomenon.[28]

In the preface to the Andrewses' and William F. Winter's *Shaker Furniture* (1937), Homer Eaton Keyes made clear that the emphasis of the book was to value and undergird American virtues and play them against the developing upheavals in America and in Europe: "It [*Shaker Furniture*] comes to hand when many dwellers in the United States are concerned about prospects of change in the social structure of the nation. Under such circumstances, information is needed regarding the causes and results of whatever social experiments have hitherto been undertaken by protagonists of the perfect state."[29] Keyes saw the Shakers as easily generating a simplicity that consciously eschewed beauty: "Thus without calling it by high-sounding names, they achieved a functionalism that functioned in fact without benefit of elaborate theory. Their intention was to eliminate beauty. But in spite of themselves they achieved it in forms so pure, so nakedly simple, so free from all self-consciousness, as to shame the artificial artlessness and meretricious chastity that characterize so many shrewdly reticent modern creations."[30]

The Collecting Network

Many of those interested in the Shakers were friends, or they associated at auctions and other specific Shaker-oriented gatherings. For example, Juliana Force, who helped Sheeler and developed Shaker Hollow at South Salem, saw the exhibition the Andrewses arranged for the Berkshire Museum in Pittsfield, Massachusetts, in 1932.[31] Beginning in November of that year she gave the Andrewses a monthly stipend of $200 and the use of a photographer. This would produce in 1937 *Shaker Furniture.*[32] She also had the Andrewses develop the 1935 *Shaker Handicrafts* show for the Whitney, which featured the Andrewses' collection.[33] Force further recommended Edward Deming Andrews for a Guggenheim Fellowship in 1937–38, during which time the Andrewses gathered material for "The Religious Arts of the Shakers"; this was published five years after Edward Andrews's death in 1964 as *Visions of the Heavenly Sphere.* Unfortunately, the Andrewses and Juliana Force had a falling-out over ownership of a group of gift drawings,[34] and her support is not acknowledged in that book, which was completed by Faith Andrews. (The history of collecting Shaker furniture in the middle of the twentieth century, as an understanding of the value of original surfaces replaced the love of the stripped, was discussed in Chapter VII, pp. 127–9).

William F. Winter, Jr.

The photographs by William F. Winter, Jr. for *Shaker Furniture* established for a generation how Shaker furniture should look and be arranged. The sensuous black and white images made sparsely arranged pieces, much of them stripped, look beautiful and proper. For example, the chest over two drawers in figure 248 looked handsome in modulated gray tones. Until fairly recently few stopped to wonder whether it had a yellow surface. It appears, in fact, much like the piece shown as figure 147. For the photographs, unused rooms at Mount Lebanon and Hancock were cleaned up by Edward Andrews, and the Andrewses' collections arranged and rearranged to create a modernist clarity of sparsely distributed forms (see figure 249). Those photographs still represent the way most people think of Shaker interiors. But actually, they speak of modernism, and they look like dealers' photographs.

The Andrewses also employed Winter to photograph their home in Richmond, Massachusetts, for an article titled "Antiques in Domestic Settings." It appeared in the January 1939 issue of *Antiques,* where they credited him as photographer. When these images were used again in the Andrewses' 1966 *Religion in Wood,* however, they were mostly not credited to Winter, although makers of other photographs, some of them further images of the Andrewses' house, were acknowledged. (A photograph Winter had taken about 1923–30—before he knew the Andrewses—of a Church Family room at Hancock was credited there to "The late William F.

248. PHOTOGRAPH BY WILLIAM F.
WINTER, JR.
Published in Edward Deming Andrews and Faith
Andrews; Photographs by William F. Winter, Jr.,
Shaker Furniture . . . ., 1937, pl. 19
Collection of Hugh Howard

249. PHOTOGRAPH BY WILLIAM F.
WINTER, JR.
Published in Edward Deming Andrews and Faith
Andrews; Photographs by William F. Winter, Jr.,
Shaker Furniture . . . ., 1937, pl. 2
Collection of Hugh Howard

250. PHOTOGRAPH BY WILLIAM F.
WINTER, JR.: *LAUNDRY AND IRONING*
ROOM, HANCOCK, MASSACHUSETTS
About 1923–30
H. 10⅛" W. 13½"
Private collection

251. TRANSITIONAL ROCKING
ARMCHAIR
Mount Lebanon, New Lebanon
1860s
Hickory and woven linen
H. 42³/₈" W. 22³/₄ " D. of seat 17¹/₄"
Kunstindustrimuseet, Copenhagen, Denmark

252. ARMCHAIR
Designed by Hans J. Wegner, Copenhagen,
Denmark, 1949; made by Johannes
Hansen, Denmark
Teak and woven cane
H. 30" W. 24³/₈" D. of seat 18¹/₂"
Philadelphia Museum of Art, Philadelphia,
Pennsylvania; gift of Mr. Carl L. Steele

Winter." He had died in 1939.) In Jerry Grant's notes from an 1983 interview with Faith Andrews, she clearly wants it understood that her husband "created" Winter as a photographer, and that it was necessary for him to approve every shot taken.[35]

However, Andrews did not "create" Winter as a photographer, or as a maker of important Shaker images. Between 1923 and 1930 Winter on his own made beautiful, rich, black and white pictures of the interiors and exteriors of Shaker buildings, group and individual shots of Shaker artifacts, and sensitive portraits of Believers, including Eldress Ann Case at Watervliet, and Eldress Rosetta Stephens and Eldress Sarah Collins of Mount Lebanon (for the latter see figure 199). In fact, Andrews met Winter when he was taking photographs at Mount Lebanon about 1930–31.[36] The pre-Andrews Winter photographs are more natural and less staged. They show actual, usable rooms, or rooms "put to bed" by the Shakers. The beautiful image in figure 250, made by Winter between 1923 and 1930, is of the laundry and ironing room at Hancock. It was shown, along with other Winter photographs, at the New York State Museum's *The New York Shakers and Their Industries* (June 1930–July 1932), and the Berkshire Museum's *Shaker Exhibition* (October 10–October 30, 1932) curated by Andrews. The latter exhibition caused Juliana Force to begin her support of the Andrewses. Winter's photographs for *Shaker Furniture* are different from his earlier images in that they show more sparsely furnished set-ups, expressing a stricter modernist and less historical accuracy. The Andrews-Winter photograph in figure 249 suggests a beautiful feeling of quiet, but it is not true to any date or place except the moment and place where it was made; it projects a beautiful placement for effect.

Danish Modern

After the Second World War Denmark became the preeminent source of wooden furniture design. What made Danish designs so popular was the use of wood, after the substitute materials featured during the war, and the lean, slightly stolid quality that could be quickly produced and looked good in the rapidly built small homes produced after years of crowded conditions. Thus the impulses behind the Danish Modern aesthetic were not unlike the needs of the Shakers early in the nineteenth century.

A copy of *Shaker Furniture* was owned by Kaare Klint, the father of Danish Modern, and he spoke with great appreciation of the quality of the Winter photographs, and of the pieces of furniture they showed.[37] Klint also knew a Shaker chair (figure 251) brought to Denmark "by a ship captain" and owned by a Copenhagen museum in which Klint had an apartment; he walked by the chair every day. It is a transitional 1860s rocking armchair with side-scrolled arms and large mushroom handholds. The latest feature is its cushion rail. Although it is not certain that the Winter photographs and the museum-owned chair influenced Danish designs, they at least acted as supporting evidence of a role for lean beauty.

In 1949 Hans Wegner created one of the finest examples of the style (figure 252). Klint admired the design, for although it appears simple, it solves many chair design problems, particularly how to relate the optimal heights from the seat for the back support at 7¹/₂ inches, and the arm supports at 8 inches. With seemingly minimal effort the chair integrates these features with careful curves; the splayed legs give it great stability.

John S. Williams, Sr.

One of the largest and most without-prejudice collections of Shaker material was formed by John S. Williams, Sr., who established the Shaker Museum and Library, Old Chatham, New York. He developed a cordial relationship in the 1940s and 1950s with the Shaker leadership at Mount Lebanon, Hancock, Canterbury, and Sabbathday Lake, and was able to form a rich collection because the leadership understood that he was forming a museum that would preserve their past, rather than benefiting from the sale of what he obtained. The Shakers accepted that the Museum would "reverently care for" the visual records of their history, "and preserve them for historical value and enlightenment in future generations." As a result of years of mutual regard, over 70 percent of the Museum's holdings have come directly from Shaker communities. In 1950 the collection became public, and now preserves about seventeen thousand museum artifacts. In 1962 Eldress Emma B. King gave to the museum the bulk of the official Church archives from Mount Lebanon and Canterbury, bringing the library's book and manuscript collection to over seventeen thousand items.

Williams's passion was machinery, and that could have skewed his collection, but his approach was to preserve all facets of Shaker life from the more than two hundred years of their existence.

He was aware that to the greatest degree possible, everything must be preserved and analyzed if a society is to be understood. Thus, while Williams collected all the well-known Shaker things—furniture, oval boxes, textiles, baskets, stoves, vehicles, herb articles, and printed and written matter—he also acquired the patterns, tools, molds, and machinery used to produce them. His intention of completeness was so certain that with great logistical difficulties he took to Old Chatham from Mount Lebanon the 1820s four-ton double trip-hammer used for forging metals.

THE SHAKERS' REVISIONIST VIEWS OF THEMSELVES

At least since the 1850s it has been increasingly easy for the Shakers to view themselves as a particular force in American society. While they ever more readily adopted the social and artistic changes occurring in the world, they contrived to present a positive image of themselves that was sufficiently different so as to be salable; and they did this while adjusting how their past was understood. From the 1870s they painted early woodwork and furniture white, or stripped it, to make it salable, while selling thousands of new chairs as communicators of traditional values. Their altering of their past to fit modern ideas has continued to recent times. Sometime before the Shakers agreed to sell Hancock in 1960 for $125,000, they stripped the orange color from much of the woodwork of the Brick Dwelling House, including the meeting room, that had been lovingly described by Brother William Deming when he wrote to Elder Benjamin S. Youngs in 1832. (In good light the orange-red color left in the grain beneath a new coat of varnish is perceptible. Fortunately the Shakers did not touch the yellow on the inside of the meeting room's cupboard doors.) The Shakers regularly refinished chairs for worldly customers. Eldress Bertha Lindsay of Canterbury remembered working with Sister Rebecca Hathaway early in the 1930s to remove red paint from chairs, and they also refinished sewing desks from Enfield, New Hampshire.

Gerald McCue recalls that the Shakers at Canterbury were particularly given to refinishing early furniture for sale in their store. Such alteration by Shakers must be seen as a natural reflections of the times as the Shakers joined into colonial nostalgia, and its commercial rewards. And, they wanted their past to be recalled as very clean. Sometimes they altered early pieces to put them to new uses, as shown in the photograph of Olive Hayden Austin at the Church Family, Hancock (figure 253). She was photographed about 1915–20 sitting on the remains of an early painted bed that has become a bench. A wonderful story about the Shakers' willingness, even desire, to move away from the encumbrances of their past is associated with this bed-bench. Austin left the Church as an adult in 1935. In 1982 or 1983, she returned to Hancock for a visit and asked if she might see the upstairs attics in the 1830 Brick Dwelling House. There she told of beds thrown out of the windows. She did not recall the number of beds, but she remembered they were in the north-west corner room, which measures 16 by 22 feet. It was packed so full of "those old beds" that a person could hardly fit through the door. She did not recall the year, but she did remember that people got tired of moving them into the hall to clean them, and under them, every spring, and they were discarded out a window. Afterward members regretted having discarded the beds, and someone suggested making garden benches from usable parts. Perhaps the bed-bench on which Austin sits in figure 253 was made from one of those tossed out of a window.[38]

As the century progressed the Shakers became ever more wary of the insistent collectors, for as Jennie Wells said in 1947, "those people would grab the chairs right out from under us if we'd let them." The Shakers knew their identity was being transferred from one of deep religious commitment to a people who made furniture—indeed, they had encouraged the idea as they benefited from sales—but ultimately they disliked the focus on their things. In 1974 Sister Mildred Barker at Sabbathday Lake made what was one of her standard retorts: "I don't want to be remembered as a piece of furniture! (I guess I will be remembered for that statement.)"[39] The Shakers became the formal purveyors of knowledge about their objects when from 1980 to 1984, and again between 1991 and 1994, Brother Arnold Hadd became Curator of Collections at Sabbathday Lake.

The Shakers are revisionist of their own history and, with the freedom with which they refinished their woodwork and furniture, they continue to recast their theological past. Helen and Charles Upton were important collectors of Shaker material in the 1950s, 1960s, and 1970s, and Helen Upton remembered Sister Mildred Barker of Sabbathday Lake saying, "Mother Ann was not Jesus, but the Spirit of Christ in female form." That statement could suggest that Christ was in Jesus and in Ann Lee, making them equal, which would be what the Shakers believed by 1790. Or, it could have meant that Jesus was a full manifestation of God and Ann Lee only a spirit-filled

253. PHOTOGRAPH: OLIVE HAYDEN AUSTIN
Hancock, Massachusetts, Church Family
1915–20
The bench was made from a bed
Private collection

person.[40] The second was probably intended, for that is how many Shakers now speak and write. Brother Theodore E. Johnson wrote in 1968, "Mother Ann was not Christ, nor did she claim to be. She was simply the first of many Believers wholly embued by His spirit, wholly consumed by His love. Mother's attitude toward her own role is reflected more than once in her own recorded sayings. 'It is not I that speaks; it is Christ who dwells in me,' she says, testifying both to the indwelling of Christ and her subservence to Him."[41] But by 1790 Ann Lee was seen as the Second Coming of Christ, who appeared first in Jesus and secondly in Mother Ann.

WORLDLY REVISIONIST THINKING

Recognizing the changes in Shaker life and thought over the Society's history helps us understand and acknowledge corresponding changes in Shaker aesthetics. Nevertheless, many worldly scholars do not easily accept Shaker developments. Two recent instances of partial blindness in otherwise interesting revisionist studies illustrate how the best scholars can carry to their writings prejudices based on personal aesthetic choices. Reviewing these helps us understand how figures like Sheeler and Andrews could unconsciously, at least to some degree, misunderstand what they loved.

Mary Lyn Ray wrote as her M.A. thesis one of the first revisionist studies of Shaker artifacts, and later published her material as an article: "A Reappraisal of Shaker Furniture and Society," in *Winterthur Portfolio* (1973). She returned to the ground the Andrewses had left in 1928, and sought out parallels between Shaker and worldly furniture; she covered a greater time span than they had by carrying her study into the post-Civil War years. Recently Ray said to me that people who loved Shaker things were "aghast" at what she wrote, "and the reaction from collectors and museum people was extreme; even at Hancock where they have the late nineteenth-century Trustees' House." What she wrote seemed to undercut Shaker uniqueness and thereby diminished the aesthetic and monetary value of Shaker art. Her presentation of "Victorian Shaker" alongside "Classic Shaker" seemed to call into question the qualities of what was most loved.

Mary Lyn Ray's work was seen as an attack on the Shakers in part because she was the first to use the Andrewses' collection of books and manuscripts since they were given to Winterthur. Faith Andrews, who was always careful of her husband's reputation, was "appalled" by what Ray had written. "It seemed," according to Ray, "to deny everything she [Faith] and Ted Andrews had spent a lifetime developing—their way of seeing the Shakers as part of American Folk Art." Twenty years later Ray understands that she was part of the new generation of scholars who were looking for the parallels between vernacular, or locally generated expressions, and Shaker work. She did not see the Shakers' artifacts as folk developments.[42]

The same dismay had occurred when Waldron Phoenix Belknap, Jr.'s, research into print-dependence in American colonial painting was published posthumously in 1955. He had found European print sources for paintings by some of the most noted American artists, including John Smibert, Joseph Badger, Robert Feke, and John Singleton Copley. The outcry that followed was the result of the confusion the discovery of sources creates: if American artists depended on European prints for parts of paintings or whole compositions, including the clothing worn—and even trees, when America was full of them—where was American individuality and separateness from Europe? And what is the economic value of a source-dependent piece? The answer, of course, is that most art is dependent on earlier examples to some degree, and originality is expressed in the way a maker's unique sensibility uses or reacts against the known.

What now seems limiting about Mary Lyn Ray's article is her inability to accept the Shakers' embracing late nineteenth-century styles. She wanted to understand their later work, but did not like it. She saw it as denying the 1845 Laws, which she thought of as the touchstone of Shaker design. Her over-emphasis on those Laws continued Andrews' mistake, and to the degree Ray disparaged the late nineteenth-century work she remained caught in one of the webs the Andrewses created. As Homer Eaton Keyes had written in his introduction to the Andrews' first *Antiques* article, "Even the [post-Civil War] Shakers appear to have yielded something to the era of bad taste."[43]

A similar displeasure that the Shakers could abandon pure rectilinear volumes to emulate late nineteenth-century forms is a slight flaw in the otherwise important work of Dolores Hayden. In 1974 she published *Seven American Utopias: The Architecture of Communitarian Socialism, 1790–1975*, and brought new understanding to the Shakers' use of architectural spaces. But when she discussed the Trustees' House at Hancock she could not refrain from writing:

Less successful adaptation occurred in the Trustees' House, one of the original farm buildings occupied by the community's founders. Numerous late nineteenth century additions, including a turret and a Palladian window, reflect the uneasy life in a declining community. With no new buildings under construction, adoption of an existing structure became an unconscious parody of the spare, functional changes effected in earlier workshops.[44]

The Society was in decline, but Hayden resisted allowing the Believers to change. Had they stayed with 1810–60 styling it would have shown a rigidity that could have caused a quicker demise. Hayden is not the first person to wish the gods would remove the Trustees' House—or at least strip off the "impure" additions: compare figures 254 and 255. Edward Deming Andrews and many others have wanted it returned to a simpler state, both inside and out.

The building is, in fact, the most untouched Shaker building remaining outside the Society's hands, for it has not been altered for ideology's sake. Inside, it is still possible to experience an authentic Shaker space, because it is simply that, and not a contrived re-creation of an imagined past. In some of the rooms, for example, the pegs have been cut from the peg boards, which have been papered over. In this building there remains an Edwardian sense of "more-is-more," and fortunately the less-is-more addicts have not been allowed to change it. Where Hayden went wrong is in believing that the Shakers had a "closed system" that ought to have stopped changes.[45] She, like many other scholars, has used as sources post-Civil War Believers who were themselves part of new theological, cultural, and aesthetic developments, and ready to rewrite the past. When Charles Nordhoff published his study in 1875, he drew heavily upon statements by Elder Frederick Evans, who was himself reinterpreting the early years. Nordhoff, however, was a good reporter and he balanced Evans's opinions by publishing extended sections of early writings. Hayden used Evans's words, as told to Nordhoff, speaking about the Shaker sense of beauty, to write against developments in Evans's own time, and to praise earlier styling. Evans, as has been quoted earlier, had said: "No, the beautiful, as you call it, is absurd and abnormal."[46] He was speaking those words as the Shakers were leaving the "classic" look behind and embracing late nineteenth-century complexity, which Evans disliked. Hayden and others have found it easy to accept such opinions as authority, particularly when they are voiced by Believers.

Another View
In 1988 I was asked to choose my favorite pieces from the collections of the Shaker Museum and Library at Old Chatham, New York, and to arrange them in their largest gallery. I undertook the project with Jerry Grant (see figure 256), because the quality of the museum's collections was obscured by an arrangement that scattered the furniture among the machinery that produced it. This is an informative display technique for some visitors, but for most it is hard to see, study, and compare related pieces when they are set far apart. Our new arrangement, which grouped more than forty objects together, might seem to fly in the face of the ever-growing movement to "contextualize" materials, but no "period" Shaker room has yet met a high standard of accuracy. Our arrangement where pieces stand like forms at Stonehenge and are free to speak to each other, offers one a way of allowing perception. The pieces included in the new display all have their original surfaces, and they range in date from the early blue Canterbury tailor's counter to a late nineteenth-century rococo-framed Shaker portrait. From the museum's point of view, the strength of the furniture collection is now more evident, and there are still many pieces displayed with the machinery.

Viewing with Open Eyes
It is difficult to be free of one's own time, and it is inevitable that each generation will rewrite the past. As Brother Arnold Hadd said to me, "Andrews and Winter invented the Shaker role-model classic."[47] That is, they focused on a particular taste in objects, and arranged settings they liked and called it "Shaker." Ultimately this has led to such abstractions from Shaker ideas as the advertisement featuring a peg board above a grid-based textile shown in figure 257, enhanced by a very non-Shaker model. (A similar textile hanging from a peg rail, perhaps the source for those features, appears in the Shaker room seen as figure 69.) The Andrewses' main handicaps were access to a disproportionate amount of mid- rather than early-nineteenth-century material, not having read the more general 1821 Laws, working from a modernist perspective, and as dealers, having a financial investment in what was then believed about the Shakers and their artifacts. To a con-

256. VIEW OF THE FURNITURE GALLERY,
THE SHAKER MUSEUM AND LIBRARY,
OLD CHATHAM, NEW YORK.
Installed by John T. Kirk and Jerry V. Grant, 1989

257. ADVERTISEMENT BY J. P. STEVENS
About 1986
Reprinted courtesy of WestPoint Stevens, Inc.

siderable degree Andrews liked the idea that during the middle of the nineteenth century the Shakers could believe that their designs came from heaven. This gave an other-worldly quality to the objects.[48] Andrews, like others, wanted the Shakers to be cheerful and gentle people. He knew about the struggle of the early Shakers—physical and psychological—but he did not like it, or at least he did not want to communicate his understanding. He quoted Horace Greeley's 1838 comment noted earlier: "At length, what was a measured dance becomes a wild, discordant frenzy; all apparent design or regulation is lost; and grave manhood and gentler girlhood are whirling round and round, two or three in company, then each for him or herself,"[49] but he edited out the final line: "in all the attitudes of a decapitated hen, or expiring top."[50]

To prefer certain times and styles is natural. The theologian Marjorie Proctor-Smith prefers the first Shaker years. She likes the struggle to find a way of logically presenting an experiential religion. Artists, and art and architectural historians, who prefer the work of Mies van der Rohe to that of Richard Morris Hunt will naturally prefer Shaker objects from 1810 to 1860, but perhaps ignore the religious frenzy that surrounded them. Enoch Jacob, who cried he would rather go to hell with Electra his wife than live among the Shakers, spoke out during the period of "Classic Shaker." To love or dislike a look, time, or idea is easy; to understand it always remains a struggle. Any study is inevitably conditioned by the personal, artistic, intellectual, and spiritual concerns of the author.

AN AWARENESS OF PERFECTION SINCE 1950

As a final stage in this study I wish to view Shaker ideas and Shaker designs as part of one recurring American attitude toward design: the urge to be reductive, to strip away and communicate by essentials, to use the least amount possible. I wish to compare early Shaker things to the art that has since 1950 communicated by spare, minimal forms that rely on shapes, repetition, color, and surfaces for their power.

From their beginning years the Shakers knew the power of repetition. Formulaic phrases, dances, songs, and artifacts make it easy for anyone to remember and affirm the identity of the individual and the community. These create inclusiveness for the insiders while distancing and mystifying outsiders. Limitations can be liberating, for controls define our freedom even as they define our boundaries. For the Shakers, multiple drawers and doors, hundreds of similar chairs, alike clothing, and identical men's haircuts visually defined their group identity and signified the saved. The Sisters' storage area in the attic of the Church Family Dwelling at Canterbury (figures 258 and 75), was constructed in 1837, and has two areas that contain a total of one entry door, seven closets, sixteen cupboards, six short doors into the crawl spaces, and one hundred drawers. In the room, two or three stacks of drawers, united by a top molding, have a cupboard above each stack. The groupings are interrupted by closet doors. Made of pine, they were painted chrome yellow; upon close inspection the woodwork appears a very dry yellow. The storage units are numbered or inscribed on white cards.

A major movement in American art since 1950 features the repetition of tight forms and incorporates the instinct to reduce parts of the world known to the artists to personal statements. A diverse cross-section of this group includes sculptors Donald Judd, Carl Andre, and Robert Gober, painters Agnes Martin and Peter Halley, and theater artist Robert Wilson.

In his wall-like sculpture of 1981 (figure 259) Donald Judd controls while introducing randomness. At first the detailing of this seventy-seven-foot-long plywood grid of ten stacks of three rectangles appears haphazard. Then it seems simple or obvious: moving from left to right, the first and fifth units seem to begin a progression of three similar units. On closer inspection, the three units in the second series are seen to be different because of the shallower angle of the lower enclosing boards. This pushes forward the lower spaces, and the greater bevel on the edge of the boards creates broader light-colored horizontal bands. The world this piece portrays is, like Shaker wall units, both repetitive and wildly diverse, and yet it is ultimately decipherable by the committed. But even when understood it remains logically fragmented; it has its own inviolable identity and mystery.

The aluminum and black Plexiglas Judd wall sculpture (figure 260) recalls the Shaker box with drawers shown in figure 84 in the way it plays with volumes and rectangles to create tensions and contrasts. The aluminum lines dividing the rectangle allow the eye to move between and around as they contain and divide. Judd's use of black at the back of his piece adds depth and mystery and eliminates the easy reading of forms.

258. DWELLING HOUSE ATTIC: DOORS, CUPBOARDS, AND DRAWERS
Church Family, Canterbury, New Hampshire, Sisters' side
1837
Shown also as figure 75
Canterbury Shaker Village, Canterbury, New Hampshire

259. UNTITLED
By Donald Judd
1981
Plywood
H. 138³/₈" W. 927⁵/₈" D. 45³/₈"
Cordiant Group, Ltd., London. © 1997 Estate of Donald Judd/Licensed by VAGA, New York

This juxtaposition of Shaker designs and the work of such artists as Judd is not an attempt to suggest an influence of Shaker images on contemporary art. Nor is it intended to celebrate a simple resemblance, or ignore cultural and historical differences. These artists are not what they are because of Shaker designs; rather, the makers in both groups are visionary in a similar manner. Some of these minimalist artists own Shaker objects, and most care about and speak enthusiastically of their sympathy for the Shaker aesthetic of the second quarter of the nineteenth century, but they do not draw inspiration from Shaker work. What the Shakers and these contemporary artists have in common is a way of conceiving and organizing objects, and they share the knowledge that limited forms have a power to evoke an experience beyond the means employed. Their use of restricted parts is not an attempt to curtail discussion, but to use singleness to encourage emotional and intellectual openness. The impulse is to do something new, not something "less." Given that the present number of Shakers is the eight members—five women and three men—

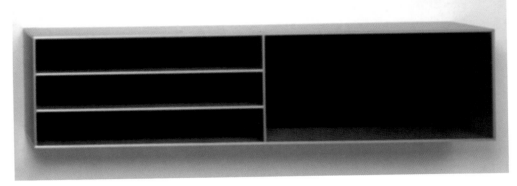

living at Sabbathday Lake, Maine, the enthusiasm is mostly, but not exclusively, one-sided. [51] The easy enjoyment by the artists is not one of nostalgia or antiquarianism, but one of kinship.

The cultural climate for the contemporary artists is different from that of the Shakers, who live apart and follow group patterns of life. However, these artists recall the Shakers in believing that simple objects and meaningful surfaces can convey a truth that pulls the committed outside normal cultural experiences. The Shakers and these artists share a firm certainty that the eye is sufficient to judge thoughts fixed in forms, and both believe in the mind's ability to understand a deeper sense of reality. Both are certain they possess the gift to judge and convey greater truths. The Shakers, conversely, have not intended their objects as initiators of a greater perception. For them what they produce records a converted state and a life of continuing commitment. The artists see their works as instigators of change, a means to disturb and lead. Both groups have a belief in the role of the restricted, balanced, and refined. All the makers see themselves as conveyors of the fact that "in the mind there is an awareness of perfection," a phrase used often by Agnes Martin to describe the inspiration of any good art.

261. CASE OF DRAWERS
New Lebanon, New York, North Family
Signed: "Galton(?)"
1830–40
Pine painted pinkish-red; cherry knobs; ivory
or bone keyhole surround
H. 70¹/₂" W. 60⁷/₈" D. 19³/₁₆"
Shown in color as figure 80
Collection of the Shaker Museum and Library,
Old Chatham, New York

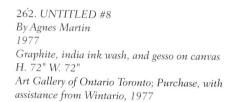

262. UNTITLED #8
By Agnes Martin
1977
Graphite, india ink wash, and gesso on canvas
H. 72" W. 72"
Art Gallery of Ontario Toronto; Purchase, with
assistance from Wintario, 1977

262A. *UNTITLED #8 (DETAIL)*

Both the Shakers and these artists can instill active small variations that result from the intrusion of the hand in work that at first seems machine-perfect. One of the supreme Shaker statements, both aesthetically and as a signifier of unity in communal living, is the New Lebanon, North Family case of sixteen drawers shown as figures 261 and 80. Sixteen nearly identical rectangles are stacked in a tight grid contained by the edges of the case. The slight variations in shape keep the surface alive, and the viewer's eyes continuously intrigued. The squared parts play

263. UNTITLED # 2
By Agnes Martin
1977
Graphite, India ink wash, and gesso on canvas
H. 72" W. 72"
The Museum of Contemporary Art, Los Angeles,
California; The Barry Lowen Collection

against the straight lines that run between and around them, which, at a slightly recessed level, allow the eye to travel among the projecting drawer fronts. The immediacy of such pieces results from several factors: their tight rectilinear outline on angled bracket feet; and the smoothness of the volume played against the projecting rectangular drawer fronts, which are punctuated by smooth knobs. (A similar movement is found in the lines of the gift drawing in figure 72.)

For Agnes Martin, "Beauty is an awareness in the mind." Since the late 1950s she has played spontaneously against a square format on canvases that have until recently been regularly 6 by 6 feet. Using an 18-inch ruler and a pencil Martin makes lines on a painted surface to suggest a plane or a patterned grid through which the eye can easily move. In figure 262, Martin arranged a grid of vertical rectangles—six across and five high—against a series of narrow lines. To create the gridness of the work, Martin intensified the lines that form the top and bottom of the rectangles (figure 262A). As Agnes Martin asserts, those who make themselves vulnerable, particularly those who have had for moments the experience of perfection, can by faith and surrender enter through the work into a state of happiness, which, according to the artist, is the goal in life. As with the Shaker case of sixteen drawers, to approach a Martin painting is to see the grid dissolve and the variation in shapes and surface increase. (The diagonal is nearly absent from art made by both the Shakers and Martin.)

In 1967 Martin left New York City, where she had worked for a decade. After more than a year traveling, seeking independence, loneliness, and freedom of the requirements of this world, she settled in New Mexico, where she lived in near isolation, and did not make art again until 1973. Since then Martin has lived in less isolated areas of the state and has produced large square paintings that are hauntingly pale, quiet, and serene. She creates bands of pencil lines or muted colors that range from warm rose to cool blue-gray. Usually the bands are oriented horizontally, although they may be vertical. Lacking symmetry or hierarchical order, the translucent washes evoke limitless depth and unhindered space. The bands in figure 263 may be read as a series of alternating complex and simple bands, or as three broad bands edged by five tightly arranged lines. Thus, like the Shaker wall hanging in figure 99, the work allows continuously shifting perception.

For Martin, "It [the painting] is not about what is seen. It is what is known in the mind." Through an openness derived from commitment, the viewer can "in the mind" experience with these paintings the happiness and "awareness of perfection" that Martin seeks to make available. When I visited Agnes Martin to discuss her art, which she prefers to call Expressionist rather than Minimalist, and objects made by the Shakers, she said: "The Shakers made their furniture smooth and tranquil to avoid awkward feelings."

Carl Andre places alike units side by side, or end to end, or at equal distances across the floor or a field to establish control of the materials, the space, and the viewers. Like a stretch of railroad ties, his units seem both dismissable and inevitable. They are ordinary and shockingly present. A stretch of rectangular steel plates on the floor, as depicted in my drawing (figure 264), secures that part of the room, makes it special, and almost unapproachable. But since one is allowed to walk on the piece—even encouraged to—the work is, while forbidding, a natural part of the environment. Walking on it is thrilling, but to do so seems almost dangerous. Like a stretched Shaker dining table the sheer length of an Andre piece becomes special, but like the table (when in use by groups of four Believers), it was conceived of as divisible into parts. The power of a very long Andre work of common materials embodies endlessness, the human act, and ordinariness. Like the Shakers' narrow path, Andre's lines provide a way along and through while encapsulating contrived and voluntary choices. The drawing in figure 265 is my understanding of an Andre work titled *Secant,* which employed one hundred blocks of Douglas fir measuring 1 x 1 x 3 feet. They were placed end to end. Moving down a field at the Nassau County Museum of Art in 1977, the work defined the contour of the land while controlling the viewer's gaze as it moved along Andre's determined path.

When I interviewed Carl Andre to ask his feelings about the Shakers, he gave three reasons for not associating his work with Shaker materials. First, that he is an atheist and they are a Christian sect. Second, he asked if it were not true that if any Shaker was enjoying a task he or she would be reassigned by the authorities to other work within the community. Andre very much believes in the value of work and a person's involvement in it. From that question I realized again how strongly the Andrewses have skewed our understanding when they wrote in *Shaker Furniture* that any Believer taking too vain a pride in his or her work was permanently assigned a different job. The Andrewses' incorrect assertion dehumanized the Shakers by removing them from the practical logic of employing every talent at hand. I told Andre that a Brother or Sister would continue in what he or she was good at for a lifetime. He asked if one could work in the kitchen all one's life, and I told him of the "kitchen Shakers." Thus the second objection was resolved. Third, Andre said, "The Shakers did not believe in art." I talked about the Shakers' concept of beauty, and how they used the word. Andre said, "A sunset is beautiful but it is not art." He meant, I think, "I consciously produce art and the Shakers did not." We did not get much further in our discussion.

I should have asked Carl Andre what he meant by art. In 1985 Andre observed: "My work is the exact opposite of the art of association. I try to reduce the image-making function of my work to the least degree."[52] I suspect that Andre rejected my attempt to compare his art to that of the Shakers because it connected his work historically, producing "association." There are so many definitions of art, and certainly Andre's focus on repeated units, his visually strong and natural materials, and his desire to control and inspire, are akin to many Shaker concerns. If one goes to the most inclusive view of art, that anything meant to be viewed aesthetically is art, then there are easy grounds for relating Andre and the Shakers. Both are and were tough-minded and dismissive of those who do not agree with them. Both have produced mind-changing visual experiences by juxtaposing the known in new ways.

Artists can control where photographs of their works are reproduced. When Carl Andre was asked for permission to include images of two of his pieces in this book, he denied permission, saying again that any relationship between his work and that of the Shakers is accidental. His toughness of mind made me even more aware of the fiber of Ann Lee, and other early Shakers, who with authoritarian control moved supplicants in and out of salvation. To provide readers visual help as they seek to understand Andre's art, I have provided drawings of my impressions of what Andre creates. The resulting distance from Andre's hand, and the introduction of me as artist, seems rather like an apostate such as Thomas Brown writing about the Shakers when he was no longer a member: The information is informative, but not as interesting as direct contact with the instigator.

Peter Halley is a younger abstract artist who has reacted against art that is solely concerned for its place in the arena of beauty and connoisseurship. Like many of his generation he allows his art to be informed by theoretical and political issues. Halley and the Shakers share a neoclassical detachment achieved by strict delineation of shapes, control of surfaces, and reliance on bright colors. Both have an almost harsh control of line.

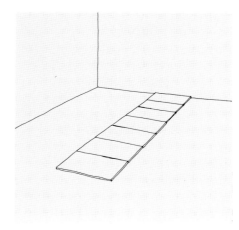

264. DRAWING OF THE SCULPTURE
SEVEN STEEL ROW BY CARL ANDRE
Sculpture made 1975
Steel; seven-unit line extending from base of wall
Each: H. ¹/₂ " W. 24¹/₈" L. 17⁷/₈"
Overall: H. ¹/₂" W. 24¹/₈" L. 125¹/₈"
Drawing by the author

265. DRAWING OF THE SCULPTURE
SECANT BY CARL ANDRE
Sculpture made 1977
Douglas fir
H. 12" W. 12" L. 300'
Installation at the Nassau County Museum
of Fine Arts, Roslyn, New York
Drawing by the author

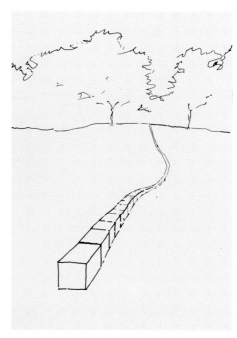

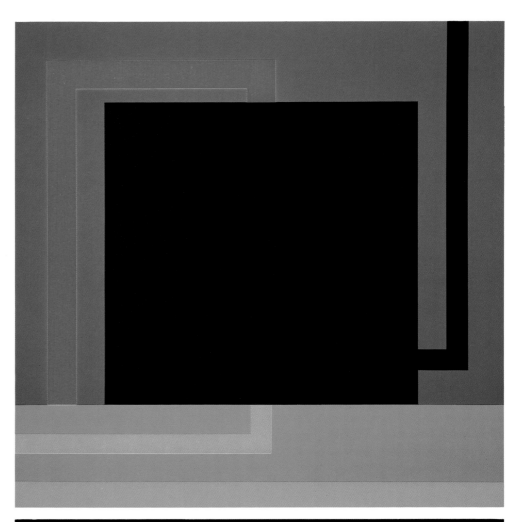

266. COLLISION CIRCUIT
By Peter Halley
1989–90
Day-glo acrylic, acrylic and Roll-a-Tex on canvas
H. 97¾" W. 95"
The Eli and Edythe L. Broad Collection

267. PRISON WITH CONDUIT
By Peter Halley
1986
Day-glo acrylic, acrylic and Roll-a-Tex on canvas
H. 58¼" W. 111"
Collection Douglas S. Cramer Foundation

Two of Halley's basic units are a plain square cell (figure 266) and a square with prison bars (figure 267). These forms signal containment and restriction, and the control imposed by society and government to limit political discussions and human freedoms. The plain cell "contains" intellectual issues. By adding prison bars Halley puts a human or group in confinement. The cells or prisons may have conduits connected to other units, or they may not. They can link the contained space or, by disappearing beyond the painting, leave viewers asking if there is another cell we cannot see. The conduits, the connectors, may take or bring effluences, such as oil or waste. They may bring or cut off sustenance; they may signal hope or mounting problems. In a world of telephones, cable television, and electrical lines, connectors are a way to or from isolated spaces; they recognize that connecting is one way of being human in modern times. Halley may show conduits rushing across the base of a work. We do not know their role, what they may carry, or whether they join some other unit we cannot see. Maybe what is on the canvas is only a tiny part

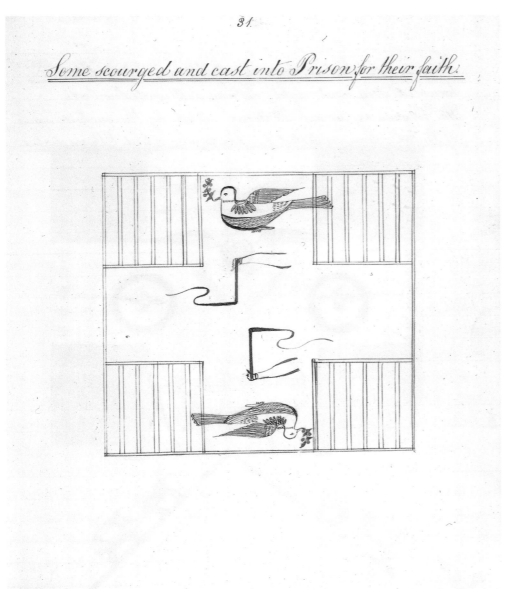

Some scourged and cast into Prison for their faith.

268. "SOME SCOURGED AND CAST INTO
PRISON FOR THEIR FAITH."
Attributed to: Miranda Barber, New Lebanon,
New York, Church Family
June, 1843
Blue and brown ink and watercolor on paper
H. 8½" W. 7"; p. 31 in an untitled manuscript
book of inspired writings and drawings
Shown also as figure 177
Western Reserve Historical Society Library,
Cleveland, Ohio

of a much larger whole. Like looking at only a small part or idea of the Shaker world, the larger context may be missed.

Like Shaker units—drawers, rooms, buildings, squared fields—the parts of Halley's paintings have their individual role, but they exist to be part of a larger pattern without which they have no long-term purpose. Shaker villages were reorganized in the early years to logical unity, with the buildings connected by thin, carefully trod paths. Halley's paintings allow us to traverse his landscapes with great consciousness. The grid-like Shaker plan of Canterbury, in figure 66, uses thin ink lines to indicate the flow of water, the underground conduit that links the buildings. Above ground, the buildings are ritualistically joined by walks, the paths the Shakers used between carefully specified buildings. Halley and the Shakers use color and surface as controlling factors that provide focus, change, and emotion. The Canterbury plan in figure 66 is dominated by yellow and red; probably before fading those Shaker colors were much brighter. For Halley, color can delineate a path to follow, and it is a means to disturb.

Throughout the nineteenth century an array of Shaker rules assured that visitors found their communities clean, peaceful, and successful. But spiritual turmoil twice closed them to the public, as leaders struggled to contain the upheavals. The public was unaware of this unless apostates spoke about it after leaving the controlled areas. As one moves through a Halley work one is both soothed and confused. The calm comes from the seemingly quiet placement, the disturbance from the ongoing demand to deal with the issues raised. Unlike the Shakers, Halley glories in the artificial, the abstract idea. Like the Shakers, he is unrelenting in his insistence on confrontation. The gift drawing "Some scourged and cast into Prison for their faith" (figures 268 and 177) fills the four corners with prison cells and the remaining cross-shaped area exhibits scourges of mortification and doves of peace. Like a work by Halley, it permits hope, but at a cost.

Peter Halley recently wrote to me concerning the relationship of Shaker design and this kind of contemporary art:

> As you know, there is little doubt that Shaker furniture and aesthetics have been an important and wide-ranging influence on postwar American art. In addition, the parallels between the development of the Shaker aesthetic and the strategies developed by various American reductivist artists are a subject of much interest. Furthermore, I find the whole issue of functionalism as it connects the Shaker phenomenon and contemporary art, to be of utmost importance.
>
> When I was a student in the early seventies, I was aware of a lively and provocative dialogue that existed on precisely this topic. It seems to me that in recent years, both curators and critics have stepped away from this issue. [53]

Peter Halley is referring to the fact that in the late 1960s and the early 1970s the relationship between Shaker and Minimalist objects was often discussed, although seldom written about.[54] In a conversation Halley told me that when one of his instructors took his class to Hancock, the purpose was to see the circular barn.

The Shakers and some contemporary artists have in common the use of sources—known images from which they draw when making personal statements. The Shakers did this automatically, and to a degree unconsciously, as they naturally took the familiar vernacular forms around them as the basis for their objects, and for theological and philosophical reasons used them to reflect their religious and social needs. In both groups this borrowing might be natural, but the process of producing a new vision is often a struggle. The "Shaker look" came from a determination to have an environment that reflected a special way of life; for contemporary artists the creative act is seldom a casual process.

Robert Wilson is an artist and performer whose work is centered in avant-garde theater. In 1991 a critic for the *New York Times* called him "the most important theater artist America has ever produced."[55] Wilson, who usually creates most aspects of his theater pieces, including sets, costumes, and texts, arrives at many of his visual effects by filtering ancient art forms or historical images through his aesthetic sensibility. The triangular shape often recurring in his groundbreaking *the CIVIL warS*, for example, was inspired by the shape of the tents in Mathew B. Brady's photographic record of the Civil War. In the theatrical production this source was clearly acknowledged in the tent scene (figure 269), but the shape recurs, albeit less recognizably, in the triangularity of the shark fins and the trailing Victorian-style dresses that appear in other scenes. Wilson's stage images are presented with direct clarity, but a scene is not meant to project a fixed message, but instead to evoke a multiplicity of resonances: what you see and what you feel depend on who you are.

During the development of a theater piece Wilson makes numerous drawings of each scene as a way of pushing further his vision of a moment, and he sells the more finished drawings as a means of funding the theater work. The drawing in figure 270 is clearly related to the tent scene, but it also echoes the shark fins and the silhouettes of the dresses. While the drawing can be understood as two steps from the Brady photographs, and one remove from the theater production, it is by the addition of further creativity an independent work of art, possessed of its own power. As with the theater moments, the independent work can awaken a variety of stored memories, visions, anxieties, and delights in a person ready to be surprised and open. Allowing vulnerability to the work in figure 270 can awaken a range of responses, from memories of images of Native-American encampments to private joys and fears, and out-of-reality experiences. Living in Seattle, it is easy for me to see Wilson's triangular shapes as Washington State's Cascade Mountains. They run north and south, dividing our lush maritime region from drier interior lands. Although these were not the artist's original references, Wilson's thought-releasing images allow his tough range of peaks to be seen as a barrier that separates the quiet familiar from the perhaps threatening unknown.

One of Wilson's great gifts is his ability to cause a suspension of the ordinary, the normally perceived reality. This is particularly true in regard to how he handles time, which he can stretch and sustain until abnormal time seems to become real. Often, particular actions, such as pouring a glass of milk, or an entire scene, are repeated many times. The slowed-down action of an actor taking a half hour to cross the stage can drive a viewer to leave the theater; it might seem as endless as Andy Warhol's eight-hour film *Empire* (1964), where a fixed camera silently recorded the Empire

Above:
269. ACT III, SCENE E FROM *the CIVIL
warS*, COLOGNE-SCHAUSPIEL
PRODUCTION
By Robert Wilson
1984

Below:
270. DRAWING FOR *the CIVIL warS*, ACT III,
SCENE E
By Robert Wilson
1982
Graphite and blue crayon on paper
H. 9" W. 31¾"
Private collection

State Building, and the changing natural and electric lights, from dusk to early morning. For the accepting viewer, however, this slowness can make stretched change, movement, and continuum—and their visual corollaries—seem normal and right. Similarly, Wilson also stretches the forms of familiar objects so that their new configurations also seem correct. He has used very tall ladders: some reach from the stage to disappear behind the proscenium arch. As in Shaker drawings, Wilson's ladders are a visual means of moving from the common to the heavenly or distant reality. On seeing the long, slender Shaker ladder shown as figure 96, Wilson let out a screech of surprise and joy as he felt a designer's instinct akin to his own, and immediately began to measure the ladder's parts with the span of his hand. The link between Wilson and the ladder-maker lies in finding it natural to break traditions, and in possessing a similar sense of rhythm and joy.

On occasion Wilson sells his theater props as individual works of art, but normally he reworks props as sculptural statements free of the restraints imposed by stage practicalities, which allows the further-developed work to evoke even greater awe and the sense of unworldly perfection. The serene and frightening *Einstein Chair* (figure 271) is a reworking of the high-seated witness chair

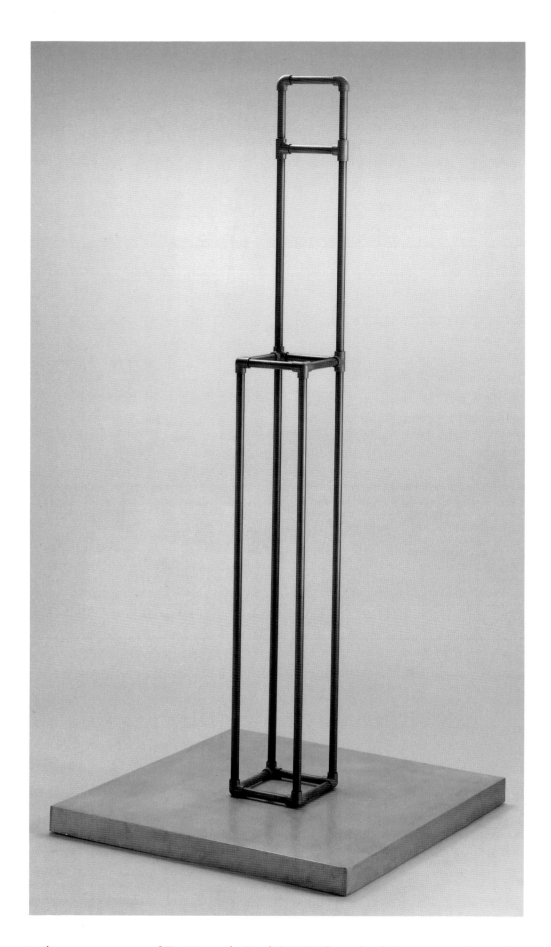

271. EINSTEIN CHAIR
By Robert Wilson
Design: 1976; edition 1985
Galvanized pipe
Chair: H. 89⅛" W. 9⅞" D. 9⅞"
Base: H. 3" W. 40" D. 40"
H. E. Bolles Fund, Museum of Fine Arts, Boston

in the courtroom scene of *Einstein on the Beach* (1976). There, the chair was not as elongated as this one, and it had a stretcher that allowed an actor to mount to a wooden seat before testifying. The precarious height made manifest the witness's vulnerability before the law. Like the Shakers' stretched forms, and their narrow paths, the exaggerated height and non-functioning aspect of the final sculpture can seem normal to those who allow the extraordinary to free their imagination. After the emotional and intellectual openness to this piece, an ordinary chair can appear uninteresting or mundane, for it can seem to lack a new understanding of the world, and what lies beyond the everyday.

Many of the Shaker objects perceived as extraordinary are of simple materials, just pine and paint. Similarly, this sculpture employs common materials: galvanized pipes and joints that allude to Einstein's remark in 1954 that if he were again young he would consider becoming a plumber rather than a scientist. As with much Shaker work, the mysterious power of Wilson's work lies not in its use of sources or materials, but in its vision, in the individual aesthetic force of the designer, and the conditions that created him.

The sculptor Robert Gober re-creates common objects in such a way that they both assume a new individual character, and project both Gober's past experiences and his vision of life. For example, his sinks, which he makes from wire, plaster, and paint, are objects laden with emotional tension. They carry explicit and implicit mysteries by being at the same time familiar pedestrian forms, and personal abstractions that would not be mistaken for actual sinks. With lines and surfaces that are not quite "real," they overlay the comfortable with a strong vision. Like the Shakers' world, which is actual to Believers but self-created to outsiders, they appear both factual and artificial. By stacking two of the sinks, as in figure 272, Gober excites and scares us, as he stretches the known into the threatening. For him this is a way of forcing a confrontation with a world unable to face the ordinary. The Shakers accepted the rightness of using the suppression of natural instincts to move closer to God. Gober asks through his sculpture for society to confront the real, to strip away what conceals the basic, and to allow it life. Reading a Gober work, like reading a Shaker yellow chest, is a way of seeing the power of tradition and the power of choice.

By evoking a child's beginnings, as in the playpen seen in figure 273, Gober makes us feel the constraints imposed by others. The neutral white bars convey the containment that can terrify or provide a sense of security. For a small child, who is rarely allowed to choose, the bars may appear permanent and unassailable. For the parents, they provide a way to confine an individual, for the child's own good or to give the parents freedom. Growing up delivers children from these constraints, but such early experiences may remain as memories that trouble their psyches.

The staircase in figure 274 probably came from the Sisters' stairhall, between the third-floor bedrooms and the attic, of the 1846 addition to New Lebanon's North Family Dwelling. Round hand rails supported by simple banisters were used in the world,[56] but their use here, on a sharply slanted staircase, enhances the sense of a plunging or a rapidly rising form. After walking slowly up and down the stairs Gober said to me, "It's like a shaft of light." He perceived the transformed

272. *THE ASCENDING SINK*
By Robert Gober
1985
Plaster, wood, wire lath, steel, semi-gloss enamel paint
Two pieces stacked, each H. 30" W. 33" D. 27"; 17" between sinks; total H. 94"
Private collection, courtesy of Paula Cooper Gallery, New York, New York

273. *TILTED PLAYPEN*
By Robert Gober
1987
Wood, enamel paint
H. 22½" W. 44⅞" D. 44⅞"
Private collection, courtesy of Paula Cooper Gallery, New York, New York

274. STAIRCASE
New Lebanon, New York; probably from the
Sisters' stairhall, between the third-floor bedrooms
and the attic of the 1846 addition to the North
Family Dwelling
Birch, cherry, and pine; colored red
H. 126" W. of stairs 46" L. 90½"
Collection of the Shaker Museum and Library,
Old Chatham, New York

ordinary as a way of affirming personal choice; by moving outside the expected, the maker achieves a greater freedom.

Little made by the Shakers or these contemporary artists asks for permission or wavers in self-knowledge. These objects, like their makers, convey an indifference to anything around them. Their creators have an awareness of place: the floor, the walls, the earth outside. The space they control is quietly secured and dominated by one or a few things, by placement, form, repetition, and surface. In 1968 Donald Judd wrote, "A shape, a volume, a color, a surface is something itself. It shouldn't be concealed as a part of a fairly different whole. The shapes and materials shouldn't be altered by their context."[57] The objects of both groups make the viewer aware of their makers—even when the parts are machine-produced, as with many Donald Judd pieces—and by paying attention we become aware of ourselves, our bodies, and our beliefs. The object's initial impact is often not one of process or study, although close inspection can reveal the stages through which they emerged.

The forms produced by both Shakers and these contemporary artists seem always to have existed. Once one has seen a body of work by either group one usually knows what to expect from the makers; the joy in them lies in experiencing variations on the familiar. As objects, they remain aloof. Touching any of them seems an invasion of the sanctity of its individual personality. Sitting on a refined Shaker chair seems as intrusive as touching a surface by Judd, Martin, or Halley. Nevertheless, all these objects convey the surety and authority of their makers. They are available to all committed observers. The delight in seeing them is in their ever-renewing power.

MILENIAL LAWS,

or Gospel statutes and ordinances, adapted to the day of Christ's second Appearing; Given & established in the Church, for the protection thereof: By the Ministry & Elders. New Lebanon, August 7th: 1821.

PRELUDIUM.

Believers, who are united in one body, possess one united and consecrated interest, & therefore must, in all things, & under all circumstances, be led, governed & influenced by one spirit, which is the spirit of God, and be subject to one general law, which is the law of Christ, in this day of his second appearing.

But as this general law comprehends all that is necessary for the moral & religious government of Believers; so it is divided into a variety of statutes & ordinances which will apply to all general cases, & teach us our duty in the various situations, circumstances & relations to which we may be called.

The first & great command enjoined upon all Believers is, "That we love the Lord our God with all our heart & with all our strength." And the second is like unto it, namely, That we love our Brethren & Sisters as ourselves

Under the influence of the first we shall always be obedient to our Parents & Elders in the gospel; and under the influence of the second we shall always do to others as we would wish others to do to us in like circumstances. On these two important points depend all the statutes and ordinances contained in the following pages.

CHAPTER I.

Orders concerning the confession of sin, and opening the mind.

1. No Believer can be justified in keeping any sin covered, under any pretence whatever; but all must make confession thereof to those who are appointed to hear them.

2. All trials must be opened according to the appointed order of God; and Believers are strictly forbidden to open their trials to those who are not set in order to hear them.

3. If any members not appointed to hear openings should attentively hear disorderly persons open their trials, or their disaffected and unreconciled feelings concerning the Ministry, Elders or Deacons, they would thereby partake of the same spirit; and it is solemnly enjoined on all such members to make confessions of the matter to their Elders, as a transgression of the order of God in hearing such opening.

4. Believers are forbidden to open matters pertaining to their own order, to other orders of people, whether believers or unbelievers.

5. All tattling, talebearing and backbiting are forbidden among Believers; and whoever offends in any of these things, cannot be allowed to stand in any rank in the worship of God, unless confession be made.

6. Believers are not allowed to call nick-names, nor to use byewords.

7. All filthy stories, and all conversation which tends to excite lustful sensations, are directly contrary to the purity of the gospel; and whoever offends in this matter must make confession before meeting, or stand behind all in the worship of God till confession be made: Also, all who hear any such story or conversation, are required to open it before meeting.

8. If any should be overcome with anger, so as to lay a brother or sister in a lie, or speak or act contrary to the gospel of Christ, or by any means try to irritate or wound the feelings of a brother or sister, the person so offending is thereby debarred from any place in our ranks, and must stand behind all in the worship of God till restored by confession.

9. If any should drink so as to be disguised thereby, the person so offending is thereby debarred from the ranks, and must also stand behind all until restored by confession and repentance.

10. No member or members of the family who may be admonished, reproved or mortified by the Elders, for any fault whatever, are allowed to make any enquiry or take pains to find out who it was that opened the matter to the Elders.

11. If any member of the family should discover any violation of the law of Christ or any thing contrary to the known doctrines of the gospel, in any person, or persons entrusted in any lot of care, either spiritual or temporal, however high & important their lot & calling may be, the person making the discovery is bound to make it known to the Ministry, or to some one in whom he or she can place the greatest confidence for salvation.

12. If any member should know of any sin, or actual transgression of the law of Christ, in any one of the family or society, and have reason to believe the same is not known, or has not been confessed in order; that member, to whom the matter is known, is bound to reveal it to the Elders, so that sin may be put away.

CHAPTER II.

Orders concerning the worship of God, religious duties and the sabbath.

1. As it is a matter of importance for all to prepare their hearts before they go into the worship of God, it is therefore required of all to retire to their rooms in silence and labour for a sense of the gospel for the space of half an hour before meeting.

2. No one is allowed to be absent from meeting without the permission of the Elders or some other person who may be authorized to give permission.

3. There must be no unnecessary conversation after evening meeting, and none in bed, except it be something of considerable importance.

4. All who sleep in the same room must kneel down together, either in ranks or facing each other, and go to bed at the same time, unless prevented by other duties.

5. Every saturday evening all the shops and work rooms must be swept, the work and tools put in good order, and the shops secured from fire and thieves.

6. No one is allowed to walk out on the sabbath day for recreation, but if any have duties to do, they may go out and do them in justification.

7. It is required of the brethren & sisters to abstain from the use of cider & distilled spirits on the sabbath, except on important occasions, such as brethren's fatiguing chores at the barns, or sisters work in the kitchen which may require it; and in such cases they can be justified in using such drinks in the morning.

8. Brethren and sisters are not allowed to read newspapers on saturday evening after supper, nor on the sabbath day.

9. No one is allowed to wear ragged nor very dirty clothes into the worship of God at any time.

10. No books may be read on the sabbath, excepting the Bible and those books which have been published by Believers, without liberty.

11. Cutting the hair, shaving the beard, pearing the nails, blacking & greasing the shoes are all forbidden to be done on sabbath, except in cases of necessity.

12. It is contrary to order to pound fresh meat on the sabbath on any occasion.

13. Brethren and sisters are not allowed to carry their dirty clothes to the washhouse on the sabbath, before sunset.

14. Fruit and vegetables must not be gathered on the sabbath except in case of necessity.

15. Shop windows must not be left open on the sabbath, except by special liberty on some needful occasion.

16. When any of the brethren or sisters are under the operation of the power of God, or on their knees, or improving in the gift of songs, all who are present should attend carefully, and not be talking, nor smoking the pipe, nor at work.

17. When a class of brethren, or sisters, or both, are together, no one should take a book & read loud without the request or union of the rest of the class; as some greater gift might be obstructed thereby.

18. It is ungodly for brethren or sisters to talk of going to the world; or to be telling how they would do if they were to got to the world.

19. Brethren and sisters must not go to each other's shops to learn songs, because it has a tendency to naturalize them, & opens a door for disorder.

CHAPTER III.

Concerning intercourse between the sexes.

1. The gospel of Christ's second appearing strictly forbids all private union between the two sexes.

2. One brother and one sister must not be together alone, except it be long enough to do a short and necessary errand, nor touch each other unnecessarily.

3. Brethren and sisters must not work together, except on special occasions, and then it must be by the permission of the Elders.

4. Brethren and sisters are not allowed to make presents to each other in a private manner.

5. It is contrary to order for brethren and sisters to pass each other on the stairs.

6. It is contrary to good order for members of the family to stop on broad stairs, or on the walks, or in the streets with those of our own order or any other order longer than to do some necessary errand or messages or to inquire after the wellfare of our friends &c. If any longer time be necessary to talk among ourselves or with our neighbors we are taught to do it within some of our buildings.

7. Brethren and sisters must not go to each other's apartments without a just and lawful occasion.

8. Brethren and sisters must not go into each other's apartments after evening meeting; except on some needful occasion.

9. When brethren have occasion to go into the sister's apartments, or sister's into the brethren's apartments, they must knock at the door and go in by liberty.

10. The brethren must all leave their rooms when the sisters go in to make the beds or clean the rooms, unless prevented by sickness or infirmity.

11. When sisters walk out into the fields, or to the barns, or to the hen-roosts, or even to the brethren's shops, there must be, at least, two in company; for it is considered unbecoming for one sister to go alone on such occasions, unless by the special liberty of the Elders of their own sex.

CHAPTER IV.

The order & office of Deacons, and the direction of temporal concerns pertaining there to.

1. As the office is the place appointed for buying and selling and transacting business with the world; and as there is an order of Deacons & Deaconesses appointed for that purpose; therefore no buying and selling can be allowed in the Ch[urc]h excepting by and through that order.

2. All monies, book-accounts, deeds, bonds, notes & the like, which belong to the Church, must be kept at the Office, except a little spending money which the family Deacons are allowed to keep for the use of the family when they ride out.

3. Believers must not run in debt to the world.

4. When any of the brethren or sisters want any thing bought, or brought in from the world, they are not to apply immediately to the Office Deacons, but must apply to the Deacons and Deaconesses in the family (those of each sex in their own order) and let them apply to the Office Deacons and Deaconesses for what is needed.

5. When any of the family go abroad they must apply to the family Deacons for spending money; and when they return, they must give an account of their expenses, to the family Deacons.

6. If those who ride out wish to purchase spectacles, or any kind of tools, they must get permission of the family Deacons before they go from home.

7. No private interest or property is, nor can be allowed of in the Church, exclusive of wearing apparel and working tools, of which each member must have the particular care and charge of his own.

8. When sisters want chests, boxes, spools or any such things made they must apply to the Deaconess; and they are to judge whether it is right for them to have such convenience or not, & if they judge such request reasonable it belongs to them to apply to the family Deacons for it & see that it is obtained in order.

9. It is contrary to Ch[urc]h order for brethren or sisters to doctor themselves, but when they need medical aid they must apply to the physicians in their own family, (those of each sex in their own order) & if they need assistance they have a right to apply for it.

10. No one is allowed to urge, or even ask, strangers nor visitors to drink distilled liquors, for it might have a bad tendency. But the order for all believers is to be free and ask for just what they need, and that which is not worth asking for is not worth having.

11. No one is allowed to drink cider & spirits the same morning before breakfast nor near together at any time.

CHAPTER V.

Rules to be observed in going abroad, & in our intercourse with the world of mankind.

1. When any of the brethren or sisters go abroad, it must be by permission of the Elders, and without such permission they ought not even to go off the farm. From this order the Deacons at the Office are exempt, having a general liberty to go when necessary.

2. Those who ride out have a general liberty to purchase such things as they need for their comfort while out, namely, such drink and eatables as are approved of at home; but they are not allowed to purchase such things to bring home with them.

3. When any are out they must not purchase nor receive any ardent spirits from the world to drink; but those who are weak, and have need of something for their health, may get a little wine: also well people, when wet and cold, may take a little wine if they cannot get cider; but they must open it to their Elders when they return home.

4. When brethren or sisters ride out they are not allowed to buy raisins and such like things at the stores near home, it does not look well, if they need such things at such times it is thought best for them to get them at our Office.

5. When brethren and sisters ride out and have ocasion to stop to feed their horses or take any refreshment, they must unhitch their horses from the carriage, so as to prevent danger, in case they should take affright and start suddenly.

6. No one is allowed, for the sake of curiosity, to go into the world's meeting houses, prisons, or towers, or to go on board of vessels, nor to see shows, or any such things as are calculated to attract the mind and lead it away from the love and fear of God.

7. Whenever any of the family go out among the world, whether it be to do business, or for a ride, when they return home they must go and see the Elders, & give an account of their proceedings and other attending circumstances which have occurred in their absence.

8. Whenever any of the family go out and stay over night, or longer, when they return they must see the Elders before they take their places in the family; and give them an account of their journey, as it respects their protection and prosperity while absent; then they may take their places in the family; but they must take their places behind all in the spiritual worship of God, until the Elders think proper to let them come into their ranks again.

9. The members of the Church of God are forbid doing any kind of work or making any kind of tools or implements for the people of the world, the uses of which are disapproved in the Church. They are also forbid making any thing for believers that will have a tendency to feed to the pride and vanity of a fallen nature, or making anything for the world that cannot be justified among ourselves, or purchasing any of their manufactures to sell with ours for the sake of temporal gain.

10. The brethren and sisters are not allowed to purchase nor borrow books nor pamphlets of the world nor of believers in other families without permission of the Elders. But if the world should offer or urge any of the believers to take some particular book or pamphlet, it would be better to accept it than to give offence; but they must not read it until they have shown it to the Elders.

11. If any member of the family should receive a letter from any person, he or she must show it to the Elders before it is read: Also, if any member should write a letter to send abroad, it must be shown to the Elders before it is sent away. But the Office Deacons are allowed to receive and write letters on temporal business without showing them to the Elders.

12. No Hymns nor anthems are allowed to go out of the family except by permission of the Elders.

13. If strangers are here at meal time they must be invited to eat.

CHAPTER VI.

Orders of safety and caution to prevent loss by fire.

1. No one is allowed to carry fire about the dooryard or among the buildings, unless safely enclosed in a lantern or fire box, or something that will secure it from danger.

2. Let no one enter a closet, or any other apartment in a building which is unoccupied, with a lighted lamp or candle, unless it be enclosed in a lantern.

3. Lighted lamps and candles must never be carried to the barns or out buildings, unless enclosed in a lantern,

4. Let no one go to a wood-box, drawer or chest with a lighted pipe in the mouth, Lest by the dropping of a spark of fire into any such place a building might be burnt.

5. Let no one go into the first house garret or any such bye places that are not inhabited with a lighted lamp or candle, unless it be enclosed in a lantern.

6. The brethren and sisters are not allowed to smoke in the kitchen, nor smoke and work at one time any where.

7. No shooting with guns is allowed near the barns, unless the wadding consists of the shavings of leather or something that will not take fire.

8. Spit boxes with sawdust in them must not be under stove hearth's, when there is a fire in them.

9. Brethren and sisters must never knock out their pipes into spit boxes; nor drop the snuff of a lamp or candle therein where there is saw-dust or any such combustible matter.

10. The last who leaves a room should be careful to shut the stove doors and see the place is secure and safe from fire.

CHAPTER VII.

Concerning prudence, care, neatness and good economy.

1. Each of the brethren and sisters are under special injunctions to take good care of all things with which they are intrusted, and to see that no loss comes through their neglect.

2. It is considered good order to lay out and fence all kinds of lots, fields and gardens in a square form where it is practicable, but the proportions, as to length and width may be left to the discretion of those who direct the work.

3. Buildings in the Church, which get out of repair, through age and decay, or any other means, must be repaired soon or taken away.

4. No kind of filthy substance may be left or remain around the dwelling houses nor shops, nor in the door yards; nor in the street in front of the dwelling houses and shops.

5. No kind of liquid matter may be emptied out of the windows of our painted buildings.

6. No apple pearings, nor the refuse of any kind of fruit may be thrown out of the windows of the dwelling houses, nor work shops.

7. When a square of glass gets broke out it must be mended before the sabbath.

8. The brethren and sisters must not throw away their old shoes & boots; but carry them to the shoe maker, and let him mend, and return them, or send them to the poor office, or rip them up, for other uses as he in his judgment may think most prudent.

9. The brethren and sisters are not allowed to give away any of their garments because they dislike them, unless they can do it in union with the Taylors or such ones as make the garments.

10. No one is allowed to go into the water to swim or bathe where it is over his head, or beyond his depth, and never go in when very warm or sweaty.

11. It is contrary to order for any slovens or sluts to live in the Church, or even for brethren or sisters to wear ragged clothes about their work.

12. Every saturday nigt and monday morning the street opposite the meeting house, and against the dwelling houses must be cleared of hay, straw and dung &c. And the outward yard of the meeting house must be cleaned every monday morning from of all such filthiness.

CHAPTER VIII.

Concerning good order in eating & the management of provisions, attending to meals &c.

1. No one is allowed to sit down at a table to eat, either at home or abroad, without kneeling before & after eating.

2. All are forbiden to throng the kitchen or to go into it unnecessarily while the cooks are employed in it.

3. Let no one attempt to instruct the cooks in their duty, nor undertake to represent the feelings of others, except those trustees whose business it is to direct them in their management of kitchen concerns.

4. If any are unwell and have need of a diet different from the family, they may freely go to the cooks and ask for it, and it is the duty of the cooks to prepare it for them. But none are to expect the cooks nor any other sister to come and urge them to have something better or different from common so long as they are able to go and ask for themselves.

5. No unripe fruit is allowed to be eaten, in its natural state, by the members of the Church.

6. Cucumbers are not to be eaten at any time, unless they are seasoned with pepper or salt, or both.

7. No one is allowed to eat any kind of raw fruit or nuts before breakfast in the morning, or after supper, unless it is eaten early, so as to eat the fruit before 6 O'clock.

8. No one is allowed to be absent from meals, unless duty requires.

CHAPTER IX.

Concerning domestic animals & dumb beasts.

1. No believer is allowed to play with cats nor dogs, nor to make unnecessary freedom with any of the beasts of the field nor with any kind of fowl.

2. No beast belonging to the Church must be allowed to suffer with hunger; but all must be kept in their proper places, and properly attended to according to their needs.

3. Neither horses, cattle, sheep nor swine ought to be allowed to feed or graze in the dooryard.

4. Horses and mares must not feed or run together in one pasture. Neither is it allowed for horses and neat cattle to run together in the same pasture, nor oxen and cows; nor sheep and swine.

CHAPTER X.

The order of the natural creation not to be violated.

1. No southern fruits, not adapted to our climate, are allowed to be propagated by believers in these parts; such as oranges, lemmons, tamarinds and the like.

2. No fruit cions or buds are allowed to be grafted or innoculated on the stock of a different kind of trees.

3. No fowls are allowed to be set on the eggs of a different kind of fowls.

CHAPTER XI.

Concerning hunting & wandering away.

1. Boys under 15 years old are not allowed to go a hunting with guns; and the longer they let the guns alone the better.

2. The brethren and sisters are not allowed to wander away from their companions in hand labour, without letting them know where they are going, so that they may be quickly found if they should be wanted.

3. Whoever borrows a tool must return it to the owner or to its proper place as soon as may be practicable.

CHAPTER XII.

Concerning Funerals.

1. Children under 15 years of age are not allowed

to attend any funeral, except in the family where they live, and even then they must not walk in the procession to the grave.

CHAPTER XIII.

The following are rules and counsel which have been given for our protection & increase.

1. Brethren and sisters must not allow themselves to sleep in retiring time, nor gape in meeting.

2. When we get up from the table we should rise up and stand erect before we kneel down.

3. When we kneel down we should come on our right knee first, and brethren should rise up in the same manner.

4. When we clasp our hands together our right thumbs & fingers should be above the left.

5. When we kneel down at a table or elsewhere it is thought improper to hold our handkerchiefs in our hands.

6. It is improper for brethren or sisters to hold conversation in the halls, or on the door steps, or on the walks where people are passing.

7. It is likewise thought improper for brethren or sisters to stop brethren or sisters of other orders in the road between the buildings. If they need to converse together any longer than to do an errand, or to enquire after the welfare of the brethren and sisters they may call them in to some house or shop.

8. Brethren are not to wash in the kitchen, except they are there to make fires, cut up meat or to do some other kitchen chores.

9. Curtains must not to be left so as to flop out of the windows.

10. Doors and gates must not be left swinging, but either shut or fastened open.

11. When brethren or sisters go up or down stairs they should not slip their feet on the carpet, but take them up and set them down plumb, so as not to wear out the carpets unnecessarily.

12. Also, when they turn at the head and foot of the stairs they should not turn their feet while on the floor, lest they wear holes in the floor; but they should turn their feet while clear of the floor.

13. It is not right to lean our chairs back against the wall in our dwelling houses nor any decent buildings; nor against any beds or furnature.

14. It is also wrong to sit with our feet on the rounds of our chairs.

15. When brethren go to each other's rooms or shops they should ask liberty before they go in: Also, when sisters go to each other's retiring rooms or shops they should ask liberty in like manner; this is necessary in order to learn how to reverence the gift of God which is or ought to be kept in all such places.

16. When we place ourselves for the worship of God our ranks should be straight, not only to the right and left, but also forward and back, and always remember to keep forward ranks as long as any of the rest.

17. It is thought imprudent to eat bread the same day it is baked.

18. All should attend Union Meeting at the hours appointed unless special duty requires them to be absent.

19. No one should get up and go out in time of union only on some necessary occasion.

20. If a brother or sister be missing in meeting or at the table the one who comes next should fill up the place, so that there may be no gap left for the devil to get between.

21. Believers, when walking or riding together, either at home or abroad, should not let an unclean creature, whether human or unhuman, get between them if they can consistently prevent it.

Father Joseph was very careful in this particular; he would, while riding on the road, turn his horse to the opposite side of the way to prevent either man or beast from passing between him and his companion.[1]

CHAPTER I

1 Thomas Brown, *An Account of the People Called Shakers: Their Faith, Doctrines, and Practice, Exemplified in the Life, Conversations, and Experience of the Author during the Time He Belonged to the Society. To Which is Affixed a History of Their Rise and Progress to the Present Day* (Troy, 1812), 288. I am indebted to Mark A. Peterson for reading the first two chapters of the manuscript and pointing out various inaccuracies and adjusting emphases.

2 Clarke Garrett, *Spirit Possession and Popular Religion: From the Camisards to the Shakers* (Baltimore and London, 1987), 10–11.

3 *Bible*, Acts 9:3–7.

4 Elie Marion quoted in Garrett, *Spirit Possession*, 32.

5 Jerry Grant outlined the basis of his understanding of the importance of the Methodists in the developing years of the Shakers in a letter to the author, June 27, 1991: In the fourth edition (1856) of Benjamin Seth Young's *The Testimony of Christ's Second Appearing* (first published in 1808), p. 616, the Shakers wrote: "*John Townley* had a measure of faith in the testimony of *James* and *Jane Wardley*; his wife was a member of the society, and had great power of God, and the gift of prophecy. *John Hocknell* was her natural brother; he lived in *Cheshire*, twenty-four miles from Manchester. According to the account of his daughter, *Mary Hocknell*, he, having separated from the Church of England, had joined the *Methodist* society, and had stated meetings at his house; till visiting the society at *Manchester* several times, and afterwards being visited by *James Wardley*, about the year 1766, he received faith in his testimony." The connection may have been even stronger than admitted in the *Testimony*, for in an untitled manuscript written at Hancock in the 1790s, there is a historical note about the connection between the Shakers and the Methodists: "This work began in England in the year of our Lord one thousand seven hundred and forty seven: in the borough of Manchester and County of Lancaster, In the manner following. First to a number in the manifestation of great Light and mighty trembling by the invisible power of God with the administration of all the spiritual gifts that was given at the day of Pentecost which is the comforter that has led us into all truth which was promised to abide with the true Church unto the end of the world. These people were or had been of the Denomination called Methodists. They formed themselves into a good degree of order and eldership was established amongst them. They professed to follow Christ in the regeneration these people were exceeding zealous and strict in their morals and discipline according to the light they had received and by the information given by Mother and the Elders, the most godly exemplary people that we have any account of since the falling away and really possest with the primitive gifts bestowed to the Church in the days of the apostles. About the year seventeen hundred sixty our Mother joined her self to this body of people . . . ." DLC, Shaker Collection, Ms. No. 185). When Brothers Ted Johnson and Arnold Hadd went to Manchester in the mid-1980s to trace the Quaker roots of the Shakers, they could not find any substantial connection, but did find that both John Townley and John Hocknell had been members of Methodist groups. Also the Shaker practice of addressing their spiritual leaders as Mother and Father, and each other as Brother and Sister, was used among the Methodists and other groups, but not among the Quakers.

6 George Fox, *The Journal of George Fox* (1694; rev. ed. Cambridge, 1952), 11, 134, 268–9. Leonard W. Levy, *Blasphemy: Verbal Offense Against the Sacred, from Moses to Salmon Rushdie* (New York, 1993), 178, 179, 182–85, 187, 195–204, and passim.

7 [Joseph Meacham], *A Concise Statement of the Principles of the Only True Church, According to the Gospel of the Present Appearance of Christ . . . .* (1790; repr., Sabbathday Lake, c. 1963), 9.

8 Using documents at Sabbathday Lake, Brother Arnold Hadd responded to my inquiry about the sect's official title in a letter of July 28, 1995: "First of all I am convinced that the first Shakers simply referred to themselves as 'the Church.' They left us no hint as to any other name. In the list of the first Believers here (date 1783) the title runs 'received faith in the Second Appearing of Christ and united with the people called Shakers.' A deed dated 1797 reads, 'being a member of the Community and united Family of Christians called Shakers.' Another deed dated 1819 states, 'deacons of the Church of Christ or Community of Believers called Shakers.' An indenture dated 1820 calls us, 'The United Society called Shakers.' Elder Calvin Green in his *Summary View* [published in 1823] entitles us 'The Millennial Church or United Society of Believers (commonly called Shakers).' Benjamin Seth Youngs in his *Testimony of Christ's Second Appearing* [1856, fourth edition] calls the Church, 'The United Society called Shakers.' Elder Frederick Evans in his *Compendium*, published in 1858, called us 'United Society of Believers in Christ's Second Appearing.' A deed from 1881 reads, 'United Society of Shakers.'"

9 Youngs, *Testimony*, 618–19; literacy: Mark A. Peterson in notes to the author, April 5, 1995. Brother Arnold Hadd responded to my inquiry about Ann Lee's ability to read in a letter of July 28, 1995: "As to the literacy of Mother Ann I suppose I think that Mother more than likely did not read or write. I have seen the banns of marriage in Manchester and

MANUSCRIPT REPOSITORIES CITED IN THE NOTES

Abbreviation	Repository and Location
DeWint	Henry Francis du Pont Winterthur Museum, Winterthur, Delaware
DLC	Library of Congress, Washington, D.C.
MPH	Hancock Shaker Village, Inc., Pittsfield, Massachusetts
N	New York State Library, Albany, New York
NN	New York Public Library, New York, New York
NOC	Emma B. King Library, Shaker Museum and Library, Old Chatham, New York
OClWHi	Western Reserve Historical Society Library, Cleveland, Ohio

by that it was certainly apparent that neither she or Abraham could write. *The Testimonies* are alive with scripture references, but when the Bible is being read to preach to the people it is always Father James who is doing the reading. Mother more than once calls on Father James to read a particular passage. I am sure that you are aware of the fact that illiterates have the ability to recall and repeat much better than those who simply know they can look it up when needed. I feel Mother Ann falls in that category. I cannot state positively that I am correct or wrong."

10 Ibid., 619.

11 [Rufus Bishop and Seth Y. Wells], eds., *Testimonies of the Life, Character, Revelation and Doctrines of Our Ever Blessed Mother Ann Lee, and the Elders with Her; Through Whom the Word of Eternal Life Was Opened In This Day of Christ's Second Appearing: Collected from Living Witnesses* (Hancock, 1816), 49.

12 *Bible*, Luke 20:34–36.

13 John Wesley, "Thoughts on a Single Life," in *The Works of the Reverend John Wesley, A.M.*, ed. John Emory (New York, 1839), 6:540–42, quoted in Garrett, *Spirit Possession*, 156.

14 Brown, *People Called Shakers*, 68.

15 *Bible*, I Corinthians 7:1–40; Ephesians 5:22; Titus 2:5.

16 Brown, *People Called Shakers*, 287; see also Youngs, *Testimony*, 97.

17 Brown, *People Called Shakers*, 357–58.

18 Bishop and Wells, *Testimonies of the Life*, 321.

19 Ibid., 21.

20 *The Virginia Gazette*, No. 964 (November 9, 1769), [1].

21 [Bishop and Wells], *Testimonies*, 66; Brown, *People Called Shakers*, 315; Youngs, *Testimony*, 621–623.

22 "Gaine's Marine List. Custom-House, New-York," *New-York Gazette and Weekly Mercury*, no. 1191 (August 8, 1774), [3].

23 Robert P. Emlen, *Shaker Village Views* (Hanover and London, 1987), 189 n.4; the 1808 edition of Youngs, *Testimony*, uses Ann Lee.

24 Brown, *People Called Shakers*, twice designated William as Ann Lee's half-brother: 289; 314.

25 Ibid., 315–16; Stephen J. Stein, *The Shaker Experience in America: A History of the United Society of Believers* (New Haven, 1992), places the date at 1776, or later, 7.

26 Dorothy M. Filley, *Recapturing Wisdom's Valley: The Watervliet Shaker Heritage, 1775–1975* (New York, 1975), 11.

27 Primary and secondary sources disagree on these early years. I have used Andrews, *People Called Shakers: A Search for the Perfect Society*; Garrett, *Spirit Possession*; Marjorie Proctor-Smith, *Women in Shaker Community and Worship: A Feminist Analysis of the Uses of Religious Symbolism* (Lewiston and Queenston, 1985); Filley, *Recapturing Wisdom's Valley*; and Bishop and Wells, *Testimonies of the Life*.

28 Edward Deming Andrews published evidence that before settling in New York State, the Shakers explored other places, particularly Bucks County, Pennsylvania. Edward Deming Andrews and Faith Andrews, *Work and Worship Among the Shakers: Their Craftsmanship and Economic Order* (1974; repr., Greenwich, 1982), 14. Mary L. Richmond (compiler and annotator), *Shaker Literature: A Bibli-*

ography, 2 vols. (Hancock and Hanover, 1977),II, 35–6, suggests that if the "date were 1775, Mother Ann and some Shakers *could* have traveled in Pennsylvania. After Ann Lee's separation from Abraham Stanley [Standerin] in 1775, Shaker sources do not chronicle her activities until she was joined in New York by Richard Hocknell and party, who had arrived in Philadelphia Dec. 25, 1775." Lee may have journeyed there to meet him. Andrews and Andrews, *Work and Worship*, 212 n. I.2, report that François Jean, Marquis de Chastellux, *Travels in North-America, in the Years 1780, 1781, and 1782* (London, 1787), 288–89, attempted to hear the Shakers preach in Philadelphia in October, 1782, but Shaker sources fail to document that Lee made any visit to Philadelphia.

29 James Thacher, *Military Journal of the American Revolution . . .* (Hartford, 1862), 141–42, quoted in Garrett, *Spirit Possession*, 162.

30 Heironymus, "To the People," *The Boston-Gazette and Country Journal*, No. 1262 (November 2, 1778), [1].

31 Garrett, *Spirit Possession*, 168.

32 Brown, *People Called Shakers*, 330; [Calvin Green and Seth Y. Wells], *A Summary View of the Millennial Church, or United Society of Believers . . .* (Albany, 1823), 25.

33 Bishop and Wells, *Testimonies of the Life*, 206.

34 Clarke Garrett, "The Shakers and 18th Century Popular Religion." Unpublished paper presented at *Shaker Religion in Context: Theology and Practice*. Old Chatham, September 23–25, 1988.

35 Garrett, *Spirit Possession*, 174.

36 Edward Deming Andrews, *The People Called Shakers: A Search for the Perfect Society* (1953; repr., enlarged ed., New York, 1993), 11–12. Andrews does not cite a source for these quotations.

37 Jean McMahon Humez, *Mother's First-Born Daughters: Early Shaker Writings on Women and Religion* (Bloomington and Indianapolis, 1993), 28 n.8.

38 Garrett, *Spirit Possession*, 170.

39 Issachar Bates, "A Sketch of the Life and Experience of Issachar Bates," *The Shaker Quarterly*, 1 (Fall, 1961), 113–14.

40 Valentine Wightman Rathbun, *Some Brief Hints of a Religious Scheme, Taught and Propagated by a Number of Europeans, Living in a Place Called Nisqueunia, in the State of New-York . . . Hartford*, (1781; repr., Boston, 1781), 14, 19.

41 Brown, *People Called Shakers*, 265.

42 Stephen J. Stein reports that although the transfer was ordered, it did not take place. *Shaker Experience*, 14.

43 Rathbun, *Some Brief Hints*, 4; Flo Morse, *The Shakers and the World's People* (Hanover and London, 1980), 5.

44 Bishop and Wells, *Testimonies of the Life*, 146–47.

45 Edward Deming Andrews, *The Gift to Be Simple: Songs, Dances and Rituals of the American Shakers* (1940; repr. New York, 1962), 144, quoting Valentine Wightman Rathbun, *An Account of the Matter, Form, and Manner of a New and Strange Religion, Taught and Propagated by a Number of Europeans, Living in a Place Called Nisqueunia, in the State of New-York . . .* (Providence, 1781), 7–8.

46 Bishop and Wells, *Testimonies of the Life*, 119–20, 95.

47 Ibid., 142.

48 Priscilla J. Brewer, *Shaker Communities, Shaker Lives* (Hanover and London, 1986), 240, n. 26.

49 Garrett, *Spirit Possession*, 180.

50 Benjamin Seth Youngs, *Testimony*, 532.

51 Morse, *Shakers and the World's People*, 30–33.

52 Garrett, *Spirit Possession*, 137–38, 178–81.

53 Brown, *People Called Shaker*, 101, 106, 279, 248–9.

54 William Plumer,"The Original Shaker Communities in New England," edited by F. B. Sanborn, *New England Magazine*, n.s. 22 (May, 1900), 303–309.

55 Theodore E. Johnson, "Life in the Christ Spirit: Observations on Shaker Theology," *The Shaker Quarterly*, 8, no. 3 (Fall, 1968), 73–74.

56 Brown, *People Called Shakers*, 98; Youngs, *Testimony*, 416–26.

57 Jon Butler, *Awash in a Sea of Faith: Christianizing the American People* (Cambridge, MA, London, 1990), Fox: 23; Wesley: 23; Mormons: 245.

58 Garrett, *Spirit Possession*, 190; Andrews, *People Called Shakers*, 48–49.

59 Bishop and Wells, *Testimonies of the Life*, 282.

60 Garrett, *Spirit Possession*, 190.

61 Brown, *People Called Shakers*, 289, 290, 293 n., 322.

62 Ibid., 296, 170–74.

63 Stein, *Shaker Experience*, 94.

64 Brown, *People Called Shakers*, 290, 324.

CHAPTER II

1 William J. Haskett, *Shakerism Unmasked, or the History of the Shakers . . .* (Pittsfield, 1828), 178.

2 Benson John Lossing, "The Shakers," *Harper's New Monthly Magazine*, 15 (July, 1857), 170.

3 Roxalana L. Grosvenor (compiler), "Sketches from Beulah Cooper's Experience . . ." in "Incidents Related by some of the Ancient Believers of Their experience & intercourse with Mother & the Elders . . ." OClWHi, Shaker Collection, VI:B-9.

4 [Joseph Meacham], *A Concise Statement of the Principles of the Only True Church According to the Gospel of the Present Appearance of Christ* (1790; repr., Sabbathday Lake, c. 1963), 11–13. The early Shakers' view on homosexuality is discussed in Chapter VIII.

5 Marjorie Proctor-Smith, "No Closed Canon: Shaker Contributions to Contemporary American Theology." Unpublished paper presented at *Shaker Religion in Context: Theology and Practice* (Old Chatham, September 23–25, 1988).

6 H[olley] G. Duffield, "Mother Ann Met Lafayette? When?" *The Shaker Messenger* 15 (October, 1993), 6, quoting the Marquis de Barbé-Marbois, "It was on Sunday [September 26] that we left [Albany] for Niskayuna"; Clarke Garrett, *Spirit Posession and Popular Religion: From the Camisards to the Shakers* (Baltimore and London, 1987), 214.

7 Garrett, *Spirit Possession*, 215, 232.

8 Joseph Meacham, "Dedication of the Meetinghouse," (New Lebanon, n.d.), DeWint, The Winterthur Library: The Edward Deming Andrews Memorial Shaker Collection, Ms. No. 790. Quoted in Edward Deming Andrews, *The People Called Shakers: A Search for the Perfect Society* (1953; repr., enlarged ed. New York, 1963), 52.

9 Andrews, *People Called Shakers*, 50; Thomas

kicked and reviled her until "a certain nobleman," who was passing by on his horse, stopped and rescued her. Another time she escaped her pursuers by lying all night on the ice of a frozen pond. She was chilled to the bone but because of her "great peace and consolation" did not even take cold. In another crisis, a friendly neighbor saved her from harm by hiding her beneath a pile of wool in an attic.

Through all vicissitudes, Ann never wavered in her conviction that she was protected by Providence. When one of her own brothers, who felt disgraced by her public behavior, tried to punish her, she said God intervened. Here is her account of their remarkable confrontation.

So he [her brother] brought a staff, about the size of a large broom handle; and came to me while I was sitting in my chair, and singing by the power of God. He spoke to me; but I felt no liberty to answer. "Will you not answer me?" said he.

He then beat me over my face and nose, with his staff, till one end of it was much splintered. But I sensibly felt and saw the bright rays of the glory of God, pass between my face and his staff, which shielded off the blows, so that he had to stop and call for drink.

While he was refreshing himself, I cried to God for His healing power. He then turned the other end of his staff, and began to beat me again. While

he continued striking, I felt my breath, like healing balsam, streaming from my mouth and nose, which healed me, so that I felt no harm from his stroke, but he was out of breath, like one which had been running a race.

No wonder Ann's followers began to say she had Godlike powers. They claimed she was the woman described in the Book of Revelations who was "clothed with the sun and crowned with the stars." That was going too far. "Blasphemy!" cried the authorities — and locked her up again.

This time they were taking no chances with Ann Lee. They put her in solitary confinement in a tiny cell of the stone prison and kept her locked up without food or water for two weeks. When they finally unlocked her door, after fourteen days of total deprivation, they expected to find her dead on the stone floor. But to their surprise, Ann Lee was alive and well. Those who watched her walk out were speechless. They thought they were witnessing a miracle; surely no one could survive such an ordeal without supernatural intervention.

There had been intervention all right, but it was not supernatural. What her persecutors did not understand was the devotion of Ann's followers. A dedicated youth named James Whittaker, who had been brought up by Ann Lee, somehow found access

while in motion, frequently touched my arm; and at every touch of her hand, I instantly felt the power of God run through my whole body.

Clearly, Mother Ann had a charismatic personality. *Charisma*, the Greek word for "divine gift," was originally used to describe miraculous powers the early Christians were said to possess, to heal, speak in tongues, and prophesy. Some of Mother Ann's disciples claimed similar gifts of grace for her; but she was careful not to presume Godlike powers for herself. To the people who came to her seeking forgiveness for their sins, *Testimonies* tells us Mother Ann would declare, "I can freely forgive you, and I pray God to forgive you. It is God that forgives you. I am but your fellow servant."

11

Ann Lee, "Spy"

Behold it is a time of war
And we have been enlisting,
Emmanuel we're fighting for,
And Satan we're resisting;
We have not in this war begun
To turn our backs as traitors,
But we will all unite as one
Against our carnal natures.

—Early Shaker Spiritual

ON MAY 10, 1780, — NEW ENGLAND'S FAMOUS "DARK day" — the sun never came out. Fearful souls were out wringing their hands and wailing, "The day of Judgement has come!" It happened that was the day Ann Lee had chosen for the first public testimony at Niskeyuna. No wonder the word went round that this woman possessed supernatural powers.

A Baptist minister named Issachar Bates gives a vivid account of that epic day in his autobiography.

There were neither clouds nor smoke in the atmosphere, yet the sun did not appear . . . No work could be done in any houses without a candle! . . . The darkness covered the whole of the land of

Brown, *An Account of the People Called Shakers: Their Faith, Doctrines, and Practice, Exemplified in the Life, Conversations, and Experience of the Author during the Time He Belonged to the Society. To Which is Affixed a History of Their Rise and Progress to the Present Day* (Troy, 1812), 326–27.

10 Garrett, *Spirit Possession*, 221–22.

11 [Rufus Bishop and Seth Y. Wells], eds., *Testimonies of the Life, Character, Revelation and Doctrines of Our Ever Blessed Mother Ann Lee, and the Elders with Her; Through Whom the Word of Eternal Life Was Opened In This Day of Christ's Second Appearing: Collected from Living Witnesses* (Hancock, 1816), 220.

12 Ibid., 219.

13 Andrews, *People Called Shakers*, 55–56, gives September 1787; Priscilla J. Brewer, *Shaker Communities, Shaker Lives* (Hanover and London, 1986), 19-20, has Wright moving to New Lebanon early in 1788 and Meacham elevating her to Mother "several months later." Clough and Hamlin were added as assistants in 1788.

14 Probably she kept her married name after she and her husband agreed to dissolve their marriage, until James Whittaker renamed her Lucy Faith in 1785. As a leader she was known as Lucy Wright, but in an 1817 letter to an apostate, she signed her name Lucy Goodrich. See: Jean McMahon Humez, *Mother's First-Born Daughters: Early Shaker Writings on Women and Religion* (Bloomington and Indianapolis, 1993), 77 n.3.

15 Bishop and Wells, *Testimonies of the Life*, 332–33.

16 Brewer, *Shaker Communities*, 28.

17 Ibid., 51; Marylynn Salmon, *Women and the Law of Property in Early America* (Chapel Hill and London, 1986), 16–18, 23–24. I am indebted to Mark A. Peterson for this reference.

18 Edward Deming Andrews, *The Gift to Be Simple: Songs, Dances and Rituals of the American Shakers* (1940; repr., New York, 1962), 21.

19 Garrett, *Spirit Possession*, 227.

20 Ibid., 229.

21 Brewer, *Shaker Communities*, 26.

22 Garrett, *Spirit Possession*, 230.

23 Brown, *People Called Shakers*, 24.

24 Brewer, *Shaker Communities*, 69.

25 Ibid., 21.

26 Garrett, *Spirit Possession*, 228.

27 Rufus Bishop, Mount Lebanon, NY, to David Darrow, Union Village, OH, July 2, 1817, OClWHi, Shaker Collection, IV:A-33.

28 Andrews, *People Called Shakers*, 106.

29 Hervey Elkins, *Fifteen Years in Senior Order of the Shakers: A Narration of Facts, Concerning That Singular People . . .* (Hanover, 1853), 21.

30 See Appendix Chapter I:2.

31 Brewer, *Shaker Communities*, 11.

32 Elkins, *Fifteen Years*, 20. For women deciding at twenty-one, see Deborah E. Burns, *Shaker Cities of Peace, Love, and Union, A History of the Hancock Bishopric* (Hanover and London, 1993), 141; 173–74.

33 Edward Deming Andrews, *The Community Industries of the Shakers* (1933; facsimile repr., Charlestown, 1971), 24.

34 Ibid., 26, quoting Charles Edson Robinson, *A Concise History of the United Society of Believers Called Shakers* (East Canterbury, 1893), 28.

35 Marjorie Proctor-Smith, *Women in Shaker Community and Worship: A Feminist Analysis of the Uses of Religious Symbolism* (Lewiston and Queenston, 1985), 44; Stephen J. Stein, *The Shaker Experience in America: A History of the United Society of Believers* (New Haven, 1992), 52–53.

36 Lucy Wright, "Mother Lucy's Sayings Spoken at Different Times and Under Various Circumstances," ed. with and introduction by Frances A Carr, *The Shaker Quarterly*, 8 (Winter, 1968), 103.

37 The year cited was 1798; Brown, *People Called Shakers*, 15.

38 Meacham, *Concise Statement*, 6–10; Ezekiel's vision: *Bible*, Ezekiel 47.

39 Joseph Meacham, "A Collection of the Writings of Father Joseph Meacham, Respecting Church Order and government; Evidently intended for waymarks, for all who were or should be called in spiritual or temporal care, In the Church," copied by Rufus Bishop, [1850]. OClWHi, Shaker Collec-tion, VII:B-59; Brewer, *Shaker Communities*, 25.

40 Garrett, *Spirit Possession*, 231.

41 Brown, *People Called Shakers*, 48; strong meat: 48, 272.

42 Humez, *Mother's First-Born Daughters*, 99.

43 Bishop and Wells, *Testimonies of the Life*, 2.

44 Garrett, *Spirit Possession*, 233–34.

45 Ibid., 235–36; Brewer, *Shaker Communities*, 28.

46 Brewer, *Shaker Communities*, 28, 30.

47 Jerry Grant in conversation with the author, April 20, 1991.

48 Humez, *Mother's First-Born Daughters*, 71, 85.

49 Sally M. Promey, *Spiritual Spectacles: Vision and Image in Mid-Nineteenth-Century Shakerism* (Bloomington and Indianapolis, 1993), 91.

50 Henry C. Blinn, "Hannah Goodrich," *The Shaker Manifesto*, 12 (July, 1882), 148; (August, 1882), 173. The saddle is now at Sabbathday Lake.

51 David Richards, "At the Museum: Mother Sarah Kendall's Saddlebags," *The Shaker Quarterly*, 17 (Summer, 1989), 67–68.

52 Humez, *Mother's First-Born Daughters*, 189–90.

53 Thomas D. Clark and F. Gerald Ham, *Pleasant Hill and Its Shakers* (1968; repr., Pleasant Hill, 1987), 5–6.

54 Brewer, *Shaker Communities*, xx.

55 Stein, *Shaker Experience*, 111.

56 Flo Morse, *The Shakers and the World's People* (Hanover and London, 1980), 47.

57 Ibid., 179.

58 This is an estimation by Jerry Grant based on his reading of Shaker documents; Grant in a letter to the author, May 23, 1993.

59 Richard Bushnell, New Lebanon, NY, to Archabald [i.e. Archibald] Meacham, Watervliet, NY, August 10, 1843, OClWHi, Shaker Collection, IV:A-38.

60 Beverly Gordon, *Shaker Textile Arts* (1980; repr., Hanover and London, 1983), 147.

61 Theodore E. Johnson, "The 'Millennial Laws' of 1821," *The Shaker Quarterly*, 7 (Summer, 1967) 36–37.

CHAPTER III

1 Clarke Garrett, *Spirit Possession and Popular Religion: From the Camisards to the Shakers* (Baltimore and London, 1987), 227.

2 William Bentley, *The Diary of William Bentley, D.D.*, 4 vols. (Salem, 1907), II, 153.

3 Garrett, *Spirit Possession*, 228.

4 Jerry V. Grant and Douglas R. Allen, *Shaker Furniture Makers* (Hanover and London, 1989), 1.

5 Later in the nineteenth century they would see themselves, and others would judge them, as progressive: Elmer Ray Pearson, Julia Neal, and Walter Whitehill, *The Shaker Image* (Hancock, 1974), 58, quotes David Austin Buckingham, 1870s: "Progression is one of the prominent points of our religious faith and we endeavor to make it manifest in things spiritual and temporal"; Charles Wingate, "Shaker Sanitation," *The Plumber and Sanitary Engineer*, 3 (September, 1880), 397. "The Shakers are a progressive people, and are always experimenting with new devices."

6 Edward Deming Andrews, *The Community Industries of the Shakers* (1933; facsimile repr., Charlestown, 1971), 29–30.

7 Mary Lyn Ray, "A Reappraisal of Shaker Furniture and Society," *Winterthur Portfolio* 8 (Charlottesville, 1973), 113.

8 Edward Deming Andrews and Faith Andrews, *Shaker Furniture: The Craftsmanship of an American Communal Sect* (1937; repr. New York, 1950), 42.

9 "Society Record," *The Shaker*, 6 (May, 1876), 40.

10 Andrews and Andrews, *Shaker Furniture*, 36. Many modern scholars continue the Andrewses' misreading of Shaker work practices, for example, Kenneth L. Ames, in an unpublished paper delivered to the American Studies Association Conference, Toronto, 1989. See also the discussion with Carl Andre in Chapter X.

11 Edward Deming Andrews and Faith Andrews, *Work and Worship Among the Shakers: Their Craftsmanship and Economic Order* (1974; repr., Greenwich, 1982), 103.

12 Ibid., 104.

13 Grant and Allen, *Shaker Furniture Makers*, 17–19.

14 Isaac N. Youngs, "A statement of those who have worked in some of the principal occupations, among the brethren," [c. 1850], in [Journal of Daily Occurrences, Church Family, New Lebanon, NY, 1834–1846], N, Shaker Collection, Ms. No. 13,500.

15 According to the present owner, Andrews sold the table, possibly as soon as he realized it was not Shaker-made, to a collector-dealer from whom the present owner purchased it. He reports that when he asked Faith Andrews about the piece, she avoided answering the question. Conversation: February 7, 1994.

16 For example, Catalogue Number 1350, *Americana*, Skinner's Auction Gallery, (Bolton, October 27, 1990), Lot Number 28.

17 Bill Samaha in conversation with the author, October 28, 1993.

18 Charles F. Hummel, *With Hammer in Hand* (Charlottesville, 1968), 97. They were used by Nathaniel Dominy V. The left and center have the initials "JD," and may originally have belonged to John Dominy, younger brother of Nathaniel Dominy's father.

19 Larrie Currie in conversation with the author, April 7, 1991.

20 I wish to thank Glendyne Wergland for bring-

ing this material to my attention: Isaac N. Youngs, "Narrative of Various Events. Beginning April 1815," DLC, Shaker Collection, Ms. No. 42. A typescript translation of the personal shorthand or code used by Youngs in this journal is available at the Hancock Shaker Village library.

21 Ibid., July 26, 1820.

22 Henry C. Blinn, "Hannah Goodrich," *The Shaker Manifesto*, 12 (August, 1882), 173.

23 Charles R. Muller and Timothy D. Rieman, *The Shaker Chair* (Canal Winchester, 1984), 63–65.

24 Alfred Collier, "[Journal] Continued from Book No 1, [December 1856–February 1859, Church Family, Harvard, MA]," OClWHi, Shaker Collection, V:B-219.

25 "Table Covers," *Fessenden's Silk Manual and Practical Farmer*, 2 (July, 1836), 37. The Shaker Museum and Library, Old Chatham, New York, owns a large basket lined with material that fits this desription.

26 Jerry Grant, "Forces Behind the Forms: Doctrines, Personalities, and Styles that Affected Shaker Designs." Unpublished talk presented as part of *Gift of the Spirit: The Life and Art of the Shakers*, Museum of Fine Arts, Boston, April 5, 1990.

27 Thomas Damon, Hancock, MA, to George Willcox, Enfield, CT, December 23, 1846, OClWHi, Shaker Collection, IV:A-19.

28 Timothy D. Rieman and Jean M. Burks, *The Complete Book of Shaker Furniture* (New York, 1993), fixed doors: 249; one drawer made to look like two drawers: 206, fig. 146.

29 Grant and Allen, *Shaker Furniture Makers*, page 41, illustrates a school desk the author thought to be made in Kentucky following these instructions. Larrie Currie, in a letter to the author, May 24, 1995, questioned that conclusion since it is of pine, a wood not used for furniture made at Pleasant Hill. She also reported that the name Samantha Newton is written in pencil under one of the desk tops. Samantha Newton was brought to the Mount Lebanon Church Family February 4, 1869, and left August 16, 1873. Therefore the desk illustrated in that volume must have been made at Lebanon.

30 Rufus Bishop, New Lebanon, NY, to David Darrow, Union Village, OH, July 2, 1817, OClWHi, Shaker Collection, IV:A-33.

31 Robert P. Emlen, *Shaker Village Views* (Hanover and London, 1987), 119–20.

32 Edwin A. Churchill, *Simple Forms and Vivid Colors: An Exhibition of Maine Painted Furniture, 1800–1850 . . .* (Augusta, 1983), 17–18; 35 n. 34.

33 For a similar Sabbathday Lake stand still owned by that community, see Theodore E. Johnson, *Hands to Work and Hearts to God: The Shaker Tradition in Maine* (Brunswick, 1969), fig. 10; a stand with ridged feet appears in fig. 29.

34 *Close Ties: The Relationship Between Kentucky Shaker Furniture Makers and Their Worldly Contemporaries* (Shaker Museum at South Union, Kentucky, 1994), 33.

35 Joseph Downs, *American Furniture: Queen Anne and Chippendale Periods* (New York, 1952), fig. 181.

36 John T. Kirk, *American Furniture and the British Tradition to 1830* (New York, 1982), 95–118.

37 Beverly Gordon, *Shaker Textile Arts* (1980; repr., Hanover and London, 1983), 149.

38 Benjamin S. Youngs, South Union, KY, to the

Ministry, Elders, and Deacons, at Lebanon, and Hancock, February 26, 1818, OClWHi, Shaker Collection, IV:A-52.

39 June Sprigg, *Shaker: Masterworks of utilitarian design created between 1800 and 1875 by the master craftsmen and craftswomen of America's foremost communal religious sect* (Katonah, 1983), 50.

40 Rieman and Burks, *Complete Book of Shaker Furniture*, 300, quoting "Daily Record of Events of the Church Family," [Union Village, OH], July 13, 1847, OClWHi, Shaker Collection, V:B-230.

41 Ibid., 346.

42 Ibid., 315.

CHAPTER IV

1 [Rufus Bishop and Seth Y. Wells], eds., *Testimonies of the Life, Character, Revelation and Doctrines of Our Ever Blessed Mother Ann Lee, and the Elders with Her; Through Whom the Word of Eternal Life Was Opened In This Day of Christ's Second Appearing: Collected from Living Witnesses* (Hancock, 1816), 265.

2 [A covenant written by the Deacons and Elders of the Church Family, New Lebanon, NY], November 23, 1802, NOC, Ms. No. 10,476. Another manuscript copy dated "Enfield February 7th 1803," titled "A Covanant Elders & Decons Coments, 1803," is in the Emma B. King Library, Shaker Museum and Library, NOC, Ms. No. 12,181.

3 Thomas Brown, *An Account of the People Called, Shakers: Their Faith, Doctrines, and Practice, Exemplified in the Life, Conversations, and Experience of the Author during the Time He Belonged to the Society. To Which is Affixed a History of Their Rise and Progress to the Present Day* (Troy, 1812), 320–21.

4 Isaac N. Youngs, "Narrative of Various Events. Beginning April 1815," March 16, 1818, DLC, Shaker Collection, Ms. No., 42.

5 [Journal Kept On a Trip To the Eastern Societies By the Ministry of Pleasant Hill and South Union, June 9–August 7, 1869], OClWHi, Shaker Collection, V:B-228.

6 Edward Deming Andrews and Faith Andrews, *Shaker Furniture: The Craftsmanship of an American Communal Sect* (1937; repr., New York, 1950), 85.

7 Ibid., 95.

8 [Journal of Domestic Occurrences, Church Family, New Lebanon, NY, 1814–1833], March 17, 20, 1825, OClWHi, Shaker Collection, V:B-68.

9 Andrews and Andrews, *Shaker Furniture*, 14 n.

10 Brother Arnold Hadd in conversation with the author, July 3, 1988.

11 "Millennial Laws, or Gospel Statutes and Ordinances Adapted to the Day of Christ's Second Appearing . . . . Revised and Re-established By the Ministry and Elders Oct'r 1845," Part IV.20, published in Edward Deming Andrews, *The People Called Shakers: A Search for the Perfect Society* (1953; repr., enlarged ed. New York, 1963), 287.

12 Ibid., Part II, Section X.2, quoted in Andrews, *People Called Shakers*, 271–72.

13 Ibid., Part II, Section XVIII.5,9, quoted in Andrews, *People Called Shakers*, 279.

14 Ibid., Part II, Section XII.4, quoted in Andrews, *People Called Shakers*, 274; Isaac N. Youngs, *A Short Abridgment of the Rules of Music* (1843; New Lebanon, 1846).

15 "Millennial Laws . . . 1845," Part I, Section II:7, quoted in Andrews, *People Called Shakers*, 255.

16 Brown, *People Called Shakers*, 293–94.

17 Andrews and Andrews, *Shaker Furniture*, 21.

18 [Calvin Green and Seth Y. Wells], *A Summary View of the Millennial Church or United Society of Believers . . .* (Albany, 1823), 248–49.

19 Marjorie Proctor-Smith, "Artifact or Icon? Clues for a Theology of Shaker Design." Unpublished paper present at *Shaker Furniture and Design: Challenging the Canon*, Old Chatham, September 26, 1987.

20 The red stain is now most easily perceived on the upper-most part of the attic balustrade.

21 *Bible*, I Kings 7:2–22. The King James Version calls the pillars brass; the 1952 Revised Standard Version sites them as bronze; Revelation, 21:12–22; [Benjamin Seth Youngs], *The Testimony of Christ's Second Appearing Containing a General Statement of All Things Pertaining to the Faith and Practice of the Church of God in This Latter-Day* (1808; 4th ed., Albany, 1856), 395–96; 439.

22 "Millennial Laws . . . 1845," Part IV:28, quoted in Andrews, *People Called Shakers*, 288.

23 Andrews and Andrews, *Shaker Furniture*, 68; Jerry Grant in conversation with the author, May 23, 1991.

24 Edward Deming Andrews and Faith Andrews, *Work and Worship Among the Shakers: Their Craftsmanship and Economic Order* (1974; repr., Greenwich, 1982), 105–07; Beverly Gordon, *Shaker Textile Arts* (1980; repr., Hanover and London, 1983), 188–94; Andrews, *People Called Shakers*, 149–50.

25 [Isaac N. Youngs], "History of the Church of Mt. Lebanon, N.Y. No. 12. The Tailors," edited by Henry C. Blinn, *The Manifesto*, 20 (June, 1890), 122.

26 Gordon, *Shaker Textiles*, 152–53.

27 Ibid., 100.

28 Andrews and Andrews, *Shaker Furniture*, 54.

29 Jerry Grant, "Forces Behind the Forms: Doctrines, Personalities, and Styles that Affected Shaker Designs." Unpublished talk presented as part of *Gift of the Spirit: The Life and Art of the Shakers*, Museum of Fine Arts, Boston, April 5, 1990.

30 Andrews and Andrews, *Work and Worship*, 153.

31 Jerry V. Grant and Douglas R. Allen, *Shaker Furniture Makers* (Hanover and London, 1989), 49.

32 Sister Marcia [Bullard], "Shaker Industries," *Good Housekeeping* 43 (July, 1906), 33–37.

33 Philemon Stewart, *A Holy, Sacred and Divine Roll and Book; from the Lord God of Heaven, to the Inhabitants of Earth . . .* (Canterbury, 1843), 333.

34 Ibid., 286.

35 Ibid., 283.

36 Jean McMahon Humez, *Mother's First-Born Daughters: Early Shaker Writings on Women and Religion* (Bloomington and Indianapolis, 1993), 241.

37 Ibid., 269.

38 Andrews and Andrews, *Shaker Furniture*, 50, quoting from "The Holy Laws of Zion."

39 Charles Nordhoff, *The Communistic Societies of the United States: From Personal Visit and Observation* (1875; repr., New York, 1966), 164–65.

40 Ibid., 186.

41 Hervey Elkins, *Fifteen Years in Senior Order of the Shakers: A Narration of Facts, Concerning That Singular People . . .* (Hanover, 1853), 56.

42 Ibid., 22, 25, 38–39. Further use of the word

beauty: "I lived with my parents in the Novitiate Order for about four months. I saw them often and conversed freely upon the harmony and exoteric beauty of our new habitation . . . . I had listened to the choir of musicians who, in that beautiful mansion almost every evening . . . . when the beautiful granite walls and blue roofs appeared more distinctly," 38; "beautiful white pine, and not a knot, blemish . . . . Within those beautiful polished walls are free stone ovens," 39.

43 Charles Dickens, *American Notes for General Circulation* (1842; New York, 1985), 195–97; Robert P. Emlen, "The Shaker Dance Prints," *Journal of the American Historical Print Collectors Society*, 17 (Autumn, 1992), 15.

44 Nathaniel Hawthorne, *The Letters, 1813–1843*, ed. Thomas Woodson, et al. (The Centenary Edition of the Works of Nathaniel Hawthorne, Columbus, 1984), 212–13.

45 Ibid., 218.

46 Ibid., 220.

47 Nathaniel Hawthorne, *The American Notebooks*, ed. Claude M. Simpson (1932; repr., Columbus, 1972), 465.

48 I am indebted for my understanding of Hawthorne to William Vance, who read this section and suggested various changes, and Edwin Haviland Miller's *Salem Is My Dwelling Place: A Life of Nathaniel Hawthorne* (Iowa City, 1991), 6–8, 90–91, 311, 314, 342–43, 348.

49 Benson John Lossing, "The Shakers," *Harper's New Monthly Magazine*, 15 (July, 1857), 166, 167, 169, 175, 177.

50 John S. Dwight, "The Shakers at New Lebanon," *The Harbinger*, 5 (August 14, 1847), 157.

CHAPTER V

1 Jean McMahon Humez, *Mother's First-Born Daughters: Early Shaker Writings on Women and Religion* (Bloomington and Indianapolis, 1993), 172 n. 3.

2 Drawing of the *Holy City*, Philadelphia Museum of Art 63-160-5. "Explanation of the Holy City with its various parts and appendixes pointed out. Drawn and partly written March 16th, 1843," Philadelphia Museum of Art 63-160-5a.

3 Robert F. W. Meader, *Illustrated Guide to Shaker Furniture* (New York, 1972), 73, fig. 141.

4 Hugh Honour, *Neo-classicism* (1968; repr., Harmondsworth, 1979), 84–85.

5 Jean-Marie Pérouse de Montclos, *Etienne-Louis Boullée (1728–1799)* (New York, 1974), figs. 57–59, 52.

6 William H. Pierson, Jr., *American Buildings and Their Architects: The Colonial and Neoclassical Styles* (1970; repr., New York, 1976), 347.

7 David R. Starbuck and Margaret Supplee Smith, *Historical Survey of Canterbury Shaker Village* (Boston, 1979), 81.

8 William Bentley, *The Diary of William Bentley, D.D.*, 4 vols. (Salem, 1907), II, 150.

9 Starbuck and Smith, *Historical Survey of Canterbury*, 93.

10 [Journal of Domestic Occurrences, kept by the Elder Sisters, Church Family, New Lebanon, NY, 1780–1841], June 20, 1824, OClWHi, Shaker Collection, V:B-60.

11 Calvin Green, "Biographic Memoir of the Life and Experience of Calvin Green . . ." [1861–1869],

June 20, 1824, OClWHi, Shaker Collection, VI:B-28; Calvin Green to Samuel Turner, July 7, 1824, copied in "Communities Expressed by diferent Sources," NNASPR American Society for Psychical Research. For further understanding of this building see: Jerry V. Grant, *Noble But Plain: The Shaker Meetinghouse at Mount Lebanon*. Shaker, [2]. Old Chatham: 1994.

12 Horatio Gates Spofford, *A Gazetteer of the State of New-York: Embracing an Ample Survey and Description of its Counties, Towns, Cities, Villages . . .* (Troy, 1825), 341–42.

13 Benson John Lossing, "The Shakers," *Harper's New Monthly Magazine*, 15 (July, 1857), 167; Charles Nordhoff, *The Communistic Societies of the United States: From Personal Visit and Observation* (1875; repr., New York, 1966), 155.

14 I am indebted to Gib Vincent for this information included in a letter of December 27, 1993. The Van Bergen overmantel is at the New York State Historical Association, Cooperstown, NY.

15 John T. Hanou, *A Round Indiana: Round Barns in the Hoosier State* (West Lafayette, 1993), 6.

16 John Michael Vlach, *Back of the Big House: The Architecture of Plantation Slavery* (Chapel Hill, 1993), 23–24, figs. 2.16, 2.17, 2.18.

17 Donald Martin Reynolds, *The Architecture of New York* (New York, 1984), 141–42; Miriam Stoffer, "John Vanderlyn's Panorama of the Palace and Gardens of Versailles," *NAHO*, 7 (Fall, 1974), 7–10.

18 Pierson, *American Buildings*, 329.

19 Jerry Grant in conversation with the author, August 21, 1990; Charles H. Walker, "Plan of a Stock Barn," *Moore's Rural New Yorker*, 8 (July 11, 1857), 221.

20 "Shaker Barn," *New England Farmer*, 5 (January 26, 1827), 215.

21 Edward Deming Andrews, *The Gift to Be Simple: Songs, Dances and Rituals of the American Shakers* (1940; repr, New York, 1962), 147, quoting Isaac Newton Youngs's 1856 manuscript "A Concise View of the Church of God and Christ on Earth ..." DeWint, the Edward Deming Andrews Shaker Collection, 861.

22 Clarke Garrett, *Spirit Possession and Popular Religion: From the Camisards to the Shakers* (Baltimore and London, 1987), 232–33.

23 Daniel W. Patterson, *The Shaker Spiritual* (Princeton, 1979), 105–106.

24 Andrews, *Gift to Be Simple*, 149–50.

25 "Arrangement of Ranks for Society meetings in large meeting House, Mt. Lebanon, N.Y.," OClWHi, Shaker Collection, I:A-8.

26 Patterson, *Shaker Spiritual*, 272.

27 Marjorie Proctor-Smith, *Women in Shaker Community and Worship: A Feminist Analysis of the Uses of Religious Symbolism* (Lewiston and Queenston, 1985); 135.

28 Andrews, *Gift to Be Simple*, 150–51.

29 Edward Deming Andrews, *The People Called Shakers: A Search for the Perfect Society* (1953; repr., enlarged ed. New York, 1963), 148, quoting [Barnabas Bates], *Peculiarities of the Shakers, Described in a Series of Letters from Lebanon Springs, in the year 1832 . . .* (New York, 1832), 59.

30 Andrews, *Gift to Be Simple*, 149; Proctor-Smith, *Women in Shaker Community*, 135.

31 La Marquise de la Tour du Pin, ed. and trans. by Walter Geer, *Recollections of the Revolution and*

the Empire (New York, 1920), 215–18.

32 The pattern in the Canterbury meetinghouse floor was brought to my attention by Jerry Grant.

33 Horace Greeley, "A Sabbath with the Shakers," *Knickerbocker*, 11 (June, 1838), 537.

CHAPTER VI

1 Jerry V. Grant and Douglas R. Allen, *Shaker Furniture Makers* (Hanover and London, 1989), 116; 6.

2 Jerry V. Grant, "Forces Behind the Forms: Doctrines, Personalities, and Styles that Affected Shaker Designs." Unpublished talk presented as part of *Gift of the Spirit: The Life and Art of the Shakers*, Museum of Fine Arts, Boston, April 5, 1990. The story was told to Grant by the Shaker apostate, Olive Hayden Austin, in the early 1980s.

3 See Appendix: Chapter VII:2; Chapter XIII: 20.

4 Ibid., Chapter VII:3; VII:4; VII:7; VII:12.

5 Hervey Elkins, *Fifteen Years in Senior Order of the Shakers: A Narration of Facts, Concerning That Singular People . . .* (Hanover, 1853), 39–40.

6 Grant and Allen, *Shaker Furniture Makers*, 37.

7 Joseph G. Dreiss, *Gari Melchers, His Works in the Belmont Collection* (Charlottesville, 1984), pl. 4; fig. 12.

8 Grant and Allen, *Shaker Furniture Makers*, 37–38.

9 "Millennial Laws, or Gospel Statutes and Ordinances Adapted to the Day of Christ's Second Appearing . . . . Revised and Re-established By the Ministry and Elders Oct'r 1845," Part II, Section XII, published in Edward Deming Andrews, *The People Called Shakers: A Search for the Perfect Society* (1953; repr. enlarged ed. New York, 1963), 273–74.

10 Grant and Allen, *Shaker Furniture Makers*, 151.

11 Beverly Gordon, *Shaker Textile Arts* (1980; repr., Hanover and London , 1983), 93; Jerry Grant in conversation with the author, June 3, 1989.

12 Freegift Wells, "Daily Journal, [Church Family, Watervliet, NY, 1819–1820]," November 27, 1819, OClWHi, Shaker Collection, V:B-287; Priscilla J. Brewer, *Shaker Communities, Shaker Lives* (Hanover and London, 1986), 69.

13 Gordon, *Shaker Textiles*, 10.

14 Daniel W. Patterson, *Gift Drawings and Gift Songs: A Study of Two Forms of Shaker Inspiration* (Sabbathday Lake, 1983), 51–52.

15 Edward Deming Andrews, *The People Called Shakers: A Search for the Perfect Society* (1953; repr., enlarged ed. New York, 1963), 24.

16 Robley Edward Whitson, ed., *The Shakers: Two Centuries of Spiritual Reflection* (New York, Ramsey, Toronto, 1983), 310; Andrews, *People Called Shakers*, 24.

17 William Deming, Hancock, MA, to [Benjamin Seth Youngs] South Union, KY, January 8, 1832, OClWHi, Shaker Collection, IV:B-35, 215–17.

18 Edward Deming Andrews and Faith Andrews, *Shaker Furniture: The Craftsmanship of an American Communal Sect* (1937; repr., New York, 1950), 77; June Sprigg and David Larkin, *Shaker Life, Work, and Art* (New York, 1987), 89.

19 Ministry, Union Village, OH, to Rufus Bishop [Ministry], New Lebanon, NY, April 8, 1845, OClWHi, Shaker Collection, IV:A-72.

20 Wallace Nutting, *Furniture Treasury*, 2 vols.

(1928; repr., New York, 1954), fig. 352.

21 *Americana*, Catalogue 1332, Skinner's Auction Gallery (Bolton, July 16, 1990), Lots 57, 58.

22 Barry A. Greenlaw, *New England Furniture at Williamsburg* (Williamsburg, 1974), fig. 78; Dean A. Fales, Jr., *The Furniture of Historic Deerfield* (New York, 1976), figs. 425, 426.

23 Robert F. W. Meader, *Illustrated Guide to Shaker Furniture* (New York, 1972), 59, fig. 124. The sides of the fall-front section were built out after the initial construction, and this moved the fall-front near the front edge. It now needs pulled out drawers to support it when in use.

24 "Millennial Laws . . . 1845," Part III, Section V.4, in Andrews, *People Called Shakers*, 283.

25 Robert E. Kinnaman and Brian A. Ramaekers, Inc., [advertisement], *The Magazine Antiques*, 137 (January, 1990), 146.

26 Grant and Allen, *Shaker Furniture Makers*, 103–04, 8, 53; letter to the author, April 26, 1995.

27 Rieman and Burks, *Complete Book of Shaker Furniture*, 175.

28 Robert Wilkins, Suzanne Courcier, Timothy Rieman, and Jerry Grant inspected this piece with one of the boxes removed.

29 Grant and Allen, *Shaker Furniture Makers,* 79, figs. 52, 53.

30 Gustave Nelson reported, in conversation with the author, that the piece once attached to the left side was in the Karl Mendel Collection, but it did not appear in the auction catalogue when the Mendel Collection was sold in 1988.

31 Charles Nordhoff, *The Communistic Societies of the United States: From Personal Visit and Observation* (1875; repr., New York, 1966), 213.

32 Gordon, *Shaker Textiles*, 99.

33 [Rufus Bishop and Seth Y. Wells], eds., *Testimonies of the Life, Character, Revelation and Doctrines of Our Ever Blessed Mother Ann Lee, and the Elders with Her; Through Whom the Word of Eternal Life Was Opened In This Day of Christ's Second Appearing: Collected from Living Witnesses* (Hancock, 1816), 268; Thomas Brown, *An Account of the People Called, Shakers: Their Faith, Doctrines, and Practice, Exemplified in the Life, Conversations, and Experience of the Author during the Time He Belonged to the Society. To Which is Affixed a History of Their Rise and Progress to the Present Day* (Troy, 1812), long tables: 360.

34 William Deming, Hancock, MA, to Benjamin Seth Youngs, South Union, KY, January 8, 1832, OClWHi, Shaker Collection, IV:B-35, 216.

35 Rieman and Burks, *Complete Book of Shaker Furniture*, 308, fig. 274.

36 Reported by Jerry Grant to the author after Grant's conversation with Brother Arnold Hadd, September 1, 1993. Brother Arnold also remarked that Brother Delmer Wilson kept Sabbathday Lake from moving away from silent meals during his lifetime.

37 Andrews, *People Called Shakers*, 183–84.

38 Richard McNemar, *A Selection of Hymns and Poems; for the use of Believers. Collected from sundry Authors, By Philos Harmoniae* [pseudo] (Watervliet, Ohio, 1833), 163.

39 Hancock Shaker Village, Inc., curatorial records.

40 Edward Deming Andrews, *The Community Industries of the Shakers* (1933; facsimile repr.,

Charlestown, 1971), 130–39. Andrews writes that the flat broom was a Shaker invention, but he does not cite a source for the assertion, 130.

41 Ibid., 130, quoting Theo. Kalandri, "Elder Goepper tells of the Philosophy of Shakerism," *The Manifesto* 17 (June, 1887), 138.

42 Ibid., 131.

43 Daniel W. Patterson, *Gift Drawings and Gift Songs: A Study of Two Forms of Shaker Inspiration* (Sabbathday Lake, 1983), pl. V.

44 Augusta Stone, [Journal, Mount Lebanon, NY, 1885–1888], August 4, 1887, NOC, Ms. No. 10,457.

45 Edward Deming Andrews and Faith Andrews, *Religion in Wood: A Book of Shaker Furniture* (Bloomington and London, 1966), x; xiii.

46 See Appendix: Chapter XIII:11–14.

47 "Millennial Laws . . . 1845," Part IV:29, in Andrews, *People Called Shakers*, 288.

48 Christopher Gilbert, *The Life and Work of Thomas Chippendale*, 2 vols. (New York, 1978), II: fig. 507.

49 Shaker Museum and Library, curatorial records, Accession Number, 7,835.

50 Grant and Allen, *Shaker Furniture Makers*, 31.

51 Susan L. Buck, Society for the Preservation of New England Antiquities Conservation Center, reporting to the author on her study of a bed belonging to Ken Hakuta, and one owned by the Winterthur Museum, May 5, 1993.

52 Brown, *People Called Shakers*, 360; op. cit., "Millennial Laws . . . 1845," Part II, Section VII:5, 8, in Andrews, *People Called Shakers*, 269–70.

53 Flo Morse, *The Shakers and the World's People* (Hanover and London, 1980), 194.

54 Grant and Allen, *Shaker Furniture Makers*, 104.

55 Bishop and Wells, *Testimonies of the Life*, 208.

56 "Millennial Laws . . . 1845," Part II, Section X:3, in Andrews, *People Called Shakers*, 272.

57 Grant and Allen, *Shaker Furniture Makers*, 109.

58 Gordon, *Shaker Textiles*, 149.

59 "A Visit to the Shakers," *Ladies Magazine*, 2 (September, 1829), 411–12.

60 Gordon, *Shaker Textiles*, 178.

61 Leonard Brooks, Sabbathday Lake, ME, to John T. Kirk, Brookline, MA, August 10, 1988.

62 "Millennial Laws . . . 1845," Part II, Section XVII:3, in Andrews, *People Called Shakers*, 277.

63 Sewing machines are mentioned in Shaker records from the early 1850s, for example: Isaac Newton Youngs' "Personal Journal," June 6, 1853. OClWHi V:B-134.

64 [Christopher Gilbert], *An Exhibition of Common Furniture: Illustrating Sub-groups within the Vernacular Tradition* (Temple Newsam, Leeds, 1982), fig. 6.

65 "Millennial Laws . . . 1845," Part I, Section V:6, in Andrews, *People Called Shakers*, 261. Elizabeth H. Rice, "A Study of Shaker Medical Practices," *The Shaker Messenger* 2, no. 2 (Winter, 1980), 3–8.

66 Fruitlands Museums, curatorial records. Thomas Hammond, [Journal, Church Family, Harvard, MA, 1831–1840], January 13, 1835, OClWHi, Shaker Collection, V:B-40.

67 Clarke Garrett, *Spirit Possession and Popular Religion: From the Camisards to the Shakers* (Balti-

more and London, 1987), 227.

68 "Report on Awards. International exhibition, Philadelphia, 1876." NOC Ms. No. 5115.

69 Andrews, *Community Industries*, 88.

70 Ibid., 107.

71 Shaker Museum and Library, curatorial records, accession number 4,625, bull blinder.

72 Shaker Museum and Library, curatorial records, drip stone, accession number 17098.

73 "Mr. Alderman's Wheelchair," *Maine Antique Digest* (August, 1989), 13-E.

CHAPTER VII

1 I am indebted to Greg Leftwich for clarifying the role of color on ancient sculpture.

2 William Salmon, M.D. *Polygraphice: or, The Arts of Drawing, Engraving, Etching, Limning, Painting, Vernishing, Japaning, Gilding, &c.*, 2 vols. (London, 1675).

3 George Hepplewhite, *The Cabinet-Maker and Upholsterer's Guide* (3rd ed. 1794; facsimile repr., New York, 1969), 2.

4 Thomas Sheraton, *The Cabinet Dictionary*, 2 vols. (1803; facsimile repr., New York, 1970), II:426-27.

5 Richard M. Candee, "Preparing and Mixing Colors in 1812," *The Magazine Antiques*, 113 (April, 1978), 849–53.

6 A[ndrew] J[ackson] Downing, *The Architecture of Country Houses* (1850; facsimile repr., New York, 1969), 367.

7 During her review of the Shaker material at the Western Reserve Historical Society, Sally M. Promey found the papers of a number of former Masons who kept their Masonic documents when they became Believers, and that these regularly display Masonic symbols; conversation with the author, June 29, 1995. Parley P. Pratt, *Autobiography of Parley P. Pratt . . .* (Salt Lake City, 1938; repr. 1985), 30–31. I am indebted for this citation to William Moore, who suggested John L. Brooke, *The Refiner's Fire . . .* (Cambridge, 1994), 61, which quoted the autobiography.

8 William J. Haskett, *Shakerism Unmasked, or the History of the Shakers . . .* (Pittsfield, 1828), 158-59.

9 Mary Marshall Dyer, *The Rise and Progress of the Serpent From the Garden of Eden to the Present Day . . .* (Concord, 1847), 190.

10 Melvin W. Chase, Concord, NH, to Robert F.W. Meader, Old Chatham, NY. Letter confirming that Joseph Dyer had been a member of the Masons. NOC, accession number, 17,325.

11 Information given to Robert F. W. Meader by Hazel Spencer Phillips, author of *Richard the Shaker*, 1973, NOC, curatorial records on Masonic membership.

12 James Stevens Curl, *The Art and Architecture of Freemasonry* (Woodstock, 1993), 46–78.

13 *Jachin and Boaz* (1767; repr. in the United States, 1801), 15.

14 Susan Montgomery was the first person to suggest to me a possible link in the meanings of colors between Shaker and Masonic practices. The discussion of the Masons and Masonic color is indebted to Henry Wilson Coil, *Coil's Masonic Encyclopedia* (New York, 1961); J. C. Cooper, *An Illustrated Encyclopedia of Traditional Symbols* (1973; repr. London, New York, 1992); Albert G. Mackey, M.D. *An Encyclopedia of Freemasonry and Its Kin-*

dred Sciences . . . (Philadelphia, 1884). Edward Deming Andrews, *Visions of the Heavenly Sphere: A Study in Shaker Religious Art*, (Charlottesville, 1969), 79 n.11, mentioned the nineteenth century Masonic frescoes on the walls of Hall's Tavern, Cheshire, Massachusetts. William Moore and John Hamilton read the sections on the Masons, suggested additions and pointed out inaccuracies.

15 I am indebted for much of the information in this section to J. J. Gerald McCue, Robert Wilkins, Suzanne Courcier, Jerry Grant, Willis Henry, and Sam Pennington.

16 Edward Deming Andrews and Faith Andrews, "Craftsmanship of an American Religious Sect," *The Magazine Antiques*, 14 (August, 1928), 132–36.

17 "Explanation of the Holy City with its various parts and appendixes pointed out. Drawn and partly written March 16th 1843," Philadelphia Museum of Art 63-160-5a.

18 Calvin Green, "Biographic Memoir of the Life and Experience of Calvin Green . . ." Copy by Alonzo G. Hollister [1861–1869], OClWHi, Shaker Collection, VI:B-31, p. 567.

19 Calvin Green, "Discourses," DLC, Shaker Collection, MS. Number 76, 33–34. A note added by Alonzo G. Hollister explains this was taken from Green's "Discourses Illustrating the System of the Gospel."

20 Brother Arnold Hadd suggested this is a preparatory drawing in a conversation with the author, May 18, 1995.

21 It is owned by the Shaker Museum and Library, Accession Number 1,108, and is pictured in black and white in Daniel W. Patterson, *The Shaker Spiritual* (Princeton, 1979), 50.

22 Beverly Gordon, *Shaker Textile Arts* (1980; repr., Hanover and London, 1983), 202–03.

23 Ibid., 14.

24 Ibid., 78–79.

25 Ibid., 196–97.

26 Ibid., 41.

27 "Silk," *New-York American*, 14 (October 15, 1833), [1].

28 Gordon, *Shaker Textiles*, 170.

29 Edward Deming Andrews and Faith Andrews, *Shaker Furniture: The Craftsmanship of an American Communal Sect* (1937; repr., New York, 1950), 117.

30 Gordon, *Shaker Textiles*, 170.

31 "Millennial Laws, or Gospel Statutes and Ordinances Adapted to the Day of Christ's Second Appearing . . . . Revised and Re-established By the Ministry and Elders Oct'r 1845," Part III, Section IV:2, published in Edward Deming Andrews, *The People Called Shakers: A Search for the Perfect Society* (1953; repr., enlarged ed. New York, 1963), 282.

32 Andrews and Andrews, *Shaker Furniture*, 117.

33 Edward Deming Andrews, *The Community Industries of the Shakers* (1933; repr., Charlestown, 1971), 215; 216–17.

34 Susan Buck in conversation with the author, April 29, 1994: Susan Buck, with funding from the Samuel Kress Foundation, has scientifically analyzed the finishes on a great number of Shaker surfaces. She has reviewed this chapter, and parts of other chapters, while in manuscript and has made many corrections and additions. Her research appears in her "Interpreting Paint and Finish Evidence on the Mount Lebanon Shaker Collection," Timothy D.

Rieman, *Shaker, The Art of Craftsmanship*, (Alexandria, 1995), 46–57, and " 'Bedsteads Should be Painted Green.' Shaker Paints and Varnishes," *Old Time New England,* 73 (Fall, 1995), 16–35. Gordon, *Shaker Textile Arts*, 10.

35 See Appendix: Chapter VII:5.

36 Ibid., Chapter XIII:13,14.

37 [Philemon Stewart] "The Holy Orders of the Church. Written by Father Joseph. To the Elders of the Church. At New Lebanon. And coppied agreeable to Father Joseph's word." February 18, 1841, NOC, Ms. No. 12,312, pp. 55–56.

38 Downing, *Country Houses*, 203–4.

39 Ibid., 186–87.

40 Andrews and Andrews, *Shaker Furniture*, 39.

41 Curatorial records, Shaker Museum and Library, Accession Number, 18,647, chest.

42 Christopher Gilbert, ed., *Loudon Furniture Designs*; three sections from J. C. Loudon's *Encyclopaedia of Cottage, Farm and Villa Architecture* (1833; facsimile of rev. 1839, London, 1970), 305.

43 Milton W. Brown et al., *American Art* (New York, 1979), fig. 127.

44 Giles B. Avery, "Memoranda [Diary, Mount Lebanon, NY], 1880," OClWHi, Shaker Collection, V:B-125.

45 Andrews and Andrews, *Shaker Furniture*, 113.

46 Isaac N. Youngs, "A Domestic Journal of Daily Occurrences . . . New Lebanon," [1856–1877], May 1,1861, OC1WHi, Shaker Collection, VB-71.

47 Daniel Boler, Watervliet, NY, to Orren Haskins, New Lebanon, NY, May 23, 1865, OClWHi, Shaker Collection, IV:A-82.

48 Freegift Wells, Watervliet, NY, to Ministry, New Lebanon, NY, [n.d., c.1860s], OClWHi, Shaker Collection, XI:A-1.

49 Andrews and Andrews, *Shaker Furniture*, 118, dated the book about 1849.

50 [David Austin Buckingham], "Receipt Book, Concerning Paints, Stains, Cements, Dyes, Inks, &c.," Watervliet, NY, c. 1860. Passed on by David Austin Buckingham to Rosetta Hendrickson, who inscribed the cover "Rosetta Hendrickson, A present from Eld Austin." She lived at New Lebanon until she moved to Watervliet in 1865. She signed the South Family Covenant in 1873. OClWHi, Shaker Collection, XI:B-14.

51 "Book of Receipts Church Family," OClWHi, Shaker Collection, XI:B-21, copal varnish: 19; [Recipe Book], OClWHi, Shaker Collection, XI:B-1, blue on wood: [16]; pink or red on wood through purple: [16]; "A Book of Receipts belonging To The Second Family Tyringham, Berkshire Co. Mass.," OClWHi, Shaker Collection, XI:B-11, cleaning woodwork: 97.

52 Isaac N. Youngs, "A Domestic Journal of Daily Occurrences . . . New Lebanon," [1834–1846], December 6, 1836, N, Shaker Collection, Ms. No. 13,500.

53 George Finny, "The Shakers' Race," in Joel Benton, "A Poet in the Rough," *Baldwin's Monthly*, 13 (July, 1876), 2.

54 Theodore E. Johnson, *In the Eye of Eternity: Shaker Life and the Work of Shaker Hands* (Gorham, 1983), 10.

55 Sheraton, *Cabinet Dictionary*, 59–62.

56 Robert P. Emlen, *Shaker Village Views* (Hanover and London, 1987), pls. XX, XXII.

57 Gordon, Shaker Textiles, 52.

58 Ibid., 188; 192; 190; 192.

59 Benson John Lossing, "The Shakers," *Harper's New Monthly Magazine*, 15 (July, 1857), 167–68.

60 James S. Prescott, "Shakers. Spirit Manifestations—among them Prior to Their Going to the World," *The Shaker and Shakeress*, 4 (April, 1874), 27. Quoted in Nordhoff, *Communistic Societies*, 235.

61 Daniel Crosman, [Journal, 1860–1880], bound with "A Confidential Journal Kept in the Elders Lot . . . [New Lebanon, NY, 1842–49]," swallowtails: January 21, 1860, OClWHi, Shaker Collection, V:B-136.

62 Rachel Spencer, New Lebanon, NY, to Ruth Farrington, Union Village, OH, July, 1819, OClWHi, Shaker Collection, IV:A-33. Quoted in Humez, *Mother's First-Born Daughters*, 188.

63 [Buckingham] "Receipt Books," [16].

64 Scott Swank in conversation with the author, June 13, 1992.

65 Susan Buck in conversation with the author, April 22, 1993.

66 David R. Starbuck and Margaret Supplee Smith, *Historical Survey of Canterbury Shaker Village* (Boston, 1979), 93; Jerry Grant in conversation with the author, September 1, 1989.

67 Ibid.

68 Jerry Grant, "Collections: [Counter, Canterbury, NH]," *Shaker Museum and Library Report* 1 (October, 1990), [3].

69 Edward E. Nickels, "The Shaker Furniture of Pleasant Hill, Kentucky," *The Magazine Antiques*, 137 (May, 1990), blue chair: 1184.

70 Charles R. Muller and Timothy D. Rieman, *The Shaker Chair* (Canal Winchester, 1984), 100.

71 Gordon, *Shaker Textiles*, 80.

72 Ibid., 58.

73 Ibid., 78.

74 For example, Calke Abbey, Derbyshire, England.

75 *Loudon Furniture Designs*, 321.

76 Eliza Leslie, *The House Book: or a Manual of Domestic Economy for Town and Country* (Philadelphia, 1841), 228.

77 John Ott in conversation with the author, June 20, 1991.

78 "Millennial Laws . . . 1845," Part III, Section IX:4, in Andrews, *People Called Shakers*, 285; John S. Cogdell, [Diary, August 7, 1810 – October 20, 1816]. The Henry Francis du Pont Winterthur Museum and Library, Joseph Downs Collection. I am grateful to Susan Buck for this reference.

79 Andrews, *People Called Shakers*, 49.

80 Sally M. Promey, *Spiritual Spectacles: Vision and Image in Mid-Nineteenth Century Shakerism* (Bloomington and Indianapolis, 1993), 91.

81 Ibid., 92.

82 "Millennial Laws . . . 1845," Part I, Section II:5, in Andrews, *People Called Shakers*, 255.

83 Patterson, *Gift Drawings*, 38.

84 "Life and Sufferings of Eunice Sagawah. Words Written On an Ancient Piece of Parchment by Mary Equemoh . . .," American Society for Psychical Research, New York, NY, p. 108. Electrostatic copy on deposit at Hancock Shaker Village, Inc., Pittsfield, MA, Accession Number, 949.

85 Ibid., 111.

86 Promey, *Spiritual Spectacles*, 149.

87 Ibid., 100–1.

88 Patterson, *Gift Drawings*, 56, fig. 19.

89 Diane Sasson, *The Shaker Spiritual Narrative* (Knoxville, 1983), 36–38.

90 "A Beautiful Present from my ever blessed & loving Mother Ann Brought by her little Angel, Jan 1st 1843," NOC 11,547.

91 *Loudon Furniture Designs*, 321.

92 "Millennial Laws . . . 1845," Part II, Section XII:6, in Andrews, *People Called Shakers*, 274.

93 "Red stain for wood, leather, paaper (sic) & c." OClWHi, Shaker Collection, XI:A-1.

94 Gordon, *Shaker Textiles*, 80.

95 Ibid., 151.

96 Canterbury, 1808: Starbuck and Smith, *Historical Survey*, 93; New Lebanon or Hancock, 1837: [Harriet Martineau], "The Shakers," *Penny Magazine*, 6 (November 18, 1837), 446.

97 Calvin Green linked together the color green, his vision of a lady in green, and his appointment as First Elder in the Gathering Order. Calvin Green, "Biographic Memoir of the Life and Experience of Calvin Green . . . ."Copy by Alonzo G. Hollister [1861–1869], OClWHi, Shaker Collection, VI:B-31, p. 566–67.

98 A.F.M. Willich, M.D. ed. by James Mease, M.D., *The Domestic Encyclopedia; or, a Dictionary of Facts . . .* 5 vols. (Philadelphia, 1801), II: 182.

99 "Millennial Laws . . . 1845," Part II, Section X:2, in Andrews, *People Called Shakers,* 271.

100 Andrews and Andrews, *Shaker Furniture*, 94.

101 Robert Emlen in conversation with the author, July 20, 1991.

102 *The Shakers: Pure of Spirit, Pure of Mind* (Duxbury, 1983), fig. 2; Timothy D. Rieman and Jean M. Burks, *The Complete Book of Shaker Furniture* (New York, 1993), 196, fig. 141.

103 Jerry Grant in conversation with the author, March 5, 1990.

104 Richard Candee in conversation with the author, February 5, 1992.

105 Abraham Perkins, Canterbury, NH, to Austin Bronson, Enfield, NH, October 19, 1858, OClWHi, Shaker Collection, IV:A-6.

106 Emlen, *Shaker Village Views*, xvi, xx.

107 Edward Deming Andrews and Faith Andrews, *Work and Worship Among the Shakers: Their Craftsmanship and Economic Order* (1974; repr., Greenwich, 1982), 108.

108 Andrews and Andrews, *Shaker Furniture*, pl. 30; 85.

109 Jerry V. Grant and Douglas R. Allen, *Shaker Furniture Makers*, (Hanover and London, 1989), 126.

110 Robert Booth and Katherine Booth, "Divine Design: A Shaker Legacy," *The 1991 Philadelphia Antiques Show* (Philadelphia, 1991), 36; Rieman and Burks, *The Complete Book of Shaker Furniture*, 195, fig. 140, has veneered drawer fronts.

111 Brother Arnold Hadd in conversation with the author, July 3, 1988.

112 Henry DeWitt, [Journal, Church Family, Mount Lebanon, NY, November 1827–September 1867], OClWHi, Shaker Collection, V:B-97.

CHAPTER VIII

1 Philemon Stewart, *A Holy, Sacred and Divine Roll and Book; from the Lord God of Heaven, to the Inhabitants of Earth . . .* (Canterbury, 1843), 364.

2 Jared B. Flagg, *The Life and Letters of Washington Allston* (New York, 1892), 198–99.

3 Washington Allston, *Lectures on Art and Poems (1850) and Monaldi (1841)* (1841 and 1850; facsimile repr. Gainsville, 1967), 15.

4 Flagg, *Life and Letters*, 204, 206.

5 Mary Pease, East Boston, MA, to Pliny Freeman, Sturbridge, MA, February 6, 1840, Freeman Family Correspondence, Manuscript Collection, Old Sturbridge Village Research Library. I am indebted to Holly Izard for bringing this letter to my attention.

6 Jon Butler, *Awash in a Sea of Faith: Christianizing the American People* (Cambridge, MA, and London, 1990), 278–79.

7 Marjorie Proctor-Smith, *Women in Shaker Community and Worship: A Feminist Analysis of the Uses of Religious Symbolism* (Lewiston and Queenston, 1985), 177.

8 Isaac N. Youngs, "A Preface, or Introduction to the Records of Sacred Communications, Given by Divine Inspiration, In the Church at New Lebanon," [c. 1842], OClWHi, Shaker Collection, VIII:B-109, 11–12.

9 Stewart, *Holy Roll and Book*, 348.

10 Rufus Bishop, "A Daily Journal of Passing Events: Begun January the 1st 1830[–May 1839]. By Rufus Bishop . . ." February 21, 1836, NN, Shaker Collection, Ms. 1.

11 Stephen J. Stein, *The Shaker Experience in America: A History of the United Society of Believers* (New Haven, 1992), 167.

12 An eleven-year-old girl falling to the ground in 1720, (Butler, *Awash in a Sea of Faith*, 84); "Hundreds of teen-age girls have been fainting en masse in classrooms, breaking out in sobs and complaining of unpleasant smells and nausea. Draped over the shoulders of teachers, they are carted off in groups to hospitals, where doctors . . . [find] no physical evidence to explain their symptoms. 'It is just hysteria.' More than a thousand young girls — between the ages of 12 and 18 . . . in some 40 schools. 'If one girl who is popular or a leader feels faint for some reason . . . the others start believing that they are suffering from the same symptoms." Chris Hedges, "Girls in Egypt Faint by Score In Classrooms, *The New York Times, International* (New York, April 18, 1993).

13 Jerry Grant in conversation with the author, November 12, 1991.

14 Horace Greeley, "A Sabbath with the Shakers," *Knickerbocker*, 11 (June, 1838), 537.

15 Youngs, "Preface," 13–15.

16 Jean McMahon Humez, *Mother's First-Born Daughters: Early Shaker Writings on Women and Religion* (Bloomington and Indianapolis, 1993), 213.

17 Stein, *Shaker Experience*, 166.

18 [Cassandana Brewster], "A Dream. Hancock Shaker Village, May 11, 1841," American Society for Psychical Research, New York, NY. Autograph copy by Alonzo G. Hollister, November 11, 1886, of document, "Found among Sister Cassandana Brewster's papers, with no name appended, I believe it is her own." Photocopy of manuscript deposited in the Hancock Shaker Village Library, MPH, Accession Number 947, pp. 341–42.

19 Hervey Elkins, *Fifteen Years in the Senior Order of Shakers: A Narration of Facts, Concerning That Singular People . . .* (Hanover, 1853), 53–54.

20 Ibid., 54–55.

21 Ibid., 43, 57.

22 Edward Deming Andrews, *The People Called Shakers: A Search for the Perfect Society* (1953; repr., enlarged ed. New York, 1963), 159, 161.

23 [Elisha Blakeman], *The Youth's Guide in Zion, and Holy Mother's Promises. Given by Inspiration at New Lebanon, N.Y., January 5, 1842* (1842; repr., Sabbathday Lake, 1963), 7.

24 Proctor-Smith, *Women in Shaker Community*, 189–91.

25 Stephen J. Stein, "Shaker Gift and Shaker Order: A Study of Religious Tension in the 19th Century." Unpublished paper presented at *Shaker Religion in Context: Theology and Practice*, Old Chatham, September 22–25, 1988.

26 Sally M. Promey, *Spiritual Spectacles: Vision and Image in Mid-Nineteenth-Century Shakerism* (Bloomington and Indianapolis, 1993), 210 n. 18.

27 Ibid., xv.

28 Stewart, *Holy Roll and Book*, 365.

29 Daniel W. Patterson, *Gift Drawings and Gift Songs: A Study of Two Forms of Shaker Inspiration* (Sabbathday Lake, 1983), 7 n. 15.

30 Walter F. Prince, "The Shakers and Psychical Research: A Notable Example of Cooperation," *Journal of the American Society for Psychical Research*, 12 (January, 1918), 69, quoted in Gerard C. Wertkin, "Given by Inspiration . . . ," *Folk Art*, 20, no. 1 (Spring, 1995), 60.

31 Fruitlands Museums, curatorial records. I am indebted to Maggie Stier for bringing the letter and the photograph of the displayed gift drawing to my attention.

32 Edward Deming Andrews and Faith Andrews, *Visions of the Heavenly Sphere: A Study in Shaker Religious Art* (Charlottesville, 1969), 3; Edward Deming Andrews and Faith Andrews, *Fruits of the Shaker Tree of Life* (Stockbridge, 1975), 96.

33 Isaac Newton Youngs, "Tour thro the States of Ohio and Kentucky by Rufus Bishop and Isaac Newton Youngs, in the Summer of 1834," vol. 1, p. 48. NOC Ms. No. 12751.

34 Originally there was a cove molding attached to the top: 1 5/16 x 7/16 x 25 5/8", and a dowel-like rod fixed to the base: 1 3/16 x 25 5/8". The rod was grooved to receive the paper. Both are made of cherry. There were strips of heavy black paper between the heads of the tacks and the paper of the drawing. A color photograph taken by Sally M. Promey, and sent to the author July 2, 1995, shows the piece before the Philadelphia Museum of Arts' conservators dismantled it for conservation. At the bottom there was a strip of woven tape – about an inch wide and three to four inches long – secured between the rod and the paper at the center of the drawing. (Its purpose is unknown.) At the top there was a strip of tape – about an inch-and-a-quarter wide and four to five inches long – secured at the center of the back of the cove molding. It projected up, away from the drawing. The tapes have been discarded. Sally M. Promey remembers them as green. A small black and white photograph taken before dismantling appears to show in the upper tape a vertical slit, near where it attaches to the cove molding. Perhaps on occasion the drawing was hung using that hole, but it seems to have remained a tight slit. Most likely the drawing was, except when shown to Believers, kept rolled up around the bottom rod with the roll

fitting neatly into the curve of the cove molding above; then the whole was secured by the upper tape being wrapped around the roll and held fast by tucking the end through the vertical slit.

35 "Millennial Laws, or Gospel Statutes and Ordinances Adapted to the Day of Christ's Second Appearing . . . . Revised and Re-established By the Ministry and Elders Oct'r 1845," Part II, Section X:7, published in Andrews, *People Called Shakers*, 272.

36 James Stevens Curl, *The Art and Architecture of Freemasonry* (Woodstock, 1993), figs. 15–17, 20, 27–29.

37 In addition to studies of gift drawings cited here, see: Sally L. Kitch, " 'As a Sign That All May Understand' Shaker Gift Drawings and Female Spiritual Power," *Winterthur Portfolio*, 24 (Spring, 1989), 1–28.

38 Promey, *Spiritual Spectacles*, 100.

39 Reuben Rathbun, *Reasons Offered for Leaving the Shakers* (Pittsfield, 1800), 6.

40 Thomas Brown, *An Account of the People Called Shakers: Their Faith, Doctrines, and Practice, Exemplified in the Life, Conversations, and Experience of the Author during the Time He Belonged to the Society. To Which is Affixed a History of Their Rise and Progress to the Present Day* (Troy, 1812), 82.

41 Ibid., 334.

42 Ibid., 322.

43 Ibid., 335.

44 Edward Deming Andrews, *The Gift to Be Simple: Songs, Dances and Rituals of the American Shakers* (1940; repr., New York, 1962), 144–45.

45 Garret K. Lawrence, New Lebanon, NY, to Isaac N. Youngs, Watervliet, NY, April 3, 1826, OClWHi, Shaker Collection, IV:A-35.

46 Elkins, *Fifteen Years*, 22.

47 Stein, *Shaker Experience*, 210; Priscilla J. Brewer, *Shaker Communities, Shaker Lives* (Hanover and London, 1986), 152, says that Jacobs joined the Shakers at Whitewater, OH, in 1846.

48 Daniel W. Patterson, "Shaker Visionary Art," *The Magazine Antiques*, 137 (February, 1990), 467.

49 Daniel W. Patterson, *The Shaker Spiritual* (Princeton, 1979), 116.

50 Andrews, *Gift to Be Simple*, 155.

51 Proctor-Smith, *Women in Shaker Community*, 134; Andrews, *Gift to Be Simple*, 149.

52 Derobigne M. Bennett and Isaac N. Youngs, "Journal of Inspired Meetings," November 1, 1840, OClWHi, Shaker Collection, VIII:B-138.

53 Patterson, *The Shaker Spiritual*, 363.

54 I am grateful to Susan von Daum Tholl for the information about the narrow path inlayed into some monastic churches, and for the citation from Peter Damian, Letter 50,4 to Stephen, a fellow monk (A.D. 1057), trans. from *The Letters of Peter Damian*, 2 vols., ed. O. Blum, II, 290.

55 A Chinese Buddhist monk, Shandao (A.D. 613–681), created a didactic tale called the "White Path Crossing Two Rivers" to warn devotees of the perils awaiting them as they sought refuge in a paradise-like realm in the west, and also to spur them on in their religious quest. The Buddhist White Path (about four or five inches wide, just wide enough for the foot) stretches from the mundane world to the sacred world. Heading west it bridges through the juncture of a river of raging fire flowing south, and a river of tumultuous water flowing north. Flames and waves from the two rivers lap over the path, making the journey to paradise difficult. I am indebted to Elizabeth ten Grotenhuis for this information. The story and a 14th-century Japanese painting of the theme are discussed in her "Visions of a Transcendent Realm: Pure Land Images in the Cleveland Museum of Art," *Bulletin of the Cleveland Museum of Art*, no. 7 (1991), 292–297; "The White Path Crossing Two Rivers: a contemporary Japanese garden represents the past," *Journal of Garden History, an International Quarterly*, 15 (1995), 1–18.

56 Patterson, *Gift Drawings*, 35.

57 Ibid., 7, 41.

58 Clarke Garrett, *Spirit Possession and Popular Religion: From the Camisards to the Shakers* (Baltimore and London, 1987), 110.

59 Brewer, *Shaker Communities*, 67, 174–75.

60 Garrett, *Spirit Possession*, 192.

61 Elkins, *Fifteen Years*, 73.

62 Ibid., 75.

63 Lucy Wright, "Mother Lucy's Sayings Spoken at Different Times and Under Various Circumstances," ed. with an introduction by Frances A. Carr, *The Shaker Quarterly*, 8 (Winter, 1968), 104.

64 "Millennial Laws . . . 1845," Part II, Section V.7, 15, 17, in Andrews, *People Called Shakers*, 266–67.

65 Viki Sand in conversation with the author, August 15, 1993, and correspondence in the files of the Shaker Museum and Library; Richard E. Williams in conversation with the author, May 16, 1995.

66 Andrews, *People Called Shakers*, 144.

67 Ibid.

68 "Three Months with the Shakers," *Bizarre, for Fireside and Wayside*, vol. IV (Philadelphia, 1854), 36. I am indebted to De Wolfe & Wood for this reference.

69 Andrews, *People Called Shakers*, 145.

70 Harvey Eads, South Union, KY, letter, November 17, 1864, OClWHi, Shaker Collection, IV:B-109, p. 177; Rufus Bishop, "A Daily Journal of Passing Events: Begun May the 19th 1839[–January 1, 1850], November 14, 1840, NN, Shaker Collection, Ms. No. 2. For further discussion of the subject, see Louis J. Kern, *An Ordered Love: Sex Roles and Sexuality in Victorian Utopias — the Shakers, the Mormons, and the Oneida Community* (Chapel Hill, 1981).

71 "Letter from James Whittaker, Minister of the Gospel in this Day of Christ's Second Appearing—to his Natural Relations in England," published in Joseph Meacham, *Concise Statement of the Principles of the Only True Church According to the Gospel of the Present Appearance of Christ . . .* (1790; repr., Sabbathday Lake, 1963), 11–14; Brown, *People Called Shakers*, 74, 111.

72 For a discussion of Christianity's many changes in attitudes toward homosexuality see: John Boswell, *Christianity, Social Tolerance, and Homosexuality: Gay People in Western Europe from the Beginning of the Christian Era to the Fourteenth Century* (Chicago and London, 1980). For an informative study of lesbianism, the church, cloistered life, spirit possession, and visions, see Judith C. Brown, *Immodest Acts, The Life of a Lesbian Nun in Renaissance Italy,* (New York and Oxford, 1986).

73 David S. Reynolds, *Walt Whitman's America* (New York, 1995), 198, 323, 391–94, 396, 398, 487, 540, 576–77.

74 Carrol Smith-Rosenberg, *Disorderly Conduct; Visions of Gender in Victorian America* (New York, 1985), 39.

75 Lillian Faderman, *Odd Girls and Twilight Lovers: A History of Lesbian Life in Twentieth-Century America* (New York: Penguin Books, 1992), 32.

76 For a discussion of changes in attitude and language during the late nineteenth and twentieth centuries, see Faderman, *Odd Girls and Twilight Lovers.*

77 Nancy F. Cott, "Young Women in the Second Great Awakening in New England," *Feminist Studies* 3 (Fall, 1975), 21, quoted in Jean McMahon Humez, *Gifts of Power: The Writings of Rebecca Jackson, Black Visionary, Shaker Eldress* (Amherst, 1981), 3.

78 Humez, *Gifts of Power*, 17.

79 Ibid., 135.

80 Ibid., 138–39.

81 Geraldine Duclow, "The Shaker Family of Philadelphia," *The Shaker Messenger*, 13 (September, 1991), 5; Humez, *Gifts of Power*, 358.

82 Humez, *Gifts of Power*, 32.

83 Stein, *Shaker Experience*, 111, 465 n. 184.

84 Elmer P. Pearson and Julia Neal, *The Shaker Image* (1974; 2nd and annotated ed., Pittsfield, 1994), 210.

85 Stein, *Shaker Experience*, 108.

86 Humez, *Gifts of Power*, 41.

87 Ibid., 9 n.10.

88 Isaac N. Youngs, Mount Lebanon, NY, to Garrett K. Lawrence, Watervliet, NY, August 11, 1833, OClWHi, Shaker Collection, IV:A-36.

89 Isaac N. Youngs, Mount Lebanon, NY, to Andrew C. Houston, Union Village, OH, June 27, 1838, OClWHi, Shaker Collection, IV:A-37.

90 Benjamin Gates, New Lebanon, NY, to Isaac N. Youngs, Watervliet, NY, March 20, 1826, NOC, Ms. No. 9,574.

91 Garrett K. Lawrence, Watervliet, NY, to Isaac N. Youngs, New Lebanon, NY, April 3, 1826, OClWHi, Shaker Collection, IV:A-35.

92 Isaac N. Youngs, [Journal of Domestic Occurrences, New Lebanon, NY, 1834–1846], January 24, 1837, N, Shaker Collection, Ms. No. 13,500; Isaac N. Youngs, "Autobiography in Verse," [1837], published in Andrews and Andrews, *Fruits of the Shaker Tree of Life*, 129–34.

93 Isaac N. Youngs, New Lebanon, NY, to Matthew Huston, Union Village, OH, June 27, 1838, OClWHi, Shaker Collection, IV:A-37.

94 Isaac N. Youngs, New Lebanon, NY, to Andrew C. Houston, Union Village, OH, August, 1827, OClWHi, Shaker Collection, IV:A-35. Titled by Youngs, "Conversation between {Andrew C. Houston May 9th & Isaac N. Youngs August} 1827. First draught;" See also: August 18, 1827, DLC, Shaker Collection, 347b, (fair copy without underlining).

95 Isaac N. Youngs, New Lebanon, NY, to Andrew C. Houston, Union Village, OH, July 9, 1828, DLC, Shaker Collection, 347b.

96 Andrew C. Houston, Union Village, OH, to Isaac N. Youngs, New Lebanon, NY, June 4, 1829, OClWHi, Shaker Collection, IV:A-70.

97 Isaac N. Youngs, New Lebanon, NY, to Andrew C. Houston, Union Village, OH, September 1, 1829, OClWHi, Shaker Collection, IV:A-35.

98 Isaac N. Youngs, New Lebanon, NY, to Andrew C. Houston, Union Village, OH, September, 11, 1836, DLC, Shaker collection, 347b. There are other letters written by or to Youngs with possibly romantic language; for example Elder Harvey Eads to Isaac N. Youngs, December 9, 1844, (letter transcribed by Alonzo G. Hollister in his "Book of Remembrances," OClWHi, Shaker Collection, VII:B-109, p. 172.

99 Jerry V. Grant and Douglas R. Allen, *Shaker Furniture Makers* (Hanover and London, 1989), 123.

100 Andrews, *People Called Shakers*, 132–33.

101 Benson John Lossing, "The Shakers," *Harper's New Monthly Magazine*, 15 (July, 1857), 165, 169.

CHAPTER IX

1 Henry C. Blinn, "The Shakers. Items of Domestic Arrangement," *The Manifesto*, 27 (May, 1897), 68.

2 William Dean Howells, "A Shaker Village," *Atlantic Monthly*, 37 (June, 1876), 707.

3 Mary Lyn Ray, "A Reappraisal of Shaker Furniture and Society," *Winterthur Portfolio*, 8 (Charlottesville, 1973), 130. Mary Lyn Ray was incorrect in placing Nicholas Briggs, who showed the washing machine, at Enfield, NH.

4 Charles Nordhoff, *The Communistic Societies of the United States: From Personal Visit and Observation* (1875; repr., New York, 1966), marriage, 35–36; separation of the sexes, 32–33, 35; eating, 32–33.

5 Ibid., 72–73.

6 Ibid., 102, 104.

7 Ibid., 271.

8 Lawrence Foster, *Religion and Sexuality, Three American Communal Experiences of the Nineteenth Century* (New York, 1981), 72.

9 Nordhoff, *Communistic Societies*, 117.

10 Priscilla J. Brewer, *Shaker Communities, Shaker Lives* (Hanover and London, 1986), 215–216. There are no data for 1890.

11 Nordhoff, *Communistic Societies*, 158–59.

12 Ibid., 187.

13 William A. Hinds, *American Communities: Brief Sketches of Economy, Zoar, Bethel, Aurora, Amana Icaria, the Shakers, Oneida, Wallingford, and the Brotherhood of the New Life* (1878; repr., New York, 1961), 110–11.

14 Nordhoff, *Communistic Societies*, 207.

15 Flo Morse, *The Shakers and the World's People* (Hanover and London, 1980), 219.

16 Nordhoff, *Communistic Societies*, 186.

17 Ibid., 145–46.

18 Ibid., 158

19 Ibid., 192–93, 211.

20 Morse, *Shakers and the World's People*, 281.

21 Theodore E. Johnson, ed., "Rules and Orders for the Church of Christ's Second Appearing . . .," *The Shaker Quarterly*, 11 (Winter, 1971), 139–165.

22 "Orders for the Church of Christ's Second Appearing, [Mount Lebanon, NY]," 1887, 56 (no. 20); 56 (no. 22); 57 (no. 27); 12 (no. 5); 12 (no. 4); 35 (nos. 2, 3), NOC, Ms. No., 10,480.

23 Nordhoff, *Communistic Societies*, 203.

24 Ibid., 203–4.

25 Ibid., 142.

26 Ibid., 184–85.

27 Ibid., 187–88.

28 Ibid., 191.

29 Ibid., 202; 210.

30 Ibid., facing 214.

31 Beverly Gordon, *Shaker Textile Arts*, (1980; repr., Hanover and London, 1983), 206.

32 Nordhoff, *Communistic Societies*, 149.

33 Ibid., 207.

34 Ibid., 207–08.

35 Charles R. Muller and Timothy D. Rieman, *The Shaker Chair* (Canal Winchester, 1984), 170–78.

36 Ibid., 206.

37 Shaker Museum and Library, curatorial records, Accession Number 18,304, rocking chair with red and black cushions; Muller and Rieman, *Shaker Chair*, photograph of Walter L. Palmer's "Library at Arbor Hill," 202.

38 For example, Dean A. Fales, Jr., *The Furniture of Historic Deerfield* (New York, 1976), fig. 19.

39 Muller and Rieman, *Shaker Chair*, 40.

40 Ibid., 152.

41 *Centennial Illustrated Catalogue and Price List of the Shakers' Chairs, Foot Benches, Floor Mats, Etc. . . .* (Albany, 1876), 11.

42 Gordon, *Shaker Textiles*, 140, 142.

43 Mary Lyn Ray, "Reappraisal," 129.

44 Muller and Rieman, *Shaker Chair*, 188.

45 *Illustrated Catalogue and Price List of Shakers' Chairs, Manufactured by the Society of Shakers. R.M. Wagan & Co., Mount Lebanon, N.Y.* (Mount Lebanon, late 1870s), [2].

46 *An Illustrated Catalogue and Price-list of the Shakers' Chairs. Manufactured by the Society of Shakers. Mount Lebanon, N.Y.: R.M. Wagan & Co.* (late 1870s; facsimile repr. Sabbathday Lake, 1992).

47 *Illustrated Catalogue of Shaker Chairs, Foot Benches, Floor Mats, etc. Mt. Lebanon, Columbia County, N.Y.* (Albany, 1874), inserted color page reproduced in Muller and Rieman, *Shaker Chair*, color plates, [3].

48 Muller and Rieman, *Shaker Chair*, 186.

49 Ibid., 228, 231.

50 Shaker Village of Pleasant Hill owns an example.

51 Herbert A. Wisbey, Jr., "Stories of the Groveland Shakers: Mother Ann's Work," *Shaker Messenger*, 14 (April 1992), 23.

52 Nordhoff, *Communistic Societies*, 150.

53 Ibid., 213.

54 Jerry V. Grant and Douglas R. Allen, *Shaker Furniture Makers* (Hanover and London, 1989), 48.

55 Howells, "Shaker Village," 707–8.

56 Ray, "Reappraisal," 117.

57 Ibid.

58 [A Domestic Journal of Daily Occurrences, New Lebanon, NY, 1856–1877], February 23, 1877, OClWHi, Shaker Collection, V:B-71.

59 Ray, "Reappraisal," 117.

60 Ibid.

61 Ibid.

62 Ibid.

63 Giles B. Avery, "[Diary], 1877," OClWHi, Shaker Collection, V:B-123, December 13, 1877.

64 A Domestic Journal of Daily Occurrences, 1856–1877, January 27, 1877.

65 Ibid. March 17, 1877.

66 Ibid., March 28, April 21, 28, 1877.

67 Jerry Grant, "Collections: [Union Porcelain Works Dishes]," *Shaker Museum and Library Report*, 1 (May, 1990), [3].

68 Grant and Allen, *Shaker Furniture Makers*, 151.

69 Ibid., 143.

70 Ibid., 154.

71 Timothy D. Rieman and Jean M. Burks, *The Complete Book of Shaker Furniture* (New York, 1993), fig. 228.

72 Ibid., 193, fig. 137.

73 Gordon, *Shaker Textiles*, 185, 214.

74 Ibid., 280–82, 211.

75 Mary Rose Boswell, "Woman's Work: The Canterbury Shakers' Fancywork Industry," *Historical New Hampshire*, 48 (Summer/Fall, 1993), 135.

76 Gordon, *Shaker Textiles*, 246

77 Grant, "Collections," (May, 1990), [3].

78 Grant and Allen, *Shaker Furniture Makers*, 12.

79 Ibid.

80 Minnie Catherine Allen, Mount Lebanon, NY, to Wallace H. Cathcart, Cleveland, OH, September 28, 1919, OClWHi, Shaker Collection, IV:A-83.

81 Jerry Grant in conversation with the author, June 13, 1991.

82 Gordon, *Shaker Textiles*, 210.

83 Edward Deming Andrews and Faith Andrews, *Shaker Furniture: The Craftsmanship of an American Communal Sect* (1937; repr., New York, 1950), 58.

84 Nordhoff, *Communistic Societies*, 151–52, 150–51.

85 Ibid., 140.

86 Ibid., 141–42.

87 Howells, "Shaker Village," 709.

88 [Amanda B. Harris], "Among the Shakers," *Granite Monthly*, 1 (April, 1877), 22.

89 [Homer Eaton Keyes], "A View of Shakerdom," *The Magazine Antiques*, 26 (October, 1934), 148.

90 Morse, *Shakers and the World's People*, 285.

91 Ibid., 286.

92 Ibid., 286.

93 Ibid., 286.

94 Ibid., 289.

95 Nordhoff, *Communistic Societies*, 186.

96 Andrews and Andrews, *Shaker Furniture*, 29.

97 Jerry Grant in conversation with the author, January 12, 1994.

98 Stephen J. Stein, *The Shaker Experience in America: A History of the United Society of Believers* (New Haven, 1992), 304, 311, 310, 318–319.

99 Charles F. Wingate, "Shaker Sanitation," *The Manifesto*, 19 (May, 1889), 114–15. Reprinted from *The Plumber and Sanitary Engineer*, 3 (September, 1880), 397.

100 Stephen A. Marini, *In Time & Eternity: Maine Shakers in the Industrial Age 1872–1918* (Sabbathday Lake, 1986), 6.

101 "Circular Concerning Photographs, Daguerreotypes, Ferrotypes &c., Ministry, New Lebanon, N.Y., Nov. 1st, 1873," NOC, accession number 9599.

102 Carl Carmer, *Listen for a Lonesome Drum* (New York, 1936), 132.

CHAPTER X

1 Frederick W. Evans, Mt. Lebanon, NY, to Count Leo Tolstoy, Yasnaya Polyana, Tula, Russia, December 6, 1890 and March 6, 1891, quoted in

"Tolstoy and the Shakers," *The Peg Board*, 4 (June, 1936), 72–76.

2 John A.H. Sweeney, *Henry Francis du Pont* (Winterthur, 1980, unpaged, facing page with picture of Mrs. Henry Algernon du Pont with her children).

3 Barbara Clark Smith, *After the Revolution: The Smithsonian History of Everyday Life in the Eighteenth Century* (New York, 1985), ix–xxv.

4 Cynthia H. Barton, *History's Daughter: The Life of Clara Endicott Sears, Founder of Fruitlands Museums* (Harvard, c. 1988), 84–85. Maggie Stier provided this reference.

5 Carol Troyen and Erica E. Hirshler, *Charles Sheeler: Paintings and Drawings* (Boston, 1987), 10.

6 Avis Berman, *Rebels on Eighth Street: Juliana Force and the Whitney Museum of American Art* (New York, 1990), 106.

7 Troyen and Hirshler, *Charles Sheeler*, 13.

8 Ibid., 10.

9 Ibid., 3.

10 Ibid., 12.

11 Ibid., 15.

12 Berman, *Rebels on Eighth Street*, 253.

13 Jerry V. Grant and Douglas R. Allen, *Shaker Furniture Makers* (Hanover and London, 1989), 82, fig. 57.

14 Rufus Bishop, "A Journal or Register of Passing Events . . . January 2, 1850[–October 19, 1859]," June 30, 1851, NN, Shaker Collection, Ms. 3. Amos Stewart performed the work assisted by Rufus Bishop. Evert A. Duyckink, editor of the *Literary World* 9 (September, 13, 1851), 201, in an article "Notes on Excursions—No. II. The Shakers at Lebanon," observed, "Several openings in the upper part of the end walls, filled with blinds, apparently acting as ventilators, are understood to be private windows for the benefit of the elders to survey in retirement what they please of the proceedings of the Millennial Church below."

15 Grant and Allen, *Shaker Furniture Makers*, 84.

16 Edward Deming Andrews and Faith Andrews, *Religion in Wood: A Book of Shaker Furniture* (Bloomington and London, 1966), 57–59.

17 Constance Rourke, *Charles Sheeler: Artist in the American Tradition* (New York, 1938), 5.

18 Ibid., 66.

19 Ibid., 77.

20 Ibid., 133–34.

21 Ibid., 134–35.

22 Ibid., 136.

23 Constance Rourke, *The Roots of American Culture, and Other Essays* (New York, 1942), 235–37.

24 Edward Deming Andrews and Faith Andrews, *Fruits of the Shaker Tree of Life* (Stockbridge, 1975), 21-22.

25 Hugh Howard, "Reinventing the Shakers." Unpublished paper presented at *The Shakers in the Twentieth Century*, Durham, NH, June 12–14, 1992. I am also indebted to Hugh Howard for reading the material on the Andrewses and suggesting revisions to the text.

26 Andrews and Andrews, *Fruits of the Shaker Tree of Life*, 22–23.

27 Edward Deming Andrews and Faith Andrews, "Craftsmanship of an American Religious Sect," *The Magazine Antiques*, 14 (August, 1928), 134.

28 Later the Andrewses again briefly mention the relationship of Shaker to worldly forms; for example: E.D. Andrews and William F. Winter's 1937 *Shaker Furniture* acknowledges "the strictly mundane origins of Shaker stylism in furniture, however, lie in the craft traditions of colonial New York and New England," and that worldly objects came in to communities. Also that a few people trained outside in furniture making later worked within the society (page 23). In the catalogue for *Shaker: Furniture and Objects from the Faith and Edward Deming Andrews Collections Commemorating the Bicentenary of the American Shakers*, Renwick Gallery, Smithsonian Institution (Washington,1973), Andrews briefly suggests, within the caption for their chest of drawers, a connection between Shaker and worldly design ideas.

29 Edward Deming Andrews and Faith Andrews, *Shaker Furniture: The Craftsmanship of an American Communal Sect* (1937; repr., New York, 1950), vii.

30 Ibid., viii.

31 Berman, *Rebels on Eighth Street*, 316.

32 Ibid., 317.

33 Ibid., 385.

34 Ibid., 403.

35 Jerry Grant, "Notes on an Interview with Faith Andrews," February 1, 1983, 10:00 A.M. to 1:30 P.M., made available to the author.

36 Andrews and Andrews, *Fruits of the Shaker Tree of Life*, 145. No date of the meeting is given.

37 I was a student of Kaare Klint and his long-term assistant Rigmor Andersen from September 1953 to June 1955. *The Shaker Chair* and *Shaker Furniture* were discussed several times by both Klint and Andersen.

38 Grant and Allen, *Shaker Furniture Makers*, 10; Jerry Grant in conversation about Olive Hayden Austin with the author, March 4, 1992; letter from Todd Burdick, Hancock Shaker Village, Inc., to the author, September 16, 1987, quoting the story from the taped interview.

39 Flo Morse, *The Shakers and the World's People* (Hanover and London, 1980), 240. Over the years Mildred Barker used different phrasing for this statement.

40 Helen M. Upton during a discussion period at *Shaker Religion in Context: Theology and Practice*, Shaker Museum and Library, Old Chatham, NY, September 23–25, 1988.

41 Theodore E. Johnson, "Life in the Christ Spirit: Observations on Shaker Theology," *The Shaker Quarterly*, 8 (Fall, 1968), 7.

42 Mary Lyn Ray. Telephone interview, September 10, 1993.

43 Andrews and Andrews, "Craftsmanship of an American Religious Sect," 133.

44 Dolores Hayden, *Seven American Utopias: The Architecture of Communitarian Socialism, 1790–1975* (Cambridge, MA, and London, 1976), 92.

45 Ibid., 101.

46 Ibid., 76.

47 Brother Arnold Hadd in conversation with the author, July 3, 1988.

48 Andrews and Andrews, *Religion in Wood*, 17.

49 Edward Deming Andrews, *The People Called Shakers: A Search for the Perfect Society* (1953; repr., enlarged ed. New York, 1963), 145.

50 Horace Greeley, "A Sabbath with the Shakers," *Knickerbocker*, 11 (June, 1838), 537.

51 During the summer of 1996, ten contemporary artists had month-long residencies with the Shakers at Sabbathday Lake. This was the central feature of a project developed by France Morin, "The Quiet in the Land: Everyday Life, Contemporary Art and the Shakers."

52 Linda Weintraub, *The Maximal Implications of The Minimal Line* (Annandale-on-Hudson, 1985), 56.

53 Peter Halley to John Kirk, October 21, 1991.

54 For an instance of the association in print see: Barbara Rose, *New Aesthetic* (The Washington Gallery of Modern Art, 1967), 14.

55 John Rockwell, "Robert Wilson: Evolution and Impact of a Theater Artist." Unpublished talk at the Museum of Fine Arts, Boston, February 13, 1991.

56 For example, in the 1795 Robert Sands House, Miller Road, Rhinebeck, NY.

57 "Portfolio: 4 Sculptors," *Perspecta* (March/May, 1968). Quoted in *Donald Judd: Complete Writings 1959–1975* (Halifax and New York, 1975), 196.

APPENDIX

1 "Milenial Laws . . . New Lebanon, August 7th: 1821," OC1WHi, Shaker Collection, I:B-37.

SUGGESTED FURTHER READING

1. EARLY SHAKER PUBLICATIONS

[Rufus Bishop and Seth Y. Wells], eds., *Testimonies of the Life, Character, Revelation and Doctrines of Our Ever Blessed Mother Ann Lee, and the Elders with Her; Through Whom the Word of Eternal Life was opened in this Day of Christ's Second Appearing: Collected from Living Witnesses* (1816).

[Calvin Green and Seth Y. Wells], *A Summary View of the Millennial Church or United Society of Believers . . .* (1823).

[Joseph Meacham], *A Concise Statement of the Principles of the Only True Church, According to the Gospel of the Present Appearance of Christ . . .* (1790).

Philemon Stewart, *A Holy, Sacred and Divine Roll and Book; from the Lord God of Heaven, to the Inhabitants of Earth . . .* (1843).

[Benjamin Seth Youngs], *The Testimony of Christ's Second Appearing Containing a General Statement of All Things Pertaining to the Faith and Practice of the Church of God in This Latter-Day* (1808).

2. EARLY WRITINGS ABOUT THE SHAKERS

Thomas Brown, *An Account of the People Called Shakers: Their Faith, Doctrines, and Practice, Exemplified in the Life, Conversations, and Experience of the Author during the Time He Belonged to the Society. To Which is Affixed a History of Their Rise and Progress to the Present Day* (1812).

Mary Marshall Dyer, *The Rise and Progress of the Serpent From the Garden of Eden to the Present Day . . .* (1847).

Hervey Elkins, *Fifteen Years in the Senior Order of the Shakers: A Narration of the Facts, Concerning That Singular People . . .* (1853).

William J. Haskett, *Shakerism Unmasked, or the History of the Shakers . . .* (1828).

Benson John Lossing, "The Shakers," *Harper's New Monthly Magazine*, 15 (July, 1857), 164–77.

Charles Nordhoff, *The Communistic Societies of the United States: From Personal Visit and Observation* (1875).

Reuben Rathbun, *Reasons Offered for Leaving the Shakers* (1800).

Valentine Wightman Rathbun, *Some Brief Hints of a Religious Scheme, Taught and Propagated by a Number of Europeans, Living in a Place Called Nisqueunia, in the State of New-York . . .* (1781).

3. SHAKER AND RELATED HISTORY

Priscilla J. Brewer, *Shaker Communities, Shaker Lives* (1986).

Deborah E. Burns, *Shaker Cities of Peace, Love, and Union, A History of the Hancock Bishopric* (1993).

Jon Butler, *Awash in a Sea of Faith: Christianizing the American People* (1990).

Dorothy M. Filley, *Recapturing Wisdom's Valley: The Watervliet Shaker Heritage, 1775–1975* (1975).

Clarke Garrett, *Spirit Possession and Popular Religion: From the Camisards to the Shakers* (1987).

William A. Hinds, *American Communities: Brief Sketches of Economy, Zoar, Bethel, Aurora, Amana Icaria, the Shakers, Oneida, Wallingford, and the Brotherhood of the New Life* (1878).

Jean McMahon Humez, *Gifts of Power: The Writings of Rebecca Jackson, Black Visionary, Shaker Eldress* (1981).

Jean McMahon Humez, *Mother's First-Born Daughters: Early Shaker Writings on Women and Religion* (1993).

Louis J. Kern, *An Ordered Love: Sex Roles and Sexuality in Victorian Utopias — the Shakers, the Mormons, and the Oneida Community* (1981).

Eliza Leslie, *The House Book: or a Manual of Domestic Economy for Town and Country* (1841).

Flo Morse, *The Shakers and the World's People* (1980).

John Harlow Ott, *Hancock Shaker Village: A Guidebook and History* (1976).

Elmer Ray Pearson and Julia Neal, *The Shaker Image* (1974; second annotated ed., 1994).

Marjorie Proctor-Smith, *Women in Shaker Community and Worship: A Feminist Analysis of the Uses of Religious Symbolism* (1985).

Diane Sasson, *The Shaker Spiritual Narrative* (1983).

Clara Endicott Sears, *Gleanings from Old Shaker Journals* (1916).

Carol Smith-Rosenberg, *Disorderly Conduct; Visions of Gender in Victorian America* (1985).

Stephen J. Stein, *The Shaker Experience in America: A History of the United Society of Believers* (1992).

4. SHAKER AND RELATED ARTS

Edward Deming Andrews, *The People Called Shakers: A Search for the Perfect Society* (1953).

Edward Deming Andrews and Faith Andrews, *Fruits of the Shaker Tree of Life* (1975).

Edward Deming Andrews and Faith Andrews, *Shaker Furniture: The Craftsmanship of an American Communal Sect* (1937).

Avis Berman, *Rebels on Eighth Street: Juliana Force and the Whitney Museum of American Art* (1990).

Susan L. Buck, " 'Bedsteads Should Be Painted Green' / Shaker Paints and Varnishes," *Old-Time New England*, 73 (Fall, 1995), 16–351.

Susan L. Buck, "Interpreting Paint and Finish Evidence on the Mount Lebanon Shaker Collection," Timothy

D. Rieman, *Shaker, The Art of Craftsmanship* (1995), 46–57.

Richard M. Candee, "Preparing and Mixing Colors in 1812," *The Magazine Antiques*, 113 (April, 1978).

Henry Wilson Coil, *Coil's Masonic Encyclopedia* (1961).

James Stevens Curl, *The Art and Architecture of Freemasonry* (1993).

A[ndrew] J[ackson] Downing, *The Architecture of Country Houses* (1850).

Robert P. Emlen, "The Shaker Dance Prints," *Journal of the American Historical Print Collectors Society*, 17 (Autumn, 1992).

Robert P. Emlen, *Shaker Village Views* (1987).

Christopher Gilbert, ed., *Loudon Furniture Designs; three sections from J. C. Loudon's Encyclopaedia of Cottage, Farm and Villa Architecture* (1833; facsimile of rev. 1839 edition, London, 1970).

Beverly Gordon, *Shaker Textile Arts* (1980).

Jerry V. Grant and Douglas R. Allen, *Shaker Furniture Makers* (1989).

Dolores Hayden, *Seven American Utopias: The Architecture of Communitarian Socialism, 1790–1975* (1976).

George Hepplewhite, *The Cabinet-Maker and Upholsterer's Guide* (3rd ed. 1794).

Hugh Honour, *Neo-Classicism* (1968).

An Illustrated Catalogue and Price-list of the Shakers' Chairs. Manufactured by the Society of Shakers. Mount Lebanon, N.Y.: R . M. Wagan & Co. (c. 1877).

Albert G. Mackey, M.D., *An Encyclopaedia of Freemasonry and Its Kindred Sciences . . .* (1884).

Charles R. Muller and Timothy D. Rieman, *The Shaker Chair* (1984).

Daniel W. Patterson, *Gift Drawings and Gift Songs: A Study of Two Forms of Shaker Inspiration* (1983).

Daniel W. Patterson, *The Shaker Spiritual* (1979).

Sally M. Promey, *Spiritual Spectacles: Vision and Image in Mid-Nineteenth-Century Shakerism* (1993).

Mary Lyn Ray, "A Reappraisal of Shaker Furniture and Society," *Winterthur Portfolio*, 8 (1973), 105–32.

Timothy D. Rieman and Jean M. Burks, *The Complete Book of Shaker Furniture* (1993).

Constance Rourke, *Charles Sheeler: Artist in the American Tradition* (1938).

Thomas Sheraton, *The Cabinet Dictionary*, 2 vols. (1803).

June Sprigg, *Shaker Design*, (1986).

Carol Troyen and Erica E. Hirshler, *Charles Sheeler: Paintings and Drawings* (1987).

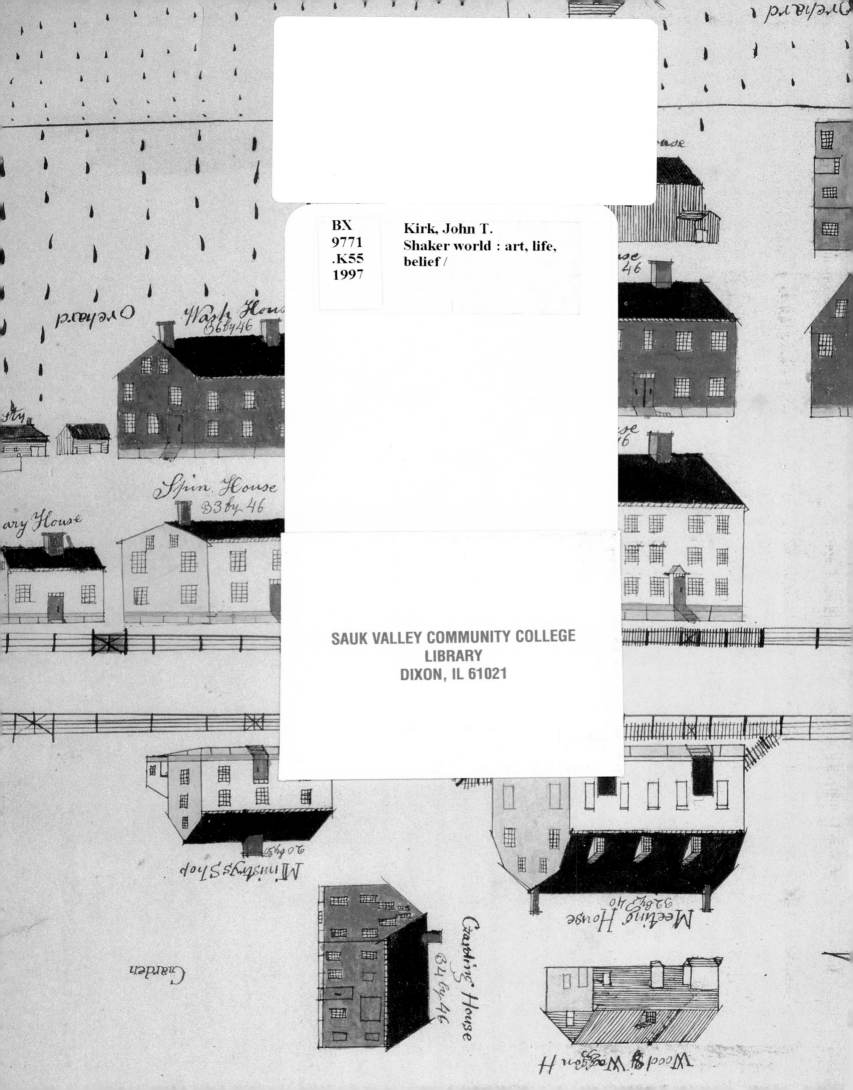